Upending American Politics

Upending American Politics

Polarizing Parties, Ideological Elites, and Citizen Activists from the Tea Party to the Anti-Trump Resistance

EDITED BY THEDA SKOCPOL
and
CAROLINE TERVO

OXFORD
UNIVERSITY PRESS

OXFORD
UNIVERSITY PRESS

Oxford University Press is a department of the University of Oxford. It furthers
the University's objective of excellence in research, scholarship, and education
by publishing worldwide. Oxford is a registered trade mark of Oxford University
Press in the UK and certain other countries.

Published in the United States of America by Oxford University Press
198 Madison Avenue, New York, NY 10016, United States of America.

© Oxford University Press 2020

CIP data is on file at the Library of Congress
ISBN 978–0–19–008353–3 (pbk.)
ISBN 978–0–19–008352–6 (hbk.)

CONTENTS

PART I.   REPUBLICANS OUTFLANKED AND RADICALIZED

FIGURES AND TABLE

Figures

Table

PREFACE

Simple curiosity is an undervalued scholarly resource. It is all too easy for university researchers to follow established academic grooves—to ask only those questions dictated by established theories and look for answers by deploying standard methodological techniques. For social scientists, such academic incrementalism has led to predictable results: one more study of congressional voting patterns; yet another model using standard indicators to predict presidential election outcomes; still another study of demographically sorted voter attitudes about health insurance. Although many valuable findings and arguments flow from such research routines, incrementalism can also create blinders, making it hard for researchers to notice new trends or patterns, let alone explain them.

How could America, somewhat surprisingly, elect its first African American president in 2008, only to turn around just eight years later to install in the White House a mendacious reality TV star who had questioned the very citizenship of that path-breaking president and promised to undo all his governing accomplishments? Why do elected Republican officeholders regularly pursue public policies that are unpopular with most Americans? After decades of erosion in local civic life, why and how did grassroots conservatives create more than a thousand local Tea Parties starting in 2009? Just eight years later, starting in late 2016, why and how did liberal-minded Americans form up to two thousand grassroots anti-Trump resistance groups? What impact have these widespread citizen movements had on the two major political parties and recent election outcomes? Most academics failed to predict such startling recent developments, and established approaches have struggled to make sense of them, even in retrospect.

Arguably, one salutary side effect of recent US political breaks has been to shock many researchers into asking new questions and using fresh methodologies. All of the contributors to this volume have certainly been among those so inspired—moved by sheer curiosity and a determination to figure out what is happening as a prelude to suggesting why. Ranging from very senior scholars to students completing fledgling research endeavors, they have probed the reverberations of increasing US partisan polarization and growing gaps in wealth and income. They focus on shifting organizational activities in politics—developing new findings about the concerted activities of wealthy donors, about recent shifts in Republican and Democratic Party organizations and allied groups, and about the roots and impact of two nationwide citizen movements: the Tea Party and the anti-Trump resistance. To learn how American civic life and politics have been upended and remade in recent times, these researchers unpack nationally consequential changes in pivotal states ranging from Florida to Wisconsin, North Carolina to Pennsylvania, Michigan to Texas. This volume cannot predict exactly what will happen in the fast-changing US political scene in 2020 and beyond, but the contributions assembled here provide telling insights about alternative futures and what could happen in the next rounds of national political conflict.

The book came together quickly in the spring of 2019 when the editors realized that more than a dozen recent and ongoing studies added up to a coherent new window into contemporary US political transformations. This is not a typical edited volume. The parts fit together like chapters in a single monograph, because all have been written by scholars at various career stages who have been in touch or collaborated with one another. The contributors have asked complementary questions about national and state-level political changes, and they have deployed similar research hypotheses and methods and shared empirical findings along the way. Many kinds of data are used in these chapters, including statistical data compilations and maps of organizational patterns, as well as ethnographically rich information gleaned from field visits in many parts of the country and interviews with civic group leaders, party officials, and organizers of election campaigns. The melding of various kinds of data, quantitative and qualitative, national and subnational, is unusual and highly valuable, especially for studies such as these that aim to describe unfolding changes in politics, rather than just measure well-known variables.

Each of the authors in this volume has many of the others to thank for mutual inspiration, constructive feedback, and shared data and names of people to contact for interviews during field visits. Individual chapters note particular debts. In addition, the editors wish to acknowledge the help many supporters and commentators have provided along the way. David McBride and his colleagues at Oxford University Press have done an amazing job of speeding this book to timely publication. Parts of the research reported here received initial hearings in sessions at the American Political Science Association and the American Sociological Association, and we are grateful for feedback from session commentators and audience members that helped us improve our work.

For similar feedback, we thank participants in research workshops at Columbia University, Harvard University, and the University of North Carolina at Chapel Hill. Harvard University student and faculty undergraduate senior thesis readers provided thoughtful and detailed comments on early research publications adapted to the chapters here. Several individual colleagues took time to read drafts and provide written feedback for which we are grateful, including Sidney Tarrow, Marshall Ganz, Robert Shapiro, Adam Joyce and Adam Reich. We also wish to thank our families: Theda's husband, Bill, and Caroline's parents, Jay and Barbara, for their insights and encouragement throughout our preoccupation with researching, writing, and wrangling this volume to fruition.

The editors are also grateful to each author for agreeing to participate in this volume. Many authors juggled other professional obligations, personal travel, or notoriously busy end-of-year graduation ceremonies while drafting their respective contributions. This volume was only possible because of their diligence, timeliness, and quick responsiveness over a tight timeline.

Most of all, we want to thank the many local leaders, American citizens of all partisan stripes, who sat with us for field interviews, filled out online questionnaires, sent us information by email, and answered our questions about conservative and liberal politics and about Republican Party and Democratic Party activities in various parts of our vast and varied country. Most informants were promised confidentiality and cannot be named, but we can thank by name Hannah Laurison of the coordinating group Pennsylvania Together, who helped us disseminate an online questionnaire to many local groups in that statewide network. Other informants likewise went beyond providing their personal insights to put us in touch with others they knew. We appreciate the trust these individuals placed in us to listen to their perspectives and report accurately on their activities. Informants may or may not agree with the scholarly conclusions we draw, but we are very grateful for their input, without which we could not accurately describe current trends in US politics that often escape media and academic attention. We respect all Americans of any persuasion who are active participants in our democracy.

Theda Skocpol and Caroline Tervo
Cambridge, Massachusetts
July 2019

CONTRIBUTORS

Alexandra Caffrey graduated cum laude with a BA in government from Harvard University in 2019. Her chapter is derived from her Thomas Temple Hoopes Prize–winning senior honors thesis. She now works in Miami for Forward Florida Action, the voter registration organization Andrew Gillum founded after the 2018 election.

Alexander Hertel-Fernandez is assistant professor of international and public affairs at Columbia University. He is the author of *State Capture: How Conservative Activists, Big Businesses, and Wealthy Donors Reshaped the American States—and the Nation* (2019), as well as *Politics at Work: How Companies Turn Their Workers Into Lobbyists* (2018), winner of the Robert A. Dahl Award from the American Political Science Association. His research focuses on the political economy of the United States, with an emphasis on the intersections among businesses, unions, donors, and public policy.

Maximilian Frank is studying for an MA in American government at Georgetown University. He graduated from Harvard in 2019 with a BA in social studies, with a focus on populism in the United States and western Europe. His chapter is adapted from his 2019 undergraduate honors thesis, winner of a Thomas Temple Hoopes Prize from Harvard College.

Leah E. Gose is a PhD student in sociology at Harvard University interested in social policy, organizational sociology, and poverty theory. Her scholarship includes research on grassroots political organizations formed in response to the Trump presidency. She is currently studying community-based organizations and their local organizational ties as vital components of hunger relief efforts and the American social safety net.

Sally Marsh is a proud Michigander whose chapter is based on her 2018 Thomas Temple Hoopes prize–winning senior honors thesis at Harvard College, which is not connected to her current employment. After graduating with a BA in Government and History from Harvard, Sally returned home to join the 2018 campaign of Jocelyn Benson for Michigan secretary of state. Sally now serves as the director of special projects at the Michigan Department of State, focusing on implementation of recent constitutional amendments calling for citizen-led redistricting and the expansion of voting rights.

Eliza Oehmler, from Memphis, Tennessee, is a member of the Harvard College class of 2021. She is concentrating in sociology with a secondary field of study in global health and health policy.

Lara Putnam is University Center for International Studies research professor in the Department of History at the University of Pittsburgh, where she has been Department Chair since 2014. She writes about Latin American and Caribbean history; migration, kinship, and gender; and the impact of digital technology on historical research. Publications include *The Company They Kept: Migrants and the Politics of Gender in Caribbean Costa Rica, 1870–1960* (2002) and *Radical Moves: Caribbean Migrants and the Politics of Race in the Jazz Age* (2013), as well as more than two dozen chapters and articles. Putnam's research on contemporary grassroots political organizing has appeared in *Vox.com, New Republic, Washington Post, Washington Monthly, Democracy Journal,* and beyond. She is active in grassroots organizing in Southwest Pennsylvania.

Theda Skocpol is the Victor S. Thomas professor of government and sociology at Harvard University. She has authored many books, articles, and reports; won major scholarly awards; and been elected to membership in the American Academy of Arts and Sciences, the American Philosophical Society, and the National Academy of Sciences. She is a proud teacher of many Harvard students, and her ongoing research focuses on US conservatives and the Republican Party, the politics of health care policy, and citizen reactions to the Obama and Trump presidencies. Skocpol is also the director of the Scholars Strategy Network, a nationwide organization with more than a thousand members and forty chapters that makes the work of university researchers understandable to civic groups, policymakers, and the media.

Caroline Tervo is currently a research coordinator in the Harvard Government Department, working with Theda Skocpol and others on studies of citizen grassroots organizing, state and local party building, and the local effects of federal policy changes. A native North Carolinian, Tervo holds a BA in government from Harvard University. Her chapter is based on her 2018 senior honors thesis, winner of two college awards, the Thomas Temple Hoopes Prize and the Seymour E. and Ruth B. Harris Prize.

Elizabeth Thom is a PhD student in government and social policy at Harvard University. She holds a BA from the University of Pennsylvania and an MSc from the University of Oxford, where she was a Thouron Scholar. Previously, Elizabeth worked at the Brookings Institution as a senior project coordinator and research assistant to E. J. Dionne Jr.

Vanessa Williamson is a senior fellow in governance studies at Brookings and a senior fellow at the Urban-Brookings Tax Policy Center. She studies the politics of redistribution, with a focus on attitudes about taxation. She is the author of *Read My Lips: Why Americans Are Proud to Pay Taxes* and the coauthor, with Theda Skocpol, of *The Tea Party and the Remaking of Republican Conservatism*.

Sophia Young graduated from Harvard University in 2019 with a BA in government and a secondary field of study in moral and political philosophy. She is continuing her research on gun violence prevention at the Brady Campaign in Washington, DC. Her chapter is based on her 2019 senior honors thesis at Harvard College.

Michael Zoorob is a PhD student in government at Harvard University from Nashville, Tennessee. He is interested in the politics of inequality and crime, and the role of organized groups in politics.

INTRODUCTION: UNDERSTANDING CURRENT TRANSFORMATIONS IN AMERICAN POLITICS

THEDA SKOCPOL AND CAROLINE TERVO

Fierce winds are rocking US politics today, swirling in ways analysts and citizens alike struggle to comprehend. In November 2008, many pundits saw the election of the nation's first African American president—backed by youthful voters and co-partisan majorities in both houses of Congress—as an irrevocable political turning point. Some even proclaimed a "New New Deal," implying that Obama Democrats might prove enduringly popular and reorient national politics for decades, just as Franklin Roosevelt Democrats did starting in the 1930s.[1] Yet just eight years later, American politics did an abrupt U-turn with the Electoral College victory of Donald Trump, who made his way to the White House with openly racist, ethno-nationalist appeals to angry white voters. Like the earlier Obama victory, Trump's win coincided with congressional victories for his party—leaving the new president poised to carry through on campaign promises to reverse or unravel everything Obama and the Democrats had done at home and abroad.

Barack Obama moved into the White House in January 2009 just as the country and the world were plunging into a steep economic recession that threatened to turn into a 1930s-style depression. The new president asked Congress to back sweeping measures to reverse the downturn, but he immediately faced concerted pushback from congressional Republicans determined to use all institutional levers at their disposal to block or slow Obama initiatives. On the far right, billionaires and multimillionaires, especially those in the tightly organized Koch network, both egged on and facilitated such GOP obstruction.[2] Within weeks, moreover, popular mobilizations added a new vector to the pushbacks against Democrats and any Republicans inclined to compromise with the new administration. Widespread Tea Party protests broke out and soon gave way to sustained local grassroots organizing all across the country.

For the following two years, Obama-era policymaking faced an uphill slog.[3] Inherited Republican tax cuts tilted toward the very rich were only belatedly and slightly modified, leaving the federal government in fiscal straights at a juncture when more, not less, public spending made sense. Immigration reform and gun safety efforts made no headway, and a comprehensive "cap and trade" effort to address global warming stalled in the Senate, far from the sixty votes it would have needed to overcome a filibuster. Even the one big legislative success of the early Obama presidency, the Affordable Care Act of 2010, barely squeaked through Congress after more than a year of fits and starts. Thereafter, the full implementation of this reform faced persistent conservative opposition, not just in the federal courts but also in dozens of states where organized free-market forces were able to block acceptance of federal funds to expand health insurance coverage.[4]

In November 2010, the Obama euphoria came to an abrupt halt amid tepid voter turnout on the left. Democrats suffered huge losses in Congress, governorships, and state legislatures. Although President Obama himself and some Democratic senators would go on to win reelection in 2012, Democratic losses multiplied again in 2014. As in 2010, the Democratic Party and its allies could not draw enough of its core supporters to the polls, not even for an important midterm election with a popular incumbent in the White House.

The next election cycle proved even more upending for both political parties. On the GOP side, a crowd of seasoned Republicans with long experience in public office contended for the presidential nomination—only to lose the primaries to a pugnacious reality TV actor and business operator. Virtually no one had given Donald Trump's candidacy any chance of success when he descended a golden Trump Tower escalator in Manhattan on June 16, 2015, and announced his presidential bid with an alarmist message describing Mexican immigrants as rapists. Candidate Trump dominated the media well beyond the Fox News sector by unleashing a daily stream of outrageous, norm-breaking personal attacks and lies. Meanwhile, below the radar, the candidate and his top aides negotiated transactional bargains with key federated organizational networks—including the National Rifle Association, conservative Christian evangelicals, and the Fraternal Order of Police. The Trump presidential effort never developed much of a campaign infrastructure of its own, but it made deals to activate well-established networks that could spread Trump's message across many states and localities, inspiring high turnout among conservative Christians and gun owners on Election Day.[5]

Trump denounced weak-kneed elites in both parties—and in a certain sense, he was correct. No one in authority seemed to know what to do with Donald

Trump. Crucially, the institutional Republican Party proved too weak to fend off a controversial interloper who hogged the stage and thrilled many GOP voters. For years, Republican politicians and officeholders had catered to the Koch network by moving so far to the free-market right that they lost touch with the passions of many ordinary Republicans. Standard GOP messages about tax cuts for the privileged and reductions in social spending for middle-class programs were not attractive to many Americans, including GOP primary voters who cared much more about the cultural and ethno-nationalist issues emphasized by the Christian right and grassroots Tea Party.

When the country got to the general election, most observers read national polls and opinion surveys and felt sure Trump could not beat the Democratic candidate, Hillary Clinton. But the Clinton campaign and the Democratic Party had stumbled into the fall of 2016 divided by a prolonged Bernie Sanders primary challenge and lacking effective organizational capacities to engage voters in most places outside of metropolitan strongholds. Outgoing president Barack Obama tried to transfer his appeal to America's first female major party presidential candidate, but one of his legacies was a failure to bolster the Democratic Party organization nationally and in the states. When he first ran for the White House, Obama and his supporters built a formidable campaign operation able to reach voters and involve people down to the neighborhood level, but they never transferred the organizational magic to the Democratic Party as a whole.[6]

In 2016, the Hillary Clinton campaign tried to use Obama's targeted voter lists one more time. In most places, the campaign did very little grassroots organizing of the sort that could have helped it keep in touch with voters, activate their social networks, and spot signs of trouble in time to reallocate efforts. In the closing months and weeks, candidate Clinton herself dodged one wild pitch after another—including dirty tricks orchestrated by Russian hackers and a nationally televised tongue-lashing from an FBI director. Voters in the middle of the road remained skeptical of Trump's honesty and presidential qualifications to the end, but Clinton never was able to pull away. The margins separating the polarized and closely balanced Democratic and Republican Parties remained sufficiently close that last-minute twists ultimately helped tip the November 8 outcomes to Trump and GOP congressional contenders, including some in close races.

Suddenly, November 2016 looked like the reverse of November 2008, as once again a polarizing president headed to the White House backed by co-partisan majorities in Congress. Just as Republican elites and citizens feared in 2008 that their political adversaries would be able to drive national politics and policy unchecked, so now did liberals and Democrats dread a Trump-GOP juggernaut. Again, the losers organized and mobilized to push back. This time the defeated party had almost no congressional levers to use, so most oppositional activities happened outside the halls of government. Within days to weeks after the November 2016 election, national and local "resistance" activists took to streets and meeting rooms determined to mobilize against the newly arriving Trump-GOP regime.[7] The day after the new president's inauguration, millions of Women's March protestors appeared not just in Washington, DC, major cities, and liberal states, but also in hundreds of other places all over the country. National advocacy groups, old and new, raised money and added staff for the battles ahead.

Important features of the new waves of anti-Trump citizens eerily resembled those of the grassroots Tea Party mobilizations that started in 2009. National elites were *not* the key actors in either drama—not the major political party leaderships, and not national advocacy or funding organizations. On the contrary, in both 2009 and 2017 local groups of volunteer citizens took the initiative, founding new grassroots organizations in many places almost simultaneously. Just as grassroots Tea Partiers organized widely starting in 2009, so too did local anti-Trump resisters form thousands of new groups after November 2016, spread across all fifty states and across many places within each state. As we will document in this book, the anti-Trump citizen mobilization has, if anything, created more groups in more places than the earlier Tea Party wave—and that is a very important finding. The grassroots anti-Trump resistance is not confined to blue states or big cities. Liberal-minded citizen volunteers, it turns out, have been able to organize much more widely across the US political geography than the Democratic Party and its legacy allies.

Along with old and new liberal organizations operating at the national level, grassroots resistance groups, led and peopled overwhelmingly by middle-class women, fought Trump-GOP policy initiatives throughout 2017, and by a hair, they won the battle to stop the repeal of the Affordable Care Act. After that, many resistance activists prepared to run for office or contact voters on behalf of Democratic candidates. Members of resistance groups and networks helped contest and sometimes win special elections in 2017, and they mobilized everywhere to contest the 2018 midterm elections. To a remarkable degree, this movement grounded in voluntarily organized grassroots groups paid off. Democrats made large 2018 gains in state legislatures, governorships, and especially the US House of Representatives—where a large new freshman class of Democratic winners, heavily female and with many minorities in its ranks, handed control to a Democratic Party majority prepared to check and oppose President Trump.

In some respects, as suggested in this quick narrative of recent American politics, the 2018 turnaround resembles the one that happened from the opposite side in 2010, when grassroots and elite conservatives delivered huge electoral setbacks to the Obama presidency. Furthermore, there are indications that grassroots anti-Trump activists are challenging and remaking state and local

Democratic Parties, much as Tea Partiers remade the GOP years earlier. Some observers are already suggesting that the Democrats may have a "Tea Party problem"—meaning that grassroots activism could push Democrats as far to the left as Tea Party activism and Koch network pressures have pushed contemporary Republicans to the right.[8]

It is too early to draw any such conclusion, however. Although the longer-term reverberations of the current wave of citizen activism remain to be seen, many parts of this book suggest that this wave will end up having different impacts on the Democratic Party—and on national politics—than the radicalizing impact of the earlier Tea Party wave.

New Questions and Sources of Evidence

The recent crosscurrents just recounted have flummoxed many observers of American politics, including political scientists and sociologists. Established perspectives such as median voter theory—the idea that parties will lean to the middle and avoid polarizing extremes—are misleading at best when applied to recent US developments. Similarly, well-worn research tools like national surveys and statistical studies of nationwide voting patterns only skim the surface. Social scientists are never very good at making political predictions, but conventional academic approaches are frequently off the mark these days.

Much of the problem lies in scholarly inattention to changing organizational configurations. In politics, organizations and networks of groups matter beyond individual participants in several important ways. Organizations have public identities and can often ensure continuity of leadership for key activities. Organizations deploy resources continuously, not just momentarily—and, over time, they can shift the balance of power in elections, public discussions, and governmental policymaking. Organizations and networks of groups connect actors to one another and help them concert their voice, plan activities, and build collective resources. In turn, well-organized actors can influence elections, policy advocacy, or governmental actions much more effectively than would be possible if they were just disconnected individual players. Unionized workers, for example, work for different goals and affect politics differently than non-unionized workers.[9] Religious adherents who belong to church networks where most congregants and lay leaders take firm stands on key issues fit into the political process differently than non-church-goers.[10] Organized wealthy donors can have much more impact by working together over time than they are likely to have by making individual one-off contributions.[11] And so forth. Ongoing relationships and connections matter in politics, especially when buttressed by formal organizational capacities.

Most scholars who study politics would assent to these assertions—yet dominant approaches nevertheless tend to ignore organizations and networks. They simply count and parse the individual characteristics, attitudes, and actions of wealthy donors, people who answer polls, citizens who vote, and legislators who answer roll calls. What is more, most analysts of American politics privilege the study of national aggregates—forgetting that the United States has a federated polity where actors in states and districts shape national outcomes.

Departing from standard approaches, contributors to this volume probe the organizations and social networks that channel action at all levels of US government, including the organizational configurations that, at times, link groups across the local, state, and national levels of politics and governance. Certainly, contributors appreciate the value of election data, attitude surveys, and demographic information, and they all make good use of such evidence. Yet the studies assembled here feature organizational analyses. They show how useful investigations of shifting organizational configurations can be for understanding key aspects of contemporary US politics—such as rightward-tilted partisan polarization, the steady movement of the Republican Party toward extremes, and the emergence and impact of widespread grassroots citizen groups on both right and left.

Studies in this volume not only highlight organizational relationships and processes but also present new kinds of empirical evidence about organized civic and political life at both ends of the partisan spectrum and all levels of the US political system. These authors have gathered and analyzed innovative evidence about organizations and their relationships in time and space. Some have ferreted out telling indicators buried in old reports; some have coded events featured on campaign websites; others have recorded evolving discussions on group Facebook pages. A number of these scholars have pieced together timelines that track the back and forth interactions of local and national entities involved in a single so-called social movement, such as the Tea Party or the anti-Trump resistance. This seemingly simple move reveals a great deal about how separately organized actors can build off one another's actions and together bring about major political shifts, even when the various organizations are not parts of any one overarching hierarchy. Likewise, researchers have examined organizations across politically relevant geographic space by preparing state or national maps from lists of kindred units—such as election campaign offices, residences of members of party committees, and the locations of local chapters of the Fraternal Order of Police and grassroots citizen groups.

Most authors of the chapters included here have also gone beyond collecting and analyzing "hard" organizational data to make field visits, conduct personal interviews, and gather questionnaire responses from founders and leaders of groups active in American politics and community life. Academics often separate so-called objective facts from such "soft" information, on the unstated assumption that interviews and questionnaires can only tap subjective attitudes. That is far from true. Observations of real-world organizational events and meetings can reveal a great deal about how politics works on the ground, in real time. Reports from key actors ranging from political strategists to organizational heads and founders can be even more revealing—if the questions posed refer not simply to attitudes but to *how* these actors go about their activities. Done right, field visits, interviews, and questionnaires—including, these days, online questionnaires that can be easy to use for all concerned—can be invaluable tools for discovering how living Americans are launching new groups and organizational networks and using them to influence elections and issue campaigns.

Looking Below the National Level

In addition to asking new questions and gathering fresh evidence about all kinds of US political organizations and their connections to one another, the contributors take very seriously the multilevel nature of American politics and government. That is why this collection includes research on subnational politics and electoral battles that have unfolded in pivotal states such as Florida, Michigan, and Pennsylvania.

As a federation, the US system is one in which power cannot be won or sustained simply by attracting a grand total of more votes regardless of district boundaries. Nor can candidates at any level prevail merely by pursuing policies that poll well in opinion surveys—unless they can get potential voters consistently to back up such expressed attitudes with action at the polls and ongoing efforts to hold elected representatives accountable. To win governing power, US political parties and their allies must organize in ways that allow them to spread messages, engage citizens, and turn out voters across many states and districts. It has never been sufficient in US politics to pile up support in the biggest cities or the most economically advanced regions. That verity has held true since the time of the Founding Fathers, and it is even truer today during an era when partisan divisions are often reinforced by geographical divides.[12]

Of course, the federated nature of US politics has always been clear to savvy politicians and strategists of all persuasions. In recent years, however, possibilities for leveraging US federalism have been more effectively realized by operatives and organization-builders on the right. From the 1970s and 1980s on, conservative elites have invested in federated networks that span most US states; and they have forged links among GOP state legislators, free-market think tanks, and organizations that can mobilize activists for elections and policy battles.[13] Elite-supported conservative organizations have also linked their operations and resources to grassroots conservatives, who are themselves spread across many states and districts and tightly networked in churches, gun clubs, and voluntary groups such as Tea Parties. In turn, allied and complementary elite and populist networks boost Republican electoral prospects—and, once GOPers take office, these networks can also pressure them to enact tax cuts, eviscerate market regulations, weaken labor rights, and adopt measures favored by religious conservatives, no matter how unpopular these steps may be with the majority of Americans.

Meanwhile, in the orbit of the Democratic Party, long-standing federated organizational networks have declined—including many labor unions buffeted not just by industrial transformations but also by stepped-up conservative assaults on union rights. Today's right-wing elites not only look for ways to tap into their own widespread grassroots networks; they also seek to use governmental power wherever they can to weaken voter turnout in Democratic areas and eviscerate the organizational capacities of their liberal opponents. Public sector unions, in particular, are three-level federated organizations that span levels of politics and bolster Democrats in elections and policy campaigns. As these unions have come under attack and experienced losses, Democrats have fallen back on presidential campaigns to extend their reach across many states and localities. The 2008 Obama campaign did that very effectively, but its organizational gains were not translated into enduring Democratic Party capacities at the grassroots. Democratic Party organs and allied groups have continued to wither in many places—creating a self-reinforcing downward spiral in which having fewer party officeholders reduces the Democratic presence in many districts and states where, in turn, it becomes even harder for liberals to influence public discussions or reach out to voters.

Not until Democratic Party fortunes hit a kind of recent rock bottom did new efforts to halt and reverse the downward spiral emerge—the election of Donald Trump quite suddenly spurred left-leaning grassroots citizens to organize across every state in communities large and small. Newly organized and energized liberal citizens are now making their voices heard, and from 2017 on, they have buoyed Democratic electoral prospects and results. The effects are still playing out. As we will see in many chapters of this volume, these new citizen activists, like right-wing Tea Party activists before them, may very well propel another round of transformations in the organizational terrain on which US politics unfolds.

The Chapters Ahead

Although we have outlined the organizational and network-oriented frame of reference used by contributors to this volume, we have not provided lengthy elaborations of theoretical concepts or posed highly general hypotheses. This volume is not a theoretical treatise, because its main purpose is to make sense of current trends and conflicts in US politics—both nationally and in important battleground states. Sometimes the best way to get around engrained assumptions and approaches is simply to show broad audiences that there are better ways to ask and answer questions. Show more than tell is what this tightly edited volume aims to do—at a juncture when many citizens as well as scholars are looking for fresh insights into US politics.

The chapters to follow are organized into two major parts. In Part I, authors look closely at the reasons that partisan polarization is so heavily tilted to the right. Chapter 1 dissects the top-down and bottom-up forces that have recently buffeted and refocused the national Republican Party, setting the stage for the current Trump presidency that fuses anti-immigrant politics with free-market economics. Chapters 2 and 3 probe the same processes of GOP radicalization as they have played out in the pivotal states of Wisconsin and North Carolina.

Then chapters 4, 5, and 6 delve more deeply into the popular outlooks, campaign activities, and conservative organizational networks that helped Donald Trump take over the Republican Party and win the 2016 presidential election—including by "flipping" the pivotal states of Pennsylvania and Michigan. The most analytically focused of these studies, reported in chapter 4, challenges the conventional pundit and academic wisdom that the 2016 Trump presidential campaign was "disorganized," dependent only on the candidate's dominance of national media coverage. Under the radar, this chapter shows, the Trump campaign worked out specific transactional bargains with key leaders of existing organizational networks, with celebrity Christian right pastors, with the heads of the National Rifle Association, and with leaders of the Fraternal Order of Police. Candidate Trump and his close associates courted these key organizational leaders early and often, promising to deliver on their policy preferences—especially on their yearning for conservative Supreme Court appointments—in return for their efforts to spread messages to millions of grassroots conservative voters who regularly participate in church networks, gun clubs, and (predominantly white) police union locals. Such local organizations just so happen to reach and connect conservative-minded Americans spread across electorally important districts and states that would tip the presidential contest to Trump in November 2016.

Part II of this volume considers what has happened to Democrats in recent years, both leading into and immediately after the cataclysmic 2016 election. Chapter 7 shines a spotlight on the ground-level capacities of Florida's Democratic and Republican Parties to reach voters in the pivotal I-4 corridor of this perennial swing state. The Obama campaigns of 2008 and 2012 effectively deployed relational organizing in Florida, but subsequently the Florida GOP adopted such practices while the state's Democrats allowed earlier connections to wither away.

Chapters 8 and 9 turn to the widespread bursts of new grassroots citizen organizing that spread across America in the wake of Donald Trump's election and the post-inaugural Women's Marches. Both chapters explore the strong role of older, mostly white, relatively highly educated middle-class women in organizing, leading, and energizing these efforts, which fought against the Trump-GOP agenda during 2017 and then turned to inspiring and supporting new candidates to run for local and state offices as well as Congress in 2018. Female-led grassroots organizations have been at the vanguard of what is often dubbed "the resistance," these chapters show. These same volunteer-led groups have been the main force behind recent turnarounds for Democrats in most places.

Additional aftereffects of the post-2016 bursts of grassroots energy on the center left figure into the remaining chapters of Part II. Chapter 10 asks why, following the January 2018 high school shootings in Parkland, Florida, public opinion and legislative agendas took surprising turns toward more support for gun control. Part of the explanation lies in timing and interactions between social movements. This chapter shows that young survivors from Marjory Stoneman Douglas High School who organized nationwide protests were able to build on prior resistance protests and garner (often behind the scenes) support from grassroots groups in many communities. In turn, Chapter 11 looks closely at the roots, strategies, and organizational legacies of Democrat Beto O'Rourke's surprisingly strong 2018 Senate campaign in the deep red state of Texas. That campaign lost, but it also worked in conjunction with the anti-Trump grassroots resistance to shift electoral margins and implant new organizational capacities for Democrats in Texas cities and suburbs.

The final two chapters of Part II—and the book—take us deep into the ground-level realities of politics in the pivotal state of Pennsylvania, describing and probing in rich detail the ways in which post-2016 resistance groups have boosted post-2016 Democratic campaigns for public office. Chapter 12 explores the dynamics and effects of resistance network efforts in the collar counties around Philadelphia plus the Lehigh Valley. Chapter 13 carries this line of investigation further, showing that in other parts of the state—in southwestern areas around Pittsburgh and in pockets of central Pennsylvania—new grassroots groups have similarly helped Democrats win or improve their margins in election contests, and they have gone on to revitalize local Democratic Party organizations in many places. Using freshly collected evidence, this chapter documents the existence of more than two hundred grassroots resistance groups that have operated since November 2016 in fifty-five of the sixty-seven counties in the vast Keystone State; and it uses questionnaire responses from more than eighty local groups to illuminate their ongoing electoral and civic activities.

Organized elite and grassroots efforts analyzed in this volume are continuing on both the right and left in US politics, and both major political parties are changing in important ways. Highly consequential shifts are proceeding apace, as tightly networked conservatives and President Trump remake the Republican Party at all levels, while organized local and national activists push for changes in the Democratic Party. Any predictions we might attempt would not likely hold for long, so we mostly refrain from making them. Instead, in the concluding chapter, we will draw on the rich analyses and provocative findings of this volume to suggest various scenarios that might unfold in American politics in 2020 election and beyond.

Notes

1. Peter Beinart, "The New New Deal," *Time*, November 24, 2008.
2. Michael Grunwald, "The Party of No," chapter 7 in *The New New Deal: The Hidden Story of Change in the Obama Era* (New York: Simon and Schuster, 2012).
3. Developments in various policy areas are analyzed in Theda Skocpol and Lawrence R. Jacobs, eds., *Reaching for a New Deal: Ambitious Governance, Economic Meltdown, and Polarized Politics in Obama's First Two Years* (New York: Russell Sage Foundation, 2011).
4. Alexander Hertel-Fernandez, Theda Skocpol, and Daniel Lynch, "Business Associations, Conservative Networks, and the Ongoing Republican War Over Medicaid Expansion," *Journal of Health Politics, Policy and Law* 41, no. 2 (April 2016): 239–86.
5. This argument is fully developed in chapter 4, "The Overlooked Organizational Basis of Trump's 2016 Victory."
6. Elizabeth McKenna and Hahrie Han, *Groundbreakers: How Obama's 2.2 Million Volunteers Transformed Campaigning in America* (New York: Oxford University Press, 2015).
7. For good overviews, see the various contributions to *The Resistance: The Dawn of the Anti-Trump Opposition Movement*, ed. David S. Meyer and Sidney Tarrow (New York: Oxford University Press, 2018).
8. Tom Davis, "Are Democrats Facing Their Own Tea Party-Style Reckoning?" *Politico*, March 18, 2019.
9. John S. Ahlquist, "Labor Unions, Political Representation, and Economic Inequality," *Annual Review of Political Science* 20 (May 2017): 409–32.
10. Robert D. Putnam and David E. Campbell, *American Grace: How Religion Divides and Unites Us* (New York: Simon and Schuster, 2010), chap. 12; Lydia Bean, *The Politics of Evangelical Identity: Local Churches and Partisan Divides in the United States and Canada* (Princeton, NJ: Princeton University Press, 2016); and Lydia Bean and Brandon C. Martinez, "Sunday School Teacher, Culture Warrior: The Politics of Lay Leaders in Three Religious Traditions," *Social Science Quarterly* 96, no. 1 (2015): 133–47.
11. Alexander Hertel-Fernandez, Theda Skocpol, and Jason Sclar, "When Political Mega-Donors Join Forces: How the Koch Network and the Democracy Alliance Influence Organized U.S. Politics on the Right and Left," *Studies in American Political Development* 32, no. 2 (October 2018): 127–65.
12. US institutional arrangements have always disfavored cities, but current economic trends are making political imbalances and partisan polarization more severe. See Jonathan A. Rodden, *Why Cities Lose: The Deep Roots of the Urban-Rural Political Divide* (New York: Basic Books, 2019).
13. Alexander Hertel-Fernandez, *State Capture: How Conservative Activists, Big Businesses, and Wealthy Donors Reshaped the American States—and the Nation* (New York: Oxford University Press, 2019).

PART I

REPUBLICANS OUTFLANKED AND RADICALIZED

1

The Elite and Popular Roots of Contemporary Republican Extremism

"The Republican Party has become . . . ideologically extreme; contemptuous of the inherited social and economic policy regime; scornful of compromise; un-persuaded by conventional understanding of facts, evidence, and science; and dismissive of the legitimacy of its political opposition." This startling description appeared not in a partisan broadside but in a wonkish book, *It's Even Worse Than It Looks: How the American Constitutional System Collided with the New Politics of Extremism*, co-authored by two sober-minded analysts of different personal political persuasions, Thomas Mann and Norman Ornstein.[1] Since the 1980s, the authors point out, partisan polarization in the United States has been propelled by the unremitting rightward movement of the Republican Party. Traditional political science models predict that a party will lean toward the middle to attract "median voters," especially after it experiences big election losses.[2] But the contemporary Republican Party defies such expectations. After Democrats won major victories in 2006, 2008, and 2012, Republicans responded by moving ever further toward the ultra-free-market right, pushing unpopular efforts to cut taxes on the rich, eviscerate labor protections, and slash spending on education, Social Security, and health care. Following the GOP's non-majority presidential victory in 2016, congressional Republicans not only continue to pursue unpopular policies; they display an increasing willingness to accede to President Trump's violations of US governing norms. Even after the 2018 midterm elections generated a "blue wave" of gains by Democrats, Republicans have responded to growing signs of voter displeasure by, if anything, doubling down on extremist governing moves.

Theda Skocpol, *The Elite and Popular Roots of Contemporary Republican Extremism* In: *Upending American Politics* Edited by: Theda Skocpol and Caroline Tervo, Oxford University Press (2020). © Oxford University Press DOI: 10.1093/oso/9780190083526.003.0001

Why have radical tendencies taken hold in one of America's two major political parties? Standard wisdom attributes contemporary Republican stances to ordinary voters—especially to Tea Partiers, Christian conservatives, and working-class nativists. In this telling, GOP candidates and elected officials are merely reflecting what their most fervent popular supporters demand. There is some truth to this claim, as this chapter will elaborate. Popular disaffection with a changing American society is generating votes for conservative politicians willing to defend traditional family and gender roles and eager to demonize African Americans and immigrants of color as (supposed) agents of disorder and decline. From the Tea Party protests that broke out early in the presidency of Barack Obama to raucous approval of Donald Trump's racially charged rhetoric in today's mass rallies, this ethno-nationalist stream of radicalism (as I label it) has unquestionably been on the rise in American public discourse, and it has been voiced in increasingly unabashed ways by many Republican politicians. Nevertheless, popular ethno-nationalism is at most only half the story, because an earlier organized elite effort to advance anti-government free-market libertarianism is an equally if not more important factor feeding today's Republican Party extremism.

Well before ethno-nationalist anxieties swelled under the nation's first African American president, uber-rich Americans advocating unpopular economic agendas had already colonized much of the Republican Party. In this undertaking, two highly ranked Forbes 400 brothers, industrialists Charles and David Koch, orchestrated other right-leaning millionaires and billionaires to construct a well-financed and tightly integrated set of political organizations at the right edge of the GOP.[3] With Americans for Prosperity at its core, the Koch political machine (often dubbed "the Koch network") grew into virtually a third major party able to work at local, state, and national levels to push and pull Republican candidates and elected officials toward a utopian ideological vision of small, elite-serving government. As I will spell out in this chapter, the Koch network has achieved major electoral and governing gains. From the early 2000s through today's Trump presidency, virtually all Republican officeholders and candidates have pushed for—and whenever possible enacted—the government-hobbling economic policies advocated by this plutocratic elite movement.

The contemporary Republican Party, in short, channels two separate currents of right-wing extremism—billionaire ultra-free-market fundamentalism and popularly rooted ethno-nationalist resentment. In this chapter, I analyze the organizational networks, outlooks, and sets of political resources that have nourished these two streams of right-wing radicalism—tendencies that have fused into an explosive mix with Donald Trump in the White House.

The Growing Clout
of Ultra-Free-Market Plutocrats

Some years ago, my research colleagues and I set out to assess shifting organizational resources in US politics—and it did not take us long to notice major, abrupt changes unfolding to the right of the Republican Party. Our first move was to assemble lists of nationally influential organizations operating in the early twenty-first century.[4] To assess underlying resources rather than spikes that occur in presidential election years, we recorded budgets for 2002 and 2014 (or the closest available year) for five kinds of groups:[5]

- *Political party committees*—including the Republican National Committee, the senatorial and congressional campaign committees, and the committees funding campaigns across state legislative and gubernatorial contests.
- *Non-party funders*—organized consortia that raise money from many rich donors and channel it into multiple campaigns and political efforts—such as Karl Rove's American Crossroads PAC, as well as the Koch seminars. This category does **not** include political action committees for individual candidates.
- *Constituency organizations*—that claim to speak for and mobilize broad constituencies, including business associations, the National Rifle Association, the Christian Coalition, and Americans for Prosperity.
- *Issue advocacy organizations*—professionally run groups that lobby on behalf of specific kinds of policies, such as antiabortion and pro-choice groups, anti-tax groups, and Washington, DC–centered environmental advocates.
- *Think tanks*—such as the Heritage Foundation, the Cato Institute, and the American Enterprise Institute.

The budget aggregates displayed in Figure 1.1 suggest recent sharp shifts in the organizational channels through which conservative political resources flow. In particular, Republican Party committees lost considerable ground compared to extra-party consortia of conservative donors—consortia that, in turn, channeled hundreds of millions of dollars to beef up extra-party think tanks, constituency mobilizing organizations, and utilities of the sort that the institutional GOP previously controlled. Tellingly, the resource shifts portrayed in Figure 1.1 occurred largely through the rise of new far-right organizations instituted after 2002. If my colleagues and I had tracked only the budgets of organizations that existed continuously from 2002 to 2014, we would still have noted some reallocations (principally from GOP party committees to constituency mobilizing organizations), but those shifts were modest. When both long-standing and post-2002 groups are included (as they are in Figure 1.1), the resource share controlled by

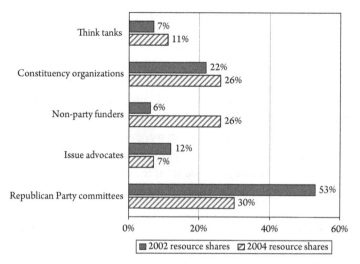

Figure 1.1 Shifting Shares of Organizational Resources on the US Right, 2002–2014.

Notes: Percentages refer to share of total budget resources in specified year (or nearest non-presidential election year).

GOP committees plunged from 53 percent of the conservative pie in 2002 to just 30 percent by 2014, at the same time as the share deployed by old and new extra-party funders burgeoned from 6 percent in 2002 to 26 percent by 2014. A closer look revealed that many of the recently founded extra-party entities deploying expanded resources are Koch-connected organizations launched after 2002.

Deciphering the Koch Network

Indeed, dramatic shifts on the contemporary US right cannot be explained without focusing on recent developments in a network of tightly coordinated organizations orchestrated by Charles Koch and his recently deceased brother, David. Their network is far more than a personal pet project because, especially between 2003 and 2012, the brothers and their allies persuaded hundreds of conservative-minded millionaires and billionaires to devote huge flows of funding to buoy the GOP and pull it to the ultra-free-market right. This deployment of pooled resources has been strategically used to build a massive political machine. Explicitly or implicitly, many previous analysts have treated the Koch operation as a corporate dark-money "front group" that scatters donations through dozens of conduits into national elections.[6] In this telling, "Kochtopus" tentacles can be found in almost every conservative cause that has ever received any kind of Koch-connected donation, including groups ranging from mainstays like the US Chamber of Commerce, the National Rifle Association, and Christian right groups to temporary operations set up to pay for advertising during one election season.[7] Taking a very different approach, my research colleagues and I hone in on the goals, personnel, and activities of a core set of major organizations heavily funded by Koch-orchestrated donors and directly controlled—and coordinated—by leaders they have installed.[8]

As the timeline in Figure 1.2 shows, the roots of Koch-orchestrated political activity go back many decades. Charles and David Koch took ideas seriously and believed that politicians "reflect" rather than create "the prevalent ideology," so they started out as major backers of the nation's leading libertarian think tank, the Cato Institute, founded in 1977.[9] In the 1980s, they became continuous sponsors of the Mercatus Center at George Mason University, which does policy studies and runs educational programs, plus the Charles G. Koch Foundation, which disburses grants to college and university-based scholars and supports programs to encourage free-market ideas and policy proposals.[10] During the 1970s, Charles and David Koch backed the Libertarian Party; and David even ran for vice president on the party's 1980 ticket. After this foray made little headway, the Kochs set up more conventional advocacy organizations to influence policymaking through lobbying and, increasingly, public outreach.

In the second phase of Koch network building, Citizens for a Sound Economy was started in 1984 to press for tax and regulatory cuts on behalf of corporate clients.[11] It functioned until 2004, when it split apart in a fight between the Kochs and the organization's erstwhile chairman, Dick Armey.[12] During the Bush senior presidential administration of the 1990s, the Kochs also sponsored

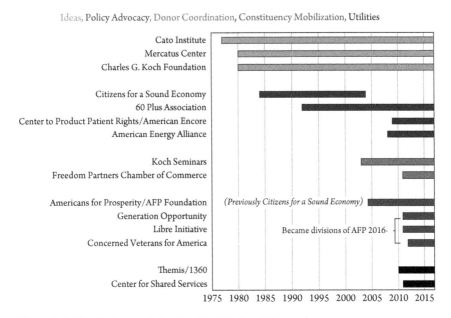

Figure 1.2 The Evolution of the Core Koch Political Network.

the 60 Plus Association to press for privatization of Social Security and Medicare and the elimination of the estate tax. In recent years, this group has campaigned against the Affordable Care Act of 2010.[13] Additional advocacy operations took to the field during the early Obama administration, including the American Energy Alliance to fight environmental regulations and cap and trade legislation, as well as the Center to Protect Patient Rights to push against the Obama health reform effort.[14] Later, the center also served as a conduit through which Koch-connected donors funded election efforts against Democrats.[15]

The long-standing proclivity of the Kochs to orchestrate other donors is perhaps the clearest reason that it is misleading to regard them as simply throwing around personal money. As heirs of a privately held corporate conglomerate, the brothers were always in a position to think big, and as men who take philosophical and normative ideas as well as material interests very seriously, they envisioned political change in a multifaceted and long-term way. With Charles in the lead, the brothers started in 2003 to go well beyond solo donor tactics by convening twice-yearly donor "seminars" at which invited wealthy conservatives, chiefly business leaders, are exposed to ultra-free-market and libertarian ideas as well as practical political strategies. At first, these Koch seminars were tiny, intellectually ponderous affairs; but after 2006 interest and attendance steadily grew.[16] By 2010, more than two hundred wealthy invited donors attended the seminars, often in husband-wife pairs, and by now attendance regularly exceeds four hundred to five hundred.[17] In 2012, the Freedom Partners Chamber of Commerce took charge of these events and the funds they raise.[18] Formal rules require guests to pledge a minimum of $100,000 per year to Koch endeavors in return for the right to participate in the seminars, yet it is clear that most give well above that minimum.[19]

Some sessions at the biannual seminars have amounted to auditions for invited GOP candidates, including congressional leaders like Paul Ryan and Mitch McConnell; governors like Scott Walker and Mike Pence and Chris Christie; Senate candidates like Cory Gardner, Tom Cotton, and Joni Ernst; and assorted presidential hopefuls.[20] The Koch network as such does not endorse particular candidates; instead, it deploys what is arguably a much more effective tactic by encouraging politicians to compete to prove that they can be effective executors of its agenda. Because the Koch seminars attract many wealthy supporters, politicians covet invitations and are glad to audition for the guests. Nevertheless, the seminars are not chiefly about "meets and greets" with politicians. Primarily, they foster like-mindedness and camaraderie and focus the assembled millionaires and billionaires on supporting interlinked Koch organizations.[21]

In recent years the Koch seminars have especially featured—and raised hundreds of millions of dollars to support—a political party–like set of organizations that constitute the third phase of comprehensive Koch network building.

Core entities include Concerned Veterans for America, launched in 2012 to deal with military veterans' issues and push for privatization of the Veterans Administration.[22] Also included are operations reaching out to constituencies liberals presume are on their side: Generation Opportunity ("GenOpp") targets young people and the Libre Initiative engages Latinos, especially in swing states.[23] Several general-utility organizations bolster Koch political efforts, including Themis/i360, a combined for-profit and nonprofit operation that has worked since 2010 to develop and deploy real-time digitized data on conservative voters and activists—resembling Catalist on the left.[24]

Within the twenty-first-century Koch network, a gigantic operation called "Americans for Prosperity" stands out as the centerpiece. Along with a coordinated nonprofit foundation led by the same board, Americans for Prosperity ("AFP" for short) was set up in 2004 as a 501(c)(4) following the break-up of Citizens for a Sound Economy, just as the Kochs were also getting their biannual donor seminars under way. By 2005, the Kochs recruited Tim Phillips, an influential Christian right organizer, to direct and vastly expand the operation at both national and state levels. As the dark gray coloring in Figure 1.3 shows, AFP achieved remarkable expansion even before Barack Obama launched his run for the presidency. By the end of 2007, AFP already had paid state directors installed in fifteen states encompassing almost half the total US population and their representatives in Congress. Well before the Democratic sweeps in the 2008 elections, AFP organizations were at work not just in conservative regions but also in the electorally contested Midwest and upper South. As later chapters in this book detail, early AFP investments in Wisconsin and North Carolina would pay off handsomely down the road.

For 2004 through 2016, the table included in Figure 1.3 tracks the overall growth in affiliated volunteer activists, budgets, and total staffing (using lists or media reports that include national staffers as well as state staffs). Every indicator points to sharp upward growth—with the caveat that the ranks of volunteer conservative activists in regular contact with AFP have increased only gradually since 2013, while paid staffing levels swelled more sharply. As it attracts generous donations from the Koch network, AFP has become more staff-heavy— and during pivotal elections or policy battles AFP raises and deploys resource "surges" to pay for advertisements and bevies of temporary field operatives in states such as Colorado and Florida.[25]

How AFP and the Koch Network Leverage the GOP

As a massive political operation, the Koch network arrayed around Americans for Prosperity combines organizational features usually found separately. It is centrally directed yet federated; it influences both elections and policymaking;

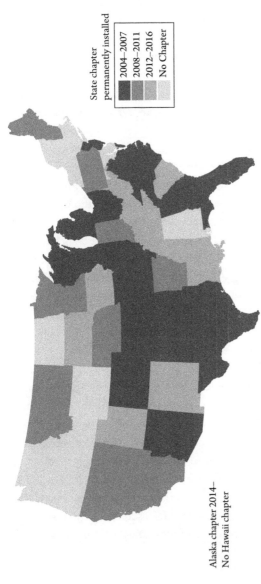

State chapter
permanently installed

- 2004–2007
- 2008–2011
- 2012–2016
- No Chapter

Alaska chapter 2014–
No Hawaii chapter

	Budget (millions $, combined AFP/Foundation)	National & state staff (AFP reported)	National & state staff (IRS reported, combined AFP/Foundation)	Millions activists nationwide	Activists per staffer (AFP reported)	State directors	% U.S. pop in staffed states
2005	3.8	19	17	0.2 est		5	16%
2007	9.2	58	50	0.7	12,069	15	47%
2009	27.1	74	88	0.9	12,162	19	61%
2011	50.8	106	177	1.58	14,868	25	70%
2013	57.6	115	437	2.24	19,443	28	75%
2015	150	500	902	2.43	4,858	34	80%
2017	At least 67.4	650		2.8	4,308	36	82%

Sources: IRS reports, AFP prospectuses; media reports.

Figure 1.3 The Rapid Growth of Americans for Prosperity.

The Elite and Popular Roots of Contemporary Republican Extremism

it combines insider lobbying with public campaigns and grassroots activation; and—perhaps most important of all—the Koch operation enforces its own highly disciplined policy agenda but at the same time is thoroughly intertwined with the Republican Party. Each of these combinations deserves elaboration. Taken together, they explain how the Koch network has gained the capacity to colonize and redirect the Republican Party.

AFP's unique combination of *corporate and federated organizational features* is its most striking characteristic. Like a privately held corporation, AFP is directed from above by centrally appointed managers operating from headquarters in Arlington, Virginia. National managers oversee functions such as fundraising, policy, and web communications—and in recent years, AFP has also deployed regional managers to shepherd groups of states. Along with the AFP board, the director and top lieutenants obviously have complete authority over personnel and resource allocations. Over-time tracking shows that AFP officials are appointed and removed at will and regularly moved around within AFP or among Koch organizations. Top AFP leaders direct special infusions of funds into various functions and states—for example, into big advertising buys during key Senate election battles or into hot campaigns to block Medicaid expansion in particular states.[26]

Yet even though AFP is highly centralized like a corporation, it also has a federated structure with important state-level organizations, just like classic voluntary associations and the US governmental system as a whole.[27] Most states have directors and other paid staffers such as "grassroots directors" who monitor and influence state and local politics and weigh in with their state's US senators and representatives. State-level AFP officials remain beholden to national managers, however. Although AFP normally appoints directors who have long-standing ties in their states, directors are *not* selected by in-state activists and, regardless of their varied career backgrounds, directors along with all other employees push the standard AFP agenda using well-honed scripts and routines. AFP is a disciplined, well-oiled machine.

In another distinctive combination, Americans for Prosperity *conducts political activities between as well as during elections*, maintaining a continuity of effort that its leaders proudly tout in public statements and private pitches to potential donors.[28] To be sure, AFP budgets and expenditures balloon during election years, as national and state operatives channel major funding into presidential contests and key Senate races. Nevertheless, AFP is not a mere pass through for electioneering monies. Every year, AFP mounts policy campaigns and maintains lobbying and grassroots pressure on legislators and public officials, especially in state legislatures. During battles in the states over Medicaid expansion under ObamaCare, for instance, AFP state directors issued press releases, pressured legislators, and mounted "grassroots" protests. The same sort of thing happens in other state-level fights over highway funding, taxes, and funding for education and social policies, as well as in battles over right-to-work legislation and curbs on public sector unions. In all such battles, AFP organizations work closely with the local legislators enrolled in the American Legislative Exchange Council (ALEC) and with conservative free-market think tanks operating in the State Policy Network.[29] In addition, many AFP-organized states put out annual "scorecards" to track votes by members of their own state legislatures, as well as publicizing the scores assigned by national AFP to their state's congressional contingents.

This brings us to the third way that AFP combines typically separated functions—*by synchronizing staff-led lobbying and publicity efforts with mobilization of volunteer citizen activists.* Most AFP-organized states have grassroots directors of some sort, whose responsibilities include maintaining lists of conservative activists, communicating regularly with them, and putting out calls for public demonstrations from time to time—such as a protest staged at a legislative hearing about a controversial piece of legislation. Overall, AFP claims to enroll more than 3 million activists nationwide—including tens to hundreds of thousands in each state (including states without paid AFP directors). Yet it is important to understand what AFP activists do—and do not—accomplish. No doubt, AFP managers pay attention to the ideas and passions of conservative voters and activists; and they certainly try to build and update contact lists so rank-and-file conservatives can be contacted for issue campaigns, turned out on Election Day, and urged to donate to AFP (which can then proudly proclaim that it has large numbers of "small donors"). However, in no sense do citizen "members" control AFP. Voluntarily affiliated citizens do not elect AFP leaders; they do not provide the bulk of organizational funding; and they do not determine AFP public messages or issue agendas. Wealthy donors and centrally orchestrated managers within the Koch political network perform all of those directive functions.

Now we get to the core question of how AFP relates to the Republican Party. In essence, *AFP is autonomous and directed from above, yet at the same time it is sufficiently intertwined with the GOP at all levels that it can pull party agendas steadily rightward—in Washington, DC, and across many states at once.* AFP pursues a broad pro-free-market agenda with a highly disciplined focus on economic and political issues, avoiding controversial social policies like gay marriage, abortion, and immigration as much as possible. Like earlier free-market advocacy groups, it pressures and pulls Republican candidates and officeholders to follow its preferred agenda. However, unlike earlier kindred organizations, AFP pursues a broader set of priorities and engages in a more integrated set of political activities across multiple levels of government. It more closely resembles a European-style political party than any sort of specialized traditional US advocacy group or election campaign organization. All the same, AFP is not a separate political party but, instead, is organized to parallel and leverage the Republican Party. AFP overlaps with the party but is not subsumed within it or beholden to GOP officials.[30] With a disciplined focus on its own agenda, AFP channels electoral support—advertisements and canvassers—to friendly Republican candidates (and away from those who do not support Koch priorities). Between elections, AFP lobbyists and citizen activists go to bat for GOP governments willing to enact the ultra-free-market agenda.

All of this has moved the needle to the right in many policy arenas. AFP and the Koch network have worked with other far-right organizations to block federal minimum wage increases and paid family leave, while also furthering efforts to slash taxes on business and wealthy Americans—even though all of these are unpopular positions.[31] Although the Koch network's efforts to prevent enactment of the Affordable Care Act of 2010 fell short, AFP has joined forces with free-market think tanks and ALEC to successfully delay or completely block ObamaCare's federally funded expansion of Medicaid to the near poor in many GOP-led states.[32] Perhaps most important of all, AFP and its state-level partners were very successful after 2010 in persuading fifteen states to eliminate or weaken the rights of public sector labor unions to collect dues or bargain for improved wages and hours.[33] This amounts to reshaping the US political terrain along with the economy, because undercutting union finances and member rolls reduces their support for Democratic candidates and limits prospects for progressive policymaking.[34] The rightward lunge of the GOP has also blocked popular compromises supported by many business elites. Most prominent US business organs favor increased government investments in infrastructure, but Koch-aligned Republicans seek to unravel federal or state highway programs and block new public infrastructure investments.

Finally, most Americans, including majorities of Republicans and GOP-leaning Independents, endorse many environmental protections and want carbon dioxide regulated as a dangerous pollutant.[35] Yet as public and even business support for action on climate change grows, AFP has persuaded more and more congressional Republicans to sign on to its "No Climate Tax Pledge."[36] With increasing unanimity, Republican politicians denounce climate science and seek to undercut environmental regulations of all kinds. As Vox reporter David Roberts has detailed, popular views are not sufficient to explain why the US Republican Party has become "the world's only major climate-denialist party," an outlier even compared to other conservative political parties worldwide.[37]

In a very short span of time, the twenty-first-century Koch network has revamped the economic policy agendas of the Republican Party—moving its officeholders and candidates far to the right on issues of public spending, taxation, and environmental and labor regulations. In the same period, AFP and other Koch political operations have helped many friendly Republicans win office at all levels of government, putting them in a position to enact the wish lists of ultra-free-market plutocrats, even when most Americans prefer very different policies.

The Tea Party Fuels Ethno-Nationalism

Of course the Koch network and its elite allies have not gotten everything they want—certainly not as soon as they hoped and planned. In the 2008 elections, Democrats led by Barack Obama won the presidency along with substantial majorities in both houses of Congress and key offices in many states. From the Koch vantage point, it was a blow for Republicans they increasingly controlled to lose so badly. Yet unbowed conservative elites at once plotted comebacks.[38] GOP leaders and their far-right funders knew that Democrats faced challenging 2010 midterm elections, and they set out to use intra-governmental obstruction and all possible extra-governmental levers to fuel opposition to the new president. In important ways, Obama's presidency turned out to be beneficial to the Koch network, as wealthy conservatives disillusioned with the institutional Republican Party clamored for invitations to the twice-yearly seminars and increased their aggregate donations via the Koch network from the tens to hundreds of millions.

Even so, the most spectacular reaction to Obama Democrats was *not* directly orchestrated either by the GOP or by its Koch outriggers. Within six weeks of the new president's inauguration, grassroots conservatives across America took heart from a television "rant" in which CNBC commentator Rick Santelli called for "Tea Party" protests.[39] In the following days and weeks, Fox News spread the word and assorted national advocacy groups on the right urged conservatives in every state and community to plan for coordinated street protests to start on Tax Day 2009, when an estimated 450,000 to 800,000 activists staged some protests in 542 counties across the country.[40] Recurrent public Tea Party protests continued thereafter, including marches on Washington, DC, as well as regional rallies timed at intervals over the next several years.

How the Tea Party Upsurge Really Worked

Public displays of anti-Obama anger—in which ordinary (mostly older white) Americans dressed up in colonial-style costumes and carried signs denouncing the president and Democratic Party initiatives—were a godsend for Republicans looking to rev up votes for 2010; and leaders of the Koch network loved these displays too. Americans for Prosperity often joined other professionally run advocacy and funding organizations to co-sponsor Tea Party branded rallies, fly in speakers, and send buses to transport grassroots citizen activists to Washington, DC, or regional marches. At the fall 2009 annual "Defending the American Dream" summit of Americans for Prosperity, David Koch spoke glowingly of the Tea Party movement in a plenary session where one paid AFP organizer after another stood up to take credit for orchestrating movement activities.[41] Much of this was unwarranted credit claiming, however.

Efforts by professionally run national political organizations to feature and leverage grassroots Tea Party energies soon led many commentators in the media and academia to conclude that this upsurge as a whole was mainly a top-down mirage, an "astroturf" creation of big-moneyed forces opposed to President Obama.[42] But Vanessa Williamson and I learned otherwise when we not only collected national survey and organizational data but also went into the field in Arizona, Virginia, and New England to attend local Tea Party meetings and interview grassroots volunteer leaders and participants.[43] Many local Tea Partiers, we discovered, knew little about national advocacy groups, including AFP. We witnessed for ourselves that their local meetings were run and attended by volunteers and, at most, were very modestly funded by bake sales, personal donations, and commissions from sales of memorabilia such as T-shirts, books like Sarah Palin's autobiography, and Tea Party pins "made in China." Local Tea Party groups turned out to be self-organized and determined to guard their autonomy. In fact, a careful look at the chronology of Tea Party activities reveals that from spring to summer of 2009, grassroots conservatives moved on from early public rallies to organize local, regularly meeting groups— ongoing grassroots citizen organizations that appear not to have been originally envisaged by national media outlets or advocacy professionals sitting in Washington, DC, offices.

Popular Tea Party organizing unfolded remarkable waves from the spring of 2009 through 2010 and beyond, as many conservative-minded Americans sought each other out to form local groups of dozens to hundreds of men and women who gathered weekly or monthly to keep up pressure against Obama Democrats and oppose any Republicans inclined to compromise. When my research colleagues and I did an exhaustive inventory of local Tea Parties with web presences of any sort in the spring of 2011, we found more than nine hundred of them spread across all fifty states.[44] Two-thirds were still meeting when we checked again in the spring of 2012. Research my colleagues and I have done more recently suggests that we missed several hundred more local Tea Parties that met for some span of time—certainly through 2010, when many avowed Tea Party adherents were elected to Congress and state-level offices.

Local Tea Parties were not creations of the Koch brothers or any other national professional operation. They were modestly funded and directed by volunteers who arranged weekly or monthly meeting spaces in libraries, back rooms of restaurants, or church halls. Most gatherings featured invited speakers, such as right-wing radio hosts, conservative preachers or professors, or lecturers dispatched from regional pro-gun or anti-tax networks or nationwide federations like AFP or FreedomWorks. Portions of meetings might also be devoted to organizing car pools to transport members to rallies or lobby days at state legislators or the US Congress. In some places, local Tea Parties cooperated in loose metropolitan or statewide networks, but most operated on their own. Indeed, local Tea Parties have almost all been fiercely autonomous, suspicious of any efforts at direction from above.

What Tea Party Supporters Want

Grassroots Tea Party organizers and members were (and still are, in places where groups continue to meet) overwhelmingly middle-class older white men and women, often married couples.[45] Tea Partiers are very conservative-minded people, many of whom previously participated in Republican politics or conservative causes such as pro-life or pro-gun organizing. Early attitude surveys sometimes mischaracterized partisan leanings, because pollsters mistook the self-labeling of Tea Partiers as "Independent" to indicate that they held middle-of-the-road views. Later research revealed that not only were grassroots Tea Partiers very conservative minded, many were disillusioned with the established GOP and held certain views well to the right of typical Republican adherents in the mass public.

In their 2014 book *Change They Can't Believe In: The Tea Party and Reactionary Politics in America*, political scientists Christopher Parker and Matthew Barreto juxtaposed Tea Party sympathizers to other self-identified Republicans and documented that the Tea Partiers were more likely to subscribe to anti-black and anti-immigrant attitudes.[46] Similarly, when Williamson and I interviewed and observed grassroots Tea Partiers, we found that they felt much more strongly about social and ethno-racial issues than about free-market economic priorities. Even participants who lived in places without many Hispanic immigrants decried immigrants to us as "illegals" who exploit taxpayer-funded services at schools and hospitals. Cultural fears and resentment were evident: one of our interviewees wondered why, after working all her life to build the country, she had to select English or Spanish on the telephone.[47] Many Tea Party people we spoke with also strongly opposed abortion rights and gay marriage. Overall, our Tea Party interlocutors expressed anger that they were "losing" the America they had built through lifetimes of hard work. They resented Obama as a symbol of immigration, black political power, and liberal welfare handouts; and they were alarmed that so many younger Americans (sometimes including their own grandchildren) celebrated his election.

Whether documented in national surveys or field interviews, grassroots Tea Party priorities were—and still are—far from the ultra-free-market priorities of the Koch network and the other right-wing elites who have gained so much policymaking clout in and through the GOP. After 2008, many professionals from right-wing donor and advocacy groups latched on to the grassroots Tea Party and appeared on television to proclaim that deep cuts in "government spending" were the top movement priority. However, during interviews and observations at the Tea Party grass roots, Vanessa Williamson and I found only one among dozens of activists who wanted the sorts of cuts in major social programs pushed by free-market elites. The spending cuts Tea Parties advocated to us—and the ones they have endorsed in national studies—target "welfare" and health coverage for low-income people. In the view of Tea Partiers, such benefits go to unworthy recipients who have not worked for them—and are paid for by their taxes or through cuts in programs like Medicare that Americans like them have earned and feel they deserve. Grassroots Tea Partiers were—and still are—far from Koch-style ultra-free-market acolytes. The vast majority are fervent ethno-nationalists and Christian conservatives—the very people who have recently become Donald Trump's most passionate supporters.[48]

Tea Party Political Clout

The Tea Party overall never has been one big integrated organization or network, so it has not been in a position simply to broker support for electoral candidates at any level. As it burst to national visibility during the early Obama presidency, the Tea Party was a congeries of organizations, some top-down, professionally run, and opulently funded, and others locally formed by citizen volunteers. Local Tea Parties and national professional organizations had common enemies, to be sure—President Obama and the Democrats. What is more, these organizations leveraged and boosted one another in many ways. The professional groups offered speakers, buses, and small grants to grassroots groups, while the local Tea Partiers picked and chose from elite offerings even as they offered a colorful popular backdrop to national conservative campaigns to block Obama Democratic initiatives. From different directions and using distinct resources of votes or big money, the two sides of the Tea Party mobilized to elect Republicans—and to pressure GOPers in office to refuse all cooperation with Obama Democrats.

Arguably, the more than one thousand local Tea Parties contributed greatly to conservative voter mobilization for the 2010 elections and beyond, not so much because their members conducted registration drives or canvassed door to door, but because these predominantly older, white citizen activists energized surrounding networks of similar people who tend to vote regularly. In contrast to the research my colleagues and I have done with center-left anti-Trump activists since 2016 (see chapter 13 of this volume), back in 2011 Vanessa Williamson and I did not hear much about voter registration or get-out-the-vote activities by grassroots Tea Partiers. Nevertheless, local Tea Parties did hold community forums and spread anti-Obama messages to other older whites, the kinds of citizens who were already inclined to vote in the pivotal 2010 midterm elections. Since that turning point, when Republicans made historic gains, grassroots Tea Party people give continuing voice to anti-immigrant and other ethnonationalist concerns, whether or not they still meet regularly. In many states and localities, Tea Party activists simply took over Republican Party positions or ran for offices themselves—in the process pulling parts of the GOP toward their ethno-nationalist world view.

Republicans have benefited from both grassroots and elite Tea Party supporters, yet no one should imagine that all forces arrayed under that label have united behind one set of candidates or a single policy agenda. Republican officials, candidates, and officeholders are cross-pressured from above and below—buffeted on the one hand by plutocratic free-market elites who deploy huge resources outside of party coffers, and confronted on the other hand by angry grassroots activists for whom anti-immigrant and religious-right priorities are paramount.

Hints of grassroots trouble ahead for the institutional GOP emerged in interviews Williamson and I conducted early in the 2011–12 presidential primary cycle, when Tea Party people expressed little enthusiasm for the available GOP choices. As it happened, we spoke with many just as Donald Trump went public with his "birther" attacks, essentially claiming that the African American president so hated and feared by Tea Partiers is not truly American. If Donald Trump had decided to run back then on the same anti-immigrant "Making America Great" platform he espoused when he descended the Trump Tower escalator in 2015, he might very well have swept away all other GOP contenders. In the next presidential cycle, he did just that.

Not surprisingly, a Pew poll taken in the spring of 2015 shortly before Trump entered the presidential sweepstakes showed that almost three-fifths of rank-and-file Republican identifiers and leaners had very little faith in party leaders.[49] Republican respondents especially faulted GOP leaders for not doing a good job on illegal immigration and same-sex marriage—precisely the issues of strong concern to grassroots conservatives, including Tea Partiers. Poll respondents also faulted their party for a poor performance on "government spending." Although that phrasing is ambiguous, I have little doubt that many of these rank-and-file Republicans meant that their party had done too little to combat ObamaCare and other programs they viewed as "welfare" for the undeserving.

Reality TV star and New York real estate operator Donald J. Trump was never the candidate either Koch network leaders or Republican Party honchos wanted on the 2016 GOP presidential ticket. But he got there anyway, in large part because he was more attuned with rank-and-file Republican anger and resentments than established primary candidates were. Eventually Trump also squeaked through to the White House—in large part because of voters living outside of big cities and in rural areas who share views with the grassroots Tea Partiers my colleagues and I have met and spoken with since 2011.[50] Trump's racially tinged anti-immigrant pledge to "Make America Great Again" resonates with many people who hate Obama-era Democrats and incline toward Republicans yet are uninspired by elitist free-market GOP nostrums. For core loyalists, Trump means welcome shakeups of political elites, including the GOP establishment.

A Radical Trump-GOP Synthesis

After November 2016, many pundits declared the incoming president to be a "populist" who would defy the GOP to work with Democrats on key issues. Even before the election, some went so far as to suggest that the previously formidable Koch network had lost clout, because the two brothers had personally refused to endorse Trump's presidential bid and their network had cut back originally projected 2016 spending from almost $900 million to a "mere" $750 million.[51] Yet such assessments seemed off the mark. During the election campaign, Trump benefited indirectly from massive Koch network resources; and afterwards an unprepared president-elect fell back on appointees and plans offered to him by the Koch network and kindred free-market players.

The Koch Network in Election 2016 and Trump's Washington

In the run-up to 2016 GOP nomination, the Koch brothers and many members of their consortium of wealthy conservatives preferred other GOP presidential contenders, especially Wisconsin governor Scott Walker and Florida senator Marco Rubio.[52] After Trump secured the nomination, some Koch-connected donors openly backed him, but the brothers themselves and the core organizations in their network never did—explicitly.[53] In practice, despite loud pronouncements from Charles Koch that his operation would not endorse Trump, some former Koch operatives—including Scott Hagerstrom of AFP-Michigan and Corey Lewandowski of AFP-New Hampshire—assumed key leadership posts in the Trump campaign, tapping their activist networks in the process.[54]

What is more, the massive Koch machine labored over many months to pinpoint and turn out Republican voters in key states.[55] AFP was deeply involved in get-out-the-vote efforts, and especially touted its efforts in the critical swing states of Florida, Wisconsin, Pennsylvania, and North Carolina.[56] In Wisconsin, for instance, AFP claims that it reached "nearly 3 million" voters in phone banking and canvassing efforts, and it also bragged about almost 300,000 "doors knocked" and nearly 4 million phone calls made in North Carolina—contact levels in both states that far exceeded Trump's margins of victory. The same was true in Pennsylvania, where AFP claimed more than 3 million "calls made" and more than 140,000 "doors knocked" in a state Trump won by less than 50,000 votes. AFP's grassroots efforts were especially extensive in Florida, where AFP boasts that its people knocked on a one million doors throughout the state to help reelect Senator Marco Rubio. Hillary Clinton lost the state by just over 100,000 votes. In all four of these states, AFP helped to reelect the incumbent Republican senators and secure important down-ballot gains. Given what researchers know about the decline of split-ticket voting, most of the same citizens AFP mobilized to vote for GOP state and congressional candidates surely also cast ballots for Trump.[57] Furthermore, both Trump and other Republicans were buoyed by Koch-supported efforts to enact state-level voter ID laws and measures to eviscerate labor union rights.[58] Such steps to undercut Democrats by depleting union resources and lowering black voter turnout may well have made the difference in Wisconsin and Michigan, two states that Trump won by a hair on November 8.[59]

After the 2016 elections installed all-GOP governance, the Koch network was well positioned to help staff and steer much of what would happen next in Washington, DC. By early January 2017, Freedom Partners issued a detailed "Roadmap to Repeal" outlining first-hundred-days and longer-term agendas for the GOP Congress and President Trump to follow in order to "repeal as many of President Obama's executive actions and regulations as possible."[60] For the emerging Trump White House, Vice President Mike Pence, long a Koch network favorite, was put in charge of transition planning for federal personnel appointments.[61] One of Pence's senior staffers for this effort was Marc Short, recent head of Freedom Partners Chamber of Commerce, the lynchpin of the Koch network's fundraising operation, who later served as the White House legislative liaison to Congress. In addition to Pence and Short, the original White House chief of staff, Reince Priebus, had strong ties to AFP's chapter in Wisconsin—a chapter that was central to all aspects of politics and policy in that state during the ascendancy of Governor Scott Walker.[62] With the exception of the Departments of Justice and Homeland Security (in which hardline anti-immigrant officials hold sway), many Koch-aligned free marketers have been seeded throughout the Trump cabinet and federal agencies, where they push through regulatory roll-backs, efforts to privatize public services, and sweetheart business contracts to loyal Trump backers. Mike Pompeo, originally the

CIA chief and later the secretary of state, also enjoys close Koch network ties, as does Secretary of Education Betsy DeVos.[63] Following the first year of the Trump administration, the watchdog group Public Citizen published a carefully documented report detailing some forty-four presidential appointees with "close ties" to Koch political groups. About half of these officials were in White House posts and the rest were peppered through the Environmental Protection Agency, Interior Department, Energy Department, and Treasury, where they could advance the Koch agenda for "weakening regulatory enforcement, lowering corporate taxes, loosening governmental regulations and opening up public land to oil and gas extraction."[64] That was 2017, and Trump administration officials tend to come and go quickly. Nevertheless, many key officials with Koch ties remain in place, circulate to new posts, or arrive as fresh replacements.

White House and executive branch staffing has been only part of the Koch influence story, because Pence, Short, and Priebus—followed by Mick Mulvaney, who took over as President Trump's "acting" chief of staff in 2018—have enjoyed close ties to congressional GOP leaders who are also closely aligned with the Koch network. After apparently denouncing and opposing GOP House Speaker Paul Ryan during the election campaign, President Trump did a quick about-face to embrace the radical government-shrinking policy agenda of this longtime "favorite of the Koch donor network."[65] After Ryan stepped down, he was followed by another Koch-aligned Speaker, Kevin McCarthy of California.[66] In the Senate, GOP majority leader Mitch McConnell has appeared at Koch meetings to advocate continued secrecy for big political donors and preview plans to undo Obama-era laws and regulations.[67] Since 2016, McConnell's caucus in the Senate has worked closely with the Trump administration to advance exactly such efforts.

Indeed, personnel is policy, as the saying goes. With key Koch-aligned congressional leaders and White House staffers calling the tune, it is hardly surprising that popular Trump campaign themes—such as his promise to trim investor-friendly tax breaks and pursue big public investments in infrastructure—soon gave way to efforts to repeal ObamaCare and enact massive upward-tilted tax cuts. Business organizations and the Koch network enthusiastically backed these early Trump administration priorities by lobbying for GOP votes and mounting costly advertising and activist campaigns at key junctures—including campaigns to tout the tax cuts after they were enacted.[68] Equally to their delight, President Trump withdrew from the Paris global warming compact, even as his administration unleashed new rounds of oil and gas production and disempowered the Environmental Protection Agency. By mid-2018, moreover, the Trump administration was signaling renewed determination to push forward with conservative and Koch-based major cuts in federal spending on an array of social safety net programs.[69]

An Uneasy Marriage of Free-Market Plutocrats
and Populist Ethno-Nationalists

Along with many other US business owners and managers, Koch-affiliated millionaires and billionaires recurrently push back against the Trump administration's trade and immigration restrictions.[70] From time to time, such elites also express displeasure about Donald Trump's "unpresidential" tweets, incessant dishonesty, and inflammatory racist rhetoric (as many have done during interviews I have conducted since 2016). Even so, America's right-leaning business leaders and wealthy donors are, as one leader said to me, "very glad Trump is president of the United States," because he is advancing big tax cuts, regulatory eviscerations, and pro-business judicial appointments. Even after Democrats made major gains in the 2018 elections, and even following Special Counsel Robert Mueller's report that the president had engaged in repeated obstruction of justice violations during his first two years in office, Republican elites in and out of public office remain virtually in lockstep behind Trump. To these elites, the president's anti-immigrant crackdowns and incendiary mass rallies seem like an unpleasant ransom. "It's what his base wants," one shrugged in a discussion with me. By mid-2019, *Politico* reported that most major GOP-leaning donors, including those who were reluctant in 2016, have gotten fully behind Trump's bid for reelection in 2020.[71]

The Koch network is at the core of this ongoing bargain. To be sure, as in 2016, the network's leaders say they will not endorse Trump formally for 2020; and tensions have developed between Koch operations and the Republican National Committee apparatus, now fully controlled by Trump-installed operatives.[72] Such kerfuffles matter less than it might seem, because the Koch machine will still weigh in for 2020, delivering votes and massive campaign resources to GOP congressional and state-level candidates and indirectly boosting Trump's reelection bid.[73] Along with most fellow US wealth-holders and business leaders, Koch-aligned plutocrats understand that they are winning—and they know that most of their policy preferences will continue to advance as long as a GOP president or a Republican Senate (either or both) remain in office.

In a broader sense, today's Trumpified GOP is likely to persist, because it is a dually radicalized synthesis years in the making—a marriage of convenience between anti-government free-market plutocrats and racially anxious ethno-nationalist activists and voters. To be sure, political and governing tensions will continue to roil the contemporary GOP, a hollowed-out party penetrated and remade by these strange-bedfellow forces. Yet the new GOP synthesis that has come of age under Donald Trump may prevail for a long time, and it certainly will not come apart from within. Strains will grow into ruptures if—and only if—this radicalized Republican Party faces repeated major defeats at the ballot box. Until then, the elite and popular extremists who have captured the Republican Party know that they have much to gain by sticking together to defeat and obstruct Democrats.

Notes

1. Thomas E. Mann and Norman J. Ornstein, *It's Even Worse Than It Looks: How the American Constitutional System Collided with the New Politics of Extremism* (New York: Basic Books, 2012), xxiv. The title of the 2016 updated edition substitutes the word *"Was"* for *"Looks."*
2. A classic statement of median voter theory appears in Anthony Downs, *An Economic Theory of Democracy* (New York: Harper and Row, 1957). For recent moves of Republicans toward extremism, see Christopher Ingraham, "This Astonishing Chart Shows How Moderate Republicans Are an Endangered Species," *Washington Post*, June 2, 2015.
3. Theda Skocpol and Alexander Hertel-Fernandez, "The Koch Network and Republican Party Extremism," *Perspectives on Politics* 14, no. 3 (September 2016)): 681–99.
4. For the list of organizations we used and their 2002 and 2014 budgets, see Alexander Hertel-Fernandez, Theda Skocpol, and Jason Sclar, "When Political Mega-Donors Join Forces: How the Koch Network and the Democracy Alliance Influence Organized U.S. Politics on the Right and Left," *Studies in American Political Development* 32, no. 2 (October 2018): 127–65, Appendix D.
5. For the funding organizations, we recorded not simply their core budgets but also the total sums each group raised and redirected from donors. Our project uses annual budgets simply to indicate the relative order of magnitude of organizational resources, and we add up budgets for organizations in each major category to give a rough sense of the resources controlled by various types of party and non-party political organizations in 2002 and 2014. This approach cannot capture all partisan resources on the right. Arguably, US conservatives benefit greatly from openly partisan media outlets, including the Fox television network and right-wing talk radio. Another consideration is how political organizations fit into the US economy. In our larger project, we include national labor unions as "constituency mobilizing organizations" on the liberal side; and the Republican/conservative list referenced here includes the US Chamber of Commerce and the National Federation of Independent Businesses. However, this conservative list does *not* include local and regional chambers of commerce, other trade groups, or individual corporations. Also omitted are evangelical church networks. As for the budgets, secret and untraceable donations are not captured by this (or any) approach that relies on public records.
6. A typical portrayal appears in the "Maze of Money" chart created by Open Secrets to display a spider-like web of some $400 million in 2012 election funding donations directly or indirectly connected to the Kochs. See Matea Gold, "Koch-Backed Political Network Built to Shield Donors Raised $400 Million in 2012 Elections," *Washington Post*, January 5, 2014; and Matea Gold, "The Players in the Koch-Backed $400 Million Political Donor Network," *Washington Post*, January 5, 2014.
7. Jane Mayer, "Covert Operations: The Billionaire Brothers Who Are Waging War Against Obama," *New Yorker*, August 30, 2010.
8. For brief descriptions of the organizations listed in Figure 1.2, see Hertel-Fernandez, Skocpol, and Sclar, "When Political Mega-Donors Join Forces," Appendix A. Further accounts appear in Gold, "The Players in the Koch-Backed Network"; Daniel Schulman, *Sons of Wichita: How the Koch Brothers Became America's Most Powerful and Private Dynasty* (New York: Hachette Book Group, 2014); SourceWatch, "The Koch Network" (Center for Media and Democracy, 2019); and Kenneth P. Vogel, *Big Money: 2.5 Billion Dollars, One Suspicious Vehicle, and a Pimp—on the Trail of the Ultra-Rich Hijacking American Politics* (New York: Public Affairs, 2014).
9. Schulman, *Sons of Wichita*, 99.
10. Dave Levinthal, "Koch Brothers Supersize Higher-Ed Funding," *Federal Politics*, December 15, 2015; updated May 7, 2018 (publication of the Center for Public Integrity, Washington, DC); and Schulman, *Sons of Wichita*, 264–66.

11. Schulman, *Sons of Wichita*, 266–70.
12. Vogel, *Big Money*, 136; and Schulman, *Sons of Wichita*, 270–71.
13. Vogel, *Big Money*, 133; and SourceWatch, "The Koch Network."
14. For details on the health reform debate, see Jane Mayer, *Dark Money: The Hidden History of the Billionaires behind the Rise of the Radical Right* (New York: Doubleday Press, 2016), chap. 7, and see chap. 8 on climate change.
15. Vogel, *Big Money*, 200–201.
16. Schulman, *Sons of Wichita*, 286–88; and Vogel, *Big Money*, 130–33 and throughout.
17. Cover Letter from Charles Koch and Enclosed Program from Spring 2010 Seminar on "Understanding and Addressing Threats to American Free Enterprise and Prosperity," held at St. Regis Resort, leaked September 24, 2010, document linked at the end of Lee Fang, "MEMO: Health Insurance, Banking, Oil Industries Met With Koch, Chamber, Glenn Beck to Plot 2010 Election," ThinkProgress, October 20, 2010, available at https://thinkprogress. org/memo-health-insurance-banking-oil-industries-met-with-koch-chamber-glenn-beck-to-plot-2010-election-3c1a0908a245/; and Andy Kroll and Daniel Schulman, "The Koch Brothers Left a Confidential Document at Their Donor Conference," *Mother Jones*, February 5, 2014.
18. Mike Allen and Jim Vandehei, "The Koch Brothers' Secret Bank," *Politico*, September 11, 2013.
19. Kenneth P. Vogel, "How the Koch Network Rivals the GOP," *Politico*, December 30, 2015.
20. Koch, Cover Letter and Enclosed Program in Fang, "MEMO"; Sam Stein, "At Koch Retreat, Top GOP Senate Candidates Credited the Network for Their Rise," HuffPost Politics, August 27, 2014; and Lauren Windsor, "Exclusive: Inside the Koch Brothers' Secret Billionaire Summit," *Nation*, June 17, 2014.
21. Carefully choreographed panels feature speakers from Koch-run political organizations and educational charities; and invited participants attend small consultations with Koch principals. For seminar programs, see Koch, "Cover Letter and Enclosed Program" and Windsor, "Exclusive." One-on-one sessions held at the winter 2014 confab are detailed in Kroll and Schulman, "The Koch Brothers Left a Confidential Document at Their Donor Conference." Further analysis appears in Hertel-Fernandez, Skocpol, and Sclar, "When Mega-Donors Join Forces.".
22. Alicia Mundy, "The VA Isn't Broken, Yet," *Washington Monthly*, March/April/May 2016; and Peter Overby, "Koch Political Network Expanding 'Grass-Roots' Organizing," NPR, October 14, 2015.
23. Angie Bautista-Chavez and Sarah Meyer [James], "The Libre Initiative—An Innovative Conservative Effort to Recruit Latino Support" (Cambridge, Massachusetts: Scholars Strategy Network, 2015); and Angie Bautista-Chavez and Sarah James, "Beyond Likely Voters: An Event Analysis of Conservative Political Outreach," forthcoming in *Political Science Quarterly*, Fall 2019. Generation Opportunity and the Libre Initiative were originally stand-alone organizations but later were moved into AFP as semi-autonomous operations.
24. On Themis/i360, see Mike Allen and Kenneth P. Vogel, "Inside the Koch Data Mine," *Politico*, December 8, 2014; for the data organizations on the left, see Eitan D. Hersh, *Hacking the Electorate* (New York: Cambridge University Press, 2015).
25. For examples of such resource surges in Colorado and Florida, see Sandra Fish, "Americans for Prosperity Colorado: Koch Brothers' Advocacy Gets Local in Colorado," *Al-Jazeera America*, August 12, 2014.; Michael J. Mishak and Phillip Elliott, "Americans for Prosperity Builds Political Machine," Associated Press, October 11, 2014; Jim Rutenberg, "How Billionaire Oligarchs Are Becoming Their Own Political Parties," *New York Times*, October 17, 2014; Kenneth P. Vogel, "How the Koch Network Rivals the GOP," *Politico*, December 30, 2015.
26. Alexander Hertel-Fernandez, Theda Skocpol, and Daniel Lynch, "Business Associations, Conservative Networks, and the Ongoing Republican Civil War Over Medicaid Expansion," *Journal of Health Politics, Policy and Law* 41, no. 2 (2016): 239–86; and Fredreka Schouten, "Koch Group Flexes Conservative Muscle in State Fights," *USA Today*, February 25, 2015.
27. Theda Skocpol, Marshall Ganz, and Ziad Munson, "A Nation of Organizers: The Institutional Origins of Civic Voluntarism in the United States," *American Political Science Review* 94, no. 3 (2000): 527–46.

28. See *Americans for Prosperity 2012 Annual Report* (Arlington, VA: Americans for Prosperity, 2013); and *Partner Prospectus* (Arlington, VA: Americans for Prosperity, 2015).
29. Alexander Hertel-Fernandez and Theda Skocpol, "How the Right Trounced Liberals in the States," *Democracy: A Journal of Ideas* 39 (Winter, 2016).
30. To determine the names, terms, and career trajectories of AFP's paid state directors, my research colleagues and I have collected earlier AFP website postings archived on the Wayback Machine. Contemporaneous lists along with real-time announcements of the arrival and departure of AFP state directors allow us to track AFP expansion across states and reconstruct the careers of many AFP state directors prior to and following their stints in those posts. Our data show that AFP state directors are frequently recruited from GOP campaign or officeholder staffs and often return to even higher-level GOP positions after time in AFP.
31. On support for raising the minimum wage, see for example CBS/New York Times Poll, May 28–31, 2015. Some 71 percent of adults supported raising the minimum wage to $10.10; 80 percent of adults according to the same poll supported an employer requirement to provide paid leave to the parents of new children or employees caring for sick family members, and 85 percent supported a paid sick leave requirement. On strong public support for higher taxes on the wealthy and large corporations, see the CBS/New York Times poll of November 6–10, 2015, where 63 percent of adults said they favored such increases.
32. Hertel-Fernandez, Skocpol, and Lynch, "Business Associations, Conservative Networks, and the Ongoing Republican Civil War Over Medicaid Expansion."
33. See the statistical results reported in Skocpol and Hertel-Fernandez, "The Koch Network and Republican Party Extremism," 694–95. Union restrictions were not favored by public opinion, and our models show that states with AFP directors were statistically more likely to enact union restrictions in 2011, even with controls for other possible causal variables.
34. James Feigenbaum, Alexander Hertel-Fernandez, and Vanessa Williamson, "From the Bargaining Table to the Ballot Box: Political Effects of Right to Work Laws," NBER Working Paper No. 24259, National Bureau of Economic Research, revised February 2019.
35. On belief in climate change among Republicans, including conservative Republicans, see Public Opinion Strategies, August 24–27, 2015.
36. Coral Davenport and Eric Lipton, "How G.O.P. Leaders Came to View Climate Change as Fake Science," *New York Times*, June 3, 2017; and Skocpol and Hertel-Fernandez, "The Koch Network and Republican Party Extremism," 693–94.
37. David Roberts, "The GOP Is the World's Only Major Climate-Denialist Party, but Why?" Vox, December 2, 2015; and David Roberts, "Republican Climate Denial: It's the Donors, Stupid," Vox, December 16, 2015.
38. Theda Skocpol and Lawrence R. Jacobs, editors, *Reaching for a New Deal: Ambitious Governance, Economic Meltdown, and Polarized Politics in Obama's First Two Years* (New York: Russell Sage Foundation, 2011), 18–20; Jonathan Alter, *The Promise: President Obama, Year One* (New York: Simon and Schuster, 2010); and Mayer, "Covert Operations."
39. Theda Skocpol and Vanessa Williamson, *The Tea Party and the Remaking of Republican Conservatism* (New York: Oxford University Press, 2012), 7 and chap. 1 and 4.
40. Andreas Madestam, Daniel Shoag, Stan Veuger, and David Yanagizawa, "Do Political Protests Matter? Evidence from the Tea Party Movement," *Quarterly Journal of Economics* 128, no. 4 (2013): 1633–85.
41. Mayer, *Dark Money*, 196–97.
42. See Mayer, *Dark Money*, especially chapter 7; and Taki Oldham, *The Billionaires' Tea Party: How Corporate America Is Faking a Grassroots Revolution*, DVD documentary (Northampton, MA: Media Education Foundation, 2011).
43. Skocpol and Williamson, *The Tea Party and the Remaking of Republican Conservatism*, especially chapter 3.
44. Skocpol and Williamson, *The Tea Party and the Remaking of Republican Conservatism*, 90–92 and Figure 3.1.
45. This draws from Skocpol and Williamson, *The Tea Party and the Remaking of Republican Conservatism*, chapters 1 and 2.
46. Christopher S. Parker and Matthew A. Barreto, *Change They Can't Believe In: The Tea Party and Reactionary Politics in America* (Princeton, NJ: Princeton University Press, 2014).

47. Skocpol and Williamson, *The Tea Party and the Remaking of Republican Conservatism*, 46.
48. See Pew Research Center, "Trump's Staunch GOP Supporters Have Roots in the Tea Party," May 2019.
49. Pew Research Center, "Republicans Say GOP Not Doing Good Job on Set of Current Issues," survey conducted May 12–18, 2015.
50. On the ethno-nationalist views of Trump supporters, see Pew Research Center, "Warmer Feelings about Trump among Republicans Critical of Immigration, Growing Diversity, Islam," survey conducted April 5–May 2, 2016. On the political geography of Trump's victory, see Lazaro Gamio and Dan Keating, "How Trump Redrew the Electoral Map from Sea to Shining Sea," *Washington Post*, November 9, 2016.
51. Matea Gold, "Charles Koch Downgrades His Political Network's Projected 2016 Spending from $889 Million to $750 Million," *Washington Post*, October 21, 2015.
52. Kenneth P. Vogel and Tarini Parti, "Koch Donors Give Rubio Early Nod," *Politico*, January 28, 2015; and Colin Campbell, "One of the Koch Brothers Just Revealed Which Republican 2016 Candidate They Support," *Business Insider*, April 20, 2015.
53. Michelle Conlin, "Powerful Koch Brothers Rebuff Big Donors' Call to Back Trump for White House," *Reuters*, August 1, 2016.
54. "Press Release—Donald J. Trump Campaign Announces Michigan State Director Scott Hagerstrom," December 21, 2015; and Maggie Haberman, "For His Unconventional Campaign, Donald Trump Looks to an Unorthodox Manager," *New York Times*, September 3, 2015.
55. Catherine Ho, "How Americans for Prosperity Gets Out the Vote," *Washington Post*, June 3, 2016.
56. The following specific claims all come from Americans for Prosperity, "By the Numbers: AFP's Activists Make the Difference," November 16, 2016, available at: http://web.archive.org/web/20161121162042/https://americansforprosperity.org/numbers-afps-activists-make-difference.
57. Jeff Stein, "Ticket Splitting Is Dead," Vox, November 17, 2016.
58. Alexander Hertel-Fernandez, "Policy Feedback as Political Weapon: Conservative Advocacy and the Demobilization of the Public Sector Labor Movement," *Perspectives on Politics* 16, no. 2 (June 2018): 364–79; and James Feigenbaum, Alexander Hertel-Fernandez, and Vanessa Williamson, "From the Bargaining Table to the Ballot Box: Political Effects of Right to Work Laws," NBER Working Paper No. 24259, National Bureau of Economic Research, revised February 2019.
59. Michael Wines, "Wisconsin's Strict ID Law Discouraged Voters, Study Finds," *New York Times*, September 25, 2017.
60. Freedom Partners Chamber of Commerce, "A Roadmap to Repeal: Removing Regulatory Barriers to Opportunity," press release January 6, 2017; introduced in a blog post by Paige Agostin, available at: https://freedompartners.org/latest-news/roadmap-repeal-removing-regulatory-barriers-opportunity/.
61. Kenneth P. Vogel and Maggie Haberman, "Mike Pence's Koch Advantage," *Politico*, August 28, 2014.
62. Mary Bottari, "Reince Priebus Promotion Another Big Win for the Koch Caucus," PRWatch, Center for Media and Democracy, November 15, 2016.
63. John Nichols, "The Koch Brothers' Favorite Congressman Will Be in Charge of the CIA," *Nation*, November 18, 2016; Adele M. Stan, "Selection of Pompeo Solidifies Trump's Position with Koch Brothers," *American Prospect*, March 14, 2018; and Jane Mayer, "Betsy DeVos, Trump's Big Donor Education Secretary," *New Yorker*, November 23, 2016.
64. Alan Zibel, "The Koch Government: How the Koch Agenda Has Infiltrated the Trump Administration," Public Citizen, Washington, DC, November 30, 2017.
65. This is from Matea Gold, "Paul Ryan Warns That the GOP Is Engaged in a 'Fight for the Soul of Our Party' over Free Market Principles," *Washington Post*, August 1, 2016.
66. McCarthy's history of aligning with Koch policy positions is detailed in "Who's On the Kochs' Shortlist for Speaker? Kevin McCarthy," *Real Koch Facts*, September 29, 2015.
67. Jonathan Weisman, "In Audio from a Koch Event, McConnell Envisions Undoing Obama Initiatives," *New York Times*, August 27, 2014.

68. Annie Linskey, "The Koch Brothers (and Their Friends) Want President Trump's Tax Cut. Very Badly," *Boston Globe*, October 14, 2017; and John McCormick, "Koch-Backed Groups Are Selling Trump's Tax Cuts Door-to-Door Ahead of the Midterms," *Bloomberg Businessweek*, May 2, 2018.
69. Glenn Thrush and Erica L. Green, "Behind Trump's Plan to Overhaul the Government: Scaling Back the Safety Net," *New York Times*, June 21, 2018.
70. Eli Stokols and Noah Bierman, "Trump Lashes Out at Koch Brothers after Their Political Network Slams White House," *Los Angeles Times*, July 31, 2018; and Jonathan Easley, "Koch-Backed Group Pushes for New Limits on Trump's Tariff Authority," *The Hill*, March 5, 2019.
71. Alex Isenstadt, "Trump Wins Over Big Donors Who Snubbed Him in 2016," *Politico*, April 22, 2019.
72. Josh Dawsey and Michelle Ye Hee Lee, "Koch Network Tells Donors It Plans to Stay Out of 2020 Race, Once Again Declining to Back Trump," *Washington Post*, January 24, 2019; and Boris Heersink, "The Koch Network Attacked Trump. Here's Why He Is Using the RNC to Fight Back," *Washington Post*, August 10, 2018.
73. Paul Waldman, Editorial: "Don't Be Fooled. The Koch Brothers Will Stick by Trump," *Washington Post*, July 30, 2018.

2

Dissecting the Conservative Triumph in Wisconsin

ALEXANDER HERTEL-FERNANDEZ

February is always chilly in Wisconsin. The winter of 2011 was no exception, yet even as the temperatures dropped, the crowds outside the state capitol in Madison kept growing with each passing day, reaching perhaps one hundred thousand at their peak.[1] Inside the capitol, hundreds of men, women, and young people had begun camping in the building's main rotunda hall. Armed with banners, signs, drums, sleeping bags, and scores of pizza boxes, these protestors took turns singing, dancing, giving speeches, and sharing stories. Many of the protestors in and out of the capitol were teachers or other public-sector workers and their families. They were there to stop a bill backed by the state's newly elected Republican governor, Scott Walker, which would strip nearly all state employees of collective bargaining rights, make it harder for public unions to collect dues and fees, and dramatically increase the cost of health care for many state workers. But the protests were ultimately to no avail. After weeks of rallies—and even an effort by Democratic state senators to leave the state to deny a legislative quorum—the GOP legislature passed, and Walker signed, the new anti-union measures into law.

Such sweeping eviscerations of the rights of public sector employees had only recently seemed unthinkable in Wisconsin, even during periods of full Republican control of state government. Public employees in the Badger State had enjoyed the right to bargain collectively for more than half a century—indeed, in 1959 Wisconsin was the first state in the nation to pass legislation granting public employees that right. Public sector unions had built a strong presence, and even though many Republican politicians had their differences with the state's unions, they had never seriously considered curbing basic union rights before 2011.

Alexander Hertel-Fernandez, *Dissecting the Conservative Triumph in Wisconsin* In: *Upending American Politics* Edited by: Theda Skocpol and Caroline Tervo, Oxford University Press (2020). © Oxford University Press
DOI: 10.1093/oso/9780190083526.003.0002

What happened to pull Wisconsin's Republican Party—and broader political terrain—to new hard-right extremes? This chapter offers an answer, and in the process sheds light on a broader set of organizations, networks, and activists at the heart of ongoing transformations of US politics across all fifty states. I highlight the long-term erosion of the American labor movement and shifts in state and local Republican Parties, and I examine key extra-party organizational networks on the right, including the Koch network and its centerpiece organization, Americans for Prosperity; the American Legislative Exchange Council; and the State Policy Network of free-market think tanks.

While acknowledging the reality of recently growing popular resentment of public sector employees, the approach I take mirrors that of the rest of this volume in focusing primarily on organizations rather than on attitudes and opinions in the mass public.[2] Similarly, although I point to the important role that certain individual political entrepreneurs and politicians have played in Wisconsin, my emphasis is on the organizations and institutions that structure the decisions leaders make and give them the capacities they need to prevail in major battles. Attention to organizational networks and capacities sets my analysis apart from other accounts of developments in the state, like Dan Kaufman's *The Fall of Wisconsin* or Jane Mayer's *Dark Money*, both of which feature individual players like Scott Walker and Charles and David Koch.[3] An organizational perspective, by contrast, helps reveal *why* those individual players have been so successful in Wisconsin and beyond—with attendant lessons about the more general exercise of power in American politics.

Putting the "Fall of Wisconsin" in Context

Before digging into Wisconsin's conservative infrastructure, it is helpful to step back and consider how the broader political balance of power has shifted over time. Between 1940 and 2011, control of the Wisconsin governorship flipped back and forth between Democrats and Republicans, but Democrats held a steady majority in both chambers from the 1970s through the mid-1990s. More recently, Democrats held the governorship from 2004 to 2010, even as control of the legislature moved back and forth between the parties. That close balance changed decisively in 2011, however, as Wisconsin Republicans gained four seats in the Senate and fourteen in the Assembly, and also won the governorship, giving the GOP a "trifecta"—that is, full control of three branches of state government. This was new. Since 1970, Republicans had enjoyed a similar level of full control only for two years in the 1990s.

Equally unprecedented was the ideological conservatism of the GOP legislators elected in 2011, as plotted in Figure 2.1, with estimates of legislator

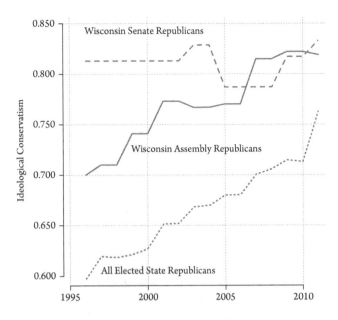

Figure 2.1 The Ideological Conservatism of Wisconsin Republicans.

Notes: Figure plots ideological conservatism of Wisconsin Senate Republicans, Wisconsin Assembly Republicans, and all elected state Republicans using Shor-McCarty ideological measures of state legislators. Higher values indicate more conservative lawmakers.

ideology devised by political scientists Boris Shor and Nolan McCarty.[4] As in many other states, Republicans in Wisconsin had been moving to the ideological right since the mid-1990s. This was especially true for Assembly Republicans, who marched steadily to the right over this period; by comparison, Senate Republicans were already quite conservative relative to their lower-chamber peers. In both chambers, Wisconsin Republicans were more conservative than the country as a whole (and this remained the case even as Republicans in other states also moved rightward after the mid-1990s).

Aided by very conservative legislative majorities, Scott Walker, the new Wisconsin GOP governor elected in 2010, was well positioned to enact a raft of hard-right priorities. That agenda included retrenchments of labor union rights, rollbacks in labor market regulations, sharply reduced taxes, a new voter ID law to make voting more cumbersome for Democratic-leaning constituencies, and reductions in environmental regulations to pave the way for ramped-up extraction of natural resources. Likewise, the new right-wing GOP government could refuse to expand Wisconsin's Medicaid program to the near-poor under the 2010 Affordable Care Act, and it could reduce public spending on schools and universities and refuse to update Wisconsin's minimum wage to reflect inflation.

Seen through the lens of the 2010 election, such policy choices might not seem all that surprising. Didn't Wisconsin's voters open the doors by installing conservative Republicans across the board and leaving the Democratic minority powerless to check their power? The evidence suggests otherwise, because the most extreme measures Governor Walker and his allies pushed through quickly in 2011—and above all the eviscerations of labor rights—had not been issues during the 2010 campaign; nor were they measures voters were clamoring to see enacted. Walker's 2010 campaign focused on boosting the state's economic development, and his signature pledge was to create 250,000 jobs during his first term in office. As part of that plan, Walker had discussed cutting taxes and curbing benefits and pay increases for state employees. But legal changes in basic union rights were not featured in his stump speeches. As one union leader argued, the eventual legislation Walker pushed "went far beyond what anybody thought he would do. He didn't talk about it during the campaign. If he had said that, some people who supported him would have had some second thoughts."[5] PolitiFact (the independent fact checker source) put it even more strikingly: "Walker, who offered many specific proposals during the campaign, did not go public with even the bare-bones of his multi-faceted plans to sharply curb collective bargaining rights."[6]

A few years later Walker and his fellow Republicans similarly surprised many Wisconsinites when they pursued right-to-work legislation decimating even private-sector union rights to collect revenues and fees. This took anti-union measures beyond the public sector. A year into his first term, Walker had batted away talk of passing such a law—not only declaring that he had "no interest in pursuing right-to-work legislation" but further proclaiming that he would "do everything in [his] power" to make sure right-to-work legislation did not end up on his desk.[7] Walker repeated the same promises two years later, just months before he reversed his position and signed a right-to-work bill into law in 2015.[8]

Both times that Governor Walker and the GOP legislature took strong steps to gut union rights they did so without any mass public mandate. In the midst of the 2011 protests about the key anti–public sector union measures embodied in Act 10, pollsters found some support for pay cuts for state employees but strong opposition to ending their collective bargaining rights.[9] A year later, support for union rights among the Wisconsin electorate remained extremely high, with around 60 percent of likely voters saying that they backed the right of public employees to collectively bargain over both wages and benefits.[10] Right-to-work legislation applicable to private-sector unions polled slightly better, but half of registered voters still opposed the enactment.

Disjunctures between anti-union legislation and Walker's campaign promises and public preferences raise questions about established political science accounts of public policymaking.[11] In the standard models, politicians campaign on issues that appeal to voters—and then carry through popular promises once in office. But that is not at all what happened in Wisconsin, when the all-GOP government, without little public discussion, quickly took sweeping anti-union steps in spite of public opposition. How did that happen? How did such anti-union Republicans, including Scott Walker, win full control of Wisconsin government after so many years of Democratic or divided governance—and how did they settle on such an ambitious and controversial agenda aimed at reshaping the political economy of the state for decades to come? It is to this question that we now turn.

Introducing the Right-Wing Troika in Wisconsin

Three organizations—what Theda Skocpol and I have elsewhere dubbed the "right-wing troika"—are at the center of this transformation of the Wisconsin Republican Party. While the troika consists of separate groups representing different constituencies and deploying different strategies, each of its three members support one another in both formal and informal ways in pursuit of a similar policy agenda.[12]

These organizations include the American Legislative Exchange Council (ALEC), an association of businesses, conservative donors, and right-leaning activists that generates "model bill" ideas and legislative supports for state elected officials to adopt; the State Policy Network (SPN), comprising state-level conservative, business-friendly think tanks promoting research reports, media commentary, and testimony backing many of the same legislative ideas ALEC promotes; and Americans for Prosperity (AFP), a federated political advocacy group run by the Koch political network that intervenes in both policy battles and elections at all levels of government. The troika's shared priorities include lower taxes and cuts to government social programs, weaker labor and environmental standards, carving out a larger role for the private sector in carrying out government services, and, above all, the defeat of labor unions, especially in the public sector.

All three networks have had a long-standing presence in Wisconsin, often previewing strategies that would be deployed in other states across the country. In turn, I review the evolution of each organization in the state and detail their relationships to the Republican Party and to the other members of the troika.

Americans for Prosperity

AFP spun off from an older Koch-supported organization, Citizens for a Sound Economy, in 2004. From the remains of that group, the Kochs inaugurated an ambitious new initiative that combined aspects of a political party—federated offices at the local, state, and national level and grassroots members—with aspects of a traditional advocacy group, including paid lobbyists. As chapter 1 details, by now the organization has a presence in over thirty-five states, over three million grassroots volunteers on its membership rolls, some five hundred paid staff, and a budget of nearly $80 million. It supports the election of conservative candidates in offices ranging from school boards to Congress and pushes for its policy agenda from city halls across the country to the White House.

AFP's Wisconsin affiliate (AFP-WI) was part of the first wave of continuously established AFP chapters, launching in 2005. Only AFP chapters in three other states (Kansas, North Carolina, and Texas) are older. AFP-WI also boasts one of the broadest grassroots volunteer bases of any other AFP chapter. According to a leaked donor prospectus from 2015, AFP-WI counts 124,816 grassroots activist-members, or 2.2 percent of the state's adult population. By comparison, the average state claimed just under 48,000 members, or 0.87 percent of the adult population. Those figures put Wisconsin in fourth place among all AFP chapters for its membership rate. And between 2015 and 2017, AFP-WI opened at least ten field offices spread out all over the state; only Florida's chapter boasts more local offices, as best as I can tell (another point of comparison for AFP's reach in the state: the state GOP has seventeen field offices). These local offices serve as focal points for grassroots training and canvassing during election-time campaigns. In between elections, they host a variety of other events, including annual conferences, training academies for grassroots lobbying, and workshops on policy issues like school choice or Social Security privatization. AFP's offices are often located in key battleground counties, mirroring the placement of the Wisconsin GOP's own posts, and thus giving AFP impressive reach across the state.

The American Legislative Exchange Council

ALEC got off the ground much earlier than AFP in the 1970s, formed by a group of social conservative movement activists, right-leaning politicians, and wealthy donors who were worried about rising liberal clout in the states. Their vision was one of a network capable of supporting conservative lawmakers in each state by offering them bill ideas, research support, and political strategy that would help enact a common agenda across the United States. Over time, as ALEC faced budget woes, private-sector businesses became a more important constituency for the organization, providing a generous source of funding in return for crafting ALEC's model bills. At its peak in the early 2000s, ALEC could claim a membership of thousands of state legislators—representing over a fifth of all elected officials—as well as hundreds of large corporations and conservative philanthropies. Those legislative members introduced some 10,000 bills and enacted around 1,500 of those bills into law over the 1990s and 2000s.[13]

Well before the Republican takeover in 2011, ALEC had deep roots within the Badger State. As I have documented in other work, ALEC lawmakers in Wisconsin had introduced a number of bills based on the group's models throughout the 1990s and early 2000s, especially related to education and health care.[14] After 2011, however, ALEC enjoyed even more leverage within Wisconsin, counting close allies in the governorship and in both legislative chambers. Incoming governor Walker was a very active member of ALEC during his time as a state legislator throughout the 1990s, and in the legislature the leader of the Senate Republicans, Scott Fitzgerald, and the speaker of the assembly, Jeff Fitzgerald (Scott's younger brother), were both longtime ALEC participants as well. Scott was a co-chair of Wisconsin's ALEC statewide delegation and had previously served on ALEC's public safety and elections task force (responsible for developing voter ID proposals), while Jeff was a member of the commerce, insurance, and economic development panel (responsible for labor policy). In all, nearly fifty individual lawmakers in the initial legislative session from 2011 to 2012, or over a third of all Wisconsin legislators, were confirmed ALEC members.

The State Policy Network

Unlike ALEC or AFP, SPN is a network of organizations, not individuals. SPN's members are state-level think tanks focused on a range of conservative issues, usually a mix of pro-business and small government policy priorities. Initially composed of a handful of think tanks that informally met to share best practices and strategy in the 1980s, SPN got a big boost when ALEC's executive director opened his donor list to the fledging think tank association and got SPN participating regularly in ALEC meetings. By the early 2000s, SPN had undergone a substantial revamp and, at its peak, had grown to a membership of nearly sixty affiliates across all fifty states. Some of their members are small, one- or two-person operations, while others, like the Mackinac Center in Michigan or the Goldwater Institute in Arizona, have budgets ranging from $5 to $10 million a year, with dozens of staff members. Just as varied are affiliates' main activities, which can include writing reports; advising political candidates and elected officials; offering testimony, media appearances, and commentary on behalf of favored legislation; and engaging in targeted litigation intended to rewrite state and federal policy.

Wisconsin counts three SPN affiliates: the Badger Institute (formerly the Wisconsin Policy Research Institute), the Wisconsin Institute for Law & Liberty, and the MacIver Institute. Established in 1987 and incorporated in the following year, the Badger Institute now employs six full-time staff and has a budget of $1.4 million per year. The institute conducts policy research and polling to support policies related to "competitive free markets, limited government, private initiative and personal responsibility."

The Wisconsin Institute for Law & Liberty is a newer organization, founded in 2011, and counts seventeen members and an annual budget of over $2 million. Like the Badger Institute, the Institute for Law & Liberty publishes research reports related to federalism, social programs, and tax policy. Unlike the Badger Institute, however, the Institute for Law & Liberty also engages in litigation to further the reach of ALEC-sponsored legislation, as when it followed up on legislative cutbacks to union fees to ensure that unions in Wisconsin were swiftly implementing the bill's requirements. The institute uses litigation to advance its agenda even when legislation is not possible, as in its efforts to further reduce campaign finance limits in the state.

Claiming the smallest budget at a little under $500,000 and six staff, MacIver launched in 2008 to promote "free markets, individual freedom, personal responsibility, and limited government." More so than either Badger or the Institute for Law & Liberty, MacIver focuses much of its effort on publicity and communications, launching grassroots and media campaigns to support many of the same priorities as ALEC and AFP in the state. That should come as no surprise, given that the institute's director of communications was a former head of ALEC's task force on health and human resources and one of its board members is a former AFP-WI state director. As we will see, MacIver was a very important supporter of Scott Walker's legislative agenda, especially Walker's controversial push to repeal public sector union rights.

The Troika: Better Together

Together, the three members of the troika have pursued a similar agenda, frequently buttressing one another's efforts. This is no coincidence, and as I have documented in previous research, leaders in, and donors for, ALEC, SPN, and AFP have encouraged the groups to work closely with one another where there are overlaps in interests.[15] SPN's network head has, for instance, fundraised from conservative foundations to cover the costs of its affiliates participating on ALEC task forces. ALEC, for its part, has found that SPN think tanks are a helpful source of policy ideas and research for developing model bills in its task forces. Those think tanks can then offer testimony and support bills once legislators introduce the models in their home states. Many state and regional AFP heads, moreover, regularly attend ALEC meetings to share strategies with the assembled lawmakers and think tanks. This coordination is especially well established in Wisconsin. One telling piece of evidence comes from ALEC's annual meetings. At ALEC's summer 2017 conference, for instance, AFP-WI sent both its state director and deputy state director to participate—something AFP affiliates in only three other states did. The Wisconsin Institute for Law & Liberty notably sent both its president and chief litigator to participate in that ALEC meeting, too.

While the troika receives financial support all across the country from wealthy individual donors, private-sector businesses, and conservative philanthropies, Wisconsin's ALEC, SPN, and AFP affiliates have been especially fortunate to have access to a deep pool of in-state conservative donors to support their operations and help coordinate efforts. Perhaps the most notable example of Badger donors is Diane Hendricks, the wealthiest self-made woman in the United States at an estimated net worth of $7 billion.[16] Hendricks lives in Rock County, Wisconsin, and has generously funded conservative causes and candidates in the state and the United States as a whole. In 2012, for instance, she became the largest single political donor in Wisconsin history for her $500,000 contribution to Scott Walker's retention campaign, and at a Koch network fundraising meeting a year earlier, she was singled out as one of the consortium's top donors for giving at least $1 million to Koch-backed groups.[17]

One of Hendricks' chief concerns is the labor movement. Days after Walker assumed office, she was caught on tape in a private conversation with the governor urging him to get Wisconsin "to be a completely red state [by working] on these unions."[18] At that point, Walker had not publicly announced any plans to tackle an overhaul of labor law. But Walker's response to her—that he would start by cutting public union rights, thus driving a wedge between government employees and the private sector, which would in turn open the door to private sector right-to-work—is exactly the divide-and-conquer strategy his administration would later deploy over the next four years.

Hendricks also serves on the board of directors of another Wisconsin philanthropy—the Bradley Foundation—that supports conservative political advocacy in the state and across the rest of the country. Bradley is a major donor to the troika and, like Hendricks, has focused special attention on supporting the troika's anti-union advocacy as a way of weakening progressive power. The foundation funds a range of tactics to advance that goal, depending on the particular political conditions in states—legislative initiatives when conservatives control legislatures, administrative action for GOP governors, and litigation to make headway in states under partial or full Democratic control.[19] Armed with funding from donors like Hendricks and Bradley, ALEC,

SPN, and AFP have all been very well positioned to build up infrastructure in Wisconsin over the years.

The Troika's Strategies for Remaking Wisconsin

But where has the troika directed those resources—and what tactics has it deployed to reshape Wisconsin politics? I examine three strategies that helped each organization establish a presence in the state, shift the governing agenda of the Republican Party, and eventually pave the way for the passage of favored bills—even when, as with union rights rollbacks, those bills were opposed by majorities of the public. These tactics include:

- Establishing overlapping career lines with Republican party staff and activists
- Building off of existing in-state networks of businesses and conservatives in early years before becoming more independent
- Fostering relationships with conservative lawmakers and supporting the development of their early careers

Establishing Overlapping Career Lines with the Republican Party

A close look at AFP and its relationship to the Republican Party reveals how this member of the troika has managed to reorient the GOP towards the troika's preferred agenda. As AFP has spread out across the states, it has gained substantial leverage over Republican Party priorities and agendas by pulling in staffers and activists who might otherwise work for local and state conservative organizations and political party committees. It has done this by hiring more frequently than these organizations—and then paying their staffers and activists much more than comparable positions in Republican party politics.

To put concrete numbers on these differences, I have assembled data on compensation self-reported by employees of all state Republican Parties and AFP in early 2019 posted on the Glassdoor online platform.[20] While undoubtedly incomplete, the Glassdoor data offer the most detailed picture to date of the hiring and pay practices of AFP and state and local political parties—and especially differences in their internal labor markets. The first important difference that emerges from the data is that AFP was more likely to provide salaried, full-time positions with benefits compared to state and local Republican Parties. Setting aside interns, 80 percent of open positions advertised with AFP were salaried, compared to 68 percent of GOP positions. And apart from having more monthly and hourly workers, state parties also tended to pay less than AFP. The average salaried state party position paid just over $40,000 per year (compared to just over $56,000 for AFP). Moreover, both the minimum ($29,000) and maximum ($92,000) reported state party salaries were lower than for AFP. This pay gap between AFP and state and local Republican Parties holds even if we consider comparable positions, like for field directors. A state GOP field director in Wisconsin can expect to receive $32,000 to $38,000; $29,000 to $31,000 in Pennsylvania; and $34,000 to $38,000 in California. By comparison, a field director for AFP can expect to receive an average salary of $40,000, ranging from $35,000 to $55,000.

Compensation is not the only perk to AFP employment, however. As part of a broader integrated advocacy group and donor network, AFP staff have many opportunities for internal advancement. AFP also budgets substantial resources for activists and leaders to use in their organizing efforts. As one former AFP employee put it in a review of time in the organization for Glassdoor: "AFP's a big name with a lot of money, and that has its benefits. An entry-level employee can get a decent salary and get flown around the country like a pri[n]ce." Another staffer agreed: "They are loyal to employees and spare no expense on accommodations on trips."

With these resources to offer to potential hires, it is not surprising that AFP manages to pull away many staff who might have otherwise worked for the GOP or allied groups. The flow of campaign and party staff goes in both directions, however, and many of the staff in AFP's orbit will eventually cycle back through Republican Party politics (and sometimes back again into the Koch network). By establishing itself as a waystation in conservative activists' careers, AFP has created a crucial source of influence. Current staffers bring with them contacts and relationships that they can use to pull GOP agendas towards Koch priorities. Indeed, in some cases, after helping to elect state legislators and governors, campaign staff will head to AFP, meaning that they are lobbying the very politicians they put in office. Many Republican staffers outside of the Koch network, for their part, may be angling for a job in AFP and may thus become more receptive to the Koch agenda to secure future employment within the network.

Wisconsin provides an excellent example of all of these mechanisms for AFP's influence. Tracing the career lines of AFP-WI's state directors, we can see that nearly all of them came from prominent positions within conservative or Republican Party politics and many of them were subsequently promoted to other positions within AFP and the Koch network.

Five men have helmed the AFP-WI chapter since its founding in 2005. These include Mark Block (2005–2010), Matt Seaholm (2011–2012), Luke Hilgemann (2012–2013), David Fladeboe (2013–2015), and Eric Bott (2015–present). Mark Block was perhaps the most fringe figure working for AFP, having been connected to a number of state conservative organizations (including the MacIver Institute) but not so directly tied to the GOP itself. Following Block's departure in 2010, however, AFP hired a string of state directors with much more traditional records of working for mainstream GOP state leaders at the center of power in the state. Block's immediate successor, Matt Seaholm, worked as the campaign manager and then chief of staff to Congressman Sean Duffy from 2010 to 2011. Luke Hilgemann served as chief of staff to Assembly Majority Leader Jeff Fitzgerald. David Fladeboe worked for the campaigns of Republican Senator Dan Kapanke and Representative Erik Severson (both of whom would eventually be elected to the legislature), then went on to work as policy director for Assembly member Scott Suder. The current head, Eric Bott, worked as budget and policy director for the Assembly Speaker Jeff Fitzgerald, helping to shepherd some of the most significant reforms the state had seen under Governor Walker, including collective bargaining and agency fee cutbacks to public-sector unions and the state's controversial voter ID law.

The destinations of AFP-WI's state directors after leaving that posting are again revealing. With the exception of Mark Block, all of the former AFP-WI state directors went on to work in other positions within AFP. Matt Seaholm left Wisconsin to serve as the national field director for AFP, which involved supervising over 150 paid staffers in more than twenty states. Seaholm then worked in political consulting and currently serves as executive director of the national plastics industry trade group. Luke Hilgemann left AFP-WI to serve as chief operating officer and then chief executive officer of AFP through 2017. Hilgemann then returned to Madison and is currently employed as a managing partner of a Wisconsin political consultancy. David Fladeboe, for his part, was promoted to director of strategy and innovation for AFP's national headquarters, which involved running the testing program at AFP to evaluate the best methods for the group's grassroots engagement across its state chapters. Fladeboe now works for the Badger Institute, SPN's affiliate in the state. All of these career trajectories are consistent with the strong internal labor market within Koch political organizations, including AFP. Still, Wisconsin stands out for the striking upward trajectory of its state directors within AFP, suggesting the strategic value and importance of the chapter for the network as a whole.

Building on Existing In-State Networks

Aside from establishing overlapping career lines with state and local Republican Parties, AFP-WI also built strength early on by capitalizing on existing conservative and business organizations. By constructing partnerships with long-standing groups with already-established memberships spread out over the state, AFP's Wisconsin chapter could get a running start in forming its own network of grassroots activists and leaders. To do this, in the first years of its operation (roughly 2006 to 2008), AFP frequently worked with other groups to put on forums with conservative leaders and pundits, town hall meetings with politicians, social events (like tailgates and happy hours), and policy issue, educational training sessions.

In AFP-WI's nascent years, the most common event co-sponsors included local and state chambers of commerce (especially the state chamber, Wisconsin Manufacturers and Commerce, and the state National Federation of Independent Business affiliate) and Grover Norquist's Americans for Tax Reform, Wisconsin chapter coalition. As a relatively new organization, these early co-sponsorships and partnerships were crucial to building out AFP's credibility and name recognition among small business owners and conservative activists who might be interested in AFP's policy advocacy efforts. Once AFP-WI had built out its membership rolls, however, it then ceased to work with these in-state, local groups and tended to host state-specific versions of national events and tours organized by AFP headquarters.

One favored set of partners during AFP-WI's initial period was local Tea Party groups—and this relationship between the Tea Party and AFP merits additional scrutiny. A conservative movement launched in 2009 to oppose the Obama administration's plans for bailing out homeowners with underwater mortgages, the Tea Party quickly expanded to encompass protests and new local organizations all across the country.[21] Blending together libertarian, populist, nativist, and conservative agendas, Tea Party activists focused particular attention on defeating the Obama administration's health care reform and climate change legislation. The movement's energy helped to elect dozens of new members to Congress in the 2010 midterm elections, as well as hundreds more in state legislatures, including in Wisconsin. According to Dan Kaufman's analysis in the *Fall of Wisconsin*, for instance, "the Tea Party wave put [GOP candidate Scott] Walker over the top." A common consensus among reporters, liberal activists, and pundits is that Americans for Prosperity and the broader Koch network were responsible for creating the Tea Party. As one investigative journalist put it in a book linking the Tea Party movement to the Koch political network and other corporate lobbies, Americans for Prosperity was "built to coordinate the [Tea Party] effort nationally."[22]

Despite the common portrayal of the Tea Party as an AstroTurf front group for the Koch network, there is good reason to doubt AFP's role in creating or launching the Tea Party—both nationally and in Wisconsin. Instead, AFP-WI, like other AFP state chapters across the country, capitalized on the grassroots energy already in place once the Tea Party was under way. Examining fine-grained data on AFP's relationship to the Tea Party through event co-sponsorship makes this difference clear. AFP-WI's first Tea Party event, like many of the other initial Tea Party mobilizations, happened on Tax Day (April 15) in 2009. "We're focused here in Wisconsin on getting members of our state legislature to take positive actions to reduce government spending and stop driving our economy deeper into recession," proclaimed then-AFP-WI state director Mark Block. "Wisconsinites agree that government spending has gotten out of control, and if our legislators don't believe me, they can see for themselves on April 15th." Block further noted that AFP nationally would be taking part in over one thousand similar rallies across the country, although not necessarily all of those events were actually organized by AFP.

Later that summer, AFP-WI hosted joint Tea Party rallies on July 4, 2009, with the La Crosse, Wausau, and Altoona Tea Parties. AFP-WI listed a number of other events organized in partnership with local Tea Parties over the next two years, invited representatives from local Tea Parties to its annual Defending the American Dream state-level summits, and also billed its own events as being part of the larger Tea Party movement. Yet crucially, AFP did not describe *creating* the local Tea Parties in any posts, suggesting instead that AFP-WI built on, but was not responsible for the creation of, the Wisconsin Tea Parties.

We can see this pattern more systematically in data on local Wisconsin Tea Parties paired with data on AFP-WI events. There was no statistically significant correlation between the counties where AFP-WI held events before the launch of the Tea Party in 2009 and the thirteen Wisconsin counties that would later have Tea Party groups.[23] Put differently, established Tea Parties were no more likely to emerge in counties where AFP had a stronger grassroots presence than in counties where AFP was less active. In contrast, *after* the Tea Party movement got going in 2009, there was a very strong correlation between the Wisconsin counties that had more AFP grassroots events and the counties that had established Tea Parties.[24] This suggests that AFP-WI was building on areas with greater Tea Party activity in its later events.

Fostering the Careers of Conservative Lawmakers

While the first two strategies involve areas where AFP shines, the final tactic reveals the comparative advantages of ALEC and SPN: nurturing relationships with conservative lawmakers, especially by supporting them early on in their careers and campaigns. As we have seen, ALEC has been in active in the state for decades, recruiting state legislators, and especially recently elected legislators, as dues-paying members. For these freshmen members, the network offers an important source of policy ideas, research assistance, and solidarity as they face the new demands associated with serving in government. Indeed, in a speech given to ALEC members in 2002, former Wisconsin governor Tommy Thompson praised the group for the support he received when he began serving in the Wisconsin assembly: "Myself, I always loved going to [ALEC] meetings because

I always found new ideas. Then I'd take them back to Wisconsin, disguise them a little bit, and declare that 'It's mine.' "[25]

Scott Walker also benefited from his long-standing association with ALEC as a junior state legislator. As he explained, reflecting back on his first days in the legislature, "Many of us, myself included, were part of ALEC . . . Clearly ALEC had proposed model legislation. And probably more important than just the legislation, [ALEC] had actually put together reports and such that showed . . . successes in other states. Those statistics were very helpful to us."[26]

Research I have conducted backs up the intuition expressed by Thompson and Walker. Studying cases of ALEC "policy plagiarism" whereby lawmakers had copied and pasted introduced legislation from ALEC model bills (as both Thompson and Walker had bragged about), I found that recently elected members of state legislatures (with one year or less of experience) relied on ALEC for more than twice as much of their authored legislation compared to members with more than a year of experience.[27]

But of course, ALEC is more than just model bills, and as the experiences of Thompson and Walker both illustrate, lawmakers benefit from the continued interactions within the community of fellow legislators, activists, donors, corporate representatives, and policy researchers that ALEC knits together at its annual meetings. These meetings, typically held at appealing (sunny) locations throughout the year, are heavily subsidized by the group's corporate and individual wealthy donor sponsors, meaning that lawmakers pay next to nothing while also having the opportunity to bring their families along for a vacation. As one corporate representative explained about his firm's support for the convenings, "We do a nice job with special events . . . We just kind of take it on ourselves because I want things to be nice for these guys who make 24,000 dollars a year."[28]

ALEC's social events and broader network thus help politicians build ties with activists and donors within their own state and across the whole country— ties that they can maintain even after they move on from legislatures to statewide or national office. ALEC conferences often invite legislative alumni, and publications regularly boast to potential corporate donor and activist participants that their group counts dozens of sitting governors and members of Congress as former legislative members. Those connections were undoubtedly very valuable for Scott Walker as he launched his campaign for the state's governorship in 2010. "Walker developed his political career with ALEC's help," argues one investigative journalist covering the group.[29] The head of the Wisconsin AFL-CIO put the role that ALEC and other conservative networks played for Walker more bluntly: "Scott Walker didn't have the stature, influence or money to become governor on his own or to end collective bargaining on his own . . . All of that flowed from . . . a network of influential conservatives," like ALEC.[30]

Within Wisconsin, moreover, both of the SPN-affiliated think tanks have made concerted efforts to establish ties with rising political stars, including Walker. Michael Grebe, the head of the Bradley Foundation, served as Walker's campaign chairman while also directing large donations through Wisconsin's SPN affiliates to support Walker's electoral bid. Bradley gave a million-dollar grant to the Wisconsin Policy Research Institute to create a legislative agenda for the next Wisconsin governor. "Some people in the Walker campaign were scratching their heads about how to deal with union health and pension costs, and we supplied the ideas," explained the former head of the Wisconsin Policy Research Institute.[31]

Bradley also funded a third of the MacIver Institute's budget, much of which was directed to a strategy for taking on public sector labor unions. In fact, the MacIver Institute made the first public call for prioritizing a full repeal of collective bargaining rights for public sector workers, which came to be seen as the blueprint for the eventual legislation. "The next 60 days should bring a sea change to Wisconsin's anti-job creation, anti-innovation labor laws," MacIver's communications director explained in the report, "two simple but fundamental steps to kick start the Wisconsin economy and get our state budget mess resolved would be to repeal collective bargaining for public employees and to make Wisconsin a right to work state, giving private sector workers the choice of whether they want to pay union dues in their workplace."[32]

Once the contentious debate was under way in the state capitol over Act 10—the public union cutback legislation—MacIver helped manage the opposition. As one GOP state senator explained, MacIver was instrumental in providing a counternarrative to the union activists protesting the legislation in and around the capitol. "All the naysayers were saying that Act 10 was the worst thing in the world, that the sky was going to fall, and that there wouldn't be enough teachers to teach classes, school sports would end . . . [MacIver] highlighted the positive things that were happening. Those weren't easy to find in the beginning."[33] "It seemed we were the only ones who were actually covering that aspect of it," one MacIver staffer explained about his group's coverage of the positive aspects of the bill.[34]

While ALEC and the SPN affiliates tended to be at the forefront of relationship-building with lawmakers, AFP was also an early backer of Scott Walker, and provided important grassroots support for his gubernatorial campaign, during the battle over Act 10, and then throughout the subsequent recall effort following the passage of the bill. As one example, Walker received a prime "MC" slot at AFP-WI's first-ever statewide Defending the American Dream Summit in 2008, which brought over eight hundred activists together to hear from leading conservative politicians, strategists, and leaders. AFP-WI also invited Walker to participate in one of their bus tours: the "Ending Earmarks Express" that crisscrossed the state calling for a repeal of congressional earmarking. "We thought here's this young, newer, local leader who is not nibbling around the edges but really getting serious about issues, especially trying to take on the unions on spending and pension issues," explained the head of AFP's national office.[35] That early attention and introduction to donors, activists, and other organizational leaders was surely helpful for the previously little-known county executive in his bid for statewide office.

Once Walker had launched his first term, AFP became a major supporter of the new administration's push for public sector collective bargaining and union fee repeal. And as the protests in the capitol over the bill got under way, AFP drew from a common playbook and organized counter-rallies in Madison, paying to bus in supporters of union cutbacks from all over the state.[36] The debate was such a high priority for the network that it flew out Tim Phillips, AFP's national president, to address the assembled AFP activists and paid for at least $500,000 worth of advertisements in support of the bill and of its Republican backers.[37] In the subsequent recall elections, AFP funneled at least $10 million into supporting Governor Walker, launching a cross-state bus tour dubbed "A Better Wisconsin" to rally voters.[38] The executive director of the Republican Governors Association would later praise the Koch network, and especially AFP, as being a "tremendous partner" who was "heavily involved" in ensuring Walker would remain as governor.[39]

The Lasting Legacy of Conservative Mobilization in Wisconsin and Beyond

Buoyed by the national backlash to the Trump presidency and historic levels of voter turnout, Democratic gubernatorial challenger Tony Evers narrowly defeated Scott Walker in the 2018 elections, although control of the state legislature remained squarely in Republican hands. Lacking outright control of state government, Democrats are thus constrained in how much they can roll back the troika's conservative victories under the Walker administration. Fully restoring cuts to state taxes, social programs, voting rights, and environmental and labor standards will require Democratic majorities in the Assembly and Senate. And some of the biggest gains that the troika has won may be much harder to reverse, even assuming stronger Democratic prospects in the future. Nowhere is this clearer than with the decimation of the state's labor movement, which is in many ways the troika's biggest and most enduring success.

Despite the massive scale of the protests described in this chapter's opening, they ultimately did not stop Republicans from passing the public sector collective bargaining cutbacks or right-to-work legislation four years later. Unlike in other Republican-controlled states where troika-backed politicians pushed through union cutbacks—like Ohio in 2011 or Missouri in 2017—union allies in Wisconsin lacked the ability to put the contested legislation up for a public referendum. That left unions with the relatively unprecedented option of trying to recall Scott Walker, a move that many voters, even Walker opponents, viewed as being a bridge too far. One indication: some 12 percent of Democrats reported that they had cast ballots to retain Walker in a post-election poll and another 18 percent stayed home.[40] If anything, Walker's resounding victory in the recall election strengthened conservatives' hand by calling into question support for the labor movement in Wisconsin and elsewhere. According to the *New York Times*, the recall election "seemed likely to embolden leaders in other states who have considered limits to unions . . . but had watched the backlash against Mr. Walker with worry."[41]

The legislation cutting back public sector bargaining rights and union fees has had immediate and deeply felt consequences for the labor movement in the state, which I document in Figure 2.2. The membership rate for all public sector unions fell from around 50 percent in 2011 to 24 percent seven years later, over a 50 percent decline. Teachers unions—which had previously been a bulwark of strength in the Wisconsin labor movement—were especially hard-hit. The statewide budget for the Wisconsin Education Association, the state's National Education Association affiliate, fell from over $21 million in 2005 to just under $8 million in 2017—a 60 percent decline.

Facing diminished membership, Wisconsin's unions have less power to wield in politics, especially in local and state-level elections and policymaking. Worried one Democratic operative in Madison: "Maybe we can win high-profile races

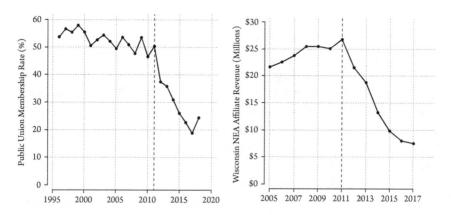

Figure 2.2 The Decline of Wisconsin Public Sector Unions.

Notes: Figure plots the annual membership rate in Wisconsin public sector unions (left-hand plot) and the annual revenue of the statewide teachers union (in millions of dollars; right-hand plot). Dashed vertical line indicates 2011, the year in which the public sector union cutback legislation passed.

because Wisconsin still leans slightly Democratic, but at the level where Walker has produced the most profound change, it may prove very difficult to turn that around. That's where [in state and local races] we pay the price."[42] A public union leader in the state grimly summed up the situation even more succinctly: "Do we have less boots on the ground? Yeah. Do we give the same amounts of money to the candidates? No."[43]

As I have documented in research with James Feigenbaum and Vanessa Williamson, the passage of cutbacks to union fees carries with it far-reaching consequences for state and national politics.[44] Such right-to-work laws durably disadvantage Democrats and liberal policymaking for years into the future. The passage of right-to-work laws, we find after comparing neighboring counties straddling state right-to-work lines, lowers Democratic vote shares and turnout up and down the ballot from the presidency down to state government. We also show that weaker unions mean that fewer working-class Americans are asked to participate in elections, one of the most important ways in which citizens are mobilized into politics. We further document that campaign contributions from unions to Democrats fall after the passage of those laws. Looking over the longer term, we find that weaker unions also have knock-on effects on other political outcomes. After the passage of right-to-work laws, states are less likely to elect working-class candidates to state legislatures and Congress and state economic policy moves sharply to the ideological right.

The destruction of the state's unions—as in other states—has thus durably shifted Wisconsin's balance of power between right and left in ways that will be difficult to reverse and have ultimately facilitated many of the troika's other wins under the Walker administration. While the state's rollback of labor rights could conceivably be reversed under a future Democratic governor and legislature, union organizers will need years to rebuild the organizations that have been weakened or even eliminated since Walker assumed office. As AFP's national leader, Tim Phillips bragged in 2017: "We have more grass-roots members in Wisconsin than the Wisconsin teachers' union has members . . . That's how you change a state."[45]

Changing a state for years to come, of course, is the troika's objective, and ALEC, SPN, and AFP have often argued that the main reason to pursue cuts to union rights is not necessarily economic but political. "Unions often have hoards [*sic*] of money to spend in political campaigns because they can use automatically deducted dues from government employee paychecks . . . Public employee unions will continue being the [political] 'big dog' as long as they have access to the taxpayer provided salaries of their members. Lawmakers should adopt [ALEC] legislation to block this process," implored one ALEC leader in a publication for his fellow members.[46]

Wisconsin's legislators, prodded on by years of mobilization by ALEC, SPN, and AFP, got on board with this offensive against labor and offered a model that would soon be followed by similar troika-guided initiatives targeting unions in Indiana, Kentucky, Michigan, and West Virginia. Lawmakers in those other states would often cite the example offered by Wisconsin as evidence of the payoff of prioritizing anti-union legislation in the face of short-term costs. The early victory in Wisconsin "sent a clear message to elected officials in the region: You can end forced [union] dues . . . and voters will reward you for it," explained one champion of right-to-work laws.[47] "When you see a Wisconsin . . . when they can get it done there," said Senator Mike Parson, a Missouri Republican, "it's pretty tough to sit here . . . with the makeup of things here and we can't get it done[.]"[48]

Indeed, SPN has documented the sharp decline in union strength in Wisconsin and used that as evidence to encourage its other affiliates to prioritize similar measures, even if it might seem controversial.[49] As a result of this diffusion through their cross-state networks, the troika's transformation of Wisconsin extends well beyond the state's borders to reverberate throughout American politics. A close understanding of these three organizations—ALEC, SPN, and AFP—and their relationship to the Republican Party and to the organized labor movement is therefore essential if we are to comprehend recent shifts in the US political terrain.

Above all, my analysis in this chapter points to the primacy of well-resourced, federated organizations operating across all (or nearly all) fifty states to influence American politics. The three organizations of the right-wing troika do command substantial financial resources, but their success is due just as much to their ability to move nimbly across the fragmented political venues of American politics. Moreover, as we have seen, many state legislators, especially more junior members, are strapped for ideas and assistance—and therefore open to the sort of agenda-setting that ALEC and SPN provide. And early victories in some states can spill over into others, as we saw with the example of labor rights retrenchment. Groups can point to initial successes to convince otherwise more reluctant lawmakers in other states of the virtues of their policies.[50]

On a related point, this chapter underscores the deepening structural weaknesses of the modern Republican Party, echoing findings from chapter 1. This is especially true in Wisconsin, where state party leaders lamented in a recent "autopsy" report that "over time the Republican Party of Wisconsin drifted from its roots as a grassroots organization and became . . . disconnected from local activists, recklessly reliant on outside consultants and took for granted money that was raised to keep the Party functioning properly."[51] This "hollowness" of the party, as political scientists Daniel Schlozman and Jake Rosenfeld have put it, meant that it was very susceptible to capture by outside interest groups like AFP that could provide staff, activists, and donors to candidates in return for setting their legislative agendas.[52] This goes well beyond the standard conception of parties as vote-maximizing entities, as groups like AFP push the party to adopt policy positions that run up against the preferences of majorities of voters, and even Republican voters, like opposing minimum wage increases, labor market protections, and environmental regulations.[53] It also means that the GOP, traditionally seen as the party friendliest to business, is now pursuing ideological, hard-right positions opposed by many mainstream and center-right corporations and trade associations—like expansion of Medicaid, spending on infrastructure, and subsidies for exporting firms. This capture, and the tension it presents, is likely to continue regardless of whether President Donald J. Trump secures reelection in 2020.

Above all, however, the research summarized in this chapter underscores the ongoing importance of states as sites for policymaking in the United States. In contrast to research that argues that the partisan balance of state governments only matters little for policy change or substantive social and economic outcomes, this chapter suggests that battles over control of state legislature and governorships can deeply shape state politics and policy.[54] Republican gains in Wisconsin after the 2010 elections changed the state's governance in important ways that would have been very different had Democrats retained control of the governorship or a legislative chamber. The troika's takeover of the GOP will leave an important imprint on the state— and the nation—for decades to come.

Acknowledgments

This chapter draws from *State Capture: How Conservative Activists, Big Businesses, and Wealthy Donors Reshaped the American States—and the Nation* (Oxford, 2019), as well as ongoing research with Theda Skocpol and Vanessa Williamson. The research on AFP would not have been possible without the Shifting US Political Terrain research assistant team, and especially Caroline Tervo for her masterful management of that team.

Notes

1. For descriptions, see especially Andy Kroll, "What's Happening in Wisconsin Explained," *Mother Jones*, March 17, 2011.
2. See Katherine J. Cramer, "Political Understanding of Economic Crises: The Shape of Resentment toward Public Employees," in *Mass Politics in Tough Times: Opinions, Votes and Protest in the Great Recession*, ed. Larry Bartels and Nancy Bermeo (New York: Oxford University Press, 2014): 72–104; and Katherine J. Cramer, *The Politics of Resentment* (Chicago: University of Chicago Press, 2016).
3. Dan Kaufman, *The Fall of Wisconsin: The Conservative Conquest of a Progressive Bastion and the Future of American Politics* (New York: W. W. Norton, 2018); and Jane Mayer,

Dark Money: The Hidden History of the Billionaires behind the Rise of the Radical Right (New York: Doubleday, 2016).

4. Boris Shor and Nolan McCarty, "The Ideological Mapping of American Legislatures," *American Political Science Review* 105, no. 3 (2011): 530–51.

5. Dave Umhoefer, "Wisconsin Gov. Scott Walker Says He Campaigned on His Budget Repair Plan, Including Curtailing Collective Bargaining," *PolitiFact: Wisconsin and the Milwaukee Journal Sentinel*, February 22, 2011.

6. Umhoefer, "Wisconsin Gov. Scott Walker Says He Campaigned on His Budget Repair Plan."

7. Patrick Marley, "Walker Says He Will Do 'Everything in My Power' to Prevent Right-to-Work Bill," *Milwaukee Journal Sentinel*, May 11, 2012.

8. Tom Kertscher, "On Supporting 2015 Right to Work Legislation, a Scott Walker Reversal," *PolitiFact Wisconsin and the Milwaukee Journal Sentinel*, February 23, 2015.

9. See, for instance, a March 2, 2011 Rasmussen poll of Wisconsin voters, available at: http://www.rasmussenreports.com/public_content/politics/general_state_surveys/wisconsin/wisconsin_poll_support_for_budget_cutting_not_for_weakening_collective_bargaining_rights.

10. See the St. Norbert College/Wisconsin Public Radio poll, conducted May 17–22, 2012, available at: https://schneiderschool.snc.edu/sri/docs/2012/201205_recallelection.pdf

11. See also Jacob S. Hacker and Paul Pierson, "After the 'Master Theory': Downs, Schattschneider, and the Rebirth of Policy-Focused Analysis," *Perspectives on Politics* 12, no. 3 (2014): 643–62.

12. Alexander Hertel-Fernandez and Theda Skocpol, "How the Right Trounced Liberals in the States," *Democracy: A Journal of Ideas*, no. 39 (Winter 2016); Alexander Hertel-Fernandez, *State Capture: How Conservative Activists, Big Businesses, and Wealthy Donors Reshaped the American States—and the Nation* (New York: Oxford University Press, 2019).

13. Hertel-Fernandez, *State Capture*, chapter 2.

14. Hertel-Fernandez, *State Capture*.

15. Hertel-Fernandez, *State Capture*, chapter 5.

16. Dylan Matthews and Byrd Pinkerton, "This Billionaire Rebuilt Her Town—While Funding a Right-Wing Revolution in Her State," *Vox*, June 12, 2019.

17. Gavin Aronsen, "Exclusive: The Koch Brothers' Million-Dollar Donor Club," *Mother Jones*, June 16, 2011; Matthews and Pinkerton, "This Billionaire Rebuilt Her Town."

18. Mary Bottari, "Weaponized Philanthropy: Document Trove Details Bradley Foundation's Efforts to Build Right-Wing 'Infrastructure' Nationwide" (Madison, WI: Center for Media and Democracy, 2017).

19. Hertel-Fernandez, *State Capture*, conclusion.

20. Glassdoor uses self-reported employee information and so is not representative of the entire population of employees. Nevertheless, it offers one way to understand the internal compensation structure within companies that would be otherwise unavailable.

21. Theda Skocpol and Vanessa Williamson, *The Tea Party and the Remaking of Republican Conservatism* (New York: Oxford University Press, 2012).

22. Jeff Nesbit, "The Secret Origins of the Tea Party," *Time*, April 5, 2016.

23. The correlation coefficient between Tea Parties and AFP events held before 2009 was 0.01 with a standard error of 0.06; Tea Party data from Skocpol and Williamson, *The Tea Party and the Remaking of Republican Conservatism*.

24. The correlation coefficient was 0.70 with a standard error of 0.09, statistically significant at the $p < 0.01$ level.

25. Quoted in John Biewen, "Corporate-Sponsored Crime Laws," *American RadioWorks*, April 2002.

26. Quoted in Biewen, "Corporate-Sponsored Crime Laws."

27. Hertel-Fernandez, *State Capture*, chapter 3.

28. Quoted in Lisa Graves, "Buying Influence: How the American Legislative Exchange Council Uses Corporate-Funded 'Scholarships' to Send Lawmakers on Trips with Corporate Lobbyists" (Common Cause, Center for Media and Democracy, and DBA Press, 2012).

29. Quoted in Ed Pilkington, "Scott Walker, First ALEC President? Long Ties to Controversial Lobby Raise Concern," *The Guardian*, July 22, 2015.

30. Quoted in Patrick Healy and Monica Davey, "Behind Scott Walker, a Longstanding Conservative Alliance against Unions," *New York Times*, June 8, 2015.

31. Quoted in Healy and Davey, "Behind Scott Walker."
32. Brian Fraley, "The Time Is Now to Reform Labor Laws Which Threaten Our State's Future" (Madison, WI: John K. MacIver Institute for Public Policy, 2010).
33. Quoted in Betsy Woodruff, "Inside Scott Walker's Secret Brain Trust," *Daily Beast*, April 16, 2015.
34. Quoted in Woodruff, "Inside Scott Walker's Secret Brain Trust."
35. Quoted in Healy and Davey, "Behind Scott Walker."
36. Hertel-Fernandez, *State Capture*, 188.
37. Hertel-Fernandez, *State Capture*, 188.
38. Brendan Fischer, "Leaked Audio Suggests Koch's AFP Violated Law During Walker Recall" (Madison, WI: Center for Media and Democracy, 2014); Chris Welch, "Crunch Time for Recall Volunteers," CNN Politics, June 4, 2012.
39. Fischer, "Leaked Audio Suggests Koch's AFP Violated Law"; Welch, "Crunch Time for Recall Volunteers."
40. See: https://law.marquette.edu/poll/2012/06/17/detailed-results-of-the-marquette-law-school-poll-june-13-16-2012/.
41. Monica Davey and Jeff Zeleny, "Walker Survives Wisconsin Recall Vote," *New York Times*, June 5, 2012.
42. Quoted in Monica Davey, "With Fewer Members, a Diminished Political Role for Wisconsin Unions," *New York Times*, February 27, 2016.
43. Quoted in Davey, "With Fewer Members."
44. James Feigenbaum, Alexander Hertel-Fernandez, and Vanessa Williamson, "From the Bargaining Table to the Ballot Box: Political Effects of Right to Work Laws" (Cambridge, MA: National Bureau of Economic Research Working Paper No. 24259, 2019); Hertel-Fernandez, *State Capture*, chapter 6.
45. Quoted in Hertel-Fernandez, *State Capture*, 189.
46. Michael Hough, "Public Employee Unions: Pushing Government to Bankruptcy," *Inside ALEC*, January 2011.
47. Healy and Davey, "Behind Scott Walker"; Monica Davey, "Unions Suffer Latest Defeat in Midwest with Signing of Wisconsin Measure," *New York Times*, March 9, 2015.
48. Healy and Davey, "Behind Scott Walker"; Davey, "Unions Suffer Latest Defeat."
49. Quoted in Ed Pilkington, "Exclusive: How Rightwing Groups Wield Secret 'Toolkit' to Plot against US Unions," *The Guardian*, May 15, 2018.
50. For a more general analysis, see e.g. Jacob M. Grumbach, "When Governments Learn from Copartisans: Partisan Policy Diffusion" (unpublished working paper, 2019).
51. 20/20 2020 RPW 2018 Review, available at https://assets.documentcloud.org/documents/6002330/RPW-Review-and-2020-Strategy-Report.pdf as of September 7, 2019.
52. Daniel Schlozman and Sam Rosenfeld, "The Hollow Parties" (unpublished working paper: 2017).
53. On parties as coalitions of activist groups: Kathleen Bawn et al., "A Theory of Political Parties: Groups, Policy Demands and Nominations in American Politics," *Perspectives on Politics* 10, no. 3 (2012): 571–97. On the disconnect between the GOP and public opinion: Theda Skocpol and Alexander Hertel-Fernandez, "The Koch Network and Republican Party Extremism," *Perspectives on Politics* 14, no. 3 (2016): 681–99.
54. John B. Holbein and Adam Dynes, "Noisy Retrospection: The Effect of Party Control on Policy Outcomes" (unpublished working paper: 2018); Matt Grossmann, *Red State Blues: How the Republican Revolution Stalled in the States* (unpublished book manuscript: 2019); Devin Caughey, Yiqing Xu, and Chris Warshaw, "Incremental Democracy: The Policy Effects of Partisan Control of State Government," *Journal of Politics* 79, no. 4 (2016): 1342–58. But see Jacob M. Grumbach, "From Backwaters to Major Policymakers: Policy Polarization in the States, 1970–2014," *Perspectives on Politics* 16, no. 2 (2018): 416–35.

3

Why Republicans Went Hard Right in North Carolina

CAROLINE TERVO

The unremitting rightward movement of the Republican Party is well documented, but nowhere has this recent shift been more rapid and apparent than in North Carolina. Republicans in this state used to be pro-business social moderates, distinct from conservative hardliners in some neighboring southern states. But in 2010 they gained control of both chambers of the state legislature for the first time in over a century. After that, GOP margins grew and a Republican governor was elected in 2012. Over the same stretch, and even during the terms of two Democratic governors, North Carolina Republicans became more conservative, pursuing a contentious legislative agenda frequently unpopular with a strong majority of North Carolinians—even troubling, at times, to moderate Republicans.

The prolonged battle over accepting federal funds to expand Medicaid to state residents just above the poverty line is an important example. Leaders of many stripes—including Republican governor Pat McCrory, Democratic governor Roy Cooper, and health care and business leaders—pushed Republicans in the North Carolina legislature to accept expansion, which is popular with most voters in the state. But ultraconservatives have resisted. By delaying Medicaid expansion for more than a decade, North Carolina has left hundreds of thousands of citizens uninsured and walked away from billions in federal funding.

In addition to refusing Medicaid expansion, in recent years the fully Republican-controlled government enacted unpopular far-right measures in policy realms ranging from voting rights and access to tax reform and environmental protection. Groups such as the National Association for the Advancement of Colored People (NAACP) and the North Carolina Association of Educators have protested ultraconservative policy measures, turning state politics into a hotbed of contention.

Caroline Tervo, *Why Republicans Went Hard Right in North Carolina* In: *Upending American Politics* Edited by: Theda Skocpol and Caroline Tervo, Oxford University Press (2020). © Oxford University Press DOI: 10.1093/oso/9780190083526.003.0003

Some Republican lawmakers elected in 2010 represented the values of Tea Party activists, but most of the party's legislative and executive leaders had already been in office for years. Such veterans had moderate backgrounds and a history of collaborating with Democrats to pass compromise legislation.[1] Recent trends in North Carolina GOP politics thus present a genuine puzzle. As Republicans have gained electoral power, why have they simultaneously shifted their policy agenda further to the right? Traditional political science predicts that parties gain and hold majority power by catering to voters in the middle.[2] But the opposite has happened among Tar Heel Republicans in recent years.

Why? Several factors have likely contributed to the North Carolina GOP's abrupt rightward movement. Geographic partisan sorting has increased as Democrats concentrate in large cities, and contentious Republican-driven gerrymandering has exacerbated geographic divisions. But these trends do not explain the whole story, because even long-serving moderate legislators and North Carolina Republicans who originally ran for office as moderates have moved very quickly toward the hard right in multiple policy areas. For example, Pat McCrory was a popular Republican mayor of Charlotte, a liberal big city, who ran a socially moderate campaign for governor. After he won, however, he signed controversial conservative bills into law and ultimately became the face of the contentious, socially conservative "bathroom bill" opposed by a majority of North Carolinians, including two of every three voters in Republican-leaning suburbs.[3]

In this chapter, I argue that a major contributor to the rapid rightward shift of the North Carolina GOP has been the crystallization of new conservative organizational networks able to link elite and grassroots activists, exacerbate divisions between big cities and non-urban areas, and pull Republican candidates and officeholders toward their policy preferences. Organizational networks perform multiple functions in contemporary politics: wealthy donors provide funding for candidates and political causes; membership organizations and activists mobilize constituencies during elections; and think tanks and advocacy groups provide research to drive lawmaking. In a partisan-aligned network, these groups can work individually and in concert to represent mobilized minority constituencies and advocate for specific policies. Grassroots organizations may boost partisan voter turnout, especially in non-presidential elections. Furthermore, when links between grassroots partisan-leaning groups and elite organizations tighten across electoral districts, legislators can more readily be persuaded to advance even extreme agendas favored by well-organized and networked advocates. Strong linkages across organizational networks can magnify the effects of slight shifts in geographic voting patterns. In turn, interconnected activist networks can exert strong influence on officeholders between elections, especially when state and local party organizations are weak. Working in concert, elite and popularly rooted organizational networks can push parties to extremes on pivotal issues such as voting rights, Medicaid expansion, and environmental protection.

To explain what happened to Republicans in North Carolina, my research examined connections between state government and conservative organizations operating outside of political parties. I find that an upsurge of conservative grassroots energy paved the way for major Republican gains in 2010, at the same time that a trio of elite-run policy think tanks and advocacy organizations built an infrastructure to influence elections and lawmaking year-round. North Carolina conservatives have effectively tightened relationships between elite organizations and networks of activists operating in districts across the state, allowing interconnected organizations to work together to reach out to voters, persuade lawmakers, and exercise growing influence over state policy agendas.

My research does not provide a comprehensive index of all organizations active in state politics; instead, it offers a window into the most politically influential. To track how networks worked together over time, I collected evidence about the geographical spread and extent of organizational activity. The WayBack Machine internet archive has been an invaluable resource. This service captures live websites at specific dates spanning many years in the past, allowing me to document organizational data such as press releases, events, and grassroots campaigns. In instances in which it was not feasible to document activities statewide, I draw on evidence from a subset of counties selected to be representative of the state, including urban, suburban, and rural counties with a mix of city sizes in eastern, central, and western North Carolina.[4] Organizational data are supplemented with insights from interviews I conducted with thirty-two North Carolinians, including citizen activists who live and work in the representative counties. Many activists also allowed me to attend civic group meetings, greatly enhancing my understanding of how conservative networks operate on the ground.

The Rising Influence of Non-Party Political Organizations

North Carolina conservatives have benefited immensely from increasing ties between elite advocacy groups and grassroots organizations operating largely outside traditional political party structures. After decades without power in the state legislature and governor's mansion, the state Republican Party organization of the mid-2000s was weak and typically raised less funding than the Democrats. Although by now most counties in the state have elected Republican Party chairs, not many have year-round staffed headquarters and regularly maintained websites. Before 2010, even fewer had such organizational capacities.[5] Instead, an upsurge of conservative grassroots energy channeled through outside organizations laid the groundwork for major electoral gains in 2010 and beyond.

Tea Partiers and Christian Conservatives

In North Carolina, as in states across the country, voluntarily created local Tea Party groups took shape before the pivotal 2010 midterm election, creating sites for activist citizens opposed to Barack Obama's presidency to meet regularly and plan events and lobbying projects. Early "Tax Day" rallies provided critical venues for Tea Partiers to engage, connect, and launch their organizing infrastructure.[6] *Jennifer*, a Tea Party leader in North Carolina, first met like-minded conservatives after a 2009 rally.[7] Afterward, she and her Tea Party counterparts liaised online to build relationships, plan demonstrations, and share information. Jennifer recounted, "We all went home and started forming our own little groups. We pretty much had to re-educate ourselves, and then decide the direction we wanted to take to fight some of these progressive, liberal policies." Her resulting Tea Party group has been active since.

The Tea Party movement was especially mighty in North Carolina at its height in early 2011. That year, a research team led by Theda Skocpol and Vanessa Williamson tracked online web presences for Tea Party groups in all fifty states. According to their findings, North Carolina's thirty-four active Tea Party groups placed it in the top third of states with the most groups, including four Tea Parties with more than five hundred online members.[8] Speaking with conservative leaders in the state and performing new searches, I expanded on this list and located fifty-two Tea Party groups that existed at some point since 2009 in forty-six of North Carolina's one hundred counties.

Although not the dominant source of new energy, some conservative organizing did flow through long-standing Christian right networks. North Carolina is home to many religious right activists, including members of the staunchly conservative Southern Baptist denomination. Southern Baptists are the largest religious group in eighty-two counties, representing 1.5 million adherents and over four thousand churches.[9] Although religiosity in general is on the decline, the Christian right continues to be a central actor for conservative organizing and maintains well-established communication networks guided by faith leaders.[10]

In fact, many emerging Tea Partiers overlapped with existing Christian right networks. Nearly half of Americans who identify with the Tea Party also say that they are part of the religious right or Christian conservative movement.[11] This certainly holds true in a state like North Carolina, where similarities between members of these groups outweigh any differences. The Tea Party leaders

I interviewed were usually just as socially conservative as their Christian right counterparts. During my visit, members of one Tea Party group were even fundraising to invite a Southern Baptist preacher to their next meeting.

Crystallization of an Elite Conservative Infrastructure

Tea Partiers and Christian right activists contributed to the 2010 red wave election in North Carolina, which occurred in tandem with the rise to prominence in state politics of a trio of elite-run policy think tanks and advocacy organizations: the John Locke Foundation, the Civitas Institute, and a part of a nationwide organization run by the Koch network called Americans for Prosperity–North Carolina (AFP-NC). All three receive funding from the John William Pope Foundation, a private family foundation named after the father of a wealthy businessman from Fayetteville, Art Pope. Pope is sometimes referred to as a lieutenant to Charles and David Koch, and his investments in North Carolina politics resemble those of wealthy Koch-affiliated donors who have sought to bolster advocacy, policy research, and grassroots organizing at the state level. Other researchers have assiduously documented Pope's politics, and liberal activists in North Carolina speak of him as a type of bogeyman. They recount how Art Pope's spending in the 2010 election facilitated crucial Republican electoral gains and allowed Republican lawmakers to draw safe districts impervious to Democratic competition.[12]

Although it is true that Pope and Pope-affiliated groups spent heavily in state elections, this chapter builds on analyses of money trails between Pope and various conservative causes to explore deeper questions. By analyzing organizational activity, as well as how groups work together and with politicians and activists, this research explores how privately sponsored organizations shape conservatism in the state and how organizational influence works above and beyond money spent during elections.

For example, Pope's financial support illuminates why all three nonprofits grew together on a convenient timeline and maintain steady partnerships. The John Locke Foundation, a think tank, was founded in 1989 and began gaining widespread legitimacy around the mid-2000s. In 2004, AFP-NC launched with seed money from the Pope Foundation, and Art Pope served on national AFP's first board of directors. The Civitas Institute, an advocacy organization, was founded in 2005. Both Locke and Civitas are affiliates of the State Policy Network, where the Pope Foundation's president serves on the board of directors. Early on, the Pope Foundation financed more than 80 percent of Locke and Civitas's respective annual budgets and today, each organization deliberately influences conservative policymaking in North Carolina.[13]

The John Locke Foundation produces a steady stream of conservative policy research and analysis and targets leaders across the state who most shape public policy. Employed researchers testify in legislative committees, respond to research requests, assist with bill writing, and serve as authoritative sources for reporters. They offer educational sessions on policy issues for legislative and statewide candidates during the primary and further workshops for party nominees.[14] The *Carolina Journal* is the organization's journalism arm that makes this research and commentary accessible to policymakers and the public. Every state elected official receives a free print copy, and the publication reaches an estimated "three-quarters of North Carolina 'influentials'—politicians, government staffers, lobbyists, CEOs, journalists, civic leaders, and political activists."[15] This vast circulation allows the organization to watchdog state politics and inform conservative activists of state and local news.

Relentless outreach to elite and grassroots leaders helped enshrine the Locke Foundation's prominence in politics and policymaking. Every two years, specialty research analysts produce an agenda book that overviews various policy areas and recommends specific actions to state lawmakers. In a humorous remark, one official observed that after including essentially the same recommendations for years, the book had to be rewritten almost entirely when Republicans won the state and the foundation's ideas were consecutively implemented.[16]

The Civitas Institute facilitates the implementation of conservative policy solutions and "hold[s] elected officials accountable when they support liberal policies."[17] Operated by a ten-person staff, Civitas invests in politically strategic tasks like citizen outreach, communications, and polling for politicians and policy issues. The non-partisan organization can act as an attack dog and negatively target liberal politicians or organizers at times of controversy. In 2008 the organization launched Civitas Action, a corresponding 501(c)(4) nonprofit arm for explicit political advocacy. Civitas Action publishes scorecards of state lawmakers' votes on key issues and advertises scores to activists and voters around the state.

As a flexible and well-resourced organization, Civitas steadfastly supports Republican leadership yet pushes legislators further to the right on both social and economic policies. The organization championed voter ID requirements and school choice measures, along with income tax cuts, and it was a stalwart supporter of the state's infamous "bathroom bill" backed by the Christian right.

Lastly, AFP-NC is a "boots on the ground" organizer and policy advocate. North Carolina housed one of the earliest AFP chapters, succeeding the state chapter of "Citizens for a Sound Economy," the first organization founded by Charles and David Koch to push for tax and regulatory cuts. That organization split in 2004 and when the Kochs launched AFP, the North Carolina affiliate started up with existing ties to activists.[18] As a 501(c)(4) nonprofit,

AFP mobilizes citizens and supports candidates in favor of ultra-free-market public policy solutions at local, state, and federal levels. In North Carolina, it has roughly half a dozen field offices in counties across the state and a year-round staff that swells during election season.

To analyze the organization's growth, I created a comprehensive dataset of every AFP-NC online post from 2007 to 2017. AFP maintains a national website to advertise events, projects, and issue positions, and subdivides the posts by state. I used internet archives to systematically categorize posts about North Carolina by date and content type. The 830 unique AFP-NC posts include information about rallies, meetings, policy briefings, and grassroots training sessions, effectively summarizing its efforts to influence candidates, elections, and policy outcomes.[19]

The AFP-NC website shows a rapidly growing network that has engaged with every level of government, worked closely with the Tea Party movement, and deployed often unconventional grassroots organizing tactics to attract new activists and media attention. The chapter launched with only a handful of staff, and its first campaign targeted state legislators for supporting a sales and income tax increase. In 2007, AFP-NC launched five county-level partnerships, engaged in aggressive organizing around the Wake County School Board, and hired a former Civitas employee as its first statewide grassroots coordinator. The organization featured erstwhile gubernatorial candidate Pat McCrory heavily at rallies and hosted a series of hot air balloon tours across the state to "highlight the economy-destroying, stealth energy tax hikes contained in legislation being pushed by global warming alarmists."[20] Despite the Democratic landslide that happened in North Carolina in 2008, AFP touted victories in thirteen counties where tax increase referenda failed.

AFP-NC has stayed prominently involved in statewide elections since. It grew rapidly to help elect former Republican Speaker of the House Thom Tillis to the US Senate. In 2012, AFP-NC had ten employees; by October 2014 it boasted nearly fifty staff and five field offices.[21] In 2016, the organization announced an unprecedented campaign to reelect incumbent Pat McCrory and, for 2020, rehired a statewide grassroots coordinator to help reelect Senator Tillis.[22]

Why Conservative Networks Are Effective

Before North Carolina Republicans had much power to shape policymaking, the state's trio of elite right-wing organizations proactively crafted a conservative agenda and built capacity at every level of government across the state. The John Locke Foundation built its reputation and readied policy proposals in the two decades leading up to the shift in legislative power, allowing it to come to the fore in conservative circles. AFP-NC's 2008 partnerships with civic groups paved the way for local conservative victories and forged connections that would help mobilize voters in 2010. In addition, Civitas started scorecard measures in 2008, creating political ammunition for subsequent election cycles. Early engagement helped the Locke Foundation, Civitas, and AFP cultivate relationships with legislators when they were still in the minority, building trust and cohesion around a new conservative policy agenda.

Once Republicans were elected to lead the state, close collaboration made this elite infrastructure extraordinarily effective. The concurrent growth of these intertwined organizations helped them jointly fashion a policy pipeline that capitalizes on each organization's unique strengths. For example, if the Locke Foundation produces a new report on wasteful government spending, AFP-NC holds a rally about this issue at the General Assembly and encourages activists to contact lawmakers in support of a bill that reduces spending. In turn, Civitas sponsors a poll surveying the attitudes of North Carolinians about "wasteful government spending," holds a Raleigh luncheon where lawmakers are invited to learn the results, and proceeds to attack Democrat-enacted legislation for embodying such spending.

Former AFP-NC state director Dallas Woodhouse described how his organization sent positive mailers to support candidates who pledged to oppose new tax increases, even as Civitas spread negative messages against incumbent Democrats. Woodhouse and Chris Hayes, then an employee at Civitas, wrote the plan for the 2010 mail campaigns on a napkin as the two sat over beers outside of the Lone Star Saloon in Hickory, North Carolina, after hosting an event for Tea Party activists. That election cycle, AFP sent mail into twenty-one legislative districts, eighteen of which Republicans won.[23] Once anti-tax legislators were in place, the Locke Foundation provided them with an arsenal of ideas to lower taxes and reduce government spending, while AFP encouraged activists to call legislators and hold them to their anti-tax pledge. In 2013, Republican lawmakers enacted ambitious laws to lower corporate and income tax rates. Those who voted in favor of the tax cuts received further praise when Civitas Action included the tax bill in its annual scorecard.

These groups are tightly linked, not just informally but by exchanges of leaders. Two of AFP-NC's state directors subsequently served as presidents of Civitas, and other personnel have served in important Republican Party positions.[24] Dallas Woodhouse and Chris Hayes even went on to serve as executive director of the North Carolina Republican Party and chief of staff to Speaker of the House Thom Tillis, respectively. In symbolic acknowledgment of close collaboration, copies of the North Carolina Constitution distributed through the Locke Foundation office emblazon AFP's logo on the back.

In addition to working closely together, this trio of elite organizations also cultivated relationships with grassroots Tea Party activists and Christian evangelicals across the state. Although the Tea Party movement emerged in response to national politics, North Carolina elite advocacy organizations benefited from the new energy. Small government and anti-tax Tea Party values perfectly aligned with the trio's ultra-free-market policy agenda, and the 2010 elections provided an opportunity for grassroots frustration to fuel state-level election success. Grassroots activists benefited from access to sophisticated policy ideas, skills training, and election and current events information. In turn, coordination between elites and geographically spread activists has enabled intertwined conservative organizational networks to persuade majorities of elected Republicans to advance their policy preferences. The Locke Foundation and Civitas offer technical expertise and resources to push for specific conservative reforms, while AFP-NC and other grassroots networks stoke voter turnout and hold legislators accountable.

In 2009, the new professional conservative infrastructure enthusiastically supported galvanized activists. AFP-NC's activity that year was defined by its close relationship with emerging Tea Parties: it coordinated sixteen Tea Party Tax Day rallies and protested impending health care reform with a bus tour to thirty-one locations. AFP and Civitas hosted eastern and western North Carolina Tea Party Summits, equipping activists with organizing skills for the upcoming election.

AFP had an exceptionally strong relationship with Tea Parties in North Carolina, even compared to other states. A content survey of Tea Party websites identified by the Skocpol-Williamson research team reveals that these thirty-four North Carolina Tea Parties linked to AFP much more frequently than their out-of-state counterparts. Nationally, one in five Tea Party groups linked to AFP; in North Carolina, half did. North Carolina was among the top five states with the highest integration between AFP and local Tea Party groups, alongside other early AFP states like Kansas and Wisconsin. North Carolina also had the largest sheer number of groups to reference AFP, even beating out states with twice the number of Tea Parties, such as Florida and Texas.

Analysis of grassroots organizing tactics employed by AFP-NC reveals how the organization cultivated close relationships with conservative activist networks and later channeled these into effective policy advocacy. It began by holding rallies and social events, and at the height of the Tea Party movement, it catered to new activists through grassroots training events. After the 2012 election, AFP-NC moved away from connection-building tactics and adopted sophisticated techniques like door knocking and phone banking tied to policy advocacy and election efforts.

The Locke Foundation and Civitas also cultivated relationships with the Christian right and other active citizens. Locke Foundation staff members travel the state to present research directly to locally meeting groups. In turn, group leaders promote the Locke Foundation as a trustworthy informational resource.[25] Linkage between Civitas and the Christian right is the likely explanation for why Civitas is one of the only elite advocacy organizations with a social and fiscal conservative mission. However, if bills included in its scorecards are any indication, social issues are not its primary agenda: of the almost five hundred bills in Civitas Action scorecards from 2008 to 2016, only 14 percent address social or cultural issues in some capacity.[26]

There are still tensions between Tea Partiers and establishment Republicans. In our conversation, Jennifer said members of her Tea Party mostly agree with the Republican Party platform; she asserted that the Republican Party, locally and nationally, had been "taken over" by defectors of Republican principles. *George*, the GOP leader in this same county, differentiated Tea Partiers from "true conservative Republicans," arguing that the former had tendencies towards libertarianism. On the contrary, speaking to conservative activists across the state, the major ideological difference I observed was that Tea Partiers take a harder stance on law-and-order issues than their Republican and Christian evangelical counterparts.

Ultimately, when the Republican Party itself is unable to bridge divisions between disparate strands of conservatism, coordination among these elite advocacy organizations can help overcome differences. Top-heavy advocacy networks work closely with grassroots networks to get conservatives of all stripes on the same page about policy priorities and singing from the same hymnbook inside and outside of government.

Conservative Networks in Action

Policy campaigns around voter ID requirements and Medicaid expansion demonstrate how conservative coordination has worked in highly consequential North Carolina policy battles.

Undermining Ballot Access

The North Carolina Republican Party has long supported voter identification laws. The measure is mentioned explicitly in every state party platform since 2001, and a voter identification requirement was, and continues to be, popular among a majority of North Carolinians.[27] Basic voter ID aside, the sharp right shift here was that Republicans took a politically popular measure like voter identification and morphed it into a more extreme outcome. During the 2013 legislative session, lawmakers enacted an omnibus election regulation bill that ended same-day registration, reduced the number of early voting days, eliminated pre-registration for sixteen- and seventeen-year olds, eliminated out-of-precinct voting, eliminated counties' ability to keep polls open in the case of long lines, and reduced Sunday voting.[28] It also required voter photo identification with severely curtailed accepted forms of ID.

The bill was contentious and unpopular. In 2016, a federal appeals panel struck down provisions of the law for targeting "African Americans with almost surgical precision," and a member of the *Wall Street Journal* editorial board called out parts of the legislation for "unnecessarily inflam[ing] minority and youth rage."[29] Majorities in North Carolina disapproved of shortening of the time allotted for early voting (including almost one in three Republicans) and opposed the elimination of same-day registration.[30]

This vast change to election law was shepherded by organizational networks to the right of the Republican Party. Tea Parties across the state regularly advertised information about alleged instances of voter fraud from the Voter Integrity Project, a state-based organization, and Civitas. In its 2011 legislative agenda, AFP-NC featured support for voter ID and the elimination of public financing for campaigns, which North Carolina had in a limited capacity prior to this law. "Repeal taxpayer financing of political campaigns" was likewise among the Locke Foundation's 2011 policy recommendations.[31]

A straightforward, if stringent, voter ID bill arrived at Democratic Governor Beverly Perdue's desk in June, 2011. AFP had bussed activists to early voter ID hearings, and when Perdue vetoed the bill, it rallied to encourage lawmakers to override that veto and others. AFP featured McCrory, then planning his second run for governor, in an automated call to activists inviting them to attend and "tell Governor Perdue she cannot veto the will of the people."[32] Ultimately Republicans did not have the votes for an override and the veto stood.

Legislators considered bringing the issue up again during the 2012 short session. To attract Democratic votes, House Republican leaders planned to lessen the stringent ID requirements. In this hypothetical bill, acceptable IDs included utility bills, bank statements, and voter registration cards. However, Civitas pushed back hard at this mention of compromise, calling the proposal a "sham" intended to "pacify" the majority of voters in the state. Civitas wanted fundamental changes to the election system such as the elimination of "one-stop" early voting and same-day registration.[33] Taking a more moderate stance, the Locke Foundation's president predicted that an uncontroversial voter ID bill would come up in the 2013 legislative session and praised the political popularity of such a measure.[34]

No compromise bill was introduced during the 2012 session. Instead, Republicans filed a voter ID bill, House Bill (HB) 589, in 2013 when they returned to Raleigh with supermajorities and a new Republican governor. But Civitas and other activists were unhappy with this bill version, too. It was only a dozen pages and permitted voters to use tribal and student ID cards.[35] Civitas staff called the bill "weak, confusing, and [bureaucratic]," and urged legislators to strengthen ID requirements.[36] Grassroots activists considered the inclusive set of acceptable IDs a fatal flaw. The Voter Integrity Project began mobilizing conservative activists to call, email, and lobby state legislators to narrow the set of permitted IDs and hosted educational events with Tea Parties and other local groups across the state.[37]

HB 589 then sat in a Senate committee for almost three months. In the meantime, the Supreme Court ruled sections of the Voting Rights Act, which required some states to get approval from federal officials before changing election law, unconstitutional. North Carolina lawmakers were now permitted to adjust election laws without preclearance by the federal government. News of this decision quickly disseminated throughout conservative grassroots networks: one jubilant Tea Party group proclaimed, "NC Legislature has no more excuses for a puny Voter ID law!" and activists lobbied their representatives to "fix" the ID bill.[38]

At the end of the legislative session, lawmakers began to reconsider HB 589. After debate in a Senate committee, the bill became forty-five pages longer and vastly more restrictive. It enumerated a narrow list of permitted IDs and eliminated same-day voter registration and a litany of other ballot access measures. In a win for AFP-NC and the Locke Foundation, the bill removed all public financing for campaigns, including a three-dollar check-off donation for political party organizations. The final legislation went farther than the 2011 voter ID bill, the bill predicted by the Locke Foundation president, and the early April 2013 bill. Lawmakers substantively altered election law, kowtowing to elite advocacy organizations and staunch conservative activists.

The NAACP filed a lawsuit the day Governor McCrory signed HB 589 into law. Civitas thanked supporters for their effort, calling the legislation "a huge success for personal responsibility, election integrity, and the future of North Carolina."[39] The Locke Foundation argued that compared to other states, North Carolina still had "pretty liberal" voting laws.[40] Before the new law took effect, the Fourth Circuit sided with the NAACP and blocked the ID requirement and other provisions, ruling that these were enacted with "racially discriminatory intent." The Supreme Court then declined review, leaving the voter ID requirement outlawed.[41] In response, Republican legislators put a voter photo identification constitutional amendment on the 2018 statewide ballot. Grassroots conservatives worked through their networks to activate support for this amendment, disseminating yard signs to Tea Parties and county Republican

Parties across the state.[42] The ballot measure passed with majority support, but as of 2019, the future of voter ID and other ballot access restrictions remains uncertain.

A Dogged Refusal to Expand Medicaid

Since the Patient Protection and Affordable Care Act (ACA) was enacted in 2010, North Carolina Republican lawmakers have repeatedly refused federal funds to expand Medicaid eligibility for individuals with incomes at or below 138 percent of the poverty line. This popular idea enjoyed majority support statewide as early as 2015 and nearly 70 percent support as of 2019.[43] What is more, refusing expansion has come with a hefty price tag. The Kaiser Family Foundation estimates more than two hundred thousand uninsured North Carolina adults miss coverage because their incomes are too high to qualify for traditional Medicaid but not high enough to receive ACA subsidies to purchase private insurance. According to a 2014 analysis by the nonprofit Cone Health Foundation, if North Carolina refused to expand Medicaid by 2016 it would lose an estimated $21 billion in federal funds and tens of thousands of jobs by 2020.[44]

Yet North Carolina GOP lawmakers have refused expansion repeatedly during the 2013, 2015, 2017, and 2019 legislative sessions, and concerted pressures from conservative organizational networks help explain why. Initially, Republicans supported certain ACA provisions. When first in the majority in 2011, they approved legislation furthering a state-based online health insurance marketplace, which the Republican sponsor of one bill argued could be superior to a "cookie-cutter" marketplace run by the federal government.[45]

But North Carolina's conservative organizations had recently helped elect almost two-dozen new Republicans to the legislature, and they quickly made their disapproval known. Civitas criticized lawmakers for supporting an "unnecessary" insurance exchange bill and argued that the federal courts should rule on the ACA's constitutionality before any state action.[46] The Locke Foundation advocated for Medicaid reform without expansion, because "when all states increase Medicaid enrollment and spending, the result is a very large tax bill."[47] Doing its part, AFP-NC issued action alerts to its activists plus instructions for contacting legislators. When efforts to set up a state-based exchange stalled, Civitas breathed a sigh of relief: "Fortunately, the Senate has yet to take up this legislation."[48] The Senate never did act.

In 2012, the Supreme Court upheld the ACA's fundamentals but not the provision allowing the federal government to require states to expand Medicaid or else lose previous core program funding. This decision threw the expansion debate squarely to states in the midst of the 2012 election. That year, conservative networks worked tirelessly to reelect Republican majorities and send Pat

McCrory to the governor's mansion. McCrory and AFP-NC had cultivated a close relationship during his first bid for governor: he was the keynote speaker for "Take Back Our State" rallies led by AFP and Civitas, and he later traveled with AFP on the "Patients First, Hands Off My Health Care" bus tour.[49] These opportunities increased the former mayor's statewide profile and connected him to conservative activists across the state before he formally kicked off his second gubernatorial bid. When McCrory declared his candidacy again, AFP-NC deployed field organizers and spent six-figures on supportive ads, fomenting distaste for the ACA and stoking conservative voter turnout.[50]

Republicans won the governorship in November 2012 along with supermajorities in the legislature. Personnel from elite advocacy groups began serving in high-level state government positions. McCrory's chief of staff and other senior advisors had ties to these networks, and Art Pope himself was selected as state budget director. Before the start of the 2013 session, the Locke Foundation issued a 220-page book of policy research and recommendations, including that lawmakers refuse to expand Medicaid and build state exchanges in order to "[blunt] the federal government's attack on federalism."[51] In the weeks that followed, all GOP lawmakers but one who originally supported a state health care exchange changed their tune. Republicans voted instead to outlaw both Medicaid expansion and a state-run exchange. McCrory signed this bill into law, declaring he would not support the growth of a "broken system."[52]

Lawmakers had another opportunity to expand Medicaid in 2015. After the midterm elections, McCrory expressed interest in expansion as part of a Medicaid reform agreement negotiated with Republican leadership, suggesting that North Carolina follow the model implemented by Indiana Governor Mike Pence.[53] But even as the governor tried to garner support for this plan, elite conservative organizations undermined his efforts. AFP-NC's state director submitted editorials to regional newspapers with the headline, "Governor, Don't Cave on Medicaid Expansion," and encouraged activists to contact McCrory directly.[54] AFP-NC made it clear to lawmakers that it intended to leverage the full weight of its organizational heft against any expansion of Medicaid. Before the start of session, an AFP-NC spokesperson told reporters, "if [legislators are] getting out of line . . . we're going to be out in their district, making phone calls and knocking on doors."[55] Civitas advertised polling results that misleadingly suggested Medicaid expansion would be unpopular with voters in the state.[56] Policy analysts for the Locke Foundation argued that Medicaid expansion amounted to "taxing future generations to provide benefits for our current generation," and instead recommended health market de-regulation.[57]

Conservative allies in the legislature agreed. When House Speaker Tim Moore and Senate President Phil Berger convened the 2015 session, they announced in a press conference that accepting federal funds to cover more

Medicaid recipients was off the table.[58] Facing pushback from other Republican leaders and the networks that helped elect him, McCrory mostly dropped his advocacy of the issue. Medicaid reform sans expansion was enacted that year.

Conservative network pressures have persisted, even as the North Carolina political landscape has shifted since 2016, when Democrat Roy Cooper defeated McCrory. Cooper's early push for Medicaid expansion was disregarded by GOP legislators, who at first maintained a majority large enough to override any vetoes. But in the 2018 elections, liberals organized widespread challenges to incumbent Republicans and elected sixteen new Democratic legislators, many of whom promised to support Medicaid expansion.

Despite mounting pressure from the governor, other Republicans, and business leaders, resistance again came from hardliners in important leadership positions with ties to conservative organizational networks.[59] In 2019, House Republicans introduced a form of expansion that included work requirements and premium charges, but GOP Senate president Berger resisted this effort. He had recently appointed as his policy advisor the Locke Foundation's longtime health care analyst, Katherine Restrepo. She has long opposed any Medicaid expansion policies, even those with "Republicanesque" components like work requirements.[60] Another key expansion opponent was Senate Finance Committee chair Ralph Hise, who was first elected in 2010 to represent a rural Tea Party–heavy district. Tellingly, Hise was an early ally of AFP-NC and one of only five senators to maintain a 100 percent ranking from Civitas Action in 2017. Like others in this orbit, Hise wants rollbacks of health care regulations instead of Medicaid expansion.[61]

Sharp divisions between Democratic governor Cooper and GOP legislative leaders have left Medicaid expansion in political limbo throughout most of the 2019 legislative session. In total, conservative organizational networks have successfully delayed expansion for close to a decade by shaping agendas early on and diligently holding lawmakers accountable through elite and grassroots advocacy. In this instance, where business profits and billions in government revenues are on the line, concerted minority opposition has managed to outweigh support for Medicaid expansion from North Carolina business and health care leaders; and it has held firm against governors of both parties, moderate legislators, and the majority of North Carolinian voters.

Effects in Other Policy Areas

New conservative organizational networks have similarly built clout in economic, environmental, and social policy areas. In 2013, AFP-NC, Civitas, and Tea Party groups joined forces to pressure North Carolina lawmakers to adopt the Locke Foundation's tax cut recommendations in the face of considerable public doubts about reducing corporate taxes while increasing sales taxes that hit lower- and middle-income residents. For years, the Locke Foundation readied proposals and articulated a clear vision for tax reform. Civitas sponsored a daylong training before the start of the legislative session, featuring expert speakers who encouraged lawmakers to enact these reforms.[62] Many newly elected lawmakers had signed AFP-NC's pledge to reform and cut taxes once in office, and AFP pressured lawmakers to adopt the Locke Foundation's proposals. It spent $500,000 on advertisements thanking lawmakers for opposing Medicaid expansion and a state-run health exchange, and encouraging them to "keep going" by passing "bold and aggressive tax reform."[63]

The product of this effort, the Tax Simplification and Reduction Act, transformed North Carolina's system from a tiered progressive tax to a flat tax, reduced the top income tax rate by 25 percent, cut corporate income taxes by more than half, and eliminated the estate tax. Although the Locke Foundation failed to convince legislators to fully eliminate personal and corporate income taxes and the sales tax, the proposal adopted by legislators closely resembled the organization's second-best "plan B," lowering and flattening most tax rates.[64] Locke experts also persuaded lawmakers to adopt a "fiscal trigger" that would automatically reduce the corporate income tax rate if state revenue reached a certain threshold.[65] Civitas Action rewarded Republicans with almost perfect scores for their votes on fiscal and economic bills that session.

New organizing also pulled North Carolina Republicans further to the right on environmental issues. Advocacy groups like AFP-NC now operate as a counterweight to the left's long-standing elite and grassroots environmental protection networks. Since early hot air balloon tours, AFP-NC has organized opposition to policies combatting climate change and encouraged conservative activists to contact lawmakers over highly technical regulatory reforms and energy policies. Recently the organization has lobbied for the repeal of the state renewable energy portfolio standards, which require electric power providers to generate some electricity through renewable resources. Although the law still stands, AFP has made strong headway with the Republican Party generally. North Carolina's renewable energy portfolio standards were enacted in 2007 with broad Republican support. But by 2014, the state Republican Party platform was newly amended to call for its repeal. Language emphasizing the importance of environmental protection was replaced with a call to eliminate the Environmental Protection Agency.[66]

Conservative activist influence over charged social issues has also grown. During the now-infamous HB 2 "bathroom bill" saga, evangelical voters placed calls to representatives and held rallies at the Capitol to convince state lawmakers to override an anti-discrimination ordinance enacted by the city of Charlotte. At the same time, the Locke Foundation authored opinion pieces and Civitas commissioned polls to suggest that state intervention would be popular. In fact, news organization-sponsored polls from this time indicate that only the self-identified "very conservative" favored legislation overriding the ordinance, while majorities of every other ideological group disagreed.[67] Passing HB 2 sparked national outcries and angered moderate, business-friendly Republicans. Governor McCrory's defense of the bill marked a significant departure from his socially moderate first campaign for governor and inflamed the 2016 gubernatorial election.

Lessons from Conservative Policy Campaigns

These policy campaigns reveal how organizational networks help shape and set policy agendas. When Republicans won power over state government for the first time in a century, they could have been paralyzed by endless legislative opportunities or unsure of how to begin implementing conservative reforms. Instead, organizational networks formulated a cohesive policy agenda. Advocacy groups like the Locke Foundation and Civitas had the expertise to push for specific conservative reforms while AFP-NC and other grassroots networks held legislators accountable and turned out conservative voters on Election Day. The central actors vary in each instance: advocacy elites exert greater influence on complex legislation like tax reform and energy policy, while grassroots and mass membership organizations are forceful for sometimes symbolic social issues like voter identification and HB 2. But top-down and bottom-up forces usually push together for policies that align with the agendas of fiscal and social conservatives and make both grassroots activists and elites happy.

These examples also show how left and right networks magnify policy consequences of the increasing gap between big city and non–big city voters and white and minority voters. Republicans were certainly going to pass conservative policies with newfound power. And even absent robust organizational activity, racism and polarizing geographic differences would still shape North Carolina politics. But when organizational networks are strengthened, final policy outcomes are more likely to reflect and heighten these tensions. An overwhelmingly white conservative network can further encourage legislators to pursue an extreme agenda, especially when Republican legislative leadership largely represents non–big city and rural conservative areas. This amplifying tendency helps explain why growing tensions coupled with active network building can cause outcomes that diverge significantly from majority public opinion and alienate moderate voters.

Can North Carolina Liberals Build Similar Clout?

This chapter argued that an upsurge of conservative grassroots energy paved the way for major GOP gains in the 2010 election, with those gains occurring at the same time that a trio of elite advocacy organizations linked up and began proactively pushing a very conservative policy agenda. Elite policy advocacy organizations successfully influenced the Republican Party through new connections with grassroots networks widespread throughout the state. During and between elections, these interconnected networks harmonize heterogeneous strands of conservatives in support of a mutual policy agenda and persuade elected legislators to take action on their preferences.

Has left-leaning organizational network building been similarly dense in North Carolina, pulling Democrats here further to extremes even as they continue to win elections? Voting records measured by advocacy organizations do indicate that Democratic legislators have moved left on Second Amendment and pro-business issues in recent years.[68] Furthermore, elite-level conservative and liberal organizations share many commonalities: the left-leaning North Carolina Justice Center frequently spars with the Locke Foundation over state policy; the Z. Smith Reynolds Foundation financially supports liberal nonprofit advocacy groups that shape state policy (and has an even larger annual budget than the Pope Foundation). There are dozens of grassroots-facing nonprofits that connect with activists, including a coalition of organizations affiliated with the NAACP's "Historic Thousands on Jones Street" movement, the precursor to 2013 "Moral Monday" demonstrations led by erstwhile NAACP North Carolina president, Reverend William Barber.

Although these commonalities exist among individual organizations in different partisan-aligned networks, liberal networks seem to lack the same dense relationships that have built highly effective conservative networks. Strategic mobilization is fractured among a large number of elite groups headquartered in the urban Raleigh-Durham area. Liberal advocacy organizations do not appear to cultivate relationships with liberal activists to the same degree that conservative elites engaged with the Tea Party. The Moral Monday movement in particular provided a venue for elites and activists to connect in protest of conservative policy change, but it faltered in its transition from rallies to meaningful grassroots organizing with a political objective.[69]

Since November 2016, however, an upsurge of grassroots anti-Trump resistance energy has emerged in the form of autonomously organized citizen-led activist groups around the state. Early analysis of these groups suggests that this new organizing may outpace the Tea Party of 2009 to 2011. Across the country, thousands of left-leaning local groups are listed on a map run by a national "Indivisible" organization. In North Carolina, there are now 115 groups that were active through the 2018 election, many more than the roughly four dozen Tea Parties active at some point since 2010.[70] Unlike liberal organizations that are only present in the biggest cities, these grassroots groups are geographically spread, comparable even to the spread of local Tea Parties at their height. There are one or more anti-Trump resistance groups in fifty-two counties, slightly more than the forty-six counties that had a Tea Party group at some point. As Figure 3.1 shows, the state was roughly divided in thirds as to whether counties had (1) both types of groups, (2) neither group, or (3) one but not the other, thus almost perfectly reflecting North Carolina's status as an evenly politically divided state.

Given that North Carolina Democrats remain in the legislative minority, it remains to be seen whether left-leaning elite and grassroots organizational networks will be able to collaborate to influence North Carolina politics as effectively as closely linked conservative networks have. The long-term role of these new grassroots groups within the existing liberal infrastructure remains unclear. The North Carolina Democratic Party itself may become a more important player than the state GOP has been. Governor Cooper raised millions to support his party's efforts during the 2018 elections, potentially strengthening the long-term capacities of state and local party organizations.[71] This could establish a different dynamic for new activists if they are able to join and cooperate with party organizations, thus enhancing their capacities to involve citizens between as well as during elections.

This analysis of conservative network building in North Carolina helps us better understand other state and national political developments. Many of the conservative groups explored here, including AFP, the Christian right, the Tea Party, and think tanks affiliated with the State Policy Network, maintain a vigorous presence in other states and in Washington, DC. Taken together, similar organizational linkages between conservative elites and activist networks have helped shape policy and politics in systematic ways similar to developments in the Tar Heel State. In fact, conservatives themselves realize the value of the North Carolina model. In 2013, the national president of AFP told *Politico* that, "Getting dramatic economic change at the federal level is very difficult . . . a few years ago, the idea we had was to create model states. North Carolina was a great opportunity to do that . . . If you could turn around a state like that, you could get real reform."[72] After the GOP speaker of the North Carolina House, Thom Tillis, ushered through the conservative overhaul of his state's tax system, he touted that legislative accomplishment in his bid for US Senate the following year. And once in the US Senate, Tillis urged congressional Republicans to look to North Carolina's tax reform as a model for what would become the 2017 Tax Cuts and Jobs Act.[73] Senator Tillis faces reelection in 2020, and he is once again running on an agenda shaped by elite advocacy groups and anticipating strong support from coordinated, widespread conservative organizational networks.

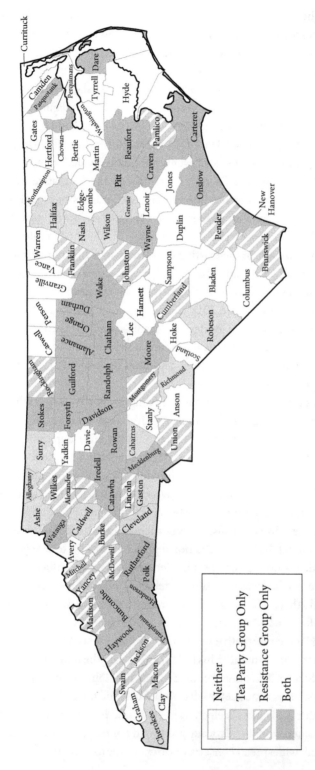

Figure 3.1 Resistance Groups and Tea Parties in North Carolina.

Notes: The map indicates North Carolina counties that have had, at any point since 2009, one or more local Tea Parties, one or more local anti-Trump resistance groups, neither type of group, or both types. Anti-Trump resistance groups are geographically widespread throughout the state—not concentrated in urban enclaves—comparable even to the geographic spread of Tea Party groups.

Like North Carolina, the United States as a whole is politically divided and grappling with partisan polarization and growing divisions between big cities and non-metropolitan areas. Understanding how organizational networks operate within and across these divides—to simultaneously energize American democracy and render it more imbalanced—can help analysts and concerned citizens alike grasp future possibilities for governance and politics. What citizens want matters, but organizations and networks among them can unequally magnify the voices of some at the expense of others, throwing public policy off-kilter in the process.

Acknowledgments

I wish to thank the active citizens of North Carolina who generously shared their time and varied perspectives on the important political work they do.

Notes

1. Scorecards from advocacy organizations show that veteran Republican lawmakers have become more conservative over time. According to the League of Conservation Voters, a pro-environment group, the average state GOP lawmaker scored above 60 percent for pro-environment votes in 2005 and zero percent in 2015. Current Speaker of the House Tim Moore scored an 80 percent as representative in 2005 and 0 percent from 2012 to 2016. Civitas Action scorecards likewise show that Republicans on average voted 30 percent more conservatively in 2011 than in 2008.
2. Anthony Downs developed the "median voter theorem" in his book *An Economic Theory of Democracy* (New York: Harper, 1957), 64–68.
3. September 29-October 3, 2016 SurveyUSA poll sponsored by WRAL-TV, quoted in Jim Morrill, "With 'Political Genes,' Pat McCrory Has Been the Face of Crises—and Controversy," *Raleigh News & Observer*, October 8, 2016.
4. Factors used to select these counties are regional population, 2016 gubernatorial votes, and demographics such as racial composition and percentage of out of state residents. They are New Hanover, Craven, Robeson, Mecklenburg, Catawba, Rockingham, Buncombe, Haywood, and Wilkes.
5. The National Institute on Money in Politics' party committee fundraising records show that the state Democratic Party maintained a fundraising edge over Republicans throughout the 2000s. In 2019, sixty-six county parties had websites listed with the NC GOP; only fifty-six did in in 2008. Recently, every county in the representative subset has elected Republican Party leadership, but only four of the nine maintain year-round office headquarters.
6. The role of rallies as precursors to autonomous groups has been studied by Theda Skocpol and Vanessa Williamson, *The Tea Party and the Remaking of Republican Conservatism* (New York: Oxford University Press, 2012), 7–9, chapter 19; and Andreas Madestam, D. Shoag, S. Veuger, and D. Yanagizawa-Drott, "Do Political Protests Matter? Evidence from the Tea Party Movement," *Quarterly Journal of Economics* 128, no. 4, (August 2013): 1633–85.
7. To protect confidentiality when applicable, I use an italicized pseudonym (e.g., *Jane Doe*) the first time an interviewee is mentioned and regular print for subsequent references.
8. Tea Party groups with more than five hundred members were in the Raleigh, Charlotte, and the Winston-Salem/Greensboro areas. Skocpol and Williamson 2012, 91.

9. Rebecca Tippett, "Religion in North Carolina: Southern Baptists Dominate, Catholicism and Non-Denominational Affiliation Rising," *Carolina Demography*, June 2, 2014. The Baptist State Convention of North Carolina self-reports 4,300 churches. Pew Research found that the Southern Baptist Convention is the third most Republican-leaning denomination in the United States. Michael Lipka, "U.S. Religious Groups and Their Political Leanings," Pew Research Center, February 23, 2016.

10. On decline in religiosity, see Robert D. Putnam and David E. Campbell, *American Grace: How Religion Unites and Divides Us* (New York: Simon & Schuster, 2010), 122–33.
    I estimated the spread of the evangelical network by identifying pastors and churches that collaborate with Christian conservative policy advocacy organizations. Two-thirds of the network I identified is Southern Baptist.

11. Survey findings reported in Daniel Cox and Robert P. Jones, "Religion and the Tea Party in the 2010 Elections: An Analysis of the Third Biennial American Values Survey," Public Religion Research Institute, October 2010.

12. Researchers like Jane Mayer have studied Art Pope's politics and influence. See Jane Mayer, "State for Sale," *New Yorker*, October 11, 2011; and Katrina Vanden Heuvel, "A Third Koch 'Brother' Hits North Carolina," *Washington Post*, June 11, 2013.

13. Author's analysis of corresponding IRS 990 forms.

14. Becki Gray, senior vice president for the Locke Foundation, in discussion with the author, August 21, 2017.

15. The *Carolina Journal* cited a "recent survey by an independent consulting firm" to derive this figure. "About Carolina Journal," *Carolina Journal Online*, https://www.carolinajournal.com/about/, accessed June 13, 2019.

16. Gray, discussion with author, 2017.

17. Civitas Institute website, https://www.nccivitas.org/mission/, accessed September 6, 2019.

18. Theda Skocpol and Alexander Hertel-Fernandez, "The Koch Network and Republican Party Extremism," *Perspectives on Politics*, 2016, 14, no. 3 (2016): 681–99.

19. This research was conducted in collaboration with members of the Shifting Terrain Project led by Theda Skocpol and Alexander Hertel-Fernandez.

20. "Nationwide Hot Air Balloon Tour to Stop in Raleigh, July 9," AFP North Carolina Newsroom, June 30, 2008 Available at https://web.archive.org/web/20090312091341/http://www.americansforprosperity.org/nationwide-hot-air-balloon-tour-stop-raleigh-july-9.

21. Fred Shropshire, "Smartphone App Helps Campaign Workers Get Your Vote." ABC11 Raleigh-Durham, October 28, 2014.

22. "Americans for Prosperity Spending Six-Figures to Defeat Roy Cooper in North Carolina," AFP North Carolina Newsroom, September 26, 2016. Available at https://americansforprosperity.org/americans-for-prosperity-spending-six-figures-to-defeat-roy-cooper-in-north-carolina/; Americans for Prosperity Job Post, "Director of Grassroots Operations, North Carolina," *LinkedIn.com*, 2019, available at: http://web.archive.org/web/20190906231325/https://www.linkedin.com/jobs/view/director-of-grassroots-operations-north-carolina-at-americans-for-prosperity-1156873419/.

23. Dallas Woodhouse, in discussion with the author, August 17, 2017.

24. Francis De Luca and Donald Bryson left AFP to lead Civitas. Joseph Kyzer left AFP to work for Speaker of the House Tim Moore. John Hood, founder and longtime president of the John Locke Foundation, became the president of the John William Pope Foundation.

25. Gray, discussion with the author, 2017. One eastern North Carolina Tea Party group lists Civitas, the Locke Foundation, and the *Carolina Journal* as recommended "Honest News Links" on its website.

26. Author analysis of Civitas Action scorecards. I coded bills into up to two categories such as economic and budget, social and cultural, crime and justice, health care, education, government reform, business regulation, and the environment.

27. GOP platforms accessed via website archives, available at http://web.archive.org/web/*/ncgop.org. Broken down by race, polls indicate that voter identification is popular with a majority of white voters in North Carolina, but increasingly unpopular among African American voters.

28. William Wan, "Inside the Republican Creation of the North Carolina Voting Bill Dubbed the 'Monster' Law," *Washington Post*, September 2, 2016.

29. Appeals panel quoted in Wan, "Inside the Republican Creation of the North Carolina Voting Bill"; Stephen Moore, "Why Are North Carolina Liberals So @&%*! Angry?" *Wall Street Journal*, July 19, 2013.

30. An Elon University poll conducted September 13–16, 2013, found 51 percent opposed reductions in early voting, including 48 percent of Independents and 30 percent of Republicans. A High Point University/*News and Record* poll conducted September 8–12, 2013, found 56 percent disapproved of the elimination of same-day registration and 55 percent disapproved of shortened early voting.

31. "Free Market Wins in Historic Legislative Session," AFP North Carolina Newsroom, June 18, 2011, available at: http://web.archive.org/web/20110706024720/http://www.americansforprosperity.org/062111-free-market-wins-historic-legislative-session; "First 100 Days: Eleven Action Items for the 2011 Legislative Session," John Locke Foundation, 2011, available at: https://www.scribd.com/document/42198695/The-First-100-Days-Eleven-Action-Items-for-the-2011-Legislative-Session.

32. "Catch the Bus to Raleigh for the Hearing for Voted [*sic*] ID," *AFP North Carolina Blog*, March 15, 2011, available at https://web.archive.org/web/20110316232737/http://www.americansforprosperity.org/031111-catch-bus-raleigh-hearing-voted-id; Laura Leslie, "Dueling Rallies Set to Open Special Session," WRAL.com, July 12, 2011; Laura Leslie, "Perdue Vetoes Voter ID," WRAL.com, June 23, 2011.

33. Susan Myrick, "Voter Photo ID 'Compromise' Is a Sham," Civitas Institute, June 18, 2012.

34. John Hood, "No Controversy about Voter ID," *Carolina Journal*, December 3, 2012.

35. North Carolina General Assembly Bill Look Up, House Bill 589, 2013–2014 Session, available at https://www.ncleg.gov/BillLookUp/2013/hb%20589.

36. Susan Myrick, "Voter Photo ID Bill on House Calendar Today," Civitas Institute, April 24, 2013.

37. See for example Caitlin Bowling, "Stopping Voter Fraud or Just Stopping Voters?" *Smoky Mountain News*, May 29, 2013.

38. Quotes from the Asheville TEA Party website from June 25 and 26, 2013, available at: https://ashevilleteaparty.org/tag/supreme-court-ruling.

39. "Governor McCrory Just Signed VOTER ID BILL!" Civitas Institute, July 12, 2013.

40. Becki Gray, "N.C. Maintains Fairly Liberal Voting Laws," *Carolina Journal*, September 5, 2013.

41. The Fourth Circuit quoted in Van R. Newkirk II, "North Carolina's Voter ID Law Is Defeated, For Now," *The Atlantic*, May 15, 2017.

42. Two county Republican Party leaders in discussion with the author, November 2, 2018.

43. A High Point University/*News and Reflector* poll conducted September 12–22, 2015, found 51 percent support for Medicaid expansion: Kate Elizabeth Queram, "HPU/N&R Poll: North Carolinians Don't Favor Health Reform Law, School Vouchers," *Greensboro News & Record*, September 24, 2015; See also the Meredith College poll conducted February 24–28, 2019 showing 68 percent support for expanding Medicaid: "Policy Issues and the 2019 Legislative Session," Meredith College Poll Report, March 8, 2019, 18.

44. Rachel Garfield, Kendal Orgera, and Anthony Damico, "The Coverage Gap: Uninsured Poor Adults in States that Do Not Expand Medicaid," Kaiser Family Foundation, March 21, 2019. Bill McCarthy, "Fact Check: Would Medicaid Expansion Add 40,000 Jobs in NC?" WRAL.com, February 25, 2019.

45. The 2011 budget read, "It is the intent of the General Assembly to establish and operate a State-based health benefits Exchange that meets the requirements of the federal Patient Protection and Affordable Care Act." North Carolina General Assembly, Session Law 2011-391, House Bill 22, 25; HB 115 in the 2011-2012 session would have established a state exchange, see https://www.ncleg.gov/BillLookUp/2011/h%20115; Adam Searing, "The Truth about the Affordable Care Act's Bumpy Start," NC Policy Watch, October 24, 2013.

46. Karen Duquette, "NC General Assembly Sending Mixed Signals about Obamacare," Civitas Institute, May 16, 2011.

47. Brian Blase and C. L. Gray, "Reforming North Carolina's Medicaid Program," John Locke Foundation, May 9, 2011.

48. Karen Duquette, "Obamacare Grant a Step in the Wrong Direction," Civitas Institute, December 5, 2011.

49. "Grassroots Activists Storm Raleigh in the Name of Limited Government and Free-Market Solutions," AFP North Carolina Newsroom, July 10, 2008, available at http://web.archive.org/web/20110710051719/http://www.americansforprosperity.org/grassroots-activists-storm-raleigh-name-limited-government-and-free-market-solutions-0; "Mayor Pat McCrory to Join AFP in Patients' Rights in Health Care Debate" AFP North Carolina Newsroom, July 2, 2009, available at https://web.archive.org/web/20100102153813/http://www.americansforprosperity.org/070209-mayor-pat-mccrory-join-afp-patients%E2%80%99-rights-health-care-debate.

50. Alex Kotch, "The Koch Brothers Set Their Sights on North Carolina State Races," *Facing South*, November 4, 2016.

51. "New JLF Book Aims to Help NC Become 'First in Freedom,'" John Locke Foundation, press release, January 29, 2013.

52. Mark Binker and Laura Leslie, "Lewis calls Medicaid vote 'a plea for help,'" WRAL.com, February 14, 2013; Mark Binker, Matthew Burns, and Renee Chou, "McCrory Backs Bill to Stop Medicaid Expansion," WRAL.com, February 12, 2013.

53. Mark Binker, "Answers on Medicaid Expansion Waiting on Supreme Court," WRAL.com, February 5, 2015; Brian Balfour "Medicaid trap awaits McCrory," *Charlotte Observer*, November 23, 2014.

54. "Tell Gov. McCrory to Oppose Obamacare Expansion," Americans for Prosperity Online, December 4, 2014, available at https://americansforprosperity.org/tell-gov-mccrory-to-oppose-obamacare-expansion/; Donald Bryson, "Governor Don't Cave on Medicaid Expansion," *Burlington Times-News*, December 8, 2014.

55. *WXII-TV Winston Salem* interview with Donald Bryson, accessed via AFP North Carolina on YouTube: www.youtube.com/watch?v=8UEp3AX0nAU, January 27, 2015.

56. Civitas cited a poll of North Carolina voters conducted by the Foundation for Government Accountability showing large opposition to Medicaid expansion when respondents were told false information that "ObamaCare's Medicaid expansion was paid for by cutting $716 billion from seniors' Medicare benefits." See Brian Balfour, "McCrory Should Listen to Voters on Medicaid Expansion," Civitas Institute, November 24, 2014; and Mary Agnes Carey "FAQ: Decoding the $716 Billion in Medicare Reductions," *Kaiser Health News,* August 17, 2012.

57. Ann Doss Helms and Tony Pugh, "North Carolina's $10B Medicaid Challenge: Pay for Other States or Take Federal Money?" *Charlotte Observer*, September 3, 2014.

58. Amanda Lehmert, "GOP Has Grand Plans as New Session Begins," *Greensboro News & Record*, January 15, 2015.

59. Greg Murphy, "Carolina Cares Is Conservative Option to Expansion," *Daily Reflector*, February 3, 2019; "N.C. CEOs: Now's the Time to Expand Medicaid," Capitol Broadcasting Company, April 30, 2019.

60. Restrepo is the author of the Locke Foundation's 2018 policy recommendation against expanding Medicaid and in favor of deregulation. See also Katherine Restrepo, "North Carolina Medicaid Reform Not a Precursor to Medicaid Expansion," *Forbes*, January 30, 2015.

61. Greg Barnes, Sarah Ovaska-Few, and Rose Hoban, "NC Health Policy and Trends to Watch For in 2019: Part 2," *North Carolina Health News*, January 2, 2019.

62. John Frank, "Laffer Lauds GOP Lawmakers for Tax Push at Civitas Lawmaker 'Training,'" *Raleigh News & Observer: Under the Dome*, January 24, 2013.

63. "Over 100 North Carolina Legislative Candidates Sign Pledge to Fight Tax Increases," AFP North Carolina Newsroom, August 12, 2010. Available at: http://web.archive.org/web/20120517020408/http://www.americansforprosperity.org/082410-over-100-north-carolina-legislative-candidates-sign-pledge-fight-tax-increases; Dallas Woodhouse, "AFP Launches 'Back in the Game' TV Ad," AFP News Release, May 28, 2013.

64. "Free-Market, Conservative Reforms Highlight 'Historic' N.C. Legislative Session," *Carolina Journal*, August 1, 2013.

65. Barry Smith, "North Carolina Gets Sweeping Tax Reform," *Carolina Journal*, August 2013.

66. Author analysis of NC Republican Party Platforms, see note 27.

67. Demi Dowdy, "Civitas Poll Shows Majority of NC Voters Feel Charlotte Ordinance Is Unsafe," Civitas Institute, March 23, 2016; a SurveyUSA poll sponsored by WRAL-TV Raleigh,

conducted March 4–7, 2016, found that 59 percent of "very conservative" respondents thought state lawmakers should override the Charlotte ordinance, but a majority each of conservative, moderate, liberal, and very liberal respondents preferred other, non-override responses.

68. Scorecards from a Second Amendment group, Grass Roots NC, indicate Democrats have become less supportive of gun rights: the average Democratic lawmaker's score dropped by roughly two-thirds between 2010 and 2016. According to scorecards issued by the National Federation for Independent Business, Democrats have also become less friendly to business interests. In North Carolina, members of the two parties received comparable scores between 2006 and 2010. However, the partisan score gap doubled between 2010 and 2016 as Democratic scores fell.

69. Moving beyond 2013 protests into the election year, the NAACP trained and placed across the state a large group of young field organizers. But this effort had limited success, as these organizers only registered five thousand new voters, or 10 percent of the initial goal, not accounting for efforts by partner organizations. Barry Yeoman, "Can Moral Mondays Produce Victorious Tuesdays?" *American Prospect*, January 19, 2015.

70. Not all 171 of the North Carolina groups contemporaneously registered with Indivisible are as active as the Tea Party groups tallied for past years. To make a more exact comparison between the two, I developed a pared-down list of 115 active North Carolina anti-Trump resistance groups using similar criteria as the 2011 Tea Party study—only counting as "active" groups that have a regularly updated website, MeetUp page, or Facebook group.

71. The state Democratic Party raised more than $7 million to assist legislative candidates, an unusual amount for an election without a high-profile statewide race. Gary Robertson, "North Carolina Democrats Break GOP's Veto-Proof Control," Associated Press, November 7, 2018.

72. Tarini Parti, "GOP, Kochs Eye NC Gains," *Politico*, May 11, 2013.

73. Thom Tillis, "Tax Reform Transformed North Carolina. Congress, Take Note," *Wall Street Journal*, September 20, 2017.

4

The Overlooked Organizational Basis of Trump's 2016 Victory

MICHAEL ZOOROB AND THEDA SKOCPOL

On September 15, 2016, less than two months prior to a presidential election win that shocked the world, Donald Trump scored a high-profile endorsement from the Fraternal Order of Police (FOP), America's largest and oldest police union. Following a vote of delegates from forty-five states, its president, Chuck Canterbury, explained that the order would enthusiastically back Trump because he "understands and supports our priorities and our members believe he will make America safe again."[1]

This was a significant Trump campaign moment for several reasons. Thematically, FOP's endorsement was perfect for a candidate who sought to heighten and benefit from racially charged polarization around US policing. Responding to the Black Lives Matter movement and swelling anger in minority communities about police killings, many Democrats, including the party's 2016 presidential candidate Hillary Rodham Clinton, embraced new rules about law enforcement practices—potential new constraints strongly opposed by most police organizations and resented by many officers, especially whites. Clinton did not seek FOP's endorsement, and the 2016 Democratic Convention from July 25 through 28 in Philadelphia featured mothers of offspring killed by police officers. In sharp contrast, the Republican Convention held in Cleveland two weeks earlier decried rising violent disorder in America and touted the need to back police authority. During the campaign, Trump regularly visited the order's lodges and boasted about FOP's endorsement at rallies. Repeatedly, Trump told police audiences that he was "on their side, 1000 percent"—as he did on August 18, 2016, to officers assembled at Lodge #27 in North Carolina.[2]

Beyond symbolic resonances, Trump's embrace of the FOP helped mobilize widespread popular support anchored in organizations and networks spread across thousands of places, including in key swing states. The FOP claims more

Michael Zoorob and Theda Skocpol, *The Overlooked Organizational Basis of Trump's 2016 Victory* In: *Upending American Politics* Edited by: Theda Skocpol and Caroline Tervo, Oxford University Press (2020). © Oxford University Press
DOI: 10.1093/oso/9780190083526.003.0004

than three hundred thousand dues-paying members and two thousand active lodges—and many lodges are concentrated in swing states like North Carolina, Ohio, and Pennsylvania. In 2012, the FOP had refused to endorse either party's presidential candidate; despite the order's qualms about Barack Obama, it saw then-GOP candidate Mitt Romney as unfriendly to unions. The order's change of heart over four years delivered an important contribution to a much-needed ground game for the GOP's reality-TV presidential contender. Not only are FOP lodges widespread, their member officers are respected figures in blue-collar and middle-class communities with ties to many other Americans through their families, churches, and neighborhoods.

The FOP was not the only widespread network of locally embedded popular organizations courted by the 2016 Trump campaign. Also hooked into the Trump campaign were Christian right networks, especially those grounded in hundreds of thousands of white Protestant evangelical churches and associated networks of pastors and counselors, along with equally massive and widespread networks of gun clubs and gun-related businesses tied to the National Rifle Association, its state affiliates, and far-right pro-gun associations. As the summer of 2016 gave way to fall, the GOP candidate sallied forth to perform at massive rallies held in mid-sized cities, yet between those events he mostly operated from his home and small campaign headquarters in Trump Tower, Manhattan. Still, it would be a mistake to imagine that the Trump campaign engaged in little popular outreach, because the candidate and his top aides managed to forge strong links to leaders in various federated conservative organizational networks, links that in turn allowed the campaign to spread messages and activate supporters in thousands of cities, towns, and rural districts.

Most commentators have paid little heed to the popularly rooted organizational basis of Trump's 2016 campaign. Conventional wisdom suggests that, despite a poorly organized staff operation and several changes in key campaign leadership posts, Trump put himself in a position to benefit from last-minute twists (like leaks of DNC emails and the Comey letter re-opening the FBI investigation of Hillary Clinton) by dominating the national media, using his personal skills as a reality TV star. This chapter makes the case for an alternative argument, positing that grassroots organizational networks helped propel Trump to victory. Of course, Donald Trump's promises to "make America great again" by defending Christians, protecting gun rights, and backing supposedly embattled police were broadcast far and wide via television, radio, and online media. But those messages also spread person-to-person through locally embedded organizations and networks, and in many places, where grassroots organizers often took it upon themselves to energize Trump supporters. On Election night, November 8, 2016, Trump eked out an Electoral College victory that depended on racking up unusually high GOP margins in thousands of non-big-city counties, including many with densely networked churches, gun clubs, and police lodges in pivotal states previously carried by Barack Obama.

In the rest of this chapter, we start with accounts of when and how leaders of the Christian right and pro-gun networks, respectively, forged transactional relationships with Trump that helped activate their federated networks of locally embedded popular organizations and members on his behalf. Then we turn back to the case of the Fraternal Order of Police in the 2016 Trump campaign. Usually, scholars find it hard to parse the electoral impact, if any, of associations that endorse and work on behalf of a candidate, because most have repeatedly backed the same party's candidates—as white evangelicals and the NRA have done. However, because the FOP refused to endorse Mitt Romney in 2012 yet got fully behind Trump four years later, we have a unique opportunity to do a statistical assessment of the order's impact in 2016.

How Trump Courted White Evangelicals

Observers regularly point out that Donald Trump is a "transactional leader" who looks for ways to exchange something of little value to him for a clear near-term pay-off.[3] The chronology of his 2016 campaign suggests that Trump used promises about issues and actions of special concern to white evangelicals to attract and hold their support. For many years, Trump displayed little personal interest in religion or the US culture wars, and he had at times seemed to endorse liberal positions on flashpoint issues like abortion.[4] Ironically, his lack of strong moral commitments probably made it relatively costless for Trump to proclaim stances such as opposition to abortion that could help him gain Christian right backing, especially from white evangelicals. Concerted efforts started in 2011, when Trump asked Florida-based pastor and televangelist Paula White to convene ministers to "pray together" over whether the time was right for him to run for president. It was not the right time, they decided, but White and her network became regular Trump advisors four years later when "Trump met early on with Pentecostal and evangelical pastors."[5]

A crowded 2015–16 GOP primary field included competitors for Christian right votes. In early primary states like Iowa and South Carolina, Texas Senator Ted Cruz and Ben Carson attracted considerable support from this constituency, especially from the most regular churchgoers. Trump gained significant shares of evangelical support from the start—and ended up the primary season with a plurality from these voters. But pollsters found that Trump's initial evangelical supporters were disproportionately *irregular* churchgoers—that is, less interconnected voters who may well have other, non-religious reasons for backing Trump.[6] Had this situation persisted, Trump could have ended up with a smaller share of general-election support from evangelical voters than the shares previously gained by Republican presidential nominees. To preclude such a scenario, the candidate and his closest advisors mounted persistent efforts to reach evangelical hearts and minds through established Christian right organizations and communication networks.

Trump glad-handed nationally influential evangelical kingpins, opened his mass rallies with showy prayers by prominent pastors, and sought well-timed endorsements from the most nationally visible Christian right leaders. Prior to the Iowa caucuses, Trump spoke in January 2016 at Jerry Falwell Jr.'s Liberty University, promising to "protect Christianity" and basking in praise as Falwell attested that "Donald Trump lives a life of loving and helping others as Jesus taught in the great commandment."[7] Not long before Iowa Republicans voted on February 1, Trump collected an effusive endorsement from evangelical and Tea Party favorite Sarah Palin at a January 19 rally in Ames, Iowa; and he also touted Falwell Jr.'s officially announced endorsement on January 26.[8] As GOP competitors fell by the wayside in one primary after another, many evangelical leaders warmed to Trump, although some continued to harbor doubts or remained behind Ted Cruz through the GOP Convention.

By June and July 2016, the Trump campaign moved to formalize tactically smart links with key organizational power brokers in the Christian right. Most Trump campaign events were televised mass rallies staged in huge arenas near medium-sized cities in swing states. Occasionally, however, Trump spoke at real-world sites—at association conventions or on visits to actual organizations such as Liberty University or police lodges. The venues for such appearances suggest the organized constituencies and institutional leaders the candidate especially tried to court. Every year, for instance, many activist Christian conservatives convene in Washington, DC, for a "Road to Majority" conference of the Faith and Freedom Coalition, founded by Ralph Reed in 2009 as a successor to the earlier Christian Coalition. On June 10, 2016, presumptive GOP nominee Trump addressed a plenary audience at this conference, telling the activists from all over the country that he would "uphold the sanctity and dignity of life" and "restore respect for people of faith."[9] His denunciations of Hillary Clinton were echoed by Reed, who urged evangelicals (17 million of whom, Reed said in chastising tones, did not show up to vote in 2012) to cast ballots this fall. "We dare not sit on the sidelines in what I believe is the most important election of our lifetimes."[10] Like other conservatives, Reed saw future Supreme Court appointments as critical—and Trump had weeks earlier released a formal list of conservative-approved judges he promised to consider.[11] Several months later, Trump again spoke at a national evangelical convention, telling the Family Research Council's Eleventh Annual Values Voter Summit hosted by Tony Perkins that "one of the greatest privileges of my journey has been the time I've spent with the evangelical community . . . There are no more decent, devoted, or selfless people than our Christian brothers and sisters here in the United States ... So let me say this right up front: A Trump administration, our Christian heritage will be cherished, protected, defended, like you've never seen before."[12] With more than two thousand volunteers and 250 paid staff working out of thirty field offices, Faith and Freedom Coalition executed a massive mobilization and outreach campaign to boost Trump electorally. Over the course of the election, organizers and volunteers from the group distributed thirty million voter guides, sent twenty-two million mailers, made fifteen million phone calls, ran twenty-six million digital ads, and canvassed more than one million religiously conservative households in twelve battleground states.[13]

Trump organized his own venues for evangelicals, too. Shortly after the June Faith and Freedom confab, on the twenty-first day of the month in New York City, Trump met for a carefully choreographed discussion and question-and-answer session with a hotel ballroom full of some one thousand conservative religious leaders, most of them white evangelicals. He won "a standing ovation," according to the *Washington Post*, when he "said he would end the decades-old ban on tax-exempt groups'—including churches—politicking, called religious liberty 'the No. 1 question,' and promised to appoint antiabortion Supreme Court justices." In essence, Trump told listeners—"who included leaders and founders of many segments of the Christian Right"—that he would take a fighting stance on their behalf. "Throughout the talk Trump emphasized that American was hurting due to what he described as Christianity's slide to become 'weaker, weaker, weaker.' "[14] He pledged to help Christian right leaders fight back.

Nor was this a one-off engagement. As the big gathering adjourned, top aides announced the names and affiliations of twenty-five Christian right leaders Trump invited to join his newly formed Evangelical Executive Advisory Board. According to the campaign, the list represented "Donald Trump's endorsement of those diverse issues important to evangelicals and other Christians and his desire to have access to the wise counsel of such leaders as needed."[15] Trump promised to continue the board if he was elected, and for the rest of the campaign, members not only met occasionally but also participated in weekly conference calls with campaign and GOP leaders. The board's composition was telling. It included various pastors of mega-churches in states like Texas, South Carolina, Georgia, and Arkansas, where white evangelicals made up a fifth to a third or more of the population. Leaders from swing states Florida and Virginia were there, too. Whether pastors or not, many board appointees were broadcast celebrities with regular nationwide Christian radio and television shows. Others were conveners of regular national meetings or principals in widespread associational networks such as American Association of Christian Counselors, the National Hispanic Christian Leadership Conference, and the aforementioned Faith and Freedom Coalition.

People named to the advisory board were *not required* to have already endorsed Trump for president, but those who had not previously done so tended to fall in line as time passed, usually at pivotal moments. Not long after Ted Cruz invoked Christian arguments to criticize Trump during the July GOP Convention in Cleveland, Dr. James Dobson—the founder of Focus on the Family and principal on the Family Talk radio program—endorsed Trump just "hours before" he "was set to take the stage to accept his party's nomination."[16] During a later two-hour interview with James Strang of Charisma Media, Dobson explained that the July meeting in New York City was pivotal in demonstrating Trump's concern for religious liberty and willingness to engage with evangelical leaders. Dobson also approved the selection of Mike Pence as Trump's running mate and the candidate's promise to nominate prospective new antiabortion judges. As Strang explained, "Dobson's role in the meeting and subsequent endorsement of Trump did a lot to persuade the evangelical community that they could overlook Trump's imperfections and vote for him, partly because Clinton was such a horrendous alternative choice."[17]

By October even advisory board member Tony Suarez, a previously skeptical leader of the Hispanic National Christian Leadership Conference, endorsed Trump at a Virginia rally.[18] What is more, when the notorious Access Hollywood tapes broke just weeks before the election, key board participants were already in so deep with Trump that they willingly rationalized away his tawdry behavior and words about women. "We're all sinners," explained Jerry Falwell Jr., as he once again pointed to Clinton's "crimes" and the fearful prospect of liberal Supreme Court justices.[19] Along with the image of Trump as an "instrument of God" willing to help beleaguered Christians fight for their way of life in a threatening world, this long-standing evangelical stress on sin and forgiveness provided rhetorical fodder for preachers, advocates, and broadcasters sending a constant barrage of messages to congregants right through Election Day.[20]

No doubt it also helped hold and deepen evangelical support when, in the third and final presidential debate on October 19, Trump declared that, if elected, he would appoint Supreme Court justices certain to overturn *Roe v. Wade*, the 1974 precedent guaranteeing women's right to choose abortion. In a Trump presidency, this "will happen, automatically" he said, because "I am pro-life."[21] Such a specific declaration went beyond the generalized allusions to nominating "constitutional conservatives" offered by previous Republican presidential candidates.

On November 8, Donald Trump, whatever his personal failings, did even better among white evangelical voters than GOP candidates before him.[22] In 2004, regular churchgoer George W. Bush got 78 percent of what Pew called the "White born-again, evangelical Christian" vote; John McCain got 74 percent in 2008 and Mitt Romney claimed 78 percent in 2012. In 2016, Donald Trump won 81 percent of these voters—whose turnout constituted 26 percent of the national electorate (as it had four years before). Only 16 percent of white evangelical voters supported Hillary Clinton. Compared even to sporadic churchgoers, weekly churchgoers of all denominations also broke strongly for Trump over Clinton.

The day after the election, Trump's Christian right advisors touted their contributions to this victory, and claimed to *Time* writer Elizabeth Dias that social media and "the reach of Christian television" was decisive.[23] This is almost certainly too simple. It did matter that Trump mobilized evangelical television and radio broadcasters to put out religiously framed messages on his behalf. But sociologist Lydia Bean has done detailed ethnographic work on evangelicals in politics, probing exactly how the Republican Party in the United States, over many years, has turned these believers into supporters who go faithfully to the polls in midterm as well as presidential years. Because they have become such loyal GOP voters who turn out every time, this religious group has political weight above its gradually waning share of the US voting-age population—as it certainly did on behalf of Trump in 2016. Yet according to Bean, "the coalition between evangelicals and the Republican Party" has not just been "constructed from the top down, by political elites who frame conservative issues in religious language."[24] Explicit political organizing is rare, Bean reports, and GOP outreach to evangelicals is certainly not confined to election seasons. Rather, ties to the GOP are "anchored from the bottom up within the worlds of local congregations," where fellow congregants and lay leaders reinforce a socially shared sense that good people vote for candidates who take righteous stands. Even more than Sunday services and sermons, everyday social interactions in Bible study groups, prayer sessions, Wednesday services, and special workshops deliver subtle, politically relevant moral messages to congregants, convincing them that they are part of a beleaguered "Christian nation" and should engage in "evangelism and community service outside of their local church." American evangelicals also learn that liberals are responsible for their country's "moral decline."[25] Framed and transmitted by national leaders and broadcasters, Donald Trump's "Make America Great Again" campaign theme obviously had the potential to resonate with these locally embedded evangelical practices. Even so, the Christian leaders who worked with Trump might not have been able to inspire so many believers to vote for him if the groundwork had not already been prepared—in the daily lives and outlooks of some tens of millions of white evangelicals who attend thousands of churches in every US state.

Trump, the NRA, and America's Gun Owners

A little over two weeks after Donald Trump effectively clinched the 2016 GOP presidential nomination in the May 3 Indiana primary, he traveled to Louisville, Kentucky, to speak to the annual convention of the National Rifle Association and collect its official endorsement. As Democratic frontrunner Hillary Clinton appeared with mothers of African Americans killed by the police, calling for "common sense" gun safety measures, and criticized her rival Bernie Sanders as too soft on gun issues, NRA leaders saw Trump as all that stood in the way of a Democratic presidency they dreaded. If Hillary Clinton is elected, "you can kiss your guns goodbye," declared hard-line NRA chief Wayne LaPierre.[26] Because he was the alternative, it took little courting for Trump to win the seal of approval of this powerhouse organization. The NRA's endorsement was delivered even before Trump was formally nominated, much earlier in the 2016 cycle than in previous presidential cycles, when the association had usually waited well into the general election period. The NRA would go on to put its money where its mouth was, spending "more than three times as much money to assist Trump as it spent backing . . . Romney in 2012, airing 4.5 times as many individual ads."[27]

The NRA's quick and enthusiastic embrace of Trump was in some ways odd. Not long before he started his presidential run, Trump had "praised President Obama's appeal for stronger gun control after the mass shooting in Newtown, Conn.," continuing a prior history of endorsing new gun control measures such as a ban on assault weapons.[28] Trump claimed to be surprised by the early NRA endorsement.[29] Nevertheless, he saw the opportunity for a mutually supportive arrangement and grabbed it in Louisville. In red-meat attacks that repeatedly brought the NRA audience to its feet, cheering, Trump denounced Hillary Clinton as someone who would "abolish the Second Amendment" and leave American women and children "defenseless" against violent criminals. Trump said the next president might appoint up to "three to five" Supreme Court Justices, and if elected he promised to nominate pro-Second Amendment candidates from a just-released list of conservatives vetted by the Federalist Society and the Heritage Foundation. " 'I will not let you down,' Trump told the NRA members . . . 'Remember that, I will not let you down.' "[30]

Trump's nakedly transactional bargain with America's pro-gun forces both paralleled and differed from his exchanges with Christian right leaders and white evangelicals. In both cases, it was a matter of working out a bargain between a positively inclined partisan constituency and Trump as a GOP outsider who had prevailed in the primaries. Evangelicals and gun owners had for years tilted toward the GOP, and their leading national organizations were tightly linked to party candidates and officeholders. Nevertheless, as the crowded, raucous GOP primaries unfolded, evangelical and pro-gun people had reason to be wary of Trump, given his past stands and his reputation for expedient turnarounds. Leaders of evangelical and pro-gun voters wanted to feel Trump out, and his willingness to publish a list of amenable Supreme Court nominees was an important step in reassuring them.

The process was much smoother on the pro-gun side, because the NRA is a heavyweight lynchpin in that universe, and its early decision to endorse Trump closed an efficient bargain. In contrast, because many Christian right leaders have their own individually run pastoral and broadcasting empires, Trump and his campaign had to do months of interpersonal wooing and herding of cats. The maneuvering stretched from Trump's January visit to Liberty University through the candidate's June 2016 New York meeting with a thousand religious leaders, during which he announced his Evangelical Advisory Board. Even then, not all board participants fully endorsed Trump, and his campaign had to do additional outreach to reach separate sets of conservative Catholics, Jews, and other religious leaders.[31]

Arguably, religious right figures were not only harder to woo and corral, they could be harder for the Trump campaign to hold in line than pro-gun leaders. Some religious leaders continued to worry about Trump's personal behavior, or at least felt the need to display consternation at morally awkward junctures like the release of the Access Hollywood tapes or the eruption of public controversies about hateful rhetoric at Trump's mass rallies. In contrast, the Trump campaign could assume loyal enthusiasm from the NRA network, as well as from most further-right "open carry" gun organizations that have recently mobilized in more than a dozen US states.[32] Pro-gun leaders and advocacy organizations cheered Trump's claims about threats to America from criminals, immigrants, and liberals, and they loved his calls for "Second Amendment people" to take bold action. The NRA and other pro-gun political actors just wanted Trump to win, so he could nominate judges maximally protective of the rights of gun owners, dealers, and manufacturers, and fend off the calls for tightened gun regulations that regularly flare up in the aftermath of America's recurrent mass shootings.

What, exactly, could the NRA writ large deliver for candidate Trump— and by what means? A first-order answer lies in the key resources of money, members, and organizational reach directly controlled or strongly influenced by the NRA. According to a compilation of "The NRA's Power: By the Numbers" in *The Hill*, the NRA took in $336.7 million in revenues in 2015, including from commercial sales, grants, royalties, advertising, and big donations. Less than half of NRA revenues ($165.7 million in 2015) comes from member dues, including one-year $40 memberships and $1,500 lifetime memberships.[33] Beyond the core association, there are several nonprofits in the NRA's coordinated orbit that channeled more than $100 million more in 2015. These include the NRA

Foundation, which supports firearms promotion, marksmanship training, and gun safety programs; the NRA Institute for Legislative Action, which does lobbying and political campaigns; the NRA Civil Rights Defense Fund, which supports litigation related to the right to bear arms; the NRA Freedom Action Fund, which encourages pro-gun citizens to vote; and the NRA's Political Victory Fund, which raises and channels tens of millions for election activities.[34] In addition to these national entities in the NRA, nominally independent but officially sanctioned state NRA affiliates do lobbying and sponsor shooting contests, gun training and safety programs, community events, and youth programs. Both the national NRA and the state affiliates also have myriad ties to commercial shooting ranges, gun-related businesses, and local and county clubs for gun owners and sportspeople. These ties provide platforms for grassroots mobilization around election time, when the NRA's Institute for Legislative Action recruits volunteers and holds events to mobilize its members and sympathizers.[35] Grassroots clout also keeps legislators in line between elections. In many key states, the percentages of residents who feel the NRA speaks for them have long rivaled the shares that say the same about the two major political parties, and NRA members and sympathizers show a fierce willingness to contact elected representatives when asked to weigh in on pending issues.[36]

In short, budgets and reach are vast indeed in America's interconnected national and state-local associational gun networks. This means that the NRA and its allies can not only fund lawsuits and do inside and outside lobbying on gun-related legislative and regulatory issues in Washington, DC, and state capitals, but they can also pay tens of millions for advertising and voter contacting to back candidates they favor, including Donald Trump in 2016.[37] NRA advertising alone can reach millions of viewers and listeners in swing states, as it apparently did for much of Pennsylvania in 2016—where a torrent of NRA ads in October 2016 are said to have played an important role in flipping a key northeastern county, Luzerne, from Obama in 2008 and 2012 to the Trump column in 2016.[38]

Beyond general lobbying and electioneering, what do we know about the NRA's capacity to reach and inspire activism from America's approximately 80 million gun owners? Answering this question starts with figuring out NRA dues-paying membership, even though detailed member totals and distributions are not publicly available. For some time, NRA leaders have touted the (suspiciously round number of) five million members, but investigative journalists arrive at lower estimates using tax data or membership-linked subscriptions to the *American Rifleman* and other official NRA magazines.[39] Such outside analysts also believe that the NRA's dues-paying membership has recently gone into slight decline.

Another kind of estimate comes from a recent Pew Research survey of US gun owners.[40] About 30 percent of US adults say they own one or more guns, and of those, 19 percent claim to be NRA members—which works out to about 14 million self-proclaimed members. Of course, more than one person in a family or household may feel they own the same gun(s); and people may be thinking of state-level memberships as well as national enrollments. NRA leaders themselves say that, beyond current dues-payers, "millions more Americans . . . support us and will tell pollsters they are members when they are not . . . For some, it could be that their membership has lapsed and for others they might consider a family member's membership part of their own . . . [T]he simple fact is that our support runs much deeper than among our members alone."[41]

In this last claim, NRA leaders are surely on to something, as both the Pew Research survey and recent scholarly studies suggest. America's gun culture is about a lot more than individuals, because gun ownership is connected to cultural understandings and to social networks of kin and friends who do activities together. Guns are bought, sold, and used especially in non-big city areas that are often thick with sporting clubs, gun ranges, and gun dealerships. The 2017 Pew poll indicates that three in ten gun owners who do *not* claim to be NRA members say they "go hunting"; half say they "go shooting"; and two-thirds say they "have taken a gun safety course"—and even higher shares of gun owners who claim NRA membership report engaging in these activities. Formal membership may not matter, however, because NRA-linked state associations, clubs, and businesses sponsor many of these activities. As sociologist Jennifer Carlson puts it, "the NRA's lobbying and social-oriented arms complement one another."[42]

Carlson spells out the implications in an ethnographically rich study of "the everyday politics of guns" that explores complementarities between NRA-certified gun safety programs and state laws mandating the issuance of "concealed carry" gun permits to all qualified applicants. The NRA and other gun lobbies have successfully persuaded dozens of states to enact such laws, most of which require applicants to take approved gun safety courses. Not coincidentally, NRA-certified instructors offer these programs everywhere, and the courses do a lot more than spread technical skills. They help the NRA attract revenue and dues-paying members. Even more important, the courses provide "a critical space in which to shape gun culture from the ground up," because instructors follow scripts that convey a morally framed social identity and worldview about "good citizenship," "a moral disposition often associated with police and soldiers."[43] Millions of (disproportionately white, male) Americans who take these courses are urged to think of themselves as civically obligated to use guns to protect themselves, their families, and their neighbors against evildoers threatening violence. This civic duty becomes not only the obligation of public officials but a much more encompassing mark of full citizenship and true belonging in the United States.

Another recent academic study of America's "social gun culture" makes an equally strong case that, for many people, gun ownership is a culturally meaningful identity reinforced by everyday interpersonal ties.[44] More than a fifth of gun owners reported that guns were part of their social lives with family and friends; and many, though lower percentages, indicated that family members and social associates "think less" of those who do not own guns. In another kind of look at daily networks, Philip Bump of the *Washington Post* mapped the locations of federally licensed gun dealers using data from the Bureau of Firearms, Alcohol, Tobacco, and Explosives showing that non–big city communities, and especially rural counties, are dense with gun dealers—a sure indication that there are many interested buyers on hand.[45]

Bump also found a very high correlation between voting margins for Trump in 2016 and the density of gun dealers, a correlation that both closely parallels and may help to explain why, as Bump puts it, "Trump country is gun country because rural America is gun country, and rural America is Trump country." In a sense there is nothing surprising here—and arguably little that can be attributed in any direct or immediate way to NRA efforts to carry through their political side of the bargain struck with Trump in June 2016. That bargain built on political and cultural realities long in the making. America's gun owners have been leaning more and more Republican since the 1980s.[46] Similarly, rural voters have increasingly put their faith in Republicans—for reasons that go well beyond enthusiasm for guns to include religious outlooks and a sense that urban Democrats are not on their side.[47] By now, the very fabric of social and commercial life carries politically relevant meanings in many smaller cities, towns, and rural counties across the country. In churches and social events, residents interact regularly with others who share "us versus them" worldviews echoed in Republican Party claims that Democrats are cosmopolitan elitists who "look down" on "real Americans" and want to confiscate guns, murder "unborn babies," and destroy the traditional family.

Still, we should not entirely write off possible specific NRA effects that may have played out in grassroots gun networks, as well as on the broadcast airwaves in 2016—not just to help all Republicans but to boost turnout for Donald Trump in particular. The Pew Research poll compared gun owners who claim to be NRA members to all other gun owners and found that guns are more important to the NRA members, who skew more heavily Republican and hold more hard-line views about gun rights than even other Republican gun owners:

- Almost half (45 percent) of NRA members say owning one or more guns is important to their identity, compared to a fifth of other gun owners.
- More than three quarters (77 percent) of NRA gun owners say they are Republicans or lean that way, compared to 58 percent of other gun owners.

- Among all Republican gun owners, the NRA members are less likely to support universal background checks, an assault weapons ban, and the creation of a federal database to track gun sales; and the Republican gun-owning NRA members are more likely to favor expanded concealed carry rights and shorter waiting periods for gun purchases.

Not only do NRA gun owners lean more toward Republicans and more strongly favor individual gun rights, when it "comes to flexing their own political muscle, NRA members are much more active than gun owners who do not belong to the NRA."[48] According to Pew, "some 46 percent of gun owners in the NRA say they have contacted a public official to express their opinion on gun policy," a quarter of them in the past year. Only 15 percent of non-NRA gun owners say they have done this, and just 5 percent in the past year. Overall, the Pew data tell us that American gun owners who claim NRA memberships are intensely, personally involved in the "social gun culture" and are extraordinarily active as citizens to press their views about gun freedoms.

The National Rifle Association's early and high-octane backing for Donald Trump surely mobilized these activists on his behalf, and they, in turn, may have influenced others in their communities. By the time of the 2016 election, a majority of Americans favored at least small steps toward gun regulation, such as universal background checks and limits on purchases by the mentally ill or persons on "no fly" lists. Many non-NRA affiliated gun owners also support such steps.[49] But NRA gun owners make up with political activism and intensity what they lack in sheer numbers—and many indicators suggest that gun enthusiasts are especially likely to live, work, and buy and use guns in non-big city districts across many electorally key states.

Trump's campaign message—that America must be made "great again" in a battle against immigrant invaders, criminals, and unpatriotic liberals—surely resonated with the sort of us-versus-them worldview that the NRA has long cultivated among its members. In an impressive recent study, political scientist Matthew Lacombe tracked themes and arguments in editorials published between 1930 and 2008 in the *American Rifleman*, the NRA's flagship magazine.[50] Furthermore, to see whether those ideas influenced gun owners, he examined pro-gun letters to the editor appearing in major newspapers in Arizona, Georgia, Chicago, and New York. Lacombe found that the NRA has long "cultivated an image of gun owners as . . . law-abiding, honest, patriotic citizens who are self-sufficient and love freedom," true Americans who are unfortunately opposed and beset by liberal elites, media and politicians trying to restrict their rights and attack their very identities. This message has gotten across, because gun owners invoke exactly these themes in their letters to newspapers. In contrast, Americans who favor gun safety regulations make technical rather than patriotic and

identity-based arguments. The NRA, as Lacombe sees it, exerts outsized influence in US politics not simply because it spends a lot of money on elections and
lobbying, but because its members and supporters have come to see themselves
as true Americans threatened by anti-gun forces. Fear and anger-based appeals to
real, patriotic Americans are, of course, exactly what Donald Trump delivered in
his NRA convention speech and at mass rallies throughout the 2016 campaign.

Trump's appeals to gun people seem to have worked on Election Day. Despite
his dalliances just a few years ago with policies anathema to pro-gun advocates,
Trump won a substantially larger share of votes from gun owners (62 percent)
than McCain in 2008 (53 percent) and Romney in 2012 (56 percent); and his
margin over his Democratic opponent was "the second-highest percentage since
1976."[51] In key states like Pennsylvania, Trump carried "gun county"—rural,
small-town, and medium city areas—by sufficiently outsized margins that he
swamped Hillary Clinton's high margins in big cities. Although statistical proof
may be hard to come by, there are many indications that the 2016 Trump campaign successfully used us-versus-them messages and organizational links into
local community networks to inspire, activate, and reap extraordinarily high
levels of support from two Republican-leaning popular constituencies: evangelical Christians and NRA-affiliated gun owners.

Trump's Boost from White Police Networks

As we dramatized at the start of this chapter, the Fraternal Order of Police was
yet another widespread federated organization with popular roots across many
districts that got fervently behind Donald Trump in 2016. Of course, this one oc-
cupationally based organization cannot rival the scope, resources, and political
clout of evangelical networks or the National Rifle Association. Nevertheless, a
closer look at the FOP helps us flesh out the Trump campaign's organizational
partnerships in 2016—and also gives us an opportunity to demonstrate statistically how federated organizational support gave Trump an added boost on
Election Day.

The FOP formed in 1915 in Pittsburgh to improve the working conditions
of police officers. Celebrating "law and order," the order originally rejected operating as a labor union, but it later embraced possibilities for collective bargaining. By now, many FOP lodges serve as collective bargaining units, while
others stick to fraternal and political activities in states that restrict collective
bargaining.[52] Nevertheless, FOP political activism has continued to tout law-
and-order themes and often promotes conservative, racially charged causes. In
1966, FOP invited Alabama segregationist Governor George Wallace to speak
at its national convention.[53] The order endorsed George Wallace for president

in 1968 and Richard Nixon in 1972, and got behind many "law-and-order" candidates in 1976.[54] On the policy side, in 2004 then president George W. Bush signed an FOP-backed act allowing law enforcement officers to carry concealed firearms in all jurisdictions, and the order's state-level lobbying has advanced measures called "Police Bill of Rights" protecting officers accused of misconduct in a dozen states.[55] More recently, the group has backed legislation making killing police officers a hate crime.

Although typically favoring Republicans in presidential races, the FOP did not endorse anyone in 2012—because it saw Obama as unfriendly to law enforcement and Romney as critical of unions.[56] Arguments in the swing state of Ohio dramatize how badly opposition to police labor union rights hurt the GOP in the 2012 cycle. Republican governor John Kasich had sponsored restrictions on all public-sector collective bargaining, and as one Ohio FOP lodge leader explained, "Some of my members have flat-out said, 'I will never again vote for someone who has an R next to their name because of what John Kasich did.'"[57] Four years later, Trump fudged this issue by responding on the FOP's candidate questionnaire that he would leave the issue to the states.[58]

Front and center in 2016 were hot-button partisan cleavages around law enforcement. The July Democratic Convention featured the mothers of people killed by police officers, a move that "shocked, angered, and saddened" the FOP according to a viral press release.[59] Posts on the FOP's private forum also branded Democratic president Barack Obama an "antipolice, antilaw and order President."[60] According to the late political sociologist Seymour Martin Lipset, throughout American history, police have gravitated to right-wing, law-and-order politicians, because the "police find few segments of the body politic who appreciate their contribution to society."[61] However, they often find unquestioning celebration on the ethnocentric right—as they did from Trump, who declared in a primary debate that police are the "most mistreated people in this country ... We have to give power back to the police because crime is rampant."[62] Such moral and patriotic I'm-on-your-side rhetoric resonated with the FOP. For example, after Trump flipped traditionally Democratic Luzerne County, Pennsylvania, a local FOP leader reflected that "We, law enforcement; and the people needed this win."[63]

Candidate Trump actively courted the FOP and police officers, especially in the weeks before the FOP's mid-September endorsement vote. On August 11, he visited Lodge #25 in Orlando, Florida "just to tell cops how appreciated they are," and on August 16, in a speech in Wisconsin, he called Clinton "against the police" and billed himself as the "law and order" candidate.[64] On August 18, he visited an FOP lodge in North Carolina, where he told members "I'm on your side 1,000 percent Trump"—and before speaking at the lodge, he practiced shooting at the lodge's gun range with the county sheriff, who told reporters

"I gotta say, this man can shoot."[65] On August 21, Trump met with a sheriff in Virginia.[66] The following day he visited the FOP lodge in Akron, Ohio, sharing pictures of the meeting on Twitter.[67]

After the FOP officially endorsed Trump, substantial campaign help followed. Back in the 2004 election, the Grand Lodge provided volunteers to the Bush campaign and launched a "get out the vote campaign" of members and their families.[68] In 2016, there are many indications that FOP efforts were at least equally wholehearted, buoyed by exceptional enthusiasm from FOP members who felt "under siege." On September 18, FOP president Chuck Canterbury explained on National Public Radio that Trump "wants to work on the systemic causes of high crime, and Mrs. Clinton wants to work on police reform. And reform in a profession that doesn't need to be reformed is not the answer to fight crime."[69] In Pittsburgh, the FOP head called Clinton's unwillingness to answer the FOP questionnaire and seek his order's endorsement "terrifying." He praised Trump as "giving the right answers . . . based on the constitution."[70] Hundreds of miles east in this pivotal state, Philadelphia's leader agreed that Clinton "blew the police off"—while Trump "cooperated" and "participated."[71] The campaign ran a television ad featuring Trump with uniformed officers, and the candidate frequently boasted of his FOP endorsement on the stump. As his campaign took every opportunity for such displays, Trump's "unwavering" support for police and other security officers like border guards became a defining theme.[72]

The FOP responded enthusiastically. Beyond helping candidate Trump define his image, the FOP's dual organizational features as both a national public-sector union and a social brotherhood helped it mobilize hundreds of thousands of members to shape politics. As a union, the FOP has experience in utilizing endorsements, deploying volunteer members for campaigns, giving contributions to candidates, and manipulating public opinion.[73] Researchers have also documented that unions influence political participation through family ties and social networks.[74] Meanwhile, the FOP also makes a difference as a federated set of socially solidary local groups. The order and its members and lodges can affect public perceptions and citizen engagement in many states and localities, much as evangelical church networks and the FOP-allied National Rifle Association and other gun groups do—and, indeed, much as federated brotherhoods and sisterhoods have done throughout US history.[75] Furthermore, police networks may be especially potent in politics—above all, in emotionally charged battles—because officers have high levels of in-group solidarity, a "police culture" nurtured by shared experiences of stressful work.[76] As we have heard in their own words, in 2016 many police officers, including FOP leaders, felt socially and physically threatened. With their consciousness as beleaguered police activated by the political climate—and facing a clear choice between Clinton and Trump—police officers in the FOP were ripe to give Trump an extra measure of support.

Did their enthusiasm matter? To see if the Trump activation of the FOP paid off, we have, first, examined individual-level political behavior of police officers. The Cooperative Congressional Election Study (CCES), a recurrent survey, allows us to compare trends in political behavior among police officers from 2012 to 2016 to similar trends among all eligible voters.[77] According to these data, in 2016 fully 69 percent of police officers reported that they were contacted by a campaign, compared to 44 percent of the general population. Ten percent reported that they volunteered for a campaign or candidate, and 36 percent reported contributing funds to a campaign—doing both of these things at about twice the rate of the general population. What is more, police officers became more politically engaged in 2016 than they were in 2012. Comparing changes from 2012 to 2016 for police officers to shifts for the general public reveals that officers were statistically more likely ($p < 0.05$) to report they were contacted by a campaign, voted GOP for president, volunteered for a campaign, and contributed to a campaign. All of these findings support the idea that Donald Trump got extra measures of police support.

Our second empirical test follows previous research efforts in political science that use local association units per person as a measure organizational presence in a community. We measured FOP lodge density per capita to assess the order's strength in various states and districts in relation to presidential vote shifts—from 2012, when the order did not endorse the GOP candidate, to 2016, when it did endorse Trump. Details appear elsewhere for our four regression models that compared the GOP vote share across counties of varying FOP presence for the 2012 and 2016 presidential cycles.[78] Our models controlled for many other politically relevant factors, including racial and economic characteristics, the percentage of county employment in protective services, and the percentage of veterans.

Our models suggest that the FOP did deliver discernably extra electoral help to Trump in 2016. Across various specifications, and holding constant other factors that explain Trump's appeal, a significant and important association persists between the density of FOP lodges and vote shifts toward Trump. Going beyond the overall analysis across all US counties, we have also been able to calculate some counterfactual electoral maps that indicate for key states the difference FOP support made for Trump. In Michigan, for example, our calculations suggest that the FOP was responsible for a GOP two-party vote swing from 2012 to 2016 of about 0.3 of a percentage point, or thirteen thousand votes—which exceeds the number of votes by which Trump won the state. In Pennsylvania, the birthplace of FOP, the swing was about 0.5 percentage points, or about twenty-seven thousand votes—in a state Trump carried by forty-four thousand votes. If we were able to do similar calculations for the extra Trump support delivered in 2016 by much more massive federated networks like the evangelical panoply and the NRA orchestrated gun networks, chances are good that we would also be able to show statistically that their extraordinarily intense engagement with his campaign made a substantial difference.

Beyond Media Celebrity

Donald Trump's victory in the November 2016 was so surprising to most scholars and pundits that their retrospective accounts stress unique events and media celebrity. Organizational factors have received next to no attention—especially not the role of federated, popularly rooted networks that likely stoked popular support for Trump. Going against the grain, this chapter pulls together evidence from campaign events and sequences involving massive organizational networks, and in particular uses uniquely available quantitative data on police political behavior and FOP lodge distributions to make the case that widespread organizational networks may have played a critical role in Trump's election.

What is more, we have suggested that three major federated networks—the white evangelical network, the NRA-connected gun owner network, and the (overwhelmingly white) FOP network—helped spread and substantiate social identity–based, conflictual partisan messages in the 2016 campaign. Donald Trump startled many observers when he took the stage at the July 2016 National Republican Convention and (misleadingly) declared that America is beset with rising waves of violence, illegal immigration, threats to law and order, and liberal Democratic attacks on religious and patriotic values. But unsettling as these claims may have been to many listeners, they certainly resonated with long-established worldviews and beliefs on the popular right. A decade ago, grassroots conservatives organized local volunteer Tea Party groups all over the United States to espouse and act upon such views.[79] By the time Trump rode down his golden escalator to launch his campaign of fear and social division in 2015, few Tea Parties were still meeting. But their surviving members are very active as Republicans in many states and districts. More to the point, the Trump message resonates just as much with other, longer-standing, deeply rooted networks of regularly meeting grassroots conservatives—including those involved in evangelical churches, gun clubs, and police groups. Such organized and interconnected Americans, most already voting for Republicans, were often thrilled to hear Donald Trump's message of racially tinged anger, fear, and resentment. They eagerly responded to his call for patriotic Americans to fight back against existential threats from liberals and Democrats. Furthermore, such voters not only heard Trump messages on national TV but also received personally tailored versions from trusted leaders and peers in churches, at gun events, and at work in law-enforcement settings. In turn, evangelicals, gun owners and NRA supporters, and law enforcement officers surely spread Trump's calls still further, to neighbors, family members, and friends. As a result, Trump garnered very high vote margins from such constituencies, even beyond usual GOP margins.

Our findings underscore the value of organizational and network research. For presidential contests, especially, widely connected organizational networks can be constructed, as they were in the 2008 Obama campaign, or they can be borrowed, as they were through the transactional bargains Donald Trump forged in 2016. Either way, they are likely to matter. Indeed, when ramified organizational networks complement an unremittingly proclaimed and emotionally laden political appeal to people who share social identities, the results can be very potent indeed. Analysts can fully grasp this symbiotic process only by going beyond polling and media studies to probe the underpinnings of organized networks in campaigns—as we have done here for key associational players and networked constituencies in the 2016 Trump campaign.

Notes

1. Ben Kamisar, "Nation's Largest Police Union Endorses Trump," *The Hill*, September 16, 2016.
2. Jesse Brynes, "Trump, Clinton Vie for Police Support," *The Hill*, August 18, 2016.
3. Debra Saunders, "Transactional President," *Real Clear Politics*, April 16, 2017.
4. Meghan Keneally, "Donald Trump's Evolving Stance on Abortion," ABC News, March 31, 2016.
5. Elizabeth Dias, "Meet the Pastor Who Prays with Donald Trump," *Time*, September 14, 2016; and Elizabeth Dias, "How Evangelicals Helped Donald Trump Win," *Time*, November 9, 2016.
6. Geoffrey Layman, "Where Is Trump's Evangelical Base? Not in Church," *Washington Post*, March 29, 2016.
7. Quoted in Robert Costa and Jenna Johnson, "Evangelical Leader Jerry Falwell Jr., Endorses Trump," *Washington Post*, January 26, 2016.
8. Alan Rappeport and Maggie Haberman, "Sarah Palin Endorses Donald Trump, Which Could Bolster Him in Iowa," *New York Times*, January 19, 2016; and Costa and Johnson, "Evangelical Leader Jerry Falwell Jr., Endorses Trump."
9. Ashley Parker, "Donald Trump, Courting Evangelicals, Fault's Hillary Clinton's Policies and Character," *New York Times*, June 10, 2016.
10. Reed is quoted in Susan Mulligan, "Trump Tamps Down the Fire in Speech to Evangelicals," *U.S. News & World Report*, June 10, 2016.
11. Alan Rappeport and Charlie Savage, "Donald Trump Releases List of Possible Supreme Court Picks," *New York Times*, May 18, 2016. By the third and final presidential debate, Trump declared that, if elected, he would specifically appoint Supreme Court justices certain to overturn *Roe v. Wade*, the 1974 precedent guaranteeing women's right to choose abortion. This went beyond the generalized assurances offered by previous Republican presidential candidates.
12. Politico Staff, "Full Text: Trump Values Voter Summit Remarks," *Politico*, September 9, 2016; and Shane Goldmacher, "Trump's Pitch to Christian Voters Evolves," *Politico*, September 9, 2016.

13. Faith and Freedom Coalition, "Faith & Freedom Volunteers Visit One Million Homes," ffcoalition.com, October 29, 2016.
14. Michelle Boorstein and Julie Zauzmer, "Thrilling Christian Conservative Audience, Trump Vows to Lift Ban on Politicking, Appoint Antiabortion Judges," *Washington Post*, June 22, 2016.
15. As quoted in Nick Gass, "Trump's Evangelical Advisory Board Features Bachmann, Falwell," *Politico*, June 21, 2016. The article also lists the names and affiliations of all 25 board members, 23 men and two women.
16. Emily McFarlan Miller, "James Dobson Joins Evangelicals Endorsing Trump," *Sojourners*, July 22, 2016.
17. Stephen Strang, "How Dr. James Dobson's Endorsement Helped Elect Donald Trump," *Strang Report*, November 13, 2017.
18. Jack Jenkins, "Meet the Latino Evangelical Pastor Who Just Endorsed Trump," *ThinkProgress*, October 26, 2016.
19. Sarah Pulliam Bailey, "'We're All Sinners': Jerry Falwell Jr. Defends Donald Trump After Video of Lewd Remarks," *Washington Post*, October 10, 2016.
20. In addition to Bailey, "'We're All Sinners,'" see Tara Isabella Burton, "The Biblical Story the Christian Right Uses to Defend Trump," Vox, March 5, 2018.
21. Dan Mangan, "Trump: I'll Appoint Supreme Court Justices to Overturn *Roe v. Wade* Abortion Case," CNBC: Stock Market & Business, October 19, 2016.
22. Gregory A. Smith and Jessica Martinez, "How the Faithful Voted: A Preliminary 2016 Analysis," *FactTank Newsletter*, Pew Research Center, November 9, 2016.
23. Dias, "How Evangelicals Helped Donald Trump Win."
24. Lydia Bean, *The Politics of Evangelical Identity: Local Churches and Partisan Divides in the United States and Canada* (Princeton, NJ: Princeton University Press, 2014), 14.
25. Bean, *Politics of Evangelical Identity*, 14–15.
26. Pierre is quoted in Jenna Johnson, "At the NRA, Trump Completes His Rapid Transformation into a Pro-Gun Voice," *Washington Post*, May 20, 2016.
27. Tom Hamburger, John Wagner, and Rosalind S. Heiderman, "Trump Returns to the NRA, which Backed Him Early and Often in 2016," *Washington Post*, April 27, 2017.
28. Johnson, "At the NRA, Trump Completes His Rapid Transformation."
29. Lois Beckett and Ben Jacobs, "Donald Trump Endorsed by NRA Despite History of Gun Control Support," *The Guardian*, May 21, 2016.
30. Passages from Trump speech quoted in Johnson, "At the NRA, Trump Completes His Rapid Transformation"; and Beckett and Jacobs, "Donald Trump Endorsed by NRA."
31. Interestingly, the June 2016 NRA convention was the only time Trump spoke before a national assemblage of gun activists, while appearances at evangelical conventions by Trump (and his running mate Mike Pence) recurred well into the fall. See Mark Woods, "Trump Campaign Makes Final Play for Evangelical Votes with Pence Video," *Christian Today*, November 4, 2016.
32. Daniel Trotta, "Local Gun Groups Flex Muscle in State Politics, Sidestepping the NRA," *Reuters*, October 8, 2018.
33. Megan R. Wilson, "The NRA's Power: By the Numbers," *The Hill*, October 8, 2017.
34. In addition to Wilson, "The NRA's Power," see the Wikipedia entry on the "National Rifle Association."
35. For example, in Ohio, see "Volunteer for the NRA-ILA in Ohio!" Buckeye Firearms Association, July 14, 2016; "Ohio Gun Voter Election Center," Buckeye Firearms Association, 2016.
36. Although a bit dated, similar patterns still hold to those documented in Ronald G. Shaiko and Mark A. Wallace, "Going Hunting Where the Ducks Are: The National Rifle Association and the Grass Roots," in *The Changing Politics of Gun Control*, ed. John M. Bruce and Clyde Wilcox (Lanham, MD: Rowman and Littlefield, 1998), 155–71,, especially Table 9.1, p. 168.
37. John Schuppe, "NRA Sticking with Trump, Breaks Own Record for Campaign Spending," NBC News, October 12, 2016; John W. Schoen, "Here Are the Congressional Candidates Who Got the Most NRA Money in the 2016 Campaign, by State—Florida Is No.3," CNBC, February 15, 2018; and Mike Spies and Ashley Balcerzak, "The NRA Placed Big Bets on the 2016 Election, and Won Almost All of Them," *OpenSecrets.org*, November 9, 2016.

38. Tom Hamburger, John Wagner, and Rosalind S. Helderman, "Trump Returns to the NRA, Which Backed Him Early and Often in 2016," *Washington Post*, April 27, 2017.

39. Christopher Ingraham, "Nobody Knows How Many Members the NRA Has, but Its Tax Returns Offer Some Clues," *Washington Post*, Wonkblog analysis, February 26, 2018; and Dave Gilson, "The NRA Says It Has 5 Million Members. Its Magazines Tell Another Story," *Mother Jones*, March 7, 2018.

40. Kim Parker, "Among Gun Owners, NRA Members Have a Unique Set of Views and Experiences," Pew Research Center, *FactTank*, July 5, 2017.

41. Blog post about the Pew Research poll from the NRA Institute for Legislative Action, quoted in Wilson, "The NRA's Power."

42. Jennifer Carlson, *Citizen-Protectors: The Everyday Politics of Guns in an Age of Decline* (New York: Oxford University Press, 2015), 63.

43. Carlson, *Citizen-Protectors*, 64, 67.

44. Bindu Kalesan, Marcos D. Villarreal, Katherine M. Keyes, and Sandro Galea, "Gun Ownership and Gun Culture," *Injury Prevention*, June 29, 2015.

45. Philip Bump, "Trump Country Is Gun Country," *Washington Post*, February 27, 2018. As Bump puts it, "the NRA probably didn't drive gun owners to support Trump in any broad sense; those voters were already there." Of course, NRA drumbeats may have helped turn out potential voters who had not necessarily gone to the polls for GOP candidates in earlier contests.

46. Mark Joslyn and Donald P. Haider-Markel, "Gun Ownership Used to Be Bipartisan. Not Anymore," *Monkey Cage*, May 9, 2017; and Mark R. Joslyn, Donald P. Haider-Markel, Michael Baggs, and Andrew Bilbo, "Emerging Political Identities? Gun Ownership and Voting in Presidential Elections," *Social Science Quarterly* 98, no. 2 (June 2017): 382–96.

47. Katherine J. Cramer, *The Politics of Resentment: Rural Consciousness in Wisconsin and the Rise of Scott Walker* (Chicago: University of Chicago Press, 2016).

48. All findings reported here come from Parker, "Among Gun Owners, NRA Members Have a Unique Set of Views and Experiences."

49. See Gallup poll trends on "Guns" at news.gallup.com/poll/1645/guns.aspx as of September 7, 2019.

50. Matthew Lacombe, "This Is How the NRA 'Politically Weaponized' Its Membership," *Monkey Cage*, October 11, 2017; and Matthew Lacombe, "The Political Weaponization of Gun Owners: The NRA's Cultivation, Dissemination, and Use of a Group Social Identity," *Journal of Politics* 81, no. 4 (2019), 2408–24.

51. Joslyn and Haier-Markel, "Gun Ownership Used to Be Bipartisan."

52. Larry Gaines and John Worrall, *Police Administration* (Clifton Park, NY: Cengage Learning, 2011), 326.

53. Stephan Lesher, *George Wallace: American Populist* (New York: DaCapo Press, 1994), 405.

54. Eric Arnesen and Joseph Lipari, *Encyclopedia of U.S. Labor and Working-Class History*, volume 1 (Abingdon, England: Taylor & Francis, 2007), 483.

55. Kevin M. Keenan and Samuel Walker, "An Impediment to Police Accountability? An Analysis of Statutory Law Enforcement Officers' Bills of Rights," *Boston University Public Interest Law Journal*, 14 (2005): 185–243.

56. Sarah Wheaton, "Police Union Meets with Trump as It Weighs Endorsement," *Politico*, August 5, 2016.

57. Quoted in Alec Magillis, "The Battleground," *New Republic*, May 18, 2012. See also Jack Torry, "Ohio Union Backs Brown in Senate Race," *Columbia Dispatch*, July 18, 2012.

58. "Donald Trump's Fraternal Order of Police Questionnaire," *Marshall Project*, July 27, 2016.

59. Jonathan Swan, "Police Union: Clinton Snubbed Us," *The Hill*, August 6, 2016. The title refers to the fact that Hillary Clinton did not respond to the FOP questionnaire.

60. Jon Swaine and George Joseph, "Hackers Post Private Files of America's Biggest Police Union," *The Guardian*, January 18, 2016.

61. Seymour Martin Lipset, "The Politics of the Police," *New Society* (March 6, 1969): 358.

62. Trump quoted in Kurtis Lee, "Campaign 2016 Updates," *Los Angeles Times*, September 20, 2016, https://www.latimes.com/nation/politics/trailguide/la-na-trailguide-updates-09202016-htmlstory.html .

63. Michael Buffer, "Trump Dominates in Luzerne County," *The Citizen's Voice*, November 10, 2016.

64. Fraternal Order of Police Orlando Lodge #25, Facebook, August 11, 2016, available at www.facebook.com/orlandofop25/photos/a.522418477768651/1301963683147456/; Jamiche Alcindor, "Trump, Rallying White Crowd for Police, Accuses Democrats of Exploiting Blacks," *New York Times*, August 16, 2016.

65. "Trump Gets Some Target Practice During Iredell County Stop," Associated Press, August 18, 2016; Donna Swicegood, "Iredell Sheriff Recalls Trump's Surprise Visit," *Statesville Record & Landmark*, September 6, 2016; and Jeff Reeves, "It's Time for a Change, Donald Trump Says at Charlotte Rally," CBS17.com, August 18, 2016.

66. "Stafford Sheriff David Decatur Hosts Trump Closed-Door Meeting," *Potomac Local*, October 19, 2016.

67. Doug Livingston and Theresa Cottom, "Trump's Day in Akron: Early Bird Catches Crowd Off Guard," *Akron Beacon Journal*, August 22, 2016.

68. Fraternal Order of Police, "F.O.P. Putting Words into Action in Support of the President," Grand Lodge FOP, October 14, 2004.

69. Rachel Martin, "The Nation's Largest Police Union Endorses Donald Trump," NPR, September 18, 2016.

70. Sarah Schneider, "Pittsburgh's Police Union Part of Vote to Endorse Trump," Radio Station WESA, September 21, 2016.

71. Quoted in Dom Giordano, "Philly FOP Chief on Presidential Endorsement," CBS Philly, September 19, 2016.

72. Michele McPhee, "The Hidden Trump Voter: The Police," *Boston Globe*, November 9, 2016. Racial controversies challenged the Trump-police link, however. In some places, white officers were disciplined for pro-Trump public displays. Furthermore, the GOP standard-bearer was opposed by organizations like Blacks in Law Enforcement of America and the Black Peace Officers Association that were formed decades ago to speak for marginalized black officers. Local black police leaders and groups also denounced Trump, as did the 2,500 member Philadelphia Guardian Civic League, which called Trump an "outrageous bigot." See Corky Siemaszko, "Black Cops at Odds with Fraternal Order of Police over Trump Endorsement," NBC News, September 22, 2016. About 30 percent of FOP members are African American police officers, but the order's historical dalliances with white racists cloud its reputation, and its seven-member governing board remains all white.

73. Ron DeLord, Jon Burpo, and Michael R. Shannon, *Police Union Power, Politics, and Confrontation in the 21st Century: New Challenges, New Issues* (Springfield, IL: Charles C. Thomas Publisher, 2008); and Jan E. Leighley and Jonathan Nagler, "Unions, Voter Turnout, and Class Bias in U.S. Elections, 1964–2004," *Journal of Politics* 69, no. 2 (2007): 430–41.

74. John S. Ahlquist, Amanda B. Clayton, and Margaret Levi, "Provoking Preferences: Unionization, Trade Policy, and the ILWU Puzzle," *International Organization* 68, no. 1 (2014): 33–75.

75. James V. Grimaldi and Sari Horwitz, "James Pasco, Fraternal Order of Police Lobbyist, Influences Gun Debate and More," *Washington Post*, December 15, 2010; and Theda Skocpol, *Diminished Democracy: From Membership to Management in American Civic Life* (Norman, OK: University of Oklahoma Press, 2003).

76. Bethan Loftus, "Police Occupational Culture: Classic Themes, Altered Times," *Policing & Society* 20, no. 1 (2010): 1–20.

77. Police were identified in the 2016 CCES using string matching of self-reported occupations; in the 2012 CCES, they were identified as those reporting working in "protective services" and working for county or local government. This process identified 243 police officers in 2012 and 109 in 2016.

78. See the article text and online appendices for Michael Zoorob, "Blue Endorsements Matter: How the Fraternal Order of Police Contributed to Donald Trump's Victory," *PS: Politics & Political Science* 52, no. 2 (2018): 243–50.

79. Theda Skocpol and Vanessa Williamson, *The Tea Party and the Remaking of Republican Conservatism* (New York: Oxford University Press, 2012).

5

How Trump Flipped Michigan

SALLY MARSH

Nearly a year after the 2016 election, the traces of Donald Trump's appeal were still visible in Manistee County, Michigan. Along county highways throughout this community in the northwest region of the Lower Peninsula, Trump/Pence signs still decorated the front of small homes, stood alongside roads through rolling farm lands, and clung to the bumpers of minivans and pick-up trucks.

In this area, where a majority of voters twice elected President Barack Obama, Trump emerged victorious in 2016 with nearly 55 percent of the vote. For nearly three weeks between August and October 2017, I lived in Northern Michigan and interviewed community leaders in Manistee County to understand how this small community flipped in just four short years. In settings ranging from local coffee shops and diners to business offices and people's homes and even the county fair, I spoke with Michiganders of all political stripes about their political preferences and the most pressing challenges facing their community. Based on this in-depth qualitative research, I use Manistee as a lens to understand how the 2016 election played out on the ground as Donald Trump, to the surprise of many observers, flipped Michigan from blue to red.

Manistee County is at the heart of the 2016 election in Michigan, because it is perhaps the most startling "flipped" jurisdiction among the twelve Michigan counties that went from delivering majorities of votes for Barack Obama in 2008 and 2012 to supporting Donald Trump in 2016. In the span of just four years, Manistee experienced a net change from Obama to Trump of 20.9 percentage points, the largest countywide net partisan change of votes in Michigan in a county that did not simultaneously experience decreased voter turnout.[1]

The electoral trends in flipped counties indicate drastic, consequential shifts at the local level. What explains these shifts, and how did presidential campaign organizations contribute to them? In order to understand the success of the Trump campaign in locales previously carried by Democrats, I investigate the interaction between voters and the campaign organizations courting their

Sally Marsh, *How Trump Flipped Michigan* In: *Upending American Politics* Edited by: Theda Skocpol and Caroline Tervo, Oxford University Press (2020). © Oxford University Press
DOI: 10.1093/oso/9780190083526.003.0005

support. Manistee County provides a useful window into the local processes at work.

By combining this case study with broader analysis of campaign and organizational dynamics statewide, I argue the Trump campaign in Michigan and its supporters benefited from strong existing conservative networks while simultaneously capitalizing on new grassroots enthusiasm inspired by his unconventional candidacy. By contrast, the Clinton campaign did not have access to the sorts of strong existing networks operating among local conservatives and did not inspire new levels of grassroots enthusiasm. Trump supporters in Manistee County were organized and energized in new ways, while the Clinton campaign left unenthusiastic Democrats without the tools or will to combat the Trump surge.

My research on relationships between presidential campaigns and local developments is rooted in interviews with community leaders and active citizens. I conducted interviews with thirty-six residents of Manistee: seventeen self-described Democrats, thirteen Republicans, and six people who do not strongly identify with a political party. Some held formal positions of leadership or involvement, and others did not, but all the people I interviewed were civically active in the county, and most were active politically. To find interview participants, I started with cold email outreach to newspaper editors and writers, political party volunteers, philanthropic and membership organizations, business leaders, and local elected officials. I also interviewed several Manistee residents at the summer county fair. At the conclusion of each interview, I asked for referrals to other members of the community. This snowball method was crucial for obtaining some of my most insightful interviews, particularly with enthusiastic Trump organizers who were not represented in typical county leadership positions. Once I earned the trust of a few community members, many more were willing to participate. When participants realized I am a native Michigander with deep family ties "Up North" near Manistee, their trust and affinity were more immediate. The quotes featured in this chapter are transcriptions from recordings and notes taken during interviews. I promised confidentiality, and to that end I use pseudonyms and remove personally identifying information from my descriptions of participants whenever possible.

I supplement interview evidence with real-time data from Facebook, Google Groups, newsletters, and newspapers. I combine this local data with a broader picture of the 2016 election in Michigan, utilizing publicly available election data, campaign-watch websites, and conversations with senior presidential campaign operatives, including Michigan for Trump state director Scott Hagerstrom.

This research approach allows me to add color, context, and in-depth analysis to understandings of the 2016 presidential election. National survey results and other aggregate data sources are limited in depth. Although my interviews with Manistee participants are not fully representative, they do allow me to understand and present the perspectives of local "opinion leaders" and politically aware citizens—who, in turn, are consequential actors quite likely to reflect widely held local sentiments and political preferences.[2] My research does not claim to reveal *the* single reason Trump was successful in Manistee or the state as a whole. Rather, I use a single flipped county as an entry point into analyzing *how* the local-level organizational differences and resonant sentiments propelling the Clinton and Trump campaigns interacted with the statewide strategy and larger narrative of the 2016 campaign. My research highlights differences in network strength and grassroots energy from the top-down and bottom-up.

Michigan and Manistee County in Election 2016

Trump's victory in Michigan—like the parallel outcome in the national Electoral College—was an unexpected and historic political upset. The *Detroit Free Press* later described Trump's win as a "stunning turnabout," because less than a month before the election polls estimated a double-digit lead for Hillary Clinton in Michigan.[3] Few predicted outsider candidate Donald Trump would be the first Republican presidential candidate to carry Michigan in nearly thirty years, and fewer still expected him to win the presidency. Before Trump, no Republican presidential candidate had carried the state since President George H. W. Bush did so in 1988.[4]

Many have theorized about the causes of this surprising victory, including commentary asserting that the outcome in Michigan can be explained by voter turnout. But low voter turnout in urban centers alone is not sufficient explanation for the electoral results in Michigan in 2016. Voter turnout in Michigan, as a whole, actually increased in 2016 compared to 2012 statewide, and less than a quarter of Michigan's eighty-three counties witnessed a decrease in turnout between those two presidential elections.[5] Furthermore, only three of the counties that did experience a decrease in turnout were Democratic strongholds; most counties with a decrease in turnout were located in the sparsely populated, conservative-trending Upper Peninsula.[6] Somewhat lower 2016 turnout in urban Democratic constituencies, as well as increased margins of victory for Trump in rural areas of Michigan, certainly played a role in the 2016 outcome, and in an extremely close election, any one factor arguably could have been decisive. But these were not surprising trends, especially given the historic unpopularity of both candidates.[7]

Flipped counties, on the other hand, indicate a substantial shift at the local level in a span of only four years. In all but one of the twelve counties that flipped in Michigan, the net change from Obama to Trump was well over 10 points, and nearly half experienced a net change in votes greater than 20 points.[8] In most flipped counties turnout increased, and even in those where turnout decreased, the effects of lower turnout were probably minimal; minor decreases in turnout accompanied substantial, double-digit electoral swings.[9] Located across the state with varied socioeconomic and demographic characteristics, these flipped counties in Michigan, highlighted in Figure 5.1, have little in common beyond their "flipped" status. Thus, local-level shifts in these locales are both puzzling and consequential for understanding the 2016 election in Michigan as a whole.

Indeed, data suggest that much of the 2016 election results can be explained by the voters and communities that flipped, rather than turnout. Nationwide, Trump flipped 30 percent of the counties Obama carried twice (while Clinton

Figure 5.1 Michigan County-Level Electoral Trends, 2008–2016.

won less than 1 percent of counties whose voters had never supported Obama).[10] Furthermore, using voter file and voter history data, Nate Cohn at the *New York Times* indicates that in select states analyzed, "large numbers of white, working-class voters shifted from the Democrats to Mr. Trump," and this trend was probably decisive.[11] Similarly, a Global Strategy Group report on the 2016 election estimates that about 70 percent of Clinton's loss can be attributed to white, working-class voters switching from Obama to Trump, and thus "turnout was less of a problem for Clinton than defections were."[12]

In Michigan, the 2016 presidential election was decided by only 10,704 votes, and the twelve flipped counties generated a 99,012-vote margin in favor of Trump.[13] Although only one of multiple significant factors, if Clinton had successfully maintained a Democratic majority in even a small handful of flipped counties, she would have won the state. Consequently, flipped counties like Manistee provide an excellent setting to investigate how Trump flipped Michigan and examine the local, interactive processes between voters and campaigns.

Why Manistee Is a Compelling Case Study

Manistee is compelling not only for its drastic shift in votes but also because of its demographic and economic characteristics. Manistee is a non-metropolitan rural county in Northern Michigan on the shores of Lake Michigan.[14] Although rural, the county is home to a historically industrial town and many blue-collar union workers, with 94 percent white residents, 17 percent of residents living in poverty, a median income of $41,395 per year, and under 5 percent of residents educated with a bachelor's degree or above.[15] In this white working-class community, Manisteeans I spoke to considered themselves aligned with the interests of working people, often discussing characteristics like hard work that they felt were especially relevant in their rural community. Given these demographics and because members of the white working class typically identify with descriptors such as "ordinary," "average," "hardworking," and "rural," the "white working class" is a useful, albeit imperfect, categorization for research in Manistee.[16] This is a portion of the electorate that remains a strong force in Michigan, and it is also a portion of the electorate analysts identify as critical for understanding the 2016 outcome.

Broadly speaking, Manistee faces economic challenges similar to those found in communities across Michigan and the United States. Local trends of declining industry and subsequent job loss leading to communitywide economic insecurity, scarcity of affordable housing, deteriorating infrastructure, and an ensuing "brain drain" of young people are familiar to many. As one longtime resident recounted, in the early 1980s "the whole town was depressed" following the loss of four key employers.[17] While the local economy had improved in the years since, it has not fully recovered. Concerns about economic development, community investment, and a deficit of "good-paying" jobs reverberated through my conversations with local leaders. On the main street, many storefronts stand empty, still waiting for new businesses to arrive someday.

Importantly, Manistee is located far outside Detroit. All competent campaigns, Republican and especially Democrat, spend time and resources in the Detroit metro area if they want to win Michigan. Removed from the main population centers in the state, including long-studied Macomb County, Manistee provides a telling lens for this research precisely because it is not the obvious recipient of resources.[18] While Detroit is certainly important, candidates have to succeed elsewhere too—in places like Manistee—in order to win Michigan.

Studying Campaigns at the Local Level

For decades, political scientists debated whether this research was even worth pursuing. Early studies of campaigns concluded that campaigns are "sound and fury signifying nothing," and subsequent findings suggested that "fundamentals" like the economy and partisanship could accurately predict election results, campaigning aside.[19] However, this "minimal effects" consensus has since been challenged by a vast literature demonstrating that in various capacities, campaigns *do* matter. The research available today indicates campaigns are capable of eliciting multiple effects, including mobilization, priming, persuasion, and voter learning.[20]

In recent years, scholars like D. Sunshine Hillygus have called for a significant scholarly shift in the study of campaigns because, "it is no longer enough for scholars to simply look for new and better ways to document that campaigns matter." Instead, as Hillygus argued, future political science research should "more fully examine the nature of the interaction between candidates and voters (as well as parties, interest groups, and the media) in political campaigns."[21] According to Hillygus, campaigns and voters make choices based on their perceptions of one another in an interactive, reciprocal process between national campaigns, local organizations, and networks in contact with voters across America.[22]

However, this framework is extremely national in its current application. Many existing studies of campaigns are useful for identifying national-level patterns and observing how voters respond in the aggregate, but there is a gap in the literature about local-level processes in crucial counties.[23] Some research has been done on the distribution of campaign field offices, but such data are static and do not necessarily reveal local dynamics as campaigns unfold.[24]

As the old adage "all politics is local" suggests, even the effects of nationwide presidential campaigns vary based on the networks and activism of individuals in local communities. To take the concept of an interactive process seriously, it is not sufficient to jump from national campaigns to the individual voters, because voters' experiences are fundamentally shaped by local organizations, political parties, unions, activists, and other networks—the intermediaries between the voter and a campaign. A holistic understanding of presidential campaigns must include study of the organizational differences between national campaigns and the intermediaries who implement them locally. Thus, my research offers a model for how to study campaigns at the local level, unpacking the outcome in Michigan through a single county. By selecting Manistee for in-depth analysis, I identify grassroots networks and resonant sentiments on the ground and the statewide campaign strategies that capitalized upon them.

How the Trump and Clinton Campaigns Approached Michigan

Both the Clinton and Trump campaigns considered Michigan an essential ingredient to winning 270 Electoral College votes.[25] Throughout the 2016 election, however, the Trump presidential campaign was repeatedly portrayed as disorganized and poorly resourced compared to the professional, well-oiled Clinton machine. One headline declared that "Donald Trump is a candidate without a campaign—and it's becoming a serious problem."[26] The candidate himself tweeted, "I am getting bad marks from certain pundits because I have a small campaign staff. But small is good, flexible, save [*sic*] money and number one!"[27] An under-staffed campaign seemed to reflect a deeper gap in monetary resources, with Clinton eventually outspending Trump by nearly two to one nationwide.[28] In Michigan, a July 2016 headline in *The Detroit News* declared that "Clinton staff dwarfs Trump's in Michigan." The article explained that Trump had only one full-time paid staffer in the state compared to Clinton's plan for a paid staff of approximately two hundred.[29] Two months later, the same newspaper reported "Trump's Michigan campaign plays catch-up with Clinton" as the Trump campaign hired only six new staff members after the RNC Convention.[30] In an interview for this project, even Michigan for Trump state director Hagerstrom described it as "a lean campaign."

However, on the ground in Michigan the Trump campaign was not nearly as disadvantaged as observers believed. The Trump campaign benefited from the infrastructure and capacity of strong conservative networks already in place across the state, in addition to grassroots enthusiasm. By contrast, the Clinton campaign did not possess the infrastructure nor corresponding enthusiasm to match the ground-level breadth and depth of the Trump campaign.

Conservative Network Building

Michigan for Trump in 2016 and the strategies it employed were made possible by both long-standing and newly developed conservative organizations. These groups provided a secure organizational base for the Trump campaign. Longtime conservative partners promulgated pro-Trump and anti-Clinton advocacy in Michigan, with active groups like Right to Life Michigan and NRA affiliates engaging in usual local gatherings and programming. As scholars like Corwin Smidt and Mikael Pelz have noted, in Michigan these networks were foundational for Trump's victory.[31] The Michigan Republican Party also provided foundational support to the Trump campaign. Regional field organizers from the Michigan GOP staffed five of the seven regions of the state for the Trump general election campaign. In addition, the Trump campaign in Michigan and other states benefited from the massive voter file data investment of over $100 million by the Republican National Committee (RNC) in the years immediately leading up to 2016.[32] The national party supported a reasonable field presence in Michigan, providing thirty-four paid field staff with seven additional staffers exclusively focused on presidential voter turnout.[33]

Pivotal to the success of the Trump campaign in Michigan was the strength of two relatively new extra-party networks: the Tea Party and the Koch network. As Theda Skocpol and Vanessa Williamson demonstrate in their research, the Tea Party is a potent amalgamation of local grassroots activists and nationwide elites advocating for extremely conservative political candidates and policies.[34] By 2011, there were over thirty local Tea Party groups in Michigan, many of which were still active in 2016.[35] Analysis in Manistee illustrates how these local groups played a valuable role in information-sharing and conservative mobilization in 2016. During the same time period, the free-market Koch network expanded in Michigan. The Koch network is growing force nationwide, spearheaded by two billionaire brothers and donors funding Americans for Prosperity (AFP) and other political organizations, with hundreds of paid staff and thousands of members.[36] AFP presence in Michigan began in 2006 but grew substantially after the 2008 election. By 2014, the organization surged from approximately seven thousand to eighty-seven thousand members, with four hundred field operatives and three permanent field offices across the state.[37] By 2016, AFP Michigan was a strong, growing presence in the Michigan conservative landscape.

Although the Trump campaign was certainly separate from AFP Michigan, it directly benefited from AFP's established networks and models of organizing. The state director for Michigan for Trump was Scott Hagerstrom, a lifelong Michigan Republican operative who previously served over six years as the AFP Michigan state director. In fact, he was initially connected to the Trump campaign via national campaign manager Corey Lewandowski, who previously served as the director of voter registration for AFP and founding director of AFP New Hampshire.[38] Hagerstrom's specialized understanding of the state was a key resource shaping the Trump operational strategy in Michigan because he was afforded significant latitude for decision making by the national campaign. Additional Koch network alumni served as both the deputy state director and the political director for the Trump campaign in Michigan.[39]

Because AFP collaborates with the Republican Party on an ad hoc basis, the AFP-alumni-led Trump campaign was not dependent on the Republican Party and some Republicans who held a deep distaste for Trump.[40] Hagerstrom's years of leadership experience in AFP channeling grassroots enthusiasm and working with Michigan-based donors, conservative organizations, and political media made him uniquely qualified for the challenge of spearheading the Michigan Trump campaign. Thus, the Trump campaign in Michigan was positioned to effectively tap preexisting networks, leveraging their organizational knowledge independent of the Michigan GOP.

Liberal Organizational Atrophy

Unlike the Trump operation, the Clinton campaign nationally and in Michigan inherited an organizational infrastructure in decline. The foundations started deteriorating years before this "blue wall" state crumbled for Trump in 2016. Until recently, in the home of the auto industry, labor unions strongly anchored the Democratic Party, but today only 14 percent of Michigan workers are union members (compared to 45 percent in 1964).[41] The passage of right-to-work legislation in late 2012 and other anti-union legislation significantly undercut union membership and resources across the state.[42] While Michigan unions were still active in 2016, their bandwidth and political clout was limited compared to previous years. For example, both the United Auto Workers (UAW) and the American Federation of State, County, and Municipal Employees fell short in their typical election-time monetary commitments for the Clinton campaign. Reciprocally, the Clinton camp did not collaborate as closely with Michigan unions as it might have done, notably failing to visit a single Michigan UAW hall.[43] This organizational deterioration precipitated electoral consequences for Clinton; Trump ultimately won 40 percent of voters in Michigan union households compared to Romney's 33 percent four years earlier.[44]

Even though Michigan voters elected Democrats in the five presidential elections prior to Trump, at the state government level the Michigan Democratic Party (MDP) struggled in the face of growing conservative strength.[45] Indeed, although the MDP and affiliated fundraising arms mostly kept up with Michigan GOP fundraising in the Obama years, in both 2014 and 2016 the Michigan

GOP and affiliates raised approximately $1 million more than Democrats for state-level offices.[46] In addition, Michigan was no exception to a Democratic Party "badly outgunned" by the RNC's new voter file database; Obama for America—the Obama campaign organization turned "Organizing for America" after the 2008 election—ultimately served mostly as a reelection vehicle for the former president without much long-term impact for state party strength or voter data.[47] Consequently, Democratic party fundraising and organization-building in Michigan and nationally relied on individual candidates and occasionally individual issues without the same long-term, consistent investment of their conservative counterparts. Prior to the Democratic successes of the 2018 midterm elections, Republicans were playing the long game in Michigan while Democrats competed one point at a time.

Differences in Statewide Campaigns

In addition to a substantial difference in the strength and utility of existing networks and organizations, the Trump and Clinton campaigns utilized different strategic tactics in Michigan. Alongside uneven partisan networks in the state, these divergent approaches resulted in an overall difference in the ground-level presence of each campaign.

Given the historic unpopularity of both candidates, the Clinton campaign made the strategic calculation to focus almost exclusively on turnout in Michigan. They built considerable organizing capacity to achieve this goal, despite the fact that Michigan was not widely considered a battleground state. In terms of paid staff and field offices, Clinton was roughly on par with her Democratic predecessor.[48] However, the Clinton approach glaringly omitted informational feedback from canvassing and neglected local-level volunteers. Liberal organizers in Michigan were concerned about lukewarm support across the state well before Election Day, but the national campaign remained disconnected from concerns on the ground and committed to a base turnout strategy.[49] The Clinton campaign built substantial capacity in Michigan, especially in comparison to Trump; they simply did not effectively leverage that capacity or partner networks to the fullest extent.

The Clinton campaign's focus on mobilization manifested in both public events and campaign infrastructure. Clinton campaign field offices in Michigan were relatively concentrated compared to both Trump and Obama before her.[50] The Trump campaign fielded offices in twenty-four counties compared to Clinton's fifteen counties. The Clinton campaign's focus on Southeast Michigan (home of Detroit) and other urban centers illustrates the degree to which it relied on base turnout at the expense of building organizational capacity elsewhere.

Poignantly, all three of Hillary Clinton's public appearances in the state took place in major metropolitan centers within the last month of the election.[51]

The Trump campaign's approach in Michigan stands in contrast to both Clinton and his recent Republican predecessors.[52] The campaign utilized existing networks along with high-visibility tactics fostering grassroots enthusiasm across the state. Crucially, the Michigan-based leadership enjoyed significant autonomy and very little management from the national Trump campaign. State director Hagerstrom, with his localized expertise, was the decision maker for most of the strategic choices in the state, including the location of Trump campaign rallies and surrogate visits. With a belief in the persuasive power of their message, the locally driven Trump campaign saw their strategy in Michigan as both mobilization and persuasion.

Trump himself consistently and increasingly campaigned in Michigan. Distributed throughout the state, the Trump rally was a unique tactic, considered the "driving force" of the campaign by Trump officials.[53] The rallies served multiple purposes: to maximize Trump's visibility and the reach of his message in earned media coverage, to galvanize thousands of supporters at a time, and to reach thousands more voters through supporters' social media postings. Trump himself held nine rallies in the state prior to Election Day (three in the primary, six during the general election), and vice presidential candidate Mike Pence held six. The campaign invested in a public presence in Michigan from the start, which only increased as Election Day grew near; approximately half of Pence and Trump rallies in the state occurred in the final month of the election. Every Trump rally in Michigan, save the three held in Grand Rapids, was located in or adjacent to one of the twelve counties that flipped from Obama to Trump.[54]

Although the exact potency of Trump rallies is difficult to measure, their sheer reach in communities across the state, with thousands of attendees, media coverage in distinct local media markets, and personal social media posts, cannot be understated. People waited in line for hours to get a seat at these rallies, and some events reached maximum capacity and turned hundreds away.[55] My conversation with *Kimberly*, chair of the Trump campaign in Manistee, provides a glimpse of the influence of these rallies.[56] She attended nearly all of the Trump rallies in Michigan, an experience she described with great enthusiasm. "They were awesome," she said. "Every time my husband and I would come back [from a rally] we were so charged, it was like a huge cheerleading rally." Many Manisteeans I spoke to, especially voters who cast their ballot for Trump, recalled a Trump campaign event held in a neighboring county early in the primary season. As one voter explained, "he went to little rural places, he went to Cadillac [Michigan] ... so he could get my vote." Trump's visits were noteworthy and memorable.

While certainly not well-oiled or steeped in immense resources, the Trump campaign's on-the-ground presence remains largely underestimated. By November 2016, the Trump campaign fielded at least thirty-two distinct field office locations, including official campaign-sponsored headquarters and grassroots partners—shown in Figure 5.2.[57] Some but not all those office locations were local Republican Party headquarters, and others were separately financed by the campaign. Still others, like the unofficial Trump "headquarters" in Manistee County discussed in the next section, were paid for and maintained entirely by volunteers. In fact, office location information distributed by Trump campaign officials in the week prior to the election does not even list the Manistee County volunteer headquarters, indicating that there were quite possibly more than thirty-two offices across the state with informal headquarters included.

As with other aspects of the campaign, the Trump camp coordinated with Republican Party locations and offices when convenient but did not rely on that infrastructure everywhere. Like the AFP model, the Trump campaign in Michigan partnered with the existing Republican infrastructure on an ad hoc basis. The campaign leadership was comfortable accommodating and encouraging divergent groups, as long as they all supported Trump. As Hagerstrom himself explained, "I said this about Tea Parties and I will say this about the campaign . . . They are sort of like churches; you find the one you are comfortable with." Similar to the Tea Party, Trump received support from different factions of people, some of whom identified as Republicans or Tea Partiers and some of whom did not. Hagerstrom and the Trump campaign "didn't want to get in the middle of those battles . . . You've got to be able to win."

This accommodating approach was essential for the campaign's success. Because they did not have the resources to facilitate many field offices or paid staff on their own, the campaign relied on local partners to maximize the campaign's capacity statewide. Although the Trump campaign's paid staff was dwarfed by Clinton's, they compensated by effectively harnessing existing networks and capitalizing upon Michigan-based ingredients for Trump's success.

On the Ground in Manistee

If you drove down the main street in downtown Manistee in the final months of the 2016 campaign, you would see the usual headquarters of both the local Manistee County Democratic and Republican Parties, advertising a range of candidates up and down the ballot. Walking into the Democratic headquarters, conciliatory volunteers might ask you to please consider voting for local candidates, even if you don't support Hillary Clinton. Walking into the Republican headquarters down the street, you might engage in conversation

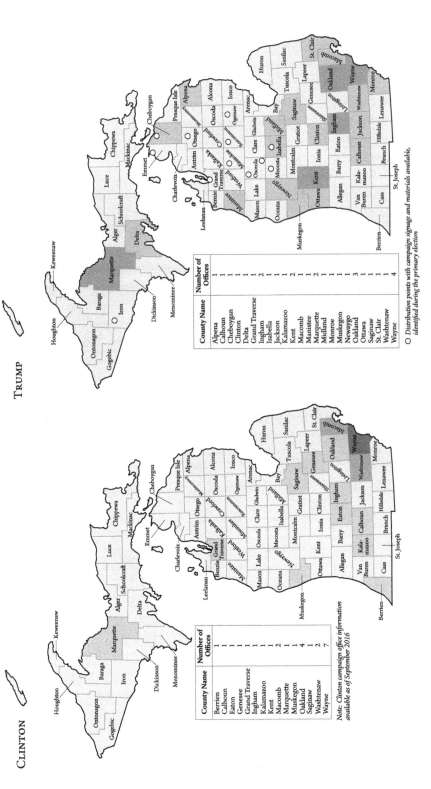

Figure 5.2 Clinton versus Trump Michigan Office Locations in 2016.

about how important it is to vote against "dodgy" Clinton and vote for the pro-America, pro-life candidate who wants to "shake things up" in Washington. Unlike previous years, however, directly next door to the Democratic Party headquarters and a block away from the Republican headquarters you would also see a Trump-only storefront, filled with Trump-Pence signs and calls to "take back America in November." Walking inside you would likely be greeted by energized volunteers, unapologetically asking if you plan to vote for Trump and offering a free yard sign.

This "Manistee Area Volunteers for Trump" headquarters was not funded by the Michigan Trump campaign and remained unaffiliated with the local Republican Party, where many local Trump volunteers felt unwelcome. Trump supporters instead asked a similarly passionate local business owner if he would open his small business as an informal Trump headquarters. As one volunteer described, "[we] weren't welcome at the Republican Party office, [we] weren't welcome at the Democrats' office, so we sandwiched ourselves between the two of them, literally a couple blocks away, and really got all the activity."

This was different from previous election cycles. As a local Democratic leader, *Liza*, described, "the Republicans really hadn't been organized before," but in 2016 the enthusiasm and activity behind Trump was noticeably different. In Manistee, Trump enjoyed the outward support of both the existing conservative infrastructure and a new set of energetic volunteers. Accordingly, Manistee provides a window into the dual forces of the Trump campaign in the state: grassroots enthusiasm combined with robust and localized conservative networks. This strength was unmatched by local Democrats who were left underutilized and isolated.

Grassroots Enthusiasm for Trump

Two middle-aged white women who had never before been involved in politics were the driving force behind the Trump campaign in Manistee. For over a year, these women—Kimberly and *Michelle*—dedicated most of their spare time to electing Donald Trump. Kimberly is a lifelong Manistee resident with deep ties in the community, especially among blue-collar voters. Despite the fact that she was the chair of the Trump campaign in the county and spent over a year mobilizing and persuading her neighbors to vote for Trump, she immediately stated in her interview that "I don't know anything about politics." She generally supported Republicans in the past, but involvement in the Trump campaign was much more intense and personal. "I got a huge Trump sticker for the back of my truck, my license plate says Trump," she told me, adding, "I wasn't shy about it . . . it was mostly a passion." Michelle, a one-time Obama voter, was also not involved in politics before, but she knew the basics of campaigns because her father was once very involved in local Republican politics. She took the initiative to contact the Trump campaign early on in the primary to help with sign distribution, at which point the Trump campaign connected Michelle and Kimberly. This connection paved the way for the two women to combine Kimberly's personal networks and passion with Michelle's know-how to lead the Manistee Area Trump volunteers independently from the Manistee Republican Party.

What the Trump campaign in this small rural county lacked in size, it made up for with committed and spirited volunteers. Like the statewide campaign, their high-visibility efforts and enthusiastic support magnified their relatively limited numbers. Through tactics like personal advocacy, sign distribution, and "Flash Mobs for Trump," Trump volunteers in Manistee campaigned to increase visibility and persuade their friends and neighbors to support Trump. In Manistee, volunteering for Trump was simple, and the volunteers welcomed all comers.

According to many interview participants, "in Manistee, Trump was *way* more present" than Clinton. While it may seem trivial, a focus on Trump sign proliferation increased Trump's visibility in Manistee without requiring hundreds of volunteers to help. During the primary and into the general election, volunteers organized sign distribution in central places like grocery store parking lots. Supplied by the statewide Trump campaign, these signs were free (unlike the local GOP's supply). When they ran out, Michelle personally purchased additional signs to distribute. This focus on signs might explain why people in Manistee repeatedly mentioned the unusual number of Trump signs compared to previous presidential elections. One Republican told me he was particularly "amazed" at how many low-income families displayed Trump signs in front of their trailers or small homes, people he thought "would normally vote Democrat."

In another high-visibility effort, the local Manistee Trump volunteers participated in statewide "Flash Mobs for Trump," which were organized by the Michigan Conservative Coalition (MCC).[58] Coordinated throughout the state on multiple days in fall 2016 leading up to the general election, these flash mobs were part visibility, part fun. The Manistee Trump volunteers participated in all of the statewide flash mob days, encouraging fellow enthusiasts to "Bring your TRUMP signs and HIGH energy!!!!" to the "Trump flash mob and sign party!"[59] Hundreds of residents driving by saw the flash mobs, which also received attention in the local press, again magnifying the impact and visibility of the effort.

Thanks in large part to social media—especially Facebook—these inexperienced grassroots volunteers organized without the formal infrastructure of county parties or other political organizations. Early on in the primary, both Kimberly and Michelle used social media to make initial contact with the

Michigan Trump campaign, and both women identified social media as their primary communication tool. Social media also allowed this new group of volunteers to connect with existing conservative groups like the Manistee Area Tea Party (MATP) and the Manistee Republican Party. Examination of these groups' Facebook pages reveals connections to a recurring set of local, statewide, and regional networks during the campaign. For example, MATP and the Trump volunteers connected with the MCC, which was the organizing force behind the flash mobs, and Trump volunteers shared information about the Michigan Republican Party's Day of Action.[60] Existing networks and their infrastructure interacted with and complemented the Trump volunteers' efforts.

Existing Conservative Networks

Indeed, existing conservative networks in Manistee played a vital role in Trump's success. Leading up to the 2016 election, these local groups were active and in some cases more prominent than in previous election years. Conservative networks promoted Trump within their organizations and bolstered his general appeal as a candidate, but even more importantly spent the years preceding the 2016 election building local conservative infrastructure and strength.

The Manistee Area Tea Party (MATP) played a particularly important and relatively new role. Prior to the Tea Party, monthly Republican Party meetings typically attracted around 15 attendees; often there were no more than four or five. However, at the peak of Tea Party activity in the area, up to 100 people would show up for a single MATP meeting. While that level of participation eventually declined, the local Tea Party is still active in Manistee and holds monthly forums for public speeches and debates. MATP does not officially endorse candidates, but its Facebook feed in the six months leading up to the general election signaled support for Trump.[61] Starting in early 2016, monthly MATP meetings featuring conservative thought leaders were recorded so they could later be aired on Manistee-area cable TV.[62] These monthly forums provide a powerful platform for conservative politicians, interest groups, and organizations like AFP and the NRA.[63] With an active Facebook page of approximately 130 followers, consistent encouragement for members to "bring friends" to meetings, and the recent, increased reach of TV broadcasts, the influence of MATP undoubtedly contributed to Trump campaign's success in the area.

Other conservative networks also played an important role locally. AFP Michigan was active in Manistee in the years leading up to the 2016 election. In the two years prior to the 2016 election, the Northern Michigan regional AFP representative Heather Cerone spoke at local MATP forums and advertised ample opportunities to participate in regional AFP programming. In addition, as in other election years, the local Republican Party opened up a headquarters, sold Trump signs along with other candidates, walked in summer parades, and hosted local candidate events. Statewide Michigan Republican Party leadership visited Manistee Republicans twice in the last few months of the 2016 election on two separate bus tours, signaling the importance of Manistee to local Republicans and attracting additional local media coverage.[64] Furthermore, Manistee and neighboring counties are home to additional conservative-allied groups and constituencies, including a local chapter of Right to Life Michigan and NRA affiliates like the Manistee Muzzleloading Club. In the year prior to the election these groups hosted usual programming to promote conservative political ideas, disseminated information, and contributed to the promotion of Trump in Manistee.[65]

Apathetic, Disconnected Democrats

Unlike their conservative counterparts, Democrats in Manistee spent the 2016 election battling an enthusiasm gap without the organizational partners to match conservative network strength. Whereas a decade or so prior there was a union office on main street, now only the temporary Democratic headquarters remained. "Hillary Clinton was failed by this [local] party and the Michigan Democratic Party," one longtime local Democrat bluntly explained. She and others described a local campaign of minimal effort with minimal support. Several highly involved Democrats I spoke with highlighted how the MDP, in both its messaging and actions, did little to empower Democrats in Manistee and similar communities in 2016.

Most active Democrats and liberal partisans in Manistee I spoke with were unenthusiastic about Clinton's candidacy, and not all of this negativity can be attributed to retrospective bias. Poignantly, the county party newsletter in October 2016 featured a letter from the chair of the Manistee Dems entitled, "Get Excited About Hillary," detailing the importance of enthusiasm for the candidate. "Stop being apologetic about her alleged flaws and stress her great policies and accomplishments," he writes. "It is up to us to set the record straight and to show our enthusiasm for Hillary."[66] It is truly striking that just weeks before the presidential election, local Democrats felt the need to encourage each other to "get excited" about their nominee. When I conducted research a full year after the election, I heard echoes of this hallow support in countless interviews with local Democrats. Tepid support for Clinton on the local level, even among her supporters, stands in stark contrast to Trump's passionate base.

Lack of enthusiasm and investment in the Clinton candidacy was reciprocal. Manistee Democrats were not asked for much from the Clinton campaign, nor did they give it, mostly opting instead to invest time and resources into local candidates. Whereas the Obama campaign helped organize local Manistee Democrats and numerous volunteers for phone banking and canvassing, the Clinton campaign provided no such support. In a review of the Manistee Democrats Google Group email listserv, the group's primary method of communication, I only found one email from a regional organizer about campaign activities for Hillary Clinton in Manistee.[67] With little communication between the state level campaign and local intermediaries, the Clinton campaign on the ground can only be described as apathetic.

The difference between the Trump and Clinton campaigns on the ground in Manistee could not be more dramatic. While Trump supporters were running out of signs, Manistee Democrats were reminding each other to "get excited about Hillary." In the absence of substantial engagement from the national or state-level campaign, Manistee Democrats focused on local candidates and mostly left the outcome of the presidential election to larger forces. By contrast, Trump supporters were passionately engaged, and the campaign benefited from the support of both new and existing networks. Through high-visibility efforts with low barriers to entry, Trump volunteers demonstrated their support proudly and with gusto.

Anti-Establishment and Identity Appeal

As active citizens and "opinion leaders" in the county, interview participants' explanations of their political choices provide a window for understanding the resonant sentiments in Manistee at large.[68] When taken together, close analysis of these conversations reveals strong anti-establishment and identity-based themes.

Donald Trump campaigned with uniquely divisive messaging during the 2016 election. In an analysis of recent presidential candidates, scholar Benjamin Enke found Trump's rhetoric had more "us" versus "them" morality than any presidential candidate from the past three cycles.[69] Conversations with Manisteeans contained echoes of this understanding of politics as "us versus them." The "us" was the white working class. "Them" took two main forms: immigrants among Trump voters, and the political establishment among Manisteeans of all political persuasions.

Overwhelming anti-establishment sentiment and dissatisfaction with the political status quo rang through the vast majority of interviews, whether Democrat, Republican, or independent. Discontent with politicians and the political elite was remarkably non-partisan in its direction. Most Manisteeans I spoke with, regardless of their political preferences, wanted a candidate who would "shake things up," and their conversations were rife with frustration at Washington. For years, regardless of the party in charge, these Manisteeans felt the political status quo did little to help their rural, economically challenged community.

Among Clinton supporters, especially among those who voted for Senator Bernie Sanders in the primary, Clinton did not offer enough change. As one woman from the Manistee League of Women Voters explained, "we need some change and we need hope for the future. Hillary wanted more of the same." While Democrats described Hillary Clinton respectfully, many spoke of her political "baggage" and their "mixed feelings" and "trust issues" with her as a candidate.

Among Trump supporters, discussion often heavily focused on his anti-establishment bona fides. Trump voters talked about their preference for a candidate who would change Washington; they spoke of Clinton's weaknesses in terms of her conformity and contributions to the undesirable political status quo. As one management professional and Obama-Trump voter described, "People were just tired of politicians, just tired of them. They said look, we don't care, this guy might be a clown, but let's put a clown in there and see what happens . . . that's why I voted for him, because I just thought, well let's just see what happens here." Similarly, *Bob*, a local Republican businessman, supported Trump despite his perceived flaws. As Bob explained, "Trump is an idiot and he proved that before he was elected, but he still got elected because a lot of people were sick of Washington, just sick of it and the way it's run."

In addition to anti-establishment sentiment, Trump supporters in Manistee positioned themselves as separate from other communities and feared a changing, declining America. Some people I interviewed revealed strong racial animus, while others displayed less outright racial resentment, but most demonstrated in their responses that their vote for Trump was informed by their identity as a white person in a rural community as opposed to more elite, urban people or communities of color. To Trump supporters, Trump gave them, and people like them, a voice.

As Skocpol and Williamson note in their analysis of the Tea Party, "fear punctuated by hope is a potent brew in politics."[70] For Manistee Trump voters, the fear of immigration was especially potent and anxiety-inducing, and Trump offered a solution. Crucially, however, Trump supporters were often less worried, if worried at all, about the role of immigration in their own community. Multiple Trump supporters described immigration in Manistee as "harmonious," but a "serious problem" on the national level. Within Manistee, even among particularly anti-immigrant Trump supporters, local migrant workers are understood as critical support for the agricultural industry and fruit orchards. As one Republican official explained, "Nowadays, if you were relying on locals to pick cherries, you ain't gonna pick too many cherries." This distinction between immigration at the local and national level demonstrates how, for these Trump voters, immigration concerns are a primarily identity-based fear.

The discussion of immigrants and the political establishment—"them"—often came alongside a clear picture of who the "us" of a Trump voter is. A construction worker and Obama-Trump voter I met at the Manistee County Fair explained that it was all suburbs and "rural places" that voted for Trump because, "If you can convince dumb white guys like me that you're going to straighten things out, then you're going to win." Similarly, *Shelley*, another Obama-Trump voter described the community of Trump voters as "the doers," and "the workers." According to Shelley, Trump voters "tend to be very down-to-earth, very simple, they're not complicated, they don't mince words. What you see is what you get—kind of honest, hardworking people." She then immediately linked white, working-class identity to anti-establishment sentiment, stating, "Of course, Donald Trump speaks that way as well, he talks about that distrust between the establishment and the blue-collar worker."

In these conversations, the picture of Trump voters is clear: less educated, working-class, rural, white Americans. It's a group in tension with the "establishment" or the "elite," as well as immigrants, who threaten the longevity of Trump voters' version of America's "common culture." Thus, voting for Trump was in many key respects about Manisteeans' identity as white, working-class Americans. They were concerned about the direction of the country culturally, politically, and economically, and consequently some voters "felt like they had no voice" until Trump. These resonant sentiments illustrate how you might support a person—even a risky candidate you know is an "idiot"—who says that they are paying attention to *people like you* and who promises to change a status quo that you believe is not working for you or your community.

Lessons from a Flipped County

Just three days after the 2016 election, a righteous essay with an unknown author titled "50 Million + Deplorables" circulated through the Manistee Area Tea Party (MATP) online community.[71] Declaring "it's midnight in America," the essay characterized the election as a "revolution" against the establishment and the status quo by a largely forgotten group of Americans. The post painted a vivid picture: "The Great Blue Wall crumbled. The impossible states fell one by one . . . The white working class that had been overlooked and trampled on for so long got to its feet . . . " After a long description of these voters' identity as the "leftovers and flyover country," the essay asserted the election was centrally about "fifty million people whose names no one except a server will ever know fighting back." It was about union members voting differently than their leadership and "the lost Democrats searching for someone to represent them" in swing states. In this vein, the essay concluded, "No one will ever interview all those men and women. We will never see all their faces. But they are us and we are them."

On the other side of the political spectrum, Manistee Democrats were "grieving." On an email thread two days after the election, members of this Democratic group wrestled with what it meant to be a Manisteean and Michigander—and by extension, an American—now that Trump won. Some felt they had lost the community they thought they knew. These Democrats were "angry" and "saddened," and found Trump's victory "disturbing" and "frightening."[72] As one member remarked, "I thought it was the Republicans who would have to do the soul searching after this election. But—guess what dude!—it's us who have the hard work to do, in spades."

From Manistee County to communities across the country, the results of the 2016 election elicited a mixture of shock, disbelief, euphoria, fear, and validation. In the days, weeks, and months since, many have debated the meaning of Trump's narrow victory. Trump's campaign was considerably underresourced with a politically divisive, inexperienced candidate. Nonetheless, Trump won against a well-funded and well-staffed campaign with a former secretary of state and US senator at the helm. With such large apparent disadvantages, how did Trump win, especially in the places Obama won, and what can we learn from it?

The outcome of the 2016 presidential campaign in Manistee County and the state of Michigan was not a foregone conclusion. Strong, localized conservative networks and grassroots energy proved to be a powerful force against a nationalized, organizationally outgunned Clinton campaign focused on mobilization. A few days after the election, one Tea Party member speculated on the MATP Facebook page, "How many of the conservative seeds the members of Tea Parties planted in people's minds beginning in 2009 [contributed] to how the electorate has voted recently?"[73] While my analysis of the networks and local leadership in Manistee does not suggest newfound dominance of conservativism, it does indicate that "conservative seeds" in the form of conservative network-building and the intermediaries it empowered, planted throughout Michigan in the past decade, grew strong enough roots to support Donald Trump's candidacy.

Indeed, this analysis warns against underinvestment at the local level for political parties and interest groups. Moving forward, the local Manistee Democrat quoted earlier was correct when he said Democrats have "hard work to do, in spades." The strength of conservative networks and their organizing in Michigan successfully offset the considerable top-level resource disadvantages of the Trump campaign. My research suggests that Democrats should focus on building local-level capacity before elections and work to maintain those networks in between election years if they hope to effectively rival conservative strength in the long term. Recent midterm election results in Michigan were promising for Democrats, but future Democratic presidential candidates should learn from both the hard-won victories in Michigan in 2018 and stinging losses in 2016. The grassroots-level party-building that Democrats began in the years after Trump's victory must continue in order to compete in the long-term.

The success of the Trump campaign in Michigan and Manistee was not immediate, nor was it inevitable. Ultimately, the presidential election was decided by individual Americans making sense of the candidates based on their own perspectives, influenced and shaped by existing organizations, grassroots leaders, and the campaigns themselves. If all politics truly is local, the study of campaigns should continue to find new frameworks and methods for understanding this interactive relationship between voters, local networks, and the campaigns of the candidates they elect.

Acknowledgments

I wish to thank my senior thesis advisor and editor Theda Skocpol for her invaluable guidance and mentorship. I am deeply grateful to my research participants in Manistee County for their candor and generosity. And to the pillars I stand on today: my grandparents Dale and Carolyn Goddard, David and Marcia Marsh, and most of all my parents, Bill and Melissa Marsh. Thank you for everything.

Notes

1. Statistics about flipped counties are gathered from the Michigan Bureau of Elections online database, "Secretary of State—Previous Election Information," *Michigan Department of State*, available at http://www.michigan.gov/sos/0,4670,7-127-1633_8722---,00.html as of March 2018. I calculated the percentage of registered voter turnout for each county by dividing the county-level "General Election Results" voter turnout by the county-level "Voter Registration Totals" for corresponding election years. I then compared registered voter turnout between 2008, 2012, and 2016 for each county.
2. For more on the merit and influence of local "opinion leaders," see Katherine J. Cramer, *The Politics of Resentment: Rural Consciousness in Wisconsin and the Rise of Scott Walker* (Chicago: University of Chicago Press, 2016); P. Lazarsfeld, *The People's Choice* (New York: Columbia University Press, 1948); John R. Zaller, *The Nature and Origins of Mass Opinion* (Cambridge: Cambridge University Press, 1992).
3. David Jesse and Matt Helms, "Donald Trump Wins Michigan by 13,225 Votes in Final Unofficial Count," *Detroit Free Press*, November 9, 2016.
4. "Secretary of State—Previous Election Information."
5. "Secretary of State—Previous Election Information."
6. The three consistently Democratic counties that experienced a decrease in turnout were Wayne (home of Detroit), Genesee (home of Flint), and Marquette counties. "Secretary of State—Previous Election Information."

7. Lydia Saad, "Trump and Clinton Finish with Historically Poor Images," Gallup.com, November 8, 2016; "How the Free Press Missed Mark on Michigan Projection for Clinton," *Detroit Free Press*, November 9, 2016.
8. Mark Fahey and Nicholas Wells, "Here's a Map of the US Counties that Flipped to Trump from Democrats," CNBC.com, n.d.
9. In the five flipped counties with decreased voter turnout, the decreases were minimal (0–4 percent), and in all but one the accompanying electoral swing was over 20 percentage points. Fahey and Wells, "Here's a Map of the US Counties that Flipped."
10. Kevin Uhrmacher, Kevin Schaul, and Dan Keating, "These Former Obama Strongholds Sealed the Election for Trump," *Washington Post*, November 9, 2019.
11. Nate Cohen, "A 2016 Review: Turnout Wasn't the Driver of Clinton's Defeat," *New York Times*, March 28, 2017.
12. Alex Roarty, "Democrats Say They Now Know Exactly Why Clinton Lost," *McClatchy DC Bureau*, May 1, 2017.
13. "Secretary of State—Previous Election Information."
14. I characterize Manistee as "non-metropolitan" and "rural" because the county is designated seven out of nine on the U.S. Department of Agriculture's Rural-Urban Continuum Code. Timothy Parker, "USDA ERS—Rural-Urban Continuum Codes," US Department of Agriculture: Economic Research Service, October 12, 2016.
15. Census estimates as of 2017, "U.S. Census Bureau QuickFacts: Manistee County," US Census Bureau, n.d. Available at https://www.census.gov/quickfacts/manisteecountymichigan as of March 2018.
16. Objective measures do not necessarily correspond to people's own perception of their social class, as class identity is based on more than income alone. For more on class, see Katherine Cramer Walsh, M. Kent Jennings, and Laura Stoker, "The Effects of Social Class Identification on Participatory Orientations towards Government," *British Journal of Political Science* 34, no. 3 (2004): 469–95; Cramer, *The Politics of Resentment*.
17. Between 1981 and 1986, four major long-term employers with factories in Manistee County left the area, resulting in hundreds of jobs lost in this small community. Source: Manistee County Historical Museum Director Mark Fedder, phone interview and email exchanges with the author, February 13, 2018.
18. Stanley Greenberg and affiliates have studied this region for decades. For example, see Stanley B. Greenberg and Nancy Zdunkewicz, "Macomb County in the Age of Trump," report by Democracy Corps, Greenberg Quinlan Rosner Research, and the Roosevelt Institute, March 10, 2017.
19. Lazarsfeld, *The People's Choice*; Bernard Berelson, *Voting: A Study of Opinion Formation in a Presidential Campaign* (Chicago: University of Chicago Press, 1954); Andrew Gelman and Gary King, "Why Are American Presidential Election Campaign Polls So Variable When Votes Are So Predictable?" *British Journal of Political Science* 23, no. 4 (1993): 409–51; D. Sunshine Hillygus, "Campaign Effects on Vote Choice" (Oxford University Press, February 25, 2010), 2.
20. On mobilization, see Gerald Kramer, "The Effects of Precinct-Level Canvassing on Voter Behavior," *Public Opinion Quarterly* 34, no. 4 (December 1, 1970): 560–72; on priming, see William Gibson, "News That Matters: Television and American Opinion," *American Journal of Sociology* 94, no. 4 (1989): 882–84; on persuasion, see D. Sunshine Hillygus and Todd G. Shields, *The Persuadable Voter: Wedge Issues in Presidential Campaigns* (Princeton: Princeton University Press, 2008); and on voter learning, see Norman H. Nie, *The Changing American Voter* (Cambridge, MA: Harvard University Press, 1979).
21. Hillygus, "Campaign Effects on Vote Choice," 13.
22. Hillygus and Shields, *The Persuadable Voter*, 4–6.
23. Gary C. Jacobson, "How Do Campaigns Matter?" *Annual Review of Political Science* 18, no. 1 (2015): 31–47.
24. For example, see Joshua P. Darr and Matthew S. Levendusky, "Relying on the Ground Game: The Placement and Effect of Campaign Field Offices," *American Politics Research* 42, no. 3 (May 1, 2014): 529–48.

25. Hillary Rodham Clinton, *What Happened* (New York: Simon & Schuster, 2017), 384; Ronald Brownstein, "Is Donald Trump Outflanking Hillary Clinton?" *The Atlantic*, November 2, 2016.

26. Benjy Sarlin, Katy Tur, and Ali Vitali, "Donald Trump Does Not Have a Campaign," MSNBC. com, June 6, 2016.

27. Sarlin, Tur, and Vitali, "Donald Trump Does Not Have a Campaign."

28. Christopher Ingraham, "Somebody Just Put a Price Tag on the 2016 Election. It's a Doozy," *Washington Post*, April 14, 2017.

29. Chad Livengood, "Clinton's Staff Dwarfs Trump's in Michigan," *Detroit News*, July 6, 2016.

30. Chad Livengood, "Trump's Michigan Campaign Plays Catch-up with Clinton," *Detroit News*, August 15, 2016.

31. Corwin Smidt and Mikael Pelz, "Michigan: The Christian Right in the Presidential Election," *God at the Grassroots, 2016: The Christian Right in American Politics* (Lanham, Maryland: Rowman & Littlefield, 2018), 69–96.

32. Clinton, *What Happened*, 421; Corey R. Lewandowski, *Let Trump Be Trump: The Inside Story of His Rise to the Presidency* (New York: Center Street, 2017), 175.

33. Livengood, "Clinton's Staff Dwarfs Trump's in Michigan."

34. Theda Skocpol and Vanessa Williamson, *The Tea Party and the Remaking of Republican Conservatism* (New York: Oxford University Press, 2012), 190.

35. Skocpol and Williamson, *Tea Party and the Remaking of Republican Conservatism*, 91.

36. Theda Skocpol and Alexander Hertel-Fernandez, "The Koch Network and Republican Party Extremism," *Perspectives on Politics* 14, no. 3 (September 2016): 684.

37. AFP Michigan data provided by the Shifting U.S. Political Terrain Project at Harvard University, led by Theda Skocpol and Alexander Hertel-Fernandez, September 21, 2017; Skocpol and Hertel-Fernandez, "The Koch Network," 688.

38. Lewandowski, *Let Trump Be Trump*, 30.

39. Deputy state director C. J. Galdes previously worked as Michigan field director for Generation Opportunity, a Koch organization targeting young people. Political director Randy Woods led field organizing for AFP Michigan. "Donald J. Trump for President Campaign Organization 2016 General Election—Michigan," Democracy in Action, May 23, 2017.

40. Paul Egan, "Michigan GOP Uneasy with Donald Trump, but Will It Matter?" *Detroit Free Press*, June 3, 2016.

41. John S. Klemanski and David A. Dulio, *Michigan Government, Politics, and Policy* (Ann Arbor: University of Michigan Press, 2017), 16.

42. For more on union decline in Michigan, see Alexander Hertel-Fernandez, "How the Right Trounced Liberals in the States," *Democracy Journal*, September 25, 2015; Klemanski and Dulio, *Michigan Government, Politics, and Policy*, 16; Keith Liang, "Michigan Union Membership Dipped in 2016," *Detroit News*, January 26, 2017.

43. Edward-Isaac Dovere, "How Clinton Lost Michigan—and Blew the Election," *Politico*, December 14, 2016; Yochi Dreazen, "Hillary Clinton's Loss in Michigan, Explained by the Last Democrat to Win in Michigan," Vox, December 21, 2016.

44. Klemanski and Dulio, *Michigan Government, Politics, and Policy*, 240.

45. Between 2008 and 2016, a Republican governor and Republican-majority legislative chambers were elected and reelected in Michigan. Jonathan Oosting, "Michigan Republicans Dominate State Elections, Grow Majorities in House and Senate," MLive.com, November 5, 2014.

46. Klemanski and Dulio, *Michigan Government, Politics, and Policy*, 207; Robert Draper, "A Post-Obama Democratic Party in Search of Itself," *New York Times*, November 1, 2017.

47. Quote from Clinton, *What Happened*, 421; Gabriel Debenedetti, "Obama's Party-Building Legacy Splits Democrats," *Politico*, February 9, 2017.

48. By the end of the campaign, Clinton fielded 211 paid staffers in Michigan; Obama had fewer than one hundred in 2012 and over three hundred in 2008. Dovere, "How Clinton Lost Michigan."

49. Sam Stein, "The Clinton Campaign Was Undone by Its Own Neglect and a Touch of Arrogance, Staffers Say," HuffPost, November 16, 2016.

50. In 2012 Obama fielded a comparable number of offices to Clinton, but in 2008 the Obama campaign fielded an impressive sixty-two offices in forty-one counties, and even then only eight were located in Wayne, home of Detroit. Source: "Obama for America 2012 Campaign Organization—Michigan," Democracy in Action, April 11, 2013; "Obama General Election Campaign Organization, Michigan," Democracy in Action, July 2, 2009; Laura Gibbons, "Hillary Clinton Campaign Opens Additional Offices in Detroit Area, Eaton County," MLive. com, August 31, 2016.

51. Data about campaign rallies compiled using "2016 Presidential Candidate General Election Events Tracker," *FairVote*, November 9, 2016; and "List of Rallies for the Donald Trump Presidential Campaign, 2016," Wikipedia, available at https://en.wikipedia.org/ w/index.php?title=List_of_rallies_for_the_Donald_Trump_presidential_campaign,_ 2016&oldid=828549644 as of March 2018.

52. In 2008 McCain pulled resources from Michigan one month before the election. In 2012 Romney relied on TV ads, only visiting twice. Michael Cooper, "McCain Abandons His Efforts to Win Michigan," *New York Times*, October 2, 2008; "Election Results 2012: Obama Wins Michigan over Romney, Grabs 16 Electoral Votes," MLive.com, November 7, 2012.

53. Lewandowski, *Let Trump Be Trump*, 9.

54. See note 51 for information on Trump/Pence rallies.

55. For example, see Karie Herringa, "Thousands of Donald Trump Supporters Attend Campaign Rally in Cadillac," *9 & 10 News*, March 4, 2016.

56. In order to protect confidentiality, I use pseudonyms when referring to most interview participants. I italicize pseudonyms the first time a participant is introduced.

57. Author analysis of Trump campaign offices from multiple sources. The tally of thirty-two Trump offices does not include thirteen campaign "distribution points," mostly located in rural areas where it is difficult to maintain an office. See "Michigan for Donald Trump" Facebook Page available at https://www.facebook.com/MichiganforDonaldTrump/ as of March 2018; and "Donald J. Trump for President Campaign Organization 2016 General Election—Michigan," Democracy in Action, May 23, 2017.

58. Information about the Michigan Conservative Coalition available at its website, https:// www.michiganconservativecoalition.com/ as of March 2018.

59. "Thank You Andrew!!," Facebook Post, Manistee County Trump Volunteers, September 10, 2016, available at https://www.facebook.com/manisteecotrump/photos/a.9270567 54072949.1073741828.927037774074847/935268673251757/?type=3&theater as of March 2018.

60. "Day of Action," Facebook Post, Manistee County Trump Volunteers, October 6, 2016, available at https://www.facebook.com/manisteecotrump/posts/956298304482127 as of March 2018.

61. For example, see "Video: Rev. Sirico on the Podesta Emails," Facebook Post, Manistee Area Tea Party Organization Facebook Page, October 20, 2016, available at https://www.face-book.com/ManisteeAreaTeaParty/posts/1171480886277722 as of March 2018.

62. "Our Meetings , . . ," Facebook Post, Manistee Area Tea Party Organization Facebook Page, June 29, 2016, available at https://www.facebook.com/ManisteeAreaTeaParty/posts/ 1083714581721020 as of March 2018.

63. Author analysis of MATP Facebook page. Further detail at "Meeting Timeline," Facebook Post, Manistee Area Tea Party Organization Facebook Page, July 12, 2015, available at https:// www.facebook.com/ManisteeAreaTeaParty/posts/894702467288900 as of March 2018.

64. "State Republican Officials, Candidates to Visit Manistee," *Manistee News*, October 30, 2016; "Chair of Michigan Republican Party to Speak at Manistee Republican Headquarters," Facebook Post, Manistee County Republican Party Facebook Page, October 5, 2016, available at https://www.facebook.com/ManisteeGOP/posts/1088731374510053 as of March 2018.

65. For example, in 2016, Right to Life Michigan–Manistee hosted its annual fundraising dinner with over 200 attendees, where the statewide Right to Life development coordinator spoke about the importance of a pro-life president. This event was covered in the local paper. "Right to Life Holds Annual Dinner," *Manistee News*, April 21, 2016.

66. "October 2016 Newsletter," Manistee County Democratic Party, available at http://www.manisteecountydemocrats.us/uploads/1/2/4/9/12495782/2016_october_newsletter.pdf as of March 2018.
67. "Clinton Campaign & Michigan Democratic Party," Email, Manistee Dems GoogleGroup, September 12, 2016, available at http://www.manisteecountydemocrats.us/contact-us.html?place=msg%2Fmanisteedems%2FCvNmR8hbuQw%2FlNM1UvRWAQAJ   as   of March 2018.
68. This approach is inspired by Katherine Cramer's ethnographic research in Wisconsin. For more on the merits of this methodology, see Cramer, *The Politics of Resentment*, chap. 2.
69. Benjamin Enke, "Moral Values and Voting: Trump and Beyond," published paper, Social Science Research Network, January 22, 2018, 1–3.
70. Skocpol and Williamson, *The Tea Party*, 46.
71. "50 Million+ Deplorables," Manistee Area Tea Party Organization Facebook Page, November 11, 2016, available at https://www.facebook.com/ManisteeAreaTeaParty/posts/1191324067626737 as of March 2018.
72. "From My Son, Clinton," Email, Manistee Dems GoogleGroup, November 9, 2016, available at http://www.manisteecountydemocrats.us/contact-us.html?place=msg%2Fmanisteedems%2F1JzFKnloFGI%2FOuxbFiUBBAAJ as of March 2018.
73. "How Many of the Conservative Seeds . . . ," Facebook Post, Manistee Area Tea Party Organization Facebook Page, November 11, 2016, available at https://www.facebook.com/ManisteeAreaTeaParty/posts/1191162407642903 as of March 2018.

6

Trump's Trump: Lou Barletta and the Limits of Anti-Immigrant Politics in Pennsylvania

ELIZABETH THOM AND THEDA SKOCPOL

On the afternoon of August 2, 2018, thousands of people snaked around the Mohegan Sun Arena outside of Wilkes-Barre, Pennsylvania, undeterred by late summer thunderstorms. Hundreds more piled up in cars on nearby Interstate-81 hoping to join them. Secret Service agents roamed through the crowds, while state troopers directed traffic off the highway. Half a mile down the road, a group of protesters assembled in a Starbucks parking lot with posters and noisemakers to counter the hats and cheers of "Make America Great Again" enthusiasts. Everyone was falling into their usual positions as President Donald Trump was due to arrive in town for another rally—his third in this arena since the 2016 primaries.

Ten miles north of the arena at the Wilkes-Barre/Scranton International Airport, Congressman Lou Barletta of Pennsylvania's eleventh district awaited the arrival of Air Force One, eager to welcome President Trump back to the region that helped put him in the White House in 2016. Trump was Barletta's loyal political booster and had personally selected the congressman to run against incumbent Democratic senator Bob Casey in 2018. Yet as the president arrived in Northeast Pennsylvania this time, Barletta was trailing in polls and needed a surge of voter support.[1] President Trump was eager to help, and when his plane touched down in the small airport the two men greeted one another with smiles and handshakes before driving off together in the presidential motorcade to greet the raucous crowd of more than ten thousand waiting in the arena.

Donald Trump has not been shy about his fondness for Pennsylvania. "I love this state and I love the people of this state," he said at a rally in Harrisburg to mark his one hundredth day in office.[2] His narrow victory there in 2016—by

Elizabeth Thom and Theda Skocpol, *Trump's Trump: Lou Barletta and the Limits of Anti- Immigrant Politics in Pennsylvania* In: *Upending American Politics* Edited by: Theda Skocpol and Caroline Tervo, Oxford University Press (2020). © Oxford University Press
DOI: 10.1093/oso/9780190083526.003.0006

about half a percentage point—secured the 270 Electoral College votes Trump needed to claim the presidency.[3] He became the first Republican presidential candidate to win Pennsylvania since 1988 by flipping once solidly Democratic counties—including Luzerne County—from blue to red.[4]

Trump's appeal to blue-collar and white working-class voters in Luzerne and other parts of the old industrial belt in northeastern Pennsylvania follows years of economic distress and political neglect in the region. As Ben Bradlee Jr. explains in his book, *The Forgotten*, Luzerne County is a mix of rural and urban communities that seems, "less Northeast Corridor than Appalachia."[5] The demise of the region's coal industry, and the subsequent decline in manufacturing, have left residents with diminished economic prospects.[6] The local economy is now dominated by warehouse and fulfillment centers for retail giants like Amazon and Walmart eager to take advantage of the area's proximity to Interstates 80 and 81.[7] Most of the new jobs require exhausting efforts to earn low hourly wages that have not kept pace with rising costs of living. The poverty rate in Luzerne County stands at 15 percent, a few points above the national estimate.[8]

In addition to wrenching economic shifts, Luzerne County has experienced an influx of Hispanic immigrants relocating from regional metropolitan centers in Philadelphia, New York and New Jersey. Most are Dominicans who have moved to the area in search of jobs, good public schools and affordable housing.[9] Although the county as a whole remains predominantly white, the city of Hazleton, just south of Wilkes-Barre, has absorbed the majority of newcomers to the region. In the span of about fifteen years, the city's population swung from 95 percent white in the year 2000, to 52 percent Hispanic by 2016.[10] Suddenly, older white residents of Italian and eastern European backgrounds felt "outnumbered" by the culturally distinct newcomers.[11]

Such rapid demographic and economic changes made Luzerne fertile ground for Donald Trump's ethno-nationalist and economically protectionist agenda. The same county that twice voted to elect President Barack Obama responded with enthusiasm to Trump's promises to build walls, ban immigrants, "take back our country," and, "Make America Great Again."[12] Indeed, many whites in the area had already found a Trump-like champion in GOP congressman, Lou Barletta, who had earlier served as mayor of Hazleton. Years before the political debut of Donald Trump, Barletta had built his political career by pushing a fierce brand of anti-immigrant politics, declaring "war on the illegals."[13] Barletta was, in essence, Trump before Trump in this part of the country.

Trump's upset victory in November 2016 catapulted Barletta from the national GOP fringe to the mainstream. He served on Trump's transition team and was rumored to have been considered for a cabinet position.[14] In the end, however, President Trump had other plans. He urged Barletta to run for the Senate in the 2018 midterms—in the hopes that the likeminded Pennsylvanian could defeat the Democratic incumbent Bob Casey to tighten the GOP hold on the Senate and further his 2020 reelection prospects. However, despite Trump's rallies, tweets, and unwavering support, Barletta's Senate campaign trailed for the entire race and ultimately lost by 13 points.[15]

Lou Barletta's tumultuous career offers a window into ethno-nationalism in US electoral politics. In this chapter, we explore Barletta's rise as the mayor of Hazleton and early Trump booster, followed by his later defeat in the 2018 Senate race, using this political rollercoaster ride to illustrate both the strengths and limits of immigrant-bashing politics in a socioeconomically variegated state. We consider why anti-immigrant messaging fell short in Pennsylvania in 2018 and, looking ahead, suggest lessons from the rise and fall of Lou Barletta that might be applicable to 2020 and beyond.

How Economic and Ethnic Change Buoyed Anti-Immigrant Politics

The early history of Hazleton, Pennsylvania, and surrounding areas in Luzerne and neighboring counties is rooted in late nineteenth century immigration waves. Situated among the Appalachian Mountains, the city was built atop a rich region of anthracite coal that attracted immigrants from Italy, Ireland, Germany and eastern Europe to its mines.[16] The coal these workers extracted was used to help fuel the mammoth Bethlehem Steel Corporation, located in the nearby Lehigh Valley. The workers established communities in Hazleton, building homes, schools and churches. The social fabric of this and nearby cities has thus always involved a diverse mix of working-class folks from different cultural and ethnic backgrounds.

Lou Barletta, born and raised in Hazleton, is a product of this history, and he often celebrates his Italian-American heritage and blue-collar roots. Both his grandfather—an immigrant from Italy—and his father worked in the coal mines before starting a family construction business.[17] When Barletta later launched his own successful road lining company, he called his experience, "like an American dream come true."[18]

Barletta's family also introduced him to local Democratic politics. The region's working-class, union-affiliated population made Hazleton and the surrounding Luzerne County a Democratic Party stronghold for much of the twentieth century.[19] For a time, Barletta's father, Rocco, was chairman of the Hazleton City Democrats; and Barletta himself started out in local politics as a self-described Reagan Democrat.[20] In the late 1980s, following a path trod by many others of that ilk, Barletta switched his party affiliation to the Republicans.

In 1998, Lou Barletta won public office as a member of the Hazleton City Council, and shortly after he was elected mayor of Hazleton. He held the office for three terms, serving from 2000 until 2010, when he rode the Tea Party wave to Congress. Mayor Barletta's top priority in his first term was turning Hazleton's financial situation around. He managed to flip the city's $1.2 million deficit into a surplus, earning him widespread popularity and an easy reelection. Yet Barletta's tenure also coincided with the height of Hazleton's immigration boom; and during his second term, Barletta changed his priorities and his political image in response to mounting pressure from older white residents to deal with the growing Hispanic population.

The "Toughest Place" on Illegal Immigration

As Barletta tells it, the city's population grew by about fifty percent from 2000 to 2005, but its tax revenue barely budged, suggesting fiscal losses from illegal immigration.[21] At the same time, he says, "gangs moved in," and, "violent crimes had gone up."[22] The actual crime records from this period are mixed—there was a brief spike in violent crime, but overall crime rates increased in tandem with the city's population growth.[23] A review of Hazleton's crime statistics by the *Philadelphia Inquirer* showed that in general, "reported offenses dropped every year between 2006 and 2011."[24] This fits with nationwide evidence that immigrant-heavy communities experience, on average, less crime per capita than native-dominated counterparts. Nevertheless, fear and financial pressures drove Barletta to search for a "solution" to the problems associated with rapid social change, including illegal immigration.

A high-profile murder gave Barletta an opening for dramatic action. In May 2006, Derek Kichline was shot in the head outside of his home by two men who were allegedly illegal immigrants from the Dominican Republic with suspected ties to drugs.[25] The murder ignited a firestorm in Hazleton as city residents demanded action. Raucous city council meetings pitted neighbors against one another along ethnic lines. Barletta wore a bulletproof vest to the meetings in an effort to demonstrate how dangerous the situation in Hazleton had become.[26] With tensions running very high, the council passed and Barletta signed into law the Illegal Immigration Relief Act. The first of its kind in the country, the measure made it a crime for employers to hire illegal workers and for landlords to rent to tenants suspected of living in the country without documentation. Violators would be subjected to a $1,000 fine and employers would have their business licenses revoked. The ordinance also made English the official language of the city and prohibited the translation of documents into other languages without prior authorization.

Almost immediately, Hazleton's law earned national and even international attention. In an interview with the *Washington Post*, Barletta admitted that the act intended to make the city "the toughest place on illegal immigrants in America."[27] He said he lay in bed at night thinking, "I've lost my city" and vowed to "get rid of the illegal people." When pressed on the racial implications of the ordinance and his rhetoric, Barletta said, "This isn't racial, because 'illegal' and 'legal' don't have a race."[28] From then on, his mantra became, "Illegal is illegal."[29]

The American Civil Liberties Union took Barletta and the City of Hazleton to court. In the ensuing legal battle lasting nearly five years, Barletta received help from law professor turned anti-immigrant politician, Kris Kobach. In 2007, a federal judge in Pennsylvania struck down the ordinance, saying that it interfered with federal law and violated due process.[30] After Barletta appealed, the act was rejected again by the Third Circuit Court of Appeals. In 2011, the Supreme Court reviewed the case and sent it back to the Third Circuit, where it was struck down for the third and final time.[31]

In the end, Luzerne prosecutors dropped the murder charges against the two suspects for lack of sufficient evidence.[32] The controversial ordinance never went into effect—and the years' long court battle left the city of Hazleton with a $1.68 million legal bill.[33] Yet even in failure the Hazleton law sparked a wave of similar anti-immigrant ordinances in localities across the country. Most of them eventually faced financial or legal setbacks, too.[34] Meanwhile, in Hazleton, the whole ordeal had lasting effects on residents and the broader community—effects that reverberated in state and national politics.

From Hazleton to Congress

The media attention Barletta received during the immigration fight propelled him into greater political celebrity, and in 2010 he decided (for the third time) to run for Congress against thirteen-term Democrat Paul Kanjorski. The midterms that year were disastrous for Democrats across the country, and Pennsylvania was no exception. In Luzerne County and surrounding areas, changing communities and a slow recovery from the economic recession set the stage for a Republican takeover. Barletta beat Kanjorski in Pennsylvania's eleventh congressional district and headed to Washington to join the new GOP majority in the House, where Barletta stayed true to his anti-immigrant pedigree and joined the ranks of other Republican immigration hardliners such as Representative Steve King of Iowa.

At the time, the extreme views of King, Barletta, and their allies put them outside of the GOP mainstream on the immigration issue. Most congressional Republicans still favored middle-of-the-road solutions to the illegal immigration problem. After all, it was President Ronald Reagan whose 1986 Immigration Reform and Control Act both cracked down on security at the Mexican border and granted amnesty to nearly three million undocumented immigrants living in the country.[35] Republican presidents thereafter also supported bipartisan efforts to address immigration issues. Former president George W. Bush backed a comprehensive immigration reform bill that would have granted legal status to some twelve million undocumented immigrants in the country, while also establishing tighter border security, workplace enforcement measures and a merit-based system for future immigrants.[36] Its ultimate failure in the Senate was one of Bush's greatest legislative disappointments.[37]

When Democratic president Barack Obama took office, he reintroduced immigration reform as a top priority for his administration. However, health care reform took precedence and it was not until Obama's second term— after the Democrats had lost their majority in the House to Tea Party-buoyed Republicans—that immigration reform took center stage again. Some momentum was generated by a bipartisan group of senators called the "Gang of Eight," who once more sought compromise on a host of immigration related reforms, including a pathway to citizenship for those living in the country illegally, improvements to visa procedures, and a better employment verification system.[38]

The Gang's bill passed the Senate with sixty-eight bipartisan votes, only to die in the Republican-controlled House, where efforts to halt progress were led by Representatives King and Barletta.[39] For months, the two men held meetings with like-minded House members to build a coalition of opposition to the bill.[40] The main sticking point for this obstructionist group was a proposed pathway to citizenship for illegal immigrants. As Barletta explained in an interview, "This will be a green light for anyone who wants to come to America illegally and be granted citizenship one day."[41] Barletta also cited political reasons for his fellow Republicans to oppose the bill, asserting that, "Anyone who believes that they're going to win over the Latino vote is grossly mistaken. The majority that are here illegally are low-skilled or may not even have a high school diploma. The Republican Party is not going to compete over who can give more social programs out. They will become Democrats because of the social programs they'll depend on."[42] Clearly, Barletta's views of immigrants had not changed much since his time as the mayor of Hazleton.

Once again, reform failed in Congress, this time amid arguments that included more openly anti-immigrant and anti-Latino rhetoric than in earlier legislative debates. No one could know it at the time, but the blocking efforts of the House hardliners were laying the foundation for a wealthy businessman named Donald Trump to come along a few years later and fuel his candidacy for president with a plan to build a wall as a part of a strategy to "Make America Great

Again." In Trump, the same politicians and voters who had refused to support reforms including a path to citizenship for America's undocumented immigrant residents found a presidential contender who spoke their language, and they would rally enthusiastically to support his bid for the White House.

Barletta Endorses Trump and Luzerne Helps Him Win

On June 16, 2015, Donald Trump descended from a Trump Tower golden escalator to proclaim he was running for president. In an announcement speech many viewed as unserious and flat-out racist, Trump declared that "Our country is in serious trouble" and observed that "Sadly, the American dream is dead."[43] The culprit? America's political leaders, who had allowed other countries to take advantage of the United States. The result? A nation overrun with low-skilled Mexican immigrants bringing drugs and crime into the country and stealing American jobs. Losing trade deals with countries like China threatened whatever was leftover.

Many dismissed the businessman's candidacy as far-fetched, especially given the GOP field crowded with experienced politicians and officeholders. Trump's views seemed plainly too extreme; and few in the Republican Party establishment realized that his message would resonate with many voters. Trump's announcement speech divided American society into two groups: "us" versus "them." The former included predominantly white working folks outside of privileged circles struggling to get ahead. The latter encompassed immigrants and the coastal elites who defended them. According to Trump, Democrats during the Obama presidency had looked after "them" and had forgotten about "us."

This Trumpian framework shifted blame away from abstract economic changes to more easily identifiable targets. Demonization of immigrants as rapists and criminals made them scapegoats for all of the country's ills—the drug crisis, unemployment, stagnant wages and rising inequality. According to Trump, the solution to these problems was to build a wall to prevent more of "them" from infiltrating "us." Moreover, he guaranteed that Mexico would pay for the wall as a kind of restitution.

Trump claimed to have spoken with American workers who pleaded with him saying, "I just want a job. Just get me a job. I don't need the rhetoric. I want a job." Whether or not anyone actually said this to Trump is beside the point. His words tapped into the psyche of Americans struggling to find work to support a middle-class lifestyle. The decline in heavy industry and subsequent decline in all kinds of manufacturing left Americans in skilled labor with few attractive employment prospects. The growing service sector and surging gig economy offered some opportunities, but the work often came with steep pay cuts and scarce benefits. Invocations of this sense of loss and falling behind became predominant themes in Trump's campaign, which again and again asserted that the United States was losing jobs to countries overseas, losing trade wars to economic foes, and losing the country's cherished white, Anglo-Saxon heritage. If Americans elected him president, Trump pledged, the country would get back to its winning ways—there would be so many victories that Americans would eventually get, "sick and tired of winning."[44]

Racial and ethnic innuendo was also in play. The slogan "Make America Great Again" served as a kind of implicit vow to Trump's overwhelmingly white and disproportionately male supporters that he would restore their power and authority.[45] Arguably, Donald Trump utilized his marketing skills to sell his presidential campaign as a cultural referendum on the cosmopolitan present. He used racially charged language in his tweets and speeches, and railed against political correctness. He refused to apologize for just about anything, and in doing so granted reprieve to Americans still clinging to racial and ethnic biases. Red "MAGA" hats turned into not-so-veiled symbols of belonging to Trump's ethno-nationalist tribe.

This approach did not appeal to most Americans—and initially it did not attract majority support from GOP primary voters, either. But the crowded Republican primary field in 2016 worked to Trump's advantage. He managed to win a plurality of votes in some of the early primary states, while his competitors split the rest.[46] It was just enough to knock off his rivals in one state at a time. Not all Republicans went down without a fight, and there was some speculation heading into the nominating convention as to whether or not the party would stage a last minute coup. A group of "Never Trump" delegates made a final stand on the convention floor, but their efforts fell far short.[47] Trump began building overwhelming Republican backing.

At first, Trump did not find many allies on Capitol Hill either. Many members hung back even as the nomination became all but certain.[48] The first official endorsement came relatively late as these things usually play out. Representative Chris Collins of New York threw his support behind Trump in late February, three weeks after he won the New Hampshire primary.[49] About a month later, Congressman Lou Barletta joined the House's small band of Trump supporters. In an interview with the *Washington Post*, Barletta admitted to Robert Costa that he had been pressured by colleagues and associates on the Hill to withhold an endorsement he wanted to make earlier.[50] Barletta said he had been impressed by the candidate since the 2015 announcement speech, where Trump "caught my attention immediately when he highlighted illegal immigration and the open southern border." In Barletta's prescient view, Trump was "resonating with average Americans who feel their voice has been lost by their party." Barletta also predicted that Trump would bring "more Democrats and independents to our party than anyone I can remember since Ronald Reagan," including "blue-collar

Democrats" in Pennsylvania and across the country who would turn out and vote for him.

Fully embracing the spirit of Trumpism, a movement rooted in his own experiences and convictions, Barletta organized support for Trump in Congress and in his home state of Pennsylvania. He became a founding member of the House Trump Caucus, which grew in numbers as Trump inched closer to the GOP nomination. Then Barletta co-chaired Trump's campaign in Pennsylvania along with another early backer, Representative Tom Marino of Pennsylvania's tenth district. Together they helped coordinate fundraising and organizing in the state. They spoke at rallies and other public events promoting Trump and his agenda. In the process, they developed a close relationship with Trump, who is known to value loyalty above all else. Trump affectionately nicknamed the two congressmen "Thunder and Lightning" for their enthusiasm on the campaign trail.

Appealing to the Pivotal Rust Belt

Representing constituencies far removed from the large urban centers of Philadelphia and Pittsburgh, both Barletta and Marino saw early on the potential for Trump's success in pivotal rust belt areas of Pennsylvania, including Luzerne County and its surrounds.[51] Trump held his first political rally in the state about two weeks ahead of the April primary. A crowd of 4,500 people showed up to support the candidate, and many more were turned away when the convention center in Pittsburgh reached capacity.[52] A week later, six thousand people eager to see and hear Trump filled an Expo Center in Harrisburg— the heart of Congressman Marino's district. The lines for that rally were so long that the event began before many could even make it into the building.[53] The day before the Pennsylvania primary, Trump held yet another Pennsylvania rally at the Mohegan Sun Arena in Wilkes-Barre—part of Congressman Barletta's district—that attracted upwards of ten thousand people. Trump himself seemed impressed by the masses, telling the packed arena, "This is amazing."[54] In an interview with the local newspaper, Barletta said he had never seen crowds or excitement like this before for a political candidate.[55]

Interviews with rally attendees illustrated the enthusiasm many people in northeastern Pennsylvania felt for Trump's candidacy. They saw him as a unifier and someone who would fight against the elites in Washington on their behalf. One woman at the rally said that, "With Trump, our voices are being heard." For many in the mostly blue-collar crowd, the rally was, "a revelation of sorts" because it demonstrated just how many people in this old Democratic stronghold sided with Trump.[56] The public display of support for him paved the way for even more fans to emerge from the shadows.

On primary day in Pennsylvania, Trump won every congressional district in the state.[57] In Luzerne County, he took home 77 percent of the vote, the largest margin of any county. Trump's campaign awakened a base of voters in the "T" counties that lie between Philadelphia and Pittsburgh. He tapped into their economic and cultural frustrations—especially their sense of being left behind and ignored—and spoke directly to their grievances. He galvanized support for his campaign by pulling these voters, some longtime conservatives and others in transition away from the Democratic Party, off the political sidelines and onto the main stage.

Sealing a Drift Away from Democrats

Trump's strong appeal was unprecedented for a GOP candidate in previously blue Luzerne County, which turned out to be the perfect breeding ground for Trumpism. The county was the fourth largest in the state by population until the 1960s, but as foreign competition and the beginnings of globalization drew jobs overseas, workers left in search of opportunities elsewhere. The population shrank to a fraction of its previous size, and the service work that remained paid much less than union salaried jobs. Median incomes in the county have not gone up significantly since 2000.[58] Amid this jarring set of changes, as we have seen, Hazleton's Latino population grew rapidly, and Lou Barletta stepped in to stoke anxiety and defend whites, drafting an anti-immigrant playbook for Trumpism's success in Luzerne County.

In this same period, many in Luzerne County were becoming disenchanted with the Democratic Party. To be sure, residents had voted Democratic in every presidential election since 1988. A brief GOP interlude during Reagan and Bush Sr.'s administrations interrupted what was otherwise a solid, union-backed tradition of supporting Democrats. Just before 2016, moreover, Luzerne twice voted to elect Barack Obama president. Yet throughout Obama's two terms in office, white working-class voters began to feel abandoned by cosmopolitan elites. Changing cultural norms combined with economic hardship to create the sense that voters like them no longer mattered much to the Democratic Party.

At the local level, the party's organizational infrastructure fell apart. The county party had difficulty filling basic leadership positions, and the state Democratic Party focused most of its efforts on the urban and suburban areas around Pittsburgh and Philadelphia. Luzerne County Democrats hemorrhaged voter registrations to the Republicans. From 2008 to 2017, nearly 13,000 voters in the county switched their registrations; and in 2016 alone about 5,800 Democrats changed their party affiliation ahead of the closed GOP primary so they could support Trump.[59] National Democrats, for their part, were either unaware or unconcerned. Neither Bernie Sanders nor Hillary Clinton visited the region during the 2016 campaign, creating a political vacuum into which Donald Trump stepped.

Trump's impressive performance in the Pennsylvania primary energized his campaign and convinced his associates that he had a shot at winning the state in the general election. Fourteen times between the April primary and the November general election he returned to Pennsylvania to hold rallies, mostly visiting non-big-city areas as Trump did everywhere during the 2016 campaign. He went to Altoona, Moon, Mechanicsburg, Hershey and Manheim; and in October, Trump returned to the Mohegan Sun Arena in Wilkes-Barre and spent the evening before the November general election in neighboring Scranton. At every arena, loyal supporters wearing red "MAGA" gear packed the venue and responded with roaring enthusiasm. A local newsman in Wilkes-Barre told us he knew something big was underway when he saw many longtime union men in the crowds.

For the most part, Trump stuck to a familiar script in Pennsylvania. The opening act usually included Barletta and Marino—Thunder and Lightning—who riled up the crowds by praising Trump's independence from the Washington swamp and his plans to stand up for workers.[60] Trump typically spoke in a rambling fashion for about an hour, making sure to touch on each of his campaign's major hits—building the wall, repealing ObamaCare, renegotiating the North American Free Trade Act (NAFTA), punishing companies for moving jobs overseas, deporting criminals, and defeating Islamic radicals. In every rally, he also denounced the "dishonest, fake news media" and "crooked" Hillary Clinton. The crowds often erupted into spontaneous chants of "Lock her up!" and "Build that wall!"

At Pennsylvania rallies, Trump also made sure to mention that he was going to bring the steel and coal industries back. As he put it on election eve in Scranton, "To all the people of Pennsylvania, I say, we are going to put the miners and the factory workers and the steel workers back to work. We are bringing our country back."[61] Whether or not Pennsylvanians believed this was even possible seemed irrelevant. After years of feeling ignored by Democrats and business-oriented Republicans, they seemed viscerally to trust Trump to fight for them and turn the tables in Washington. In a kind of closing statement, Trump said to his followers, "You have one magnificent chance to beat this corrupt system and to deliver justice for every forgotten man, every forgotten woman, and every forgotten child in this nation."[62]

On November 8, 2016, Trump upset Hillary Clinton in Pennsylvania by less than 1 percentage point. His victory in the state secured the Electoral College and the White House. Trump carried fifty-six of Pennsylvania's sixty-seven counties, which earned him just enough votes to overcome Clinton's totals in the cities and populous southeastern districts. As his enthusiastic white working- and middle-class base turned out in large numbers, Trump flipped the rustbelt areas of Erie, Luzerne, and Northampton Counties that had backed Obama in 2012.[63] Where previous GOP presidential contenders had failed to tap the growing disenchantment with Democrats, Trump succeeded big time.

In a larger sense, for many voters in Pennsylvania—especially in rust belt and in rural areas—Trump's election validated anxieties about economic and cultural changes and offered reassurance that building walls and banning immigrants might "take our country back."[64] Even voters who sensed this might not succeed were glad the new president would try, would be on their side. Perhaps no one in Pennsylvania felt more vindicated by Trump's victory than Lou Barletta—who, to his credit, had predicted early on that Trump would win Luzerne County and the state of Pennsylvania. After Trump won, he rewarded Barletta and several other early supporters with positions on his transition team that worked to fill important posts in various executive agencies. Members of Congress who once chided Barletta for backing Trump now came to him seeking access to the new president's administration. Although Barletta was not appointed to an administration post, he returned to Capitol Hill as a strong presidential ally—until Trump called on him again.

The Promise and Limits of a Trumpian Senate Campaign

Seeking a Senate candidate to carry his message and help protect the slim Republican majority in the Senate, Trump called Barletta at home in the summer of 2017 and urged him to run. The president made the case that Barletta, as a politician in Trump's own image, could stage a formidable challenge to Democratic incumbent Bob Casey. Indeed, despite the incumbent Democratic senator's moderate politics and broad popularity, pundits initially considered the Pennsylvania Senate race a potential toss-up, given Trump's surprise success there in 2016.

But Barletta would soon face an uphill battle when it came to fundraising and statewide name recognition. Although he had enjoyed some time in the spotlight, he was not widely recognizable across the state outside of conservative circles. Bob Casey, on the other hand, was seeking his third term in statewide office with one of the most recognizable names in state politics, shared with his late father, Bob Casey Sr., a popular pro-life Catholic Democrat who served as governor of Pennsylvania. Both Casey's grew up in the city of Scranton, the same hometown as another local favorite, former vice president Joe Biden. Like neighboring Wilkes-Barre and Hazleton, Scranton is another old coal mining and industrial town in the state's Appalachian northeast, giving both Casey and Barletta roots in a swing area outside the state's two major metropolitan areas.

Doubling Down against Immigration

From the outset, Barletta took a gamble by embracing Trumpism to its fullest, issuing an announcement video proudly declaring that he would work to, "make Pennsylvania and America great again."[65] This may have personally been an easy choice given Barletta's faith as a true believer and his overriding need for the president's strong backing, but it flew in the face of polling heading into the midterms showing that 53 percent of Pennsylvanians disapproved of how Trump was handling his duties in the White House.[66]

Senate candidate Barletta also stuck to his radical ethno-nationalist rhetoric on immigration. A fundraising mailer sent to some Republican households during the state's primary race tried to stoke fears that Pennsylvania was being overrun by illegal immigrants living in so-called sanctuary cities. Using bold-faced and underlined lettering, the mailer featured a warning from Barletta, who declared "I won't sugarcoat it . . . America is at war." In the span of a couple hundred words, the mailer declared the country at war three times and suggested Barletta was building a conservative "army" to fight the battle over illegal immigration.[67] "With every day that passes more Americans are killed or victimized," continued the mailer message, "whether by violent criminal aliens who are *untouchable* within the 'Sanctuary Cities' of the left or by radical terrorists who sneak across our border or walk right through the front door via liberal schemes like the 'Diversity Visa Lottery Program.' "[68] The mailer's language was even more extreme than some of Barletta's previously strong words about undocumented immigrants in his hometown of Hazleton. In an interview with the *Philadelphia Inquirer*, Barletta tried to backpedal on some of the mailer's explicit fearmongering, but his efforts were mostly futile.[69]

After Barletta easily won the GOP primary in May of 2018, President Trump tweeted "Lou is a friend of mine and a special guy, he will very much help MAKE AMERICA GREAT AGAIN!" That summer, Barletta's campaign received assistance and fundraising support from other immigration hardliners and Trump loyalists, including Vice President Mike Pence, Brexit crusader Nigel Farage, and members of the Trump family.

Despite all of this help, Barletta had trouble making inroads with voters across the state. His poll numbers hovered around 35 percent and barely budged even in response to supportive presidential tweets. He had a particularly difficult time gaining traction in the southeastern portion of the state where Trump's job approval ratings were low. In August 2018, just 10 percent of Philadelphians held a favorable view of Trump. In the populous Philadelphia suburbs, where Barletta needed to earn a substantial amount of support from GOP voters and independents, Trump's approval stood at 30 percent.[70]

Not even the much-hyped fall migrant crisis at the southern US border did much to move moderate voters in Pennsylvania. In an attempt to deter Central American migrants from crossing into the country, the Trump administration instituted a "zero tolerance" policy that resulted in thousands of children being separated from their parents at the border and placed in makeshift shelters with no clear plans for reunification.[71] A fierce backlash from the public ensued, as images of crying children in holding facilities circulated in the media. Barletta was virtually the only member of Congress to openly defend the policy. In an interview with a Pittsburgh area television station, he explained that "The laws of the country state that when you commit a criminal offense, children, you will be separated during the custody." He added, "I don't think we should have separate laws for people who come in the country illegally and other laws for American citizens."[72] Such extreme views displayed Barletta's loyalty to his ally, President Trump, but did not help his prospects in many parts of Pennsylvania.

A Last-Ditch Effort Falls Short

Toward the end, Barletta turned to Trump in an attempt to reprise a reelection strategy that had apparently worked in 2016—holding raucous rallies across the state. As we glimpsed at the start of this chapter, the first stop was a return to the Mohegan Sun Arena in Barletta's home district—ironically, an arena situated in a large retail complex called Casey Plaza, in honor of Bob Casey's late father. Barletta kicked off the event by claiming that Casey favored sanctuary cities and open borders, while praising President Trump for the progress he was making on immigration and the economy. Trump then took the stage and spoke for over an hour, mostly about himself. He issued one of his fiercest attacks on the media and christened Barletta's opponent with one of his infamous nicknames, calling him "Sleepin' Bob," a senator who is "boring" and "overrated." He also threw out red meat on immigration, declaring that "Bob Casey doesn't mind MS-13 coming in," referring to the Central American gang, and falsely accused Casey of supporting the abolition of Immigration and Customs Enforcement (ICE), the federal immigration enforcement agency.[73] Trump told the crowd to vote for Barletta, who would fight to protect the border and help carry out his America First agenda.

At another rust belt rally in Erie in early October, Trump called Barletta a "special man" and a "total winner," which was curious given that the polls continued to show Barletta trailing Casey by double digits. Trump had previously made a habit of dropping people he did not believe would win, but this time he continued to heap praise on Barletta, who he said had been "an incredible

Congressman." Trump admitted that he was the one who had convinced Barletta to run, saying, "I got him into this."[74]

As we have noted, even with Trump's vocal and persistent support, Barletta ultimately lost the Senate race. Voter turnout in Pennsylvania was high, especially for a midterm election, and it was especially high in the Democratic-leaning counties of southeastern Pennsylvania, helping Casey to win by a larger margin than he did back in 2012.[75] Barletta underperformed Trump in the southeastern part of the state and lost the independent vote by almost 20 points. All in all, Barletta lost four counties that Trump carried in 2016: Beaver, Berks, Erie and Northampton. Barletta won his native Luzerne County by 8 points, but that was less than half of Trump's commanding margin over Clinton in 2016.

Why Did Barletta Fail in 2018?

Of course, Democrats performed well in the 2018 midterms across the country, not just in Pennsylvania. Still, few Republicans embraced Trump's ethno-nationalist agenda as avidly as Barletta, whose defeat in Pennsylvania, a pivotal swing state, offers important insights into the limits of anti-immigrant and ethno-nationalist politics.

Exit polls showed that anti-immigrant messaging never really resonated in Pennsylvania during the 2018 election cycle, because voters said the most important issue facing the country was health care, followed by the economy.[76] Republican pollster David Winston concluded that Trump and the GOP's supreme emphasis on illegal immigration and the migrant caravan cost them 12 points nationwide with undecided voters, who ultimately went with the Democrats.[77] In Pennsylvania specifically, when it came to immigration, 52 percent of Keystone voters believed Trump's policies were "too tough." One third of Democrats and roughly two thirds of Republicans thought the policies were "about right." Just 17 percent of voters saw them as "not tough enough."[78] Most Pennsylvanians simply did not support more extreme immigration measures. In post-election polling, they said they found Barletta's positions on health care to be more concerning than Casey's immigration record.[79]

Indeed, Democratic senator Casey recognized voter priorities and ran a disciplined campaign that focused almost exclusively on health care. The majority of his political advertisements showed him fighting to defend health care benefits for Pennsylvanians, especially those with preexisting conditions. One poignant ad was narrated by a northeastern Pennsylvania coal miner who told the story of how Casey had stepped in to protect health care coverage for miners.[80] Casey routinely attacked Barletta for his votes in the House to repeal the Affordable Care Act and protections for preexisting conditions.

Developments in Barletta's own hometown of Hazleton point to yet another possible contributor to his ultimate Senate shortfall. The influx of immigrants has by now changed the face and prospects of the city, which is undergoing an economic revival of sorts thanks in large part to Latino residents there who have opened new restaurants, stores and other small businesses. *El Mensajero*, the city's Spanish newspaper, estimates that one hundred Latino-owned businesses have opened in Hazleton since 2006.[81] Nonprofits and civic organizations, such as the Hazleton Integration Project, are bringing together members of the community from all ethnic and social backgrounds.[82] As a result, a "fledgling Anglo-Hispanic" culture is taking root.[83] Unlike the situation even a decade ago when Barletta was on the rise, growing numbers of voters living in cities like Hazleton are seeing the benefits of the influx of young, hardworking families. Fearmongering and ethno-nationalism may ring hollow with remaining whites as time passes, and newcomers register to vote eventually. Recent elections in Hazleton suggest that these processes are under way. In his 2016 congressional reelection bid, Barletta carried his home county, but did not carry Hazleton city proper, the area where most of the growing Latino population lives.[84]

In Luzerne County as a whole, anti-immigrant politics surely still has considerable appeal, even if not quite as many of the area's voters responded in 2018 to Lou Barletta's reprise of themes that helped Trump win by huge margins in 2016. In other parts of Pennsylvania, fear-mongering about immigrants seems to have been even less appealing.

In some urban and upscale suburban areas, immigration crackdowns—once witnessed in actual practice—raise concerns for many. Since taking office in January 2017, Trump has instituted a travel ban, a policy of "extreme vetting" and new limits on the number of refugees and asylum seekers admitted into the country. The promised wall is now to be paid for by American taxpayers, not Mexico. And the Trump administration has unleashed federal immigration agents to round up and deport immigrants living in the country without proper documentation. An investigation by the *Philadelphia Inquirer* and *ProPublica* found that in 2017 the Philadelphia branch of ICE arrested more undocumented immigrants without criminal records in Pennsylvania and its neighboring states than any other office in the country.[85]

This high arrest rate is noteworthy given that the size of Pennsylvania's undocumented population does not even fall within the top ten in the nation. According to the report, ICE officers feel "emboldened" by President Trump to track down illegal immigrants by any means necessary.[86] Amid what they regarded as "indiscriminate" raids targeting law-abiding people, authorities in the city of Philadelphia stopped sharing information with ICE just months before the 2018 midterms, arguing that ICE actions were making residents less likely to cooperate with local police. "How anyone can define this as making America great again is beyond me," explained the mayor.[87]

In some of Pennsylvania's rural areas, as in others across the country, ICE raids have broken apart families and caused labor shortages. Reports pointed to this downside of Trump administration policies for Pennsylvania's mushroom farmers and dairy producers.[88] In such labor markets, immigration's effects run contrary to Trump and Barletta's claims that immigrants are stealing American jobs, because newcomers are often the only ones willing to work grueling hours for low pay on farms. Agricultural businesses often depend on immigrant labor for their very survival.

Declining industrial areas can see immigrants as more than just threats even before new arrivals revitalize entire local economies, as has happened in Hazleton. In the northwest corner of Pennsylvania, for example, the city of Erie receives more refugees than any other small city in America.[89] They hail from Africa, Asia and the Middle East and have repopulated pockets of the old manufacturing city—the positive impact can be seen in the city's schools, businesses and grocery stores. Erie remains predominantly white, but a racially diverse group of refugees now makes up 18 percent of the population. Some locals told the *Wall Street Journal* that they fear the Trump administration's increasingly draconian refugee cap will jeopardize the city's economic progress.[90] Electoral reverberations of this worry are, of course, hard to pin down. But we do know that in 2016, the city of Erie voted for Hillary Clinton, while the county was one of three, along with Luzerne and Northampton, to flip from Obama in 2012 to Trump (narrowly) in 2016. In 2018, however, both Northampton and Erie Counties switched back and voted for Casey over Barletta. Erie, moreover, switched back into the Democratic column by 18 points, suggesting at the very least that the Barletta anti-immigrant message did not resonate there.[91]

Looking Ahead

Donald Trump's 2016 campaign for president obviously resonated with voters across the country who felt left behind by demographic and economic change, including many in exurban and rural counties in Pennsylvania. In the northeast part of the state, especially, Trump's plans to build a wall to keep immigrants out and promises to bring back jobs and industries from overseas struck a chord, because recent economic and cultural trends had created perfect conditions for nostalgic politics.

But 2016 may not prove prophetic. As suggested by the story of Lou Barletta's rise to 2016 heights followed by a clear electoral failure two years later, the 2018 midterm elections in Pennsylvania revealed some weaknesses for the Trump brand and appeal. Far from proving to be another 2016-style winner, Lou Barletta's Trumpism not only fell short statewide and especially around the big cities, but it also faltered more or less obviously in rust belt areas.

That is not to say that President Trump himself will necessarily lose Pennsylvania in 2020. Despite Barletta's 2018 failure, there are signs that the Trump version of Republicanism remains popular in politically crucial parts of this contested state. Republicans continue to gain supporters in the northeast and southwestern regions. From the fall of 2018 to the spring of 2019 Republicans netted more than one thousand voters to their registration totals in Lackawanna, Luzerne, Northampton, Beaver, Cambria, Fayette, Washington and Westmoreland Counties.[92] Pennsylvania will once again be a key battleground state in the 2020 presidential election, and Democratic candidates hoping to wrestle the state from Trump will have to improve on Clinton's margins in rust belt counties like Luzerne and turn out the city and suburban vote in the state's two metropolitan areas.

We can be a bit more certain in arguing that ethno-nationalist, anti-immigrant politics is unlikely to be enough to win the day in 2020. Trump's narrow victory in Pennsylvania in 2016 and Barletta's subsequent loss in 2018 suggest that while ethno-nationalism may deliver some temporary electoral successes in rapidly changing places, it may not be a broadly popular long-term political strategy. That Barletta, Trump's political godfather, could not reprise his ally's formula for electoral success suggests that issues such as improving health care can take precedence over demonizing immigrants. Even more fundamentally, recent trends in Hazleton, Erie and other parts of Pennsylvania point to a familiar story in American history—immigrants are eventually woven into the fabric of social and political life. As this process unfolds, attacking the newcomers and using them as scapegoats becomes a less viable political strategy. Republicans in and beyond Pennsylvania might do well to learn these lessons from Lou Barletta's failed Senate campaign. If Trump's Trump was vulnerable in Pennsylvania in 2018, perhaps Trump himself—and other Republicans who echo his raw, hardline nativism—will be at risk in 2020. In larger, socioeconomically vibrant and varied states, politicians may not find electoral success marching in lockstep with President Trump under the banner of tough immigration crackdowns.

Notes

1. NBC News/Marist Poll, August 12–16, 2018.
2. "President Trump Remarks in Harrisburg, Virginia," C-SPAN, April 29, 2017.
3. "Election 2016: Pennsylvania Results," New York Times, September 23, 2017.
4. Trip Gabriel, "He's a G.O.P. Immigration Hard-Liner. So Why Is He Trailing in Trump Country?" New York Times, August 2, 2018.

5. Ben Bradlee Jr., *The Forgotten: How the People of One Pennsylvania Country Elected Donald Trump and Changed America* (New York: London, Brown, and Company, 2018), 15.
6. Bradlee, *The Forgotten*, chapter 1.
7. Suzette Parmley, "The Great Warehouse Boom in Lehigh Valley and Beyond," *Philadelphia Inquirer*, June 30, 2017.
8. "Luzerne County, PA," Data USA. Available at https://datausa.io/profile/geo/luzerne-county-pa as of September 7, 2019.
9. Bradlee, *The Forgotten*, chapter 2.
10. Michele Norris, "As America Changes, Some Anxious Whites Feel Left Behind," *National Geographic*, April, 2018 available at https://www.nationalgeographic.com/magazine/2018/04/race-rising-anxiety-white-america/.
11. Norris, "As America Changes."
12. Aaron Blake, Amber Philips, and Callum Borchers, "The First Hillary Clinton vs. Donald Trump Showdown of 2016, Annotated," *New York Times*, September 7, 2016.
13. Michael Powell and Michelle García, "Pa. City Puts Illegal Immigrants on Notice 'They Must Leave,' Mayor of Hazleton Says After Signing Tough New Law," *Washington Post*, August 22, 2006.
14. Marianne Levine, "Rep. Lou Barletta under Consideration for Labor Secretary," *Politico*, September 29, 2016.
15. "Election 2018: Pennsylvania Election Results," *New York Times*, January 28, 2019.
16. Bradlee, *The Forgotten*, chapter 2.
17. Bradlee, *The Forgotten*, chapter 3.
18. Bradlee, *The Forgotten*, 63.
19. Eleanor Klibannoff, "Luzerne County Voted for Trump, and Has Matched Pa.'s Outcome Since 1932," WHYY, November 18, 2016.
20. Bradlee, *The Forgotten*, chapter 3.
21. Bradlee, *The Forgotten*, chapter 3.
22. Chris Brennan, "As Lou Barletta's Immigration Law Failed His Political Brand Was Born," *Philadelphia Inquirer*, July 16, 2018.
23. Powell and García, "Pa. City Puts Illegal Immigrants on Notice."
24. Michael Matza, "10 Years after Immigration Disputes, Hazleton Is a Different Place," *Philadelphia Inquirer*, April 1, 2016.
25. Brennan, "As Lou Barletta's Immigration Law Failed."
26. Powell and García, "Pa. City Puts Illegal Immigrants on Notice."
27. Powell and García, "Pa. City Puts Illegal Immigrants on Notice."
28. Powell and García, "Pa. City Puts Illegal Immigrants on Notice."
29. Bradlee, *The Forgotten*, 65.
30. Julia Preston, "Judge Voids Ordinance on Illegal Immigrants," *New York Times*, July 27, 2007.
31. Brennan, "As Lou Barletta's Immigration Law Failed."
32. "Murder Case Fails Against Immigrants in Pennsylvania City," *New York Times*, July 8, 2007.
33. Brennan, "As Lou Barletta's Immigration Law Failed."
34. Chico Harlan, "In These Six American Towns, Laws Targeting 'The Illegals' Didn't Go as Planned," *Washington Post*, January 27, 2017.
35. "A Reagan Legacy: Amnesty for Illegal Immigrants," NPR, July 4, 2010.
36. Donna Smith, "Senate Kills Bush Immigration Reform Bill," *Reuters*, June 28, 2007.
37. "President Bush Disappointed by Congress's Failure to Act on Comprehensive Immigration Reform," White House press release from June 28, 2007. Available at https://georgewbush-whitehouse.archives.gov/news/releases/2007/06/text/20070628-7.html.
38. Ramsey Cox, "Schumer Introduces Comprehensive Immigration Reform Bill," *The Hill*, April 17, 2013.
39. Seung Min Kim and Carrie Budoff Brown, "The Death of Immigration Reform," *Politico*, June 27, 2014.
40. Kim and Brown, "The Death of Immigration Reform."
41. Colby Itkowitz, "Congressman Lou Barletta Opposes Emerging Immigration Plan," *Morning Call*, January 28, 2013.
42. Itkowitz, "Barletta Opposes Emerging Immigration Plan."

43. "Here's Donald Trump's Presidential Announcement Speech," *Time*, June 16, 2015.

44. Tom Lutey, "Trump: 'We're Going to Win So Much, You're Going to Be So Sick and Tired of Winning,'" *Billings Gazette*, May 26, 2016.

45. Mugambi Jouet, "Trump Didn't Invent 'Make America Great Again,'" *Mother Jones*, January/February, 2017.

46. "Election 2016: Republican Party CNN Delegate Estimate," CNN, July 2016.

47. Kyle Cheney, "Chaos Erupts on GOP Convention Floor after Voice Vote Shuts Down Never Trump Forces," *Politico*, July 18, 2016.

48. Nick Gass, "Rep. Hunter on Colleagues Reluctant to Back Trump: 'Toughen Up,'" *Politico*, May 31, 2016.

49. Jeremy Diamond, "First Congressman to Back Trump: 'We Need a Chief Executive'" CNN, February 24, 2016.

50. Robert Costa, "Lou Barletta, an Immigration Hard-Liner in Congress, Endorses Trump," *Washington Post*, March 22, 2016.

51. Laura Olson, "Pennsylvania Congressmen Who Backed Trump Early Pitch in to Promote Him," *Morning Call*, July 21, 2016.

52. Chris Potter and Sean D. Hamill, "Trump Promises to Revive Steel, Asks about Joe Paterno During Stop in Pittsburgh," *Pittsburgh Post-Gazette*, April 14, 2016.

53. Laura Olson, "Donald Trump Rally in Harrisburg Draws Thousands," *Morning Call*, April 21, 2016.

54. Bill O'Boyle, "One Word for Trump Crowd: 'Huge,'" *Times Leader*, April 25, 2016.

55. Bill O'Boyle, "One Word for Trump Crowd.

56. Bradlee, *The Forgotten*, 14.

57. Ed O'Keefe and Katie Zezima, "Trump Won at Least 39 Unbound Pa. Delegates, According to Washington Post Tally," *Washington Post*, April 27, 2016.

58. O'Keefe and Zezima, "Trump Won at Least 39 Unbound Pa. Delegates.

59. O'Keefe and Zezima, "Trump Won at Least 39 Unbound Pa. Delegates, 32.

60. Melanie Mizenko, "Donald Trump Promises to Return Jobs to US during Stop in Scranton," *Times Leader*, July 27, 2016.

61. Bill O'Boyle, "Candidates Make Closing Arguments Day before Polls Open," *Times Leader*, November 7, 2016.

62. O'Boyle, "Candidates Make Closing Arguments."

63. Maria Panaritis, Dylan Purcell, Chris Brennan, and Angela Couloumbis, "How Trump Took Pennsylvania: Wins Everywhere (Almost) But the Southeast," *Philadelphia Inquirer*, November 9, 2016.

64. Elizabeth Chuck, "Donald Trump: 'Don't Worry, We'll Take Our Country Back,'" NBC News, July 11, 2015.

65. Sheryl Gay Stolberg, "Trump Republicans Invigorate, and Complicate, Party's Fight for Senate," *New York Times*, August 29, 2017.

66. NBC News/Marist Poll, August 12–16, 2018.

67. Jonathan Tamari, "'America Is at War' with 'Violent Criminal Aliens,' Says GOP Senate Candidate Lou Barletta," *Philadelphia Inquirer*, February 16, 2018.

68. Tamari, " 'America Is at War.' "

69. Tamari, " 'America Is at War.' "

70. NBC News/Marist Poll, August 12–16, 2018.

71. Julie Hirschfeld Davis and Michael Shear, "How Trump Came to Enforce a Practice of Separating Migrant Families," *New York Times*, June 16, 2018.

72. Jon Delano, "GOP Senate Candidate Defends Separating Children from Parents Who Enter U.S. Illegally," *KDKA Pittsburgh*, June 15, 2018.

73. Delano, "GOP Senate Candidate Defends Separating Children."

74. "Speech: Donald Trump Holds a Political Rally in Erie," *Factbase*, July 12, 2016.

75. Michelle Merlin and Eugene Tauber, "Voter Turnout in Some Pennsylvania Counties Neared Presidential Election Levels," *Morning Call*, November 21, 2018.

76. NBC News Exit Polls, November 2019.

77. Francis Wilkinson, "Trump Is Making Americans More Immigrant-Friendly," *Bloomberg*, December 19, 2018.

78. NBC News Exit Polls, November 2019.

79. "Immigration Hub Post-Election Survey Results Pennsylvania," available from The Global Strategy Group at https://static1.squarespace.com/static/5b60b2381aef1dbe876cd08f/t/5beaf8f20ebbe8e566741e46/1542125846350/PDF+Immigration+Hub+PA+%28ONLY%29++Slides+D11.12.2018.pdf.

80. Video called "Tony" from Bob Casey for Senate, available at https://www.youtube.com/watch?time_continue=4&v=6_gfbevbQuA as of May 25, 2019.

81. Michael Matza, "10 Years after Immigration Disputes, Hazleton Is a Different Place," *Philadelphia Inquirer*, April 1, 2016.

82. Matza, "10 Years after Immigration Disputes."

83. Bradlee, *The Forgotten*, 67.

84. From the Luzerne County Certified Election Results, available at http://results.enr.clarityelections.com/PA/Luzerne/64171/184324/Web01/en/summary.html as of September 7, 2019.

85. Deborah Sontag and Dale Russakoff, "In Pennsylvania, It's Open Season on Undocumented Immigrants," *ProPublica*, April 12, 2018.

86. Sontag and Russakoff, "In Pennsylvania, It's Open Season."

87. Claudia Lauer, "Philly Cuts Off Cooperation with ICE, Citing Indiscriminate Raids, Arrests," Talking Points Memo, July 28, 2018.

88. Katie Park, "'There's No One Around': Pa. Farmers Faced with Labor Shortage," *Philadelphia Inquirer*, May 7, 2019.

89. Miriam Jordan, "The Town That Can't Do Without Refugees," *Wall Street Journal*, February 28, 2017.

90. Jordan, "The Town That Can't Do Without Refugees."

91. Andrew Seidman and Jonathan Tamari, "Election Results in Pa., Rust Belt Hint at Cracks in Trump's Coalition," *Philadelphia Inquirer*, November 9, 2018.

92. Nick Field, "Here's What the Latest Voter Registration Numbers Tell Us about the State of the Commonwealth," *Pennsylvania Capital-Star*, May 6, 2019.

PART II

DEMOCRATS AT BAY
AND RESURGENT

7

From Obama Victories to a GOP Edge in Florida

ALEXANDRA CAFFREY

"They say that whoever wins the I-4 corridor wins Florida, and whoever wins Florida, wins America."
—Adam Gabbatt, *The Guardian*, January 31, 2012

In December 2012 the state of Florida seemed like it was on its way to becoming
a little less purple and a bit more blue. Barack Obama had won two elections
in a row in the Sunshine State, Democrats had a five hundred thousand person
lead over Republicans in the voter rolls, and the rapidly growing state population was shifting in a direction thought to be favorable for the Democrats.
Furthermore, Obama's campaign had won with an extremely effective, locally
based, grassroots organizing approach, seemingly laying the groundwork for sustained Democratic success in the state.

But that is not what happened. In 2014 and 2018 Florida elected a Republican
governor and in 2016 a majority of Floridians voted for Donald Trump for president. In fact, since 2014 Republicans have won ten out of eleven statewide
elections.[1] Although many external factors affected these close elections, almost
all of the Republicans still won—leaving Florida leaning red, not blue.

Why have Republicans continued to win consistently in a swing state where
demographic trends and other factors seemed to favor the Democrats? What are
the political dynamics involved? Demographics matter in elections, but so does
political organizing, which can help a party or candidate realize demographic
possibilities. The evidence I report here indicates that Democrats made strong
headway in grassroots organizing through the 2012 Obama reelection campaign, but since then the two parties have switched sides in this crucial aspect of
electioneering. Florida Republicans have been out-organizing their Democratic
counterparts on the ground. In a state where elections are won and lost on the

Alexandra Caffrey, *From Obama Victories to a GOP Edge in Florida* In: *Upending American Politics* Edited by: Theda
Skocpol and Caroline Tervo, Oxford University Press (2020). © Oxford University Press
DOI: 10.1093/oso/9780190083526.003.0007

margins, this recent change, if it continues, may very well tip additional election outcomes and cement the state of Florida into the GOP column.

Political Organizing in Pivotal Places

Grassroots organizing has not always been central to modern US campaign strategies, but in the last decade it has made a comeback. This began in 2004, when campaigns began to realize the consistent returns effective grassroots organizing could provide.[2] Then, in 2008, Obama made organizing grounded in personal connections a key component of his campaign. As political scientists Alan Gerber and Donald Green show in many of their studies, grassroots organizing does not necessarily yield huge gains, but it can steadily boost candidates by about 1 to 2 percentage points.[3] In Florida, this means that on-the-ground organizing can be critical to victory, especially in the Interstate 4 (I-4) corridor, the swing part of the swing state. Realizing this, many campaigns since 2008 have invested significantly in field organizing arms—and my research focuses on these dynamics.

In 2016, the *Tampa Bay Times* published an article entitled "Florida's I-4 Corridor: Where Presidents Get Picked."[4] Hillary Clinton and Donald Trump both visited the area over fifteen times during the 2016 campaign, in line with the campaign habits of presidential candidates from 2004 to 2012. Statewide campaigns in Florida usually build significant infrastructure and spend massive resources in this region and its media markets. Swing voters cluster in the I-4 corridor, where substantial Democratic and Republican bases also need to be turned out. This area is therefore the best place to look closely at political organizing in Florida.

As many as fifteen counties can be considered part of the corridor, but most definitions encompass around nine or ten. For the purpose of this research I focus on nine central counties directly intercepted by the I-4 highway or very close to it, specifically Pinellas, Hillsborough, Pasco, Polk, Lake, Osceola, Orlando, Seminole and Volusia Counties, as displayed in Figure 7.1. These counties are all traditionally considered part of the corridor, and population and voting statistics employed here refer to them unless otherwise noted.[5]

A main reason the I-4 corridor is not consistently blue or red is its demographics. The I-4 counties include rural and suburban populations, as well as rapidly growing urban areas. Demographically and politically, these counties add up to a microcosm of the state as a whole. I chose to zoom in on the I-4 because it is varied as well as essential for both Republicans and Democrats, and thus provides a window into organizing conditions statewide.

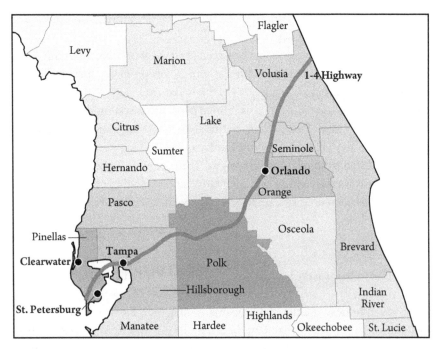

Figure 7.1 Map of Florida's Interstate 4 Corridor.

To analyze and understand the use of grassroots organizing in recent election cycles, I narrowed the scope of my research to one campaign per cycle for an executive office, not the Senate. Because candidates for president and governor sit at the top of the ticket every four years, they are more directly comparable to each other than Senate candidates are to executive candidates. I also chose to begin my analysis in 2012. Although the rise of locally based grassroots organizing as a campaign strategy can be traced to the 2004 presidential campaign cycle and Obama's massive field organizing army in 2008, the techniques most relevant to grassroots organizing today are encompassed in my analysis of the 2012 campaign cycle. Those techniques especially include the use of neighborhood team structures, reliance on person-to-person organizing styles, and long-term preparation of the Obama campaign's ground game.[6]

My analysis about grassroots organizing in recent campaign cycles in the I-4 corridor draws especially from thirty-one in-depth interviews with people who are and have been deeply involved in politics in the area. I interviewed local county party chairs from a sample of counties in the corridor as well as staff members in the state parties, current and former state politicians, Republican and Democrat consultants, former campaign organizers, and other local political activists. Although my approach to evidence collection could not ensure a representative sample of everyone politically involved in the I-4 corridor, it did build a wide interview pool that allowed me to form a comprehensive picture of recent statewide campaigns.

To supplement the interviews, I analyzed print media stories about the 2012, 2016, and 2018 election cycles, with a specific focus on newspapers in Florida and especially high-circulation papers in the I-4 corridor such as the *Tampa Bay Times* and *Orlando Sentinel*. I also examined press releases from the Republican National Committee, Democratic National Committee, Florida Democratic Party, and the Republican Party of Florida, as well as blog posts from political analysts and staff from relevant campaigns. The goal of both the interviews and media analysis was to create a rich qualitative understanding of how grassroots organizing has been used by campaigns and how it connects to larger dynamics of Florida politics.

How Obama Organized Florida

When asked to describe the 2012 Obama campaign in Florida, Brett Doster, a well-known Republican consultant, began by saying that "Obama was the best community organizer on the planet" and continued to note that his ground game was unlike anything Florida had ever seen before.[7] Although Obama's grassroots efforts in 2008 were arguably transformational, the 2012 presidential election cycle was where his campaign's ground game methods were codified and refined. Understanding what happened on the ground in 2012 is essential to understanding what happened after, because the 2012 election highlighted the power of effective field organizing. This organizing subsequently caused a shift in how ground operations have been conducted in Florida and nationwide, particularly by those on the other side of the political spectrum.

In 2012 Obama won Florida by just 0.9 percent of the vote, or under one hundred thousand votes.[8] This is the kind of margin that can be directly connected to field organization and ground game. Although causal effects of campaign components on election outcomes can be hard to prove, a study of the 2012 election by Masket, Sides, and Vavreck found that the portion of the vote share they could credit to Obama's ground game was decisive in the presidential election outcome in Florida.[9] So what made this ground game so successful?

Longevity Matters

The 2012 ground operation for the Obama campaign was built on top of a structure that was already in place from the 2008 election. When Obama was elected on November 6, 2008 the Obama for America campaign morphed into

Organizing for America (OFA)—a community organizing project that sustained relationships, energy, and activism in communities from November 7, 2008, until the 2012 election.[10] This effort was valuable because the most effective grassroots organizing is sustained year-round, not just transactional during an election cycle. As a veteran political organizer in Hillsborough County noted to me, it's nearly impossible to come into a community and build an effective field organization that hinges on volunteer efforts in just six months; serious grassroots organizing takes longer than that.[11] Yet many campaigns before Obama and after have tried to use a short-term, transactional model, which consistently has limited success. The Obama campaign recognized that short-term organizing was not the best strategy and instead built a ground game on the principles of community organizing and infused the basic structure with the power of a presidential campaign.[12] They focused on creating relationships, making commitments based on shared values and common interests, and going beyond the basic acts of phone banking and canvassing.[13] So when the 2012 election rolled around, the OFA team had been using this type of organizing in I-4 communities for over four years.

Brick and Mortar Matters

The Obama ground game in Florida was widespread, well-funded, and active in communities all across the state, not just in Democratic strongholds. The Obama 2012 campaign had 106 field offices across Florida's sixty-seven counties. Almost 2 offices per county was an unprecedented commitment. In addition, the campaign had around eight hundred full-time staff members and a budget of $50 million. In the nine I-4 corridor counties alone Obama had 32 offices. The Romney campaign on the other hand had only 18 offices in the I-4 and, with just 47 statewide offices, had fewer than half the number of Florida field offices as Obama, seen in Figure 7.2.[14] The offices that Romney did have were also not as effective as Obama's. In their analysis of the 2012 campaign, John Sides and Lynn Vavreck estimate that to match the effectiveness of Obama's ground game, Romney needed 2 field offices for every 1 of Obama's. Obama's locally sourced, long-term volunteer-based campaign style was more impactful than the traditional, imported system of the Romney campaign.[15]

Although field offices are not a perfect measure of organizing capacity, they have an impact in election cycles. Notably, Sides and Vavreck found that in Florida, the impact of an Obama field office in a county was equal to the impact of "roughly three additional ads per person on the day before the election."[16] This is particularly relevant because of where Obama's offices were located within the I-4 corridor. There was an office in every one of the nine I-4 counties, even the

1-4 Corridor Obama Offices 2012

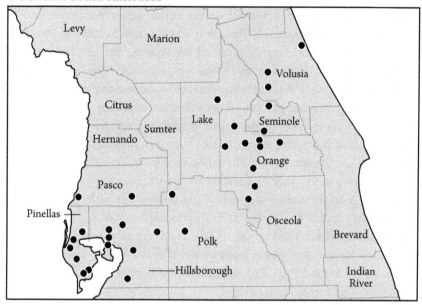

1-4 Corridor Romney Offices 2012

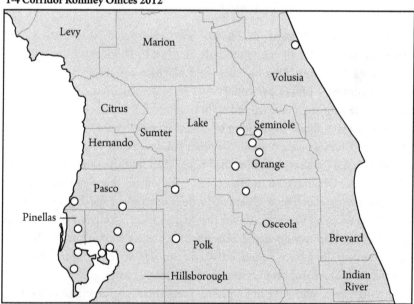

Figure 7.2 Obama versus Romney Florida Interstate 4 Corridor Office Locations in 2012.

red counties with significantly smaller and mostly rural populations like Lake, Pasco, Polk, and Volusia. By placing field offices in these areas and in other Republican areas across the state, the Obama campaign was acknowledging that there were Democratic votes to be had in these counties. Campaign staff were taking a chance on the idea that a bit of Democratic organizing could harness key votes in these areas, as winning a statewide election in Florida is often about managing the margins–and they were right.[17] Obama technically lost in Lake, Pasco, Polk and Volusia. Yet, had the margins in these counties shifted just 2 percentage points towards Romney, that would have cost Obama Florida as a whole.

Volunteers Matter

The 2012 Obama campaign was also effective because it was locally rooted and emphasized volunteer responsibility. Campaign leaders strived to hire organizers who were from the areas they were organizing, because teams that are built on local foundations quickly become effective.[18] Yet even in communities without paid organizers, the Obama campaign reaped many of the same benefits through its neighborhood team structure and empowerment of volunteers with leadership responsibilities. In these places Obama organizers were tasked with finding volunteers, but their jobs did not stop there: organizers cultivated relationships with volunteers, created commitments, and then trained them to be leaders themselves. The most successful volunteer leaders were then tasked with leadership of their own volunteer teams which became central components of the campaign's organizing efforts. This allowed the campaign to be active in communities it would not have had the capacity to reach otherwise in both breadth and depth.

Personal Connections Matter

Another central component of the Obama 2012 organizing structure was the campaign's heavy focus on door-to-door and face-to-face contact with voters, and when that was not possible, personal phone calls instead of automated. This was based on the idea that personal contacts and actual boots on the ground have an impact beyond just the conversation that a staffer or volunteer has with a voter.[19] Wes Hodge was one of the many active Obama volunteers in the Orlando area in 2012. Wes is also a cancer survivor, and when his cancer came out of remission during the 2012 campaign, he put in canvassing shifts in between sessions of chemotherapy. Although Wes deeply believed in Obama as a president and a candidate, he was truly motivated to get involved because he had a preexisting condition and saw Barack Obama's reelection as the only way to ensure he would have health care in the future. When Wes was going to door-to-door talking to voters, he would share a portion of his story with them. This personal connection was a key component of the ground campaign strategy.

Wes recounted one canvassing shift where he was in a predominantly black community and had a conversation with a voter who described feeling apathetic and uninterested in voting in this election, especially since America had now already had its first black president. Wes, who is white, responded by saying that he understood the sentiment, and that just as it was really important for this voter to have a black president in 2008, it was really important for people like Wes, who had preexisting conditions, to continue to have access to affordable health care. That is what this voter would support if he voted in this election. Wes connected with this voter on a personal level and gave him a concrete example of why his vote would matter. This story conveys the impact that personalized grassroots organizing and field efforts can have. The sentiment that Wes was able to convey is different from what could have been conveyed through a TV advertisement or a mailer. The impact of this interaction was probably farther-reaching than just the individual conversation, as political scientists Gerber and Green found that "about 60 percent of the direct impact of canvassing appears to be transmitted to voters' housemates."[20]

In sum, the Obama ground game was so successful in the I-4 corridor and nationwide because it was long term in nature, robust in both its office and staff numbers, locally based, and focused on personal connections. Furthermore, the campaign kept detailed data on its ground efforts and targeted voters and then used these metrics to scale its efforts.[21] As Marshall Ganz, one of the main architects of the Obama organizing model noted, the Obama campaign "was able to combine the enthusiasm, contagion, and motivation of a movement, with the discipline, focus, and organization that it takes to win."[22]

After 2012, Florida Parties Switch Sides on the Ground

On Monday, March 17, 2013, the Republican National Committee (RNC) released an "autopsy report" that analyzed the causes of its 2012 loss.[23] The report, officially titled "The Growth and Opportunity Project," identified the Republican Party's insufficient ground game as a major reason for its loss. Determined not to continue conceding grassroots organizing superiority to the Democratic Party, the national Republican Party immediately took action after the report was released and began investing in sustained, locally based organizing, especially in swing states. By the end of October 2013, the RNC stated that it had hundreds of staffers hired in swing states working with the state parties to build a "bottom-up boots on the ground operation." Sean Spicer, then RNC communications director, noted this change in a 2014 press release: "the lesson from 2012 is we must have a permanent ground game. We must engage with voters year-round in their communities."[24] According to David Johnson, a well-known Republican consultant in Florida, this change was evident in Florida as the RNC and the Republican Party of Florida (RPOF) "increased ten-fold how many people they were paying on the ground," and they did this by "shifting some of the large pot of money to field organizing."[25] The Republican Party did not follow all of the report's suggestions, such as diversifying the Republican Party coalition and appealing less to extreme conservatism; but the party, especially in Florida, has followed the grassroots organizing suggestions explicitly.

Republicans Build, Democrats Dissolve

At the same time that the Republican Party was building an organizing system that was directly "modeled on the Obama field organization," the Democratic Party was letting the robust grassroots organizing system of the Obama campaigns disappear.[26] Although Obama's organizing arm technically morphed (again) into Organizing for Action after the 2012 election, it was not sustained at the same level as after 2008. In most places the local networks completely dissolved, severely hampering the ground games of future campaigns at both the state and national levels. Future Democratic campaigns were forced to re-build from scratch; while at the same time, in swing states around the country the Republican Party was hard at work building a sustained organizing structure that was interacting with voters year-round. This direct role-reversal carried Republicans to victory in Florida in the 2014 midterm elections and set the stage for Donald Trump's success in the 2016 presidential election in the state.

Since November 9, 2016, political scientists, journalists and politicians have been clamoring to understand the outcome of the 2016 election and the factors that allowed Donald Trump to succeed. Some attribute Trump's victory to the power of populist rhetoric, others speak of the impact of widespread racial resentment and economic insecurity, and still others emphasize a deep-seated desire among the electorate to rebuke the establishment along with the vestigial effects of inherent sexism in many voters. Most of these explanations and others are well-supported by a range of evidence, and there was clearly a cocktail of factors that led to Donald Trump's election. But as RNC co-chair Sharon Day put it, "2016 also had an X factor the pundits and analysts weren't prepared for: the Republican National Committee's unprecedented ground game operation."[27] This organizing effort, glossed over during the election and in many post-election analyses, was a crucial component of Trump's success, and it was directly copied from the organizing system that Obama had used just four years before.

In fact, RPOF executive director George Riley noted that the RNC staff who came to Florida in early 2015 to help build the GOP campaign told the RPOF executive team to "go and buy *Groundbreakers* and read it because that is what we are doing."[28] *Groundbreakers* is the book by Elizabeth McKenna and Hahrie Han that explicitly outlines the Obama organizing structure and details the reasons it was innovative and successful. To say that Florida Republicans were literally reading the Obama organizing textbook and learning from its secrets would hardly be an exaggeration.

Media Looks Left, Missing the Right on the Ground

During the election the media did not focus on the state or national party structure, instead the majority of reporting only focused on the two campaigns. Journalistic accounts from the election point to the superiority of the Clinton ground game over the Trump ground game. Headlines such as, "Clinton Has More Than 3 Times as Many Campaign Offices as Trump. How Much of an Advantage Is This?," "No, Donald Trump—You Still Don't Have A Ground Game," and "Democratic Insiders: Clinton's Ground Game Will Sink Trump" ran in major news outlets throughout fall 2016, promulgating the overarching message that Clinton had a far better ground effort in Florida and around the county.[29] These headlines were correct in the sense that Donald Trump himself did not have a significant ground game. By August he had very few offices open, but the state and national Republican Parties had been building a robust ground game in Florida for years, with the local Republican Party offices throughout the state actively participating in traditional field operation activities. In an interview with *The Hill* in August 2016, former Trump campaign strategist for Florida, Karen Giorno noted that the campaign has 67 county party chairs that "actively produce Trump events and Trump activities weekly that contribute to voter registration drives."[30]

The Republicans were completely underestimated by the media and by the left. According to a staffer from Clinton's Brooklyn headquarters, most Clinton staffers thought their campaign's ground efforts far surpassed Trump's. No one on the campaign even discussed the underlying ground efforts of the Republican Party. Moreover, not only were the Republicans' efforts overlooked by the media and the Clinton campaign, but also the Clinton campaign's grassroots organizing capacity was grossly overestimated.[31]

Clinton's Top-Down Grassroots

The 2016 Hillary Clinton campaign aimed to replicate the Obama coalition that was comprised of millennials, minorities, and white working-class voters, but they particularly focused on minority communities and millennials while giving far less time to working-class white voters.[32] Many journalists and political scientists around the country have highlighted this omission of the white working class as one of the central downfalls of the campaign.[33] Yet beyond the omission of this target group, the Clinton campaign had serious structural weaknesses in its ground game that were detrimental in the long term. As one Hillary for America organizer from the I-4 described the campaign, "the nicest way I can put it, is that it was a crap show."

The first issue for the Clinton campaign was that, unlike the Obama campaign in 2012, it did not have the benefit of a robust community-organizing group like Organizing for America that it could simply morph into the base of its field organizing system. As noted previously, the Obama organizing network slowly dissolved after 2012, leaving the Clinton campaign to start essentially from scratch. Beyond the lack of a preexisting system, the Clinton campaign was also far more top-down in its structure. It did not directly employ the neighborhood team model, volunteers were not given as much responsibility, and the organizers were not predominantly local to the communities in which they were organizing. Interviews with multiple organizers for the Clinton campaign in Florida indicate that staffers were sent in from all around the country, often to places where they lacked knowledge of the community and had no personal connections. This led to tensions with local Democratic leaders and undercut the efficiency of organizing.[34] As one county party chair from the I-4 corridor explained, it was off-putting and inefficient to have "twenty-somethings from Connecticut" attempting to tell her what to do to organize in her own community.[35] Moreover, she described how the orders from Brooklyn were often delayed and out of touch with the needs of her specific county.

To some, it seemed the entire field operation was dictated from Brooklyn, which does not make for a very locally oriented campaign. As one Miami-Dade-based Clinton staffer put it:

> Brooklyn's narrow focus on data was frustrating for the political and field operatives on the ground advocating for more of a human touch. There was no attempt to train organizers how to seek out community leaders, mobilize local organizations or build relationships with the grassroots.[36]

This led to a "very transactional" campaign and unfortunately, as basic organizing principles indicate, transactional interactions do not build effective organizing networks.[37]

The Clinton ground effort was also significantly smaller than the Obama ground effort. In 2012 the Obama campaign had 106 field offices in Florida. In 2016, the Clinton campaign had 82.[38] So, not only were the offices less effective than Obama's because of the lack of localization, but there were also simply fewer of them. In 2017, Joshua Darr, a political scientist who studies the impact of field organizing noted that "Clinton did not open fewer offices because of a strategic decision to prioritize Democratic areas over rural Republican ones: she invested substantially less in both."[39] And then, on top of the weak Clinton ground game, the Florida Democratic Party was also moribund. Before the 2016, cycle the Democratic Party had not spent any time building a sustained ground game and offered little guidance to its county party chairs.

What is more, the Clinton campaign's long, tough primary battle against Bernie Sanders delayed general election campaigning until the beginning of the summer of 2016. Although the Trump campaign was also unable to focus on the general until the beginning of the summer, the campaign had the benefit of the RPOF and the RNC doing voter contact and building on a preexisting grassroots system throughout the primary season. The Florida Democratic Party and the DNC were not doing anything at a similar scale on the left during the primary season which highlights the large-scale negative externalities that come from a weak state party.

The RNC as Trump's Secret Weapon

When Donald Trump secured the Republican Party nomination in July 2016, there was an active, widespread, relationship-based ground game awaiting him in Florida (as well as in many other swing states). For Hillary Clinton there was no such network. On a conference call in October of 2016, RNC political director Chris Carr stated that the party was doing "most of the heavy lifting" regarding the Trump ground game, because it had built a system that was already in place before the election began. Carr went on to note that "before Clinton had staff focused on the general election, the RNC's staff, organizers, and volunteers had tallied well over 1.2 million hours of organizing. That's the equivalent to 50,000 days, or 137 years of organizing."[40] On the surface it may have seemed like the Clinton campaign had a more robust and effective ground game than the Trump campaign, but the reality of the situation was far more complicated.

The Trump campaign in 2016 only had twenty-nine field offices, but there were RPOF/RNC offices on top of the Trump offices, as well as local county Republican Party offices that were actively engaging in the Trump ground game. When Susie Wiles, the Trump campaign director in Florida was asked in September about how many offices she would consider actively working for the Trump campaign, she said sixty offices.[41] This puts the total number of active Trump campaign offices, even if they were not explicitly branded as Trump offices, at double the twenty-nine offices reported by multiple journalists. The RNC/RPOF also had 1,040 paid staff members on the ground in Florida in 2016. In 2012, it only had 84 paid staff members.[42] This size growth was also was coupled with localization and strong emphasis on relationship building.[43] The party hired local staff and emphasized principles of community organizing by splitting the state into 254 distinct turfs.[44] As Josh Kivett, the RNC regional policy director for the Southeast during the campaign, noted, "we effectively put together 254 individual campaigns throughout the state."[45] So while the Clinton campaign staffers were getting blanket, data-driven direction from Brooklyn for areas with which they were unfamiliar, the RNC and the RPOF were running a locally targeted campaign with staffers who knew their areas well and had read *Groundbreakers*.

Josh Kivett also noted that the Republicans were "running up the score in areas where I don't believe the Democrats thought they could get additional votes . . . such as the Tampa exurbs."[46] I have already noted that Florida is a state for which margins are crucial, and nowhere is that more evident than in the suburban and urban counties of the I-4. These places were not lost causes for the Democratic Party in Florida. Although Hillary Clinton likely could not have won these counties, she could have done a bit better in all of them which in aggregate would have made a difference in Florida.[47] Obama received 46.38 percent of the vote in the suburban and rural counties in the I-4, while Clinton only received 41.26 percent.[48] If Clinton had matched Obama's numbers and received 5.00 percent more of the vote total, adjusted for population shifts, she would have received 86,894 more votes across these six I-4 counties. Hillary Clinton lost in Florida as a whole by just under 120,000 votes, and there were plenty of other suburban and rural counties across the state where Obama's margins were slightly better than Clinton's. Field organizing efforts by the Democrats likely could have shifted vote totals, had they invested at all in these places.

Although Trump's appeal to the white working class and his populist style of campaigning helped propel him to victory in Florida, it is essential to acknowledge the Republican ground efforts. By glossing over the failings of the Democratic ground game, many post-election analyses neglect a central piece of the 2016 election. Furthermore, this misses a bigger picture trend of influential, sustained, locally based organizing in recent elections. This organizing has roots in the 2004 election but can be directly traced from Obama in 2008 and 2012 through to Trump in 2016, by way of the Republican Party. As such, we have to start on the ground to understand the complex political landscape of Florida and what happened in 2018.

The 2018 Reckoning

In October 2018, Mayor Andrew Gillum was ahead of Congressman Ron DeSantis in nearly all polls measuring the race for Florida governor. Nationally, everyone was talking about the blue wave about to sweep Washington, DC, as Democrats dreamed of winning swing districts across the country and taking back the House of Representatives. A blue wave seemed likely in Florida, too. Gillum was a dynamic gubernatorial candidate who generated massive enthusiasm on the left, especially with young voters and minority communities; Bill Nelson, the incumbent Democratic Senate candidate, had not lost a general election in his forty-six years in politics. One could easily argue that the Democrats in Florida were finally poised to win some statewide races in the perennial swing state. While a blue wave did hit Washington, DC, giving the Democrats a majority in the House of Representatives, it did not make it to Florida. Both Gillum and Nelson lost, as did the Democratic candidate for attorney general. What happened? Why did the blue wave that carried so many other Democrats to victory in 2018 not make it to the Sunshine State, especially when the margins (as usual) were so close?[49] Although many factors impact election outcomes, grassroots organizing undoubtedly played a key role in the 2018 Florida election. During this cycle, the absence of an existing organizing infrastructure proved detrimental for Democrats, while Republicans benefited from their previous investment in a locally sourced ground game. Moreover, statewide Republican success this cycle indicated that Trump's success in 2016 was not just an aberration stemming from a populist politician but potentially the product of something systemic on the grassroots level.

Where Was the Florida Democratic Party?

One of the central issues for Democratic candidates in the 2018 election cycle was the lack of any infrastructure built by the state party. As an I-4 organizer for a liberal independent expenditure group noted, "The Florida Democratic Party was honestly just not there."[50] The primaries in Florida did not take place until August 28, 2018, leaving nominees only two months until Election Day—an insufficient amount of time to build an effective grassroots effort from the bottom up. For reasons that remain unclear, the Florida Democratic Party (FDP) did not invest in building a ground game prior to August 2018.

In a February 2019 appearance, Andrew Gillum himself highlighted this problem. He noted that "you can't be a party organization that only activates in an election year. Voters actually don't operate that way, they live 365 days a year."[51] Statewide, the Florida Democratic Party was not organizing in advance of the primary. The party did not hire organizers, find locations for offices, or even encourage local Democratic Executive Committees to start organizing.[52] Although it seems that party leadership was waiting for a gubernatorial candidate before officially starting a coordinated campaign, they certainly could have put the pieces of a field organization together ahead of time. As one Gillum organizer, Misha Nadel, put it, "I can't imagine the idea of a 'coordinated campaign' was thought up on August 29th."[53]

Scaling up a primary campaign to a general election size campaign is an immense task and in 2018 it was made even more difficult by the late primary date. Moreover, during the primary, Andrew Gillum ran a lean campaign as he was not the front runner and did not start receiving major donations until later in the primary cycle. During the primary he only had seven full-time staff.[54] Once he became the nominee he was somehow expected to scale up to a staff of over four hundred, and as he noted in an interview, "there was no real groundwork done in anticipation or to help prepare—I did not absorb an infrastructure from the state party to help me become the Governor of Florida."[55] This was highly problematic for his campaign.

The lack of a Democratic Party ground structure was harmful to Andrew Gillum's campaign on many levels, but most detrimentally, it lost time in the field; and as the general political adage goes, the only thing you cannot get more of on a campaign is time. Despite the fact that the Florida Democratic Party knew it was going to be implementing a coordinated campaign for the general election, it took the FDP, in conjunction with the Gillum and Nelson campaigns, a full four weeks to put staff on the ground after the primary. In fact, as Misha Nadel points out, "The Florida Democratic Party held its statewide training for its very-newly-hired Coordinated Campaign field team on September 24th–25th . . . we didn't start making voter contact until September 28th . . . and *we weren't making targeted voter contact until five weeks after the primary*."[56] The RPOF, with funding from the RNC, had hired sixty people in April.[57] As a seasoned I-4 area organizer put it, the problems that the lack of prior organizing created were directly connected to the fact that "there is a built-in function that the state party/DNC is supposed to do and they just did not do it in 2016 or 2018."[58]

The Democratic side lost crucial momentum when it was not ready to expand right after the primary.[59] Andrew Gillum generated massive enthusiasm throughout his primary campaign and once he became the nominee, excitement increased exponentially. This was evident in the rallies that the party held right after primary. Andrew Gillum, Senator Bill Nelson, and the Democratic gubernatorial candidates who lost in the primary held a "UNITY" rally in Orlando where several hundred people packed into an arena.[60] But the Florida Democratic Party had no plan to translate this excitement into action. When people at the rally asked how to help and get involved, they were told to wait while the party got the coordinated campaign up and running. It was not until four weeks later that the campaign was ready for volunteers, at which point the post-primary enthusiasm it sought to capture had waned.

Again, Right-Wing Boots Were on the Ground

As the Democrats were losing momentum by putting their ground game on hold to set up a coordinated campaign, the Republicans were ramping up an effort that they had been building since the 2016 election. The RPOF, via funding from the RNC, hired a 2018 election campaign state director in mid-2017, according to a top official at the state party.[61] It had its first statewide "day of action" on April 28, 2018 where it hosted thirty-four training events across the state, and by July staff and volunteers had knocked on one million doors.[62] On October 1, 2018, the Republicans announced that they had knocked on over two million doors in Florida this election cycle. October 1 was also the day cited by many involved with the Democratic campaign as the first day that the Democratic co-ordinated campaign even had organizers on the ground.[63] This was just over a month before Election Day and only one day before 2018 Vote-by-Mail ballots were sent out. Notably, approximately 31.5 percent of the electorate in Florida voted by mail.[64] In addition, the Gillum campaign / Florida Democratic coordi-nated campaign never even made it to persuading voters; they almost solely fo-cused on getting out the vote of known supporters due to the time constraint. As organizer, Misha Nadel highlighted, "The persuasion target list had zero people in it, statewide."[65] By comparison, in March, Republicans split Florida into 255 organizing turfs, divided so that each had approximately equal numbers of per-suadable voters for organizers to target.[66] The Republican ground efforts were miles ahead of the Democratic efforts and certainly impacted the outcome of the 2018 election. The early investment from the right and the lack thereof from the left was crucial to the Republican success.

Local Organizing and Small Blue Waves

The post-2016 Democratic energy that was visible nationwide still existed in Florida in some areas during the 2018 election cycle. This energy was harnessed in places in the I-4 corridor where there were effective local leaders who built their own ground efforts in their communities and thus made an impact. These singular successes, despite the lack of organizing on a statewide level, demon-strate the impact that grassroots organizing can have. For Democrats, they indi-cate a potential road to electoral success in Florida. The first example of this in the I-4 corridor is in Hillsborough County, which is home to Tampa and is one of the most populous counties in the state.

The day after Donald Trump was elected president of the United States, Christine Hanna was distraught. She, along with many throughout America, had not expected him to win. Christine needed to figure what to do about it. She had been involved in political organizing in different capacities throughout her life and felt that action was far better than words, so she decided that she would do something in Hillsborough County. She started by forming a "Pantsuit Nation Tampa Bay" Facebook group which grew exponentially and eventually led to the formation of Indivisible Action Tampa Bay (IATB) which became a key actor in the 2018 election in Hillsborough.[67] The IATB Facebook group now has over 6,200 members and the group is one of the largest and most successful in the nation. Through the Facebook platform, IATB built and cultivated a large and sustainable grassroots organizing network in Hillsborough that is consistently advocating for progressive causes via protests, meetings with representatives, and fundraisers.

During the 2018 primary season, IATB was also the ground game for the Gillum campaign in Hillsborough and Pinellas Counties. The group tapped Gillum as its candidate of choice early on and, starting in January 2018, IATB was running phone banks, Hustle text-a-thons, and canvasses for his campaign.[68] Christine Hanna, the IATB founder, Justin Diaz, the IATB policy director, and Shay DeGolier, the Indivisible organization staff member for Florida, all suggested that IATB's efforts were a central part of the reason Andrew Gillum secured the Democratic nomination in Florida. IATB organized on the ground in a populous county and secured Gillum an endorsement from national Indivisible, increasing his national profile before the primary.

In the general election, IATB continued working hard on the ground for Gillum, as well as for Bill Nelson, and other down-ballot candidates. They ran multiple canvasses every weekend, along with phone banks and a near-perpetual texting effort. But beyond IATB, Hillsborough also had a highly effective Democratic Executive Committee (DEC), which is what the local Democratic Party system in Florida is called. After the 2016 election, the increased progressive energy was not just seen in the development of groups like IATB but also in the growth of previously established progressive entities—the Hillsborough County DEC membership went from 69 people in December 2016 to 340 people by January 2018.[69] It was clear that the blue wave potential was there in Hillsborough just as it was state- and nationwide.

Lacking guidance from the state party, the Hillsborough County Democratic Chair Ione Townsend took matters into her own hands. As she began knocking on doors and building relationships in January 2018, Ione realized the traditional precinct captain structure was not working well for Hillsborough and therefore built a more regional leadership model to make sure that every part of the county was covered. When I asked Ione to describe how she thought about local organizing, she often referred back to her experience volunteering on the Obama campaigns in 2008 and 2012 which she said "worked because they empowered local communities."

Both IATB and the Hillsborough County DEC employed tactics that were reminiscent of tactics used by the Obama campaigns in 2008 and 2012 (and by the Republican Party in 2016 and 2018). The result was a blue wave in Hillsborough County. Andrew Gillum and Bill Nelson both won here with better margins than Hillary Clinton in 2016.[70] The midterm turnout for Democrats in Hillsborough County also increased significantly– in 2014 the turnout percent of registered Democrats was 50 percent, in 2018 it was up to 65 percent.[71] Four of the Hillsborough County Commission seats flipped from Republican to Democrat and two of the eight total Florida House of Representatives seats that flipped from red to blue were in Hillsborough County.[72] Although there were plenty of factors at play in Hillsborough during this election cycle, the robust and comprehensive organizing efforts of IATB, the local DEC, and other independent expenditure groups like For Our Future and Next Gen, clearly amplified the blue wave in Hillsborough and also held back the red tide that was strongly supported by a RPOF ground game.

Seminole County, Flipped

A similar correlation between effective local leadership and a local blue wave can be seen across the corridor in Seminole County, a traditionally red county comprised of the Orlando suburbs. Seminole County went blue for the first time in thirty years in 2018. The county voted to support both Andrew Gillum for governor and Bill Nelson for Senate and one of the state house seats in the county flipped from Republican to Democrat.[73] Much of this Democratic success can be traced back to the local Seminole DEC and their chair Rob Bial.

Rob became involved with the Seminole County Democrats after the 2016 election. He had volunteered for the Clinton campaign and after she lost, he felt like he could not just stop working. When Rob first started attending Seminole County Democrats meetings, "the energy was there but the mission and organization were not," and Rob felt that he and the general Democratic energy around him would be most effective working through an organized county party structure. So, Rob became more involved with the DEC. He was eventually elected chair, and then helped the organization rebrand as SemDems. Rob made SemDems a safe space for all of the different grassroots groups in Seminole that had developed from the post-2016, anti-Trump energy. Due to this shift and Rob Bial's continued work, the SemDems had a significant presence in the 2018 election cycle. They were organizing and reaching out to voters throughout the spring and ran a serious ground operation throughout the general election. During the general the SemDems hosted multiple canvasses per week, ran phone and text banks, and sent their own direct mail. This is especially important because the FDP did not invest in Seminole in 2018. They gave the county party no money, did not put a coordinated campaign office in Seminole, and according to Rob, told him not to even bother running candidates for local seats (the same seats where the Democrat ended up only losing by 1 percent).

Seminole County is a clear success story for Democratic grassroots organizing that is locally based and people-centered. When I asked Rob about what he thought happened in 2018 in Seminole he noted that "there is no secret sauce, it was the hard work of grassroots organizing. It was knocking on doors and getting to know our neighbors." Boots on the ground make a difference and Seminole County Democrats were extraordinarily effective because they understood this and acted on it. It seems that Democrats did so well in Seminole County, partially because of shifting demographics but primarily because of dynamic and effective leadership that was prepared to channel the massive Democratic enthusiasm.

Party Infrastructure Still Matters

The 2018 campaign reveals that it is not a winning strategy for Democrats in Florida to simply bet on having effective local DEC chairs who are willing to devote massive amounts of time to the Democratic cause; or to bet on the potential existence of a robust independent expenditure group (like IATB) in every county. This is especially true when the Republican Party now has an organized ground effort up and running months in advance of each election cycle. Grassroots organizing impacts election outcomes, especially in a state where elections are constantly decided on the margins. The FDP needs to address this fact in a structural manner if it wants to build a consistent winning strategy. In addition, the right benefits from a very effective independent expenditure group, Americans for Prosperity (AFP). AFP organizes around conservative issues and directly supplements the Party's efforts.[74] So, the right has the two structures working in concert, while the left only has sporadically effective independent expenditure groups.

Better margins in the I-4 counties might not have led to a victory for Andrew Gillum, because many factors impacted the outcome of the 2018 gubernatorial election in Florida. Democratic turnout rates in Miami-Dade, Broward, and Palm Beach Counties were much lower than people were expecting; new Puerto Rican voters in Orlando did not vote en masse; and racial views were clearly a more significant factor than many pundits and journalists predicted they would be—inducing some people to vote for Nelson and not Gillum. However, in this incredibly close election more effective grassroots organizing—reinforcing preexisting efforts—might well have improved margins statewide and boosted turnouts in the critical places that fell short. The results might have been enough to garner the approximately thirty-five thousand additional votes Gillum needed to win.

What Next?

In Florida an odd electoral reversal that bears resemblance to national trends has occurred. Since 2012, Florida Republicans have become the "Obama-ites" in their campaign strategy. As the executive director of the RPOF put it, they have literally read the Obama organizing textbook and implemented a systemic strategy that invests in sustained grassroots organizing.[75] In the same period, Florida Democrats have allowed their own grassroots organizing system to fall into disarray.

As this chapter illustrates, the Republican Party has employed and expanded on the organizing tactics that were central to Obama's winning strategy in 2008 and 2012, using this approach to win ten out of eleven statewide elections since 2014. Although this research does not prove statistical causation, the evidence in this chapter indicates that the notable differences between the Republican and Democratic ground efforts in recent election cycles have likely influenced the outcomes. By allowing Republicans to gain the upper hand in organizing after 2012, Democrats created fertile ground for Donald Trump's 2016 campaign.

Trump tapped into voters who felt they were being ignored by the establishment, who felt they were being left behind and forgotten. He told them that he would work for them— and they believed him. Although this populist rhetoric was clearly vital to his success, the RNC grassroots organizing system was Trump's secret weapon. Political analysts and social scientists have consistently emphasized the role of Obama's ground organization in his success, yet they fail to acknowledge the analogous benefits for Trump of the 2016 Republican ground game that explicitly imitated Obama's system. Instead of falling into a one-sided analysis of ground efforts, this chapter shows that grassroots organizing has been a key factor in all Florida election cycles since 2008. When implemented well, ground-level voter outreach is regularly connected to electoral success.

The demographics of Florida are theoretically shifting in favor of Democrats as the urban centers grow rapidly and the population of minority residents increases, especially as more Puerto Ricans move to the state.[76] Yet even with beneficial demographic trends leading into 2018, it was difficult for Florida Democrats to counter long-term statewide organizational efforts by the right with merely sporadic and non-systemic efforts on the left. Although Democrats did relatively well in some places where local leaders took matters into their own hands, it was not enough to turn the tide. As Andrew Gillum often notes, "demographics are not destiny."

Looking towards 2020 and the presidential election, grassroots organizing will likely be the key to winning Florida—and thus, very possibly, the White House. Millions of potential Florida voters are not registered. The Puerto Rican population is growing along the I-4 corridor. And up to one million formerly incarcerated people had their voting rights restored in 2018. For all these reasons—in addition to roiling views about the Trump presidency—nothing about the state's politics is set in stone. Time is of the essence and the future of Florida politics could well come down to how effectively Democrats and Republicans engage with voters on the ground. Currently, Democrats are behind, and if they do not find ways to reach new voters and communicate specifically how the party can work in their favor, Florida's future will likely be red, not blue.

The situation in Florida highlights broader trends, because the power of grassroots organizing is not unique to the Sunshine State. In swing states nationwide, party investments in organizing infrastructures that can support persistent local outreach are among the keys to winning elections. This type of organizing provides consistent returns, is not complicated to implement, and is not very vulnerable to online hackers. Grassroots organizing does, however, require time and commitment, and in the current Florida political situation, Republicans have made stronger commitments than Democrats. This commitment helped the Florida Republican Party fend off surging Democratic candidates in 2018, and the GOP's system is already expanding for the 2020 election cycle.

After 2018, there is still energy on the left and a clear desire to work for liberal candidates. Grassroots progressive energy drove the nationwide blue wave in the 2018 elections, but the results would have been even better had there been better channels for newly active citizens in all parts of the Democratic Party. If Democrats wish to be successful in the future of American politics, they should build and sustain a serious grassroots operation—one that is locally sourced and coordinated through existing county and precinct party structures. Democrats should have paid staff on the ground in swing states organizing year-round, not just for four months in advance of Election Day. Although year-round organizing cannot consistently be as extensive as in presidential campaigns, having some type of party presence is important, even if it is small in many places. A visible and welcoming Democratic presence needs to be constructed in both red and blue areas of swing states—not just in liberal urban strongholds. Furthermore, the DNC and state parties should provide funds and resources to empower and engage volunteers, because it is clear that effective volunteers can exponentially increase the impact of paid staff efforts at the grassroots.

Organizational shortcomings for Democrats in many areas currently put party candidates in Florida, and beyond, at a disadvantage before they even begin campaigns. The Florida story told in this chapter suggests that if Democrats do not figure out how to fix their organizing systems in swing states and counties— if they do not build outreach networks comparable to recent Republican undertakings—they may well continue to lose otherwise winnable statewide and presidential elections for the foreseeable future.

Notes

1. The only Democrat who has won statewide in the past three election cycles is Nikki Fried, who won the race for Agricultural Commissioner in 2018.
2. John Kirtley, Florida non-profit director in an interview with author, October 31, 2018.
3. Donald P. Green and Alan Gerber, "Voter Mobilization, Experimentation, and Translational Social Science," *Perspectives on Politics* 14, no. 3 (2016): 738–49.
4. Adam Smith, "Florida's I-4 Corridor: Where Presidents Get Picked," *Tampa Bay Times*, November 4, 2016.
5. "Florida Election Results Archive," Florida Division of Elections, n.d. Available at https://results.elections.myflorida.com/ as of January 2019.
6. "Ground game" encompasses all of the grassroots systems that are built throughout states and tends to refer to coalition building efforts along with voter registration, persuasion, and turnout.
7. Doster immediately clarified that he did not feel similarly about Obama's abilities as president.
8. "2012 Florida Election Results Archive," Florida Division of Elections, n.d. Available at https://results.elections.myflorida.com/Index.asp?ElectionDate=11/6/2012&DATAMODE= as of January 2019.
9. Seth Masket, John Sides, and Lynn Vavreck, "The Ground Game in the 2012 Presidential Election," *Political Communication* 33, no. 2 (April 2, 2016).
10. Robert Crew and Mary Ruggiero Anderson, *The 2014 Elections in Florida: The Last Gasp from the 2012 Elections* (Lanham, MD: Hamilton Books, 2018), 17.
11. Ione Townsend, chair of the Hillsborough County Democratic Executive Committee was interviewed by the author, November 27, 2018.
12. Elizabeth McKenna and Hahrie Han, *Groundbreakers: How Obama's 2.2 Million Volunteers Transformed Campaigning in America* (New York: Oxford University Press, 2015), 7.
13. Marshall Ganz, "Organizing Obama: Campaign, Organization, Movement," In the Proceedings of the American Sociological Association Annual Meeting San Francisco, August 8, 2009.
14. Romney and Obama campaign statewide field office figures from Robert Crew and Mary Ruggiero Anderson, *2012 Elections in Florida* (Lanham, MD: University Press of America, 2015), 20. Locations of Romney and Obama I-4 field offices presented in Figure 7.2 generously provided by John Sides, in communication with the author, January 2019.
15. John Sides and Lynn Vavreck, *The Gamble: Choice and Chance in the 2012 Presidential Election* (Princeton, NJ: Princeton University Press, 2013), 220.
16. Sides and Vavreck, *The Gamble*, 220.
17. Steve Schale, "Florida 2016 in the Rearview Mirror," accessed January 14, 2019, http://floridapolitics.com/ archives/227371 -steve-schale-florida-2016-rear-view-mirror. David Johnson, leading Republican consultant in Florida, was interviewed by the author on January 11, 2019.
18. McKenna and Han, *Groundbreakers*, 100.

19. McKenna and Han, *Groundbreakers*, 125.
20. Donald P. Green, *Get Out the Vote: How to Increase Voter Turnout* (Washington, DC: Brookings Institution Press, 2015), 42.
21. McKenna and Han, 158.
22. Ganz, "Organizing Obama: Campaign, Organization, Movement."
23. "Growth and Opportunity Project," Republican National Committee, n.d., available at https://gop.com/growth-and-opportunity-project as of January 2019.
24. "MEMO: Follow the Money—RNC Investing," *GOP* (blog), October 28, 2013.
25. Johnson, interview, January 11, 2019.
26. Crew and Ruggiero Anderson, *The 2014 Elections in Florida*, 7.
27. Sharon Day, "How the RNC's Ground Game Made Florida Red Again | Opinion," *Sun Sentinel*, December 24, 2016.
28. George Riley, executive director of the Republican Party of Florida in a phone interview with the author, February 22, 2019.
29. Seth Masket and Jennifer Victor, "Clinton Has More Than 3 Times as Many Campaign Offices Than Trump. How Much of an Advantage Is This?" Vox, October 5, 2016. Chris Cillizza, "No, Donald Trump—You Still Don't Have a Ground Game," *Washington Post*, September 2, 2016; Steven Shepard, "Democratic Insiders: Clinton's Ground Game Will Sink Trump," *Politico*, November 4, 2016.
30. Jonathan Swan, "Trump Campaign Plans Rapid Florida Expansion," *The Hill*, August 13, 2016.
31. Susan MacManus, "A Look Back at the 2016 Presidential Race in Florida: Another 1 Percent Margin-of-Victory Election," *Sayfie Review*, December 20, 2018.
32. Susan MacManus, David Bonanza, and Anthony Cilluffo, "The I-4 Corridor: The Sunshine State's Premier Battleground," chapter 4 in *Florida and the 2016 Election of Donald J. Trump*, ed. Matthew Corrigan and Michael Binder (Gainesville: University Press of Florida, 2019).
33. Nate Cohn, "Why Trump Won: Working-Class Whites," *New York Times*, November 9, 2016; Stephanie Coontz, "2016 Election: Why the White Working Class Ditched Clinton," CNN, November 11, 2016.
34. MacManus, "A Look Back at the 2016 Presidential Race in Florida: Another 1 Percent Margin-of-Victory Election."
35. Townsend, interview, November 27, 2018.
36. Amory Beldock, "How Clinton Lost the Ground Game: A View From the Trenches," *Progressive Policy Institute* (blog), December 22, 2016.
37. Liz Johns (pseudonym) was interviewed by the author, December 19, 2018.
38. Sabrina Siddiqui and Ben Jacobs, "Battle for Florida: Trump and Clinton Home in on Crucial State as Voting Begins," *The Guardian*, October 27, 2016, sec. US news.
39. Joshua Darr, "The Incredible Shrinking Democratic Ground Game," Vox, November 16, 2017.
40. "ICYMI: Ground Game Press Briefing Call with RNC Political Director," *GOP* (blog), October 6, 2016.
41. Adam C. Smith, "Democrats Distressed about Hillary Clinton's Ground Game in Florida," *Tampa Bay Times*, September 29, 2016.
42. "MEMO: Sleight of Hand: Clinton Ground Game Lags Trump and RNC," *GOP* (blog), September 12, 2016.
43. Day, "How the RNC's Ground Game Made Florida Red Again | Opinion."
44. Patricia Mazzei, "In Florida, 'Underestimated' RNC Takes Victory Lap | Naked Politics," *Miami Herald*, November 15, 2016.
45. Mazzei, "In Florida, 'Underestimated' RNC Takes Victory Lap | Naked Politics."
46. Mazzei, "In Florida, 'Underestimated' RNC Takes Victory Lap | Naked Politics."
47. Schale, "Florida 2016 in the Rearview Mirror."
48. Suburban I-4 counties: Pinellas, Seminole, Volusia. Rural I-4 counties: Pasco, Polk, Lake, Osceola. Urban I-4 counties: Hillsborough, Orange.
49. The Senate race was decided by 10,033 votes—less than 0.1 percent of the vote. The gubernatorial race was decided by 32,463 votes—less than a 4.0 percent difference. The Agricultural Commissioner race which was decided by just 8,753 votes—less than 0.1 percent of the vote.
50. Grayson Lanza, I-4 organizer for Next Gen, was interviewed by the author on January 7, 2019.

51. Andrew Gillum at a John F Kennedy Jr. Forum event, Harvard University Kennedy School of Government, February 11, 2019.

52. This information was confirmed by the DEC chairs in Orange, Seminole, and Hillsborough, as well as the head Gillum field organizer for the Orlando area.

53. Misha Nadel, "The Five Weeks That Doomed the Campaign," *Medium* (blog), December 20, 2018.

54. Andrew Gillum, in discussion with the author, February 25, 2019.

55. Gillum, in discussion with the author, February 25, 2019.

56. Nadel, "The Five Weeks That Doomed the Campaign."

57. "Florida Republicans Kick Off 2018 Ground Game with National Day of Action," *GOP* (blog), April 15, 2018.

58. Lanza, interview, January 7, 2019.

59. Darnell Roberts, "Fumbling on the Goal Line . . ." *Medium* (blog), December 27, 2018.

60. Kirby Wilson and Elizabeth Koh, "At Orlando Rally, Democrats Hope Gillum and Nelson Are the Winning Ticket," *Miami Herald*, August 31, 2018.

61. Riley, interview, February 22, 2019.

62. "Florida Republicans Kick Off 2018 Ground Game with National Day of Action," *GOP* (blog), April 15, 2018. Ryan Nicol "Sore Knuckles Much? Florida GOP Knocks on 1 Million Doors," *Florida Politics* (blog), July 30, 2018.

63. "RNC, RPOF Knock on Over Two- Million Doors," *GOP* (blog), October 1, 2018.

64. "2018 Florida Election Results Archive," Florida Division of Elections, n.d., available at https://results.elections.myflorida.com/Index.asp?ElectionDate=11/6/2018&DATAMODE=, as of January 2019.

65. Nadel, "The Five Weeks That Doomed the Campaign."

66. Johnson, interview, January 11, 2019.

67. The development of the Pantsuit Nation group into an Indivisible group that was influential in the 2018 election is similar to the shifts that many other anti-Trump resistance groups went through in 2017. See chapters 9, 12, and 13 in this volume.

68. Hustle is an innovative platform that allows volunteers to text voters instead of calling them.

69. Townsend, interview, November 27, 2018.

70. Hillsborough County, FL: In 2016 Hillary Clinton received 50.62 percent of the vote. In 2018 Andrew Gillum received 53.86 percent of the vote and Bill Nelson received 54.03 percent of the vote.

71. Craig Latimer "District Voter Turnout Analysis for 2018 General Election," Hillsborough Supervisor of Elections, n.d.

72. The seat for the Florida House District 59 is now held by Democrat Adam Hattersley and the seat for Florida House District 63 is now held by Democrat Fentrice Driskell. Both seats were formerly held by Republicans.

73. Democrat Joy Goff-Marci beat Republican incumbent Bob Cortes to represent Florida House District 30.

74. Theda Skocpol and Alexander Hertel-Fernandez, "The Koch Network and Republican Party Extremism," *Perspectives on Politics* 14, no. 3 (2016): 681–99.

75. Riley, interview, February 22, 2019.

76. Twenty-four percent of Floridians as of 2018 are Hispanic, up from 17 percent in 2000. The population is also growing faster than the population of the state as a whole. Antonio Flores, Mark Hugo Lopez, and Jens Manuel Krogstad, "Hispanic Voter Registration Rises in Florida," *Pew Research Center* (blog), October 12, 2018.

8

Middle America Reboots Democracy

*The Emergence and Rapid Electoral Turn of
the New Grassroots*

LARA PUTNAM

Nancy Reynolds looks like no one's idea of a revolutionary, least of all her own. She has a quick and contagious smile, shiny coiffed hair, a bad knee, and four grandchildren. Heartbroken after the defeat of Hillary Clinton—for whom Reynolds had spent long hours canvassing in the fall of 2016—she marched in protest in January 2017. When the 2018 anniversary march rolled around, she made sure to fit it in, but it wasn't easy. By then Nancy Reynolds had campaigns to run: as Hampton Township coordinator for one friend's Pennsylvania State Senate campaign; as canvass organizer for the slate of first-time candidates she helped elect to Hampton town council in November 2017, breaking decades of Republican dominance; and as signature-gatherer for her own campaign for election to her local Democratic Party committee. A retired librarian, Nancy had long been a powerhouse within her local community, nestled in Pittsburgh's comfortable northern suburbs. Prior to 2016, local and state politics were not on her radar screen. Since 2017 they have dominated her to-do list every day.

Similar stories to Nancy's unfolded in suburbs and towns across her home state and the country in 2017. She and tens of thousands of other women, mostly mothers and grandmothers ranging in age from their thirties to seventies, had begun fueling a political transformation. It was not a top-down project or centrally coordinated movement, but something more diffuse, more personal, and more powerful. Nancy's story is that of a "generation" in the making: a co- hort of Americans for whom life-cycle stage and personal trajectory collided with public events—the election of Donald Trump; the Women's Marches and calls to action that followed—in ways that changed life after life in similar, and consequential, directions. It is no happenstance that this change was felt first and foremost in the suburbs, those middle-class, Middle American spaces that grew

Lara Putnam, *Middle America Reboots Democracy* In: *Upending American Politics* Edited by: Theda Skocpol and Caroline Tervo, Oxford University Press (2020). © Oxford University Press
DOI: 10.1093/oso/9780190083526.003.0008

up alongside a generation—the baby boomers—whose last act of generational transformation seems to have now arrived.

Some high-profile indicators of nationwide civic rumblings made the papers in the year after Donald Trump's inauguration: big turnouts at hundreds of Women's Marches in January 2017 and again a year later; the flood of Democratic congressional challengers who stepped forward for 2018, with a record-breaking proportion of women among them. But the most critical transformations were happening off stage and behind the scenes. Day in and day out, through one church-basement meeting after another, a demographic swathe of forgotten Americans had begun rebuilding the basic infrastructure of center-to-left participatory politics.

The change was not centered in the cosmopolitan urban enclaves where most national pundits live, nor among the grizzled men in coal country diners who had come to symbolize Trump's rural pull in media narratives. Neither of those geographic poles typifies the bulk of America in any case. Fully half the country lives in the suburbs, twice the number who live in either entirely urban or rural settings. More than half of Americans are also women—and of those, half are in their thirties to sixties.[1] It was in this Middle America, and among these Middle Americans, that political developments after the November 2016 election moved fastest and farthest.

The political uprising underway had little in common with the precedents pundits reached for. It was not Sanders versus Clinton redux: that "last year's news" divide was flatly irrelevant to the people working shoulder-to-shoulder in the present. It was not an Occupy Wall Street-type questioning of liberal democracy, because these new activists believed laws and votes could make good government as strong and transparent as possible. It was not the 1960s, with young people leading the way—although there were lots of helpful teenagers in the background, saying, "Mom, it's fine: go to your meeting; I'll get dinner myself."

The protagonists of these trends have been, in their majority, college-educated suburban white women. Their stories are critical not because college-educated white women are the most Democratic slice of the electorate (they aren't—data suggest about 36 percent of college-educated white women nationwide voted for Trump), nor because they are the most progressive voices within the Democratic Party (they aren't), nor because they have a special claim to lead the left moving forward (they don't: nor do they pretend to).[2] Crucially, however, it was among college-educated, middle-aged women in the suburbs that political practices changed most in response to Donald Trump's election. If our question is how America's panorama of political possibility began changing in the wake of November 2016, the story needs to begin here.

Local Initiative and Supralocal Connections

Across the country we heard similar origin stories.[3] Regular citizens bitterly disappointed with the November 2016 results emerged from what many called a "period of mourning" to start planning activities, coordinated by pairs or trios or handfuls of self-appointed leaders. Some of these sparkplugs already knew one another. Others connected on buses chartered for the 2017 Women's Marches or "met" online, sometimes facilitated by the Pantsuit Nation Facebook group that connected hundreds of thousands of women in anticipation of the first female president. Although some men also stepped forward to join (and occasionally even lead) the face-to-face groups of allies for action that emerged, women were very much in the vanguard, making up about 70 percent of the participants and most members of leadership teams.[4]

In the wake of Trump's election, many voices had called for a national movement of active opposition. A unitary label became a common shorthand: "The Resistance." Our local-level observations showed this was a misnomer. While the metropolitan leaders of national-level efforts like the Women's March, Indivisible, and MoveOn seemed to take for granted the left-progressive issue focus of the activism underway, and their own importance in coordinating it, on the ground we found a pattern of engagement that was ideologically diverse and far less issue-focused. The groups we found were nationally aware, but locally initiated and guided. They were also increasingly regionally networked.

Since this mobilization was both decentralized and based in face-to-face rather than virtual actions, it was impossible to scope from a distance. Nancy Reynold's revolution was not being tweeted. Even in the private Facebook groups most local groups created and maintained, the most prolific posters were not necessarily representative of the views of the members most active in real life. Local interviews and observations were essential, we found, to understand what was going on. The source base for this chapter combines the author's immersive observations as participant in grassroots organizing efforts in Southwest Pennsylvania, plus two dozen formal interviews she conducted with leaders and activists there over the course of 2017 and 2018, with Theda Skocpol's findings from repeated field trips to eight non-metropolitan counties in North Carolina, Wisconsin, Ohio, and Pennsylvania, and questionnaires that Skocpol and Leah Gose collected from organizers and participants in some three dozen local groups active across all regions of Pennsylvania in late 2017.[5]

Though not nationally directed, the new activism was not just local either. New national organizations like Indivisible, Sister District, Run for Something, Action Together, Swing Left, Women's March, and many others had stepped up—and staffed up—to offer encouragement and tools via internet outreach, and many of these aspired to coordinate and speak for the new local activists.[6] And most local founders of post-November 2016 grassroots groups did sooner or later read the *Indivisible Guide*, and eagerly borrowed ideas and tools from many of these national organizations. Nevertheless, it is clear that the national organizations did not themselves create the dizzying array of local groups—the "pop-up groups," one bemused but grateful Virginia campaign manager called them—that spread like wildfire in the days, weeks, and early months after November 2016.[7]

As similar small groups emerged in parallel in place after place, they took inspiration from one another, looked for ways to link up within regions and states, and continued to take pointers from national outlets. Yet none of the local groups we interviewed limited their vision, plans, or ties to those offered by just one national-level advocacy organization. Instead, local leaders sought out a wide range of ideas, tools, and connections, actively picking and choosing what they and their fellow members found most relevant to their particular circumstances. The leaders and funders of national "resistance" organizations may not have themselves understood the degree to which local citizen activists eclectically leveraged varied menus of assistance, taking what they need from various offerings rather than lining up under any particular flagship.

Often employed or retired from teaching, business, nonprofit, or government social service posts, the newfound activists already knew how to put out messages, plan gatherings, and share information. Word spread through churches, unions, PTAs, and local good government groups, and dozens of friends, neighbors, and co-workers assembled for founding meetings in living rooms, libraries or church basements, or at local restaurants.

In the early months of 2017, entire groups met often face to face. Soon, many of them hived-off committees or task forces started focusing on particular projects, like coordinating calls to congressional offices, organizing town halls, gathering petitions for anti-gerrymandering referenda, or putting out newsletters. Aware of the homogeneity of their communities, many groups sought to take on board the calls for attention to race-based disparities that came to the fore around the first Women's March. Leaders organized discussions of racial justice issues and sought to cosponsor events or campaigns with NAACP chapters and immigrant-supporting groups. Everywhere, participants worked through much of 2017 to save the Affordable Care Act health reform, and many undertook campaigns to fight gerrymandering or address educational and environmental issues or speak out on behalf of refugees and immigrants. Yet in a departure for recent organizing on the left, these new groups did not seek to be issue advocacy specialists. Rather, we heard over and over a much broader refrain: centered on protecting American democracy and reclaiming citizen ownership of public life.

"I had never really been involved," explained one Southwest Pennsylvania volunteer. "I did one GOTV [Get Out The Vote canvass] on Election Day for John Kerry. That was really all I had done. Through the Obama years, I was busy with my kids, I was happy. Once Trump won I was like, okay, it is *absolutely* time to get involved." By the time we interviewed this volunteer in March 2018, she had: found a new local grassroots group to join; ended up as its leader; run monthly meetings of forty to sixty active members and an email list of six hundred; coordinated volunteer canvass shifts that helped win a congressional special election in a district Donald Trump won by 20 points; arranged a training on "How to Run for Democratic Precinct Person" that drew a hundred people; and was currently running for her county Democratic committee and the Democratic state committee simultaneously. (She won both.)[8]

Self-avowed Democrats were key participants in this new form of engagement, but many local groups deliberately reached out to Independents and disaffected Republicans, intentionally adopting names and practices that allowed them to remain welcoming and inclusive across partisan lines. Among Democrats too they practiced pragmatic inclusivity. In contrast to the factional battles at the Democratic National Committee and in some state Democratic Parties as well as on social media, in these local groups former Bernie and Hillary supporters— joined by others who supported neither—spent little time rehashing the past. Shock at the November 2016 results and horror at the stances and rhetoric of President Donald Trump drove their start. But the time spent on venting about 2016 was everywhere limited, as people asked what could be done to get democracy back on track: and found answers right in front of them.

More than a national movement, then, what Trump's election sparked among the mothers, grandmothers, and allies of Middle America was a nationwide pattern of mutually energizing local engagement. Sociologically, it was an inflection point—a shift in long-standing trends—concentrated in one large demographic group, as college-educated women ramped up their political participation en masse. The visible collective protests they joined in response to national events were just one piece of a far more consequential rebuilding of the face-to-face structures of political life that the same people very quickly took up. Suburban women were leaning in, and their little-d democratic commitments were as important as their capital-D Democratic alignment.

The Local Electoral Turn

If you spent time around people like Nancy Reynolds, the national messaging from the Women's March and Indivisible, which began announcing it was "time to turn to elections" as January 2018 loomed, seemed weirdly clueless about the very people they purported to lead. By January 2018 many of the local groups whose emergence had been linked to Indivisible and the Women's March a year earlier were already ten months into an electoral turn. They had one election cycle under their belt, and concrete targets in their sights for 2018, 2019, and 2020.

Although weekly protests—such as the "Tuesdays with Toomey" events across Pennsylvania in which groups of activists gathered with signs, chants, and song at the offices of Republican senator Pat Toomey to make their concerns known—might have seemed to be the simple enactment of a national "resistance" agenda, in fact these gatherings reinforced personal connections that sped local engagement. Weekly protests turned out to provide the ideal setting for incubating electoral plans, as participants shared knowledge about incumbents and potential candidates, discussed the strengths and weaknesses of organizational allies, and turned weak ties created through Facebook into strong personal bonds.[9] It is not surprising that Americans who reported attending protests were nearly ten times as likely as non-rally-goers to report having volunteered for a political party, candidate, or campaign.[10] Not only were folks inclined to do the one already more inclined to the other, but the very act of showing up to protest built contacts that pulled people deeper into activism.[11]

And that activism offered schooling in turn. As a federal polity with multiple gerrymandered layers, the United States is maze of overlapping, oddly shaped jurisdictions that do not line up well with natural communities—a fact that came to the fore for the new local activists who had taken it on themselves to work face to face (rather than just via clicks and links) to contact officeholders and change electoral equations. "Pop up" groups rapidly coalesced around the multiple geographic units that make up the elections system, from wards to townships to counties. In the greater Pittsburgh area alone, for instance, about three dozen such groups had emerged and engaged by summer 2017. This might seem a sign of disorganization or factionalism, but on the ground was recognizable as a logical reflection of their pragmatic focus on local elections, given the distinct but overlapping geographies these involved. The need to contest "every seat, every election" became a mantra among activists in red or purple communities, who were appalled by the range of elective offices they discovered all around them for which Democrats had stopped even fielding candidates over the preceding decade.

They made remarkable progress, first visible in the kind of affluent "country club Republican" suburbs that had voted for Mitt Romney in 2012 but Hillary Clinton in 2016, and then with increasing impact beyond that peri-metropolitan core as the 2018 midterm campaigns gained steam.[12] As activists expanded their knowledge of local politics with stunning speed in the tumultuous first half of 2017, they recruited and supported Democratic candidates for offices ranging from coroner to borough council member to state senator. In states like Virginia and New Jersey where state legislatures were up for reelection in that year, grassroots dived into those campaigns with a vengeance.[13] Meanwhile, in every US congressional district where current Republican incumbents coincided with a critical mass of left-leaning grandmothers, district-defined grassroots groups— such as "PA 12 for Progress" and "PA 18 for Progress" (renamed Progress PA and Partners for Progress SWPA in the wake of Pennsylvania's court-ordered redistricting in February 2018)—formed, seeking to vote those incumbents out of office. In turn, statewide umbrella organizations—like Pennsylvania Together, a statewide coalition encompassing over a hundred new grassroots groups, or Virginia Grassroots Coalition, which brought together a similar number— emerged to share resources and build capacity, hosting regional training sessions in different parts of the state, leadership Slack channels, conference-call webinars, and more.[14]

Pennsylvania Together identified more than sixty candidates who ran for local or municipal office in Pennsylvania with new grassroots groups' support in November 2017. Most were first-time candidates; more than half were women; four out of five won.[15] That last fact is all the more striking because the candidates were often running in places presumed to be so heavily Republican that Democrats hadn't fielded campaigns there in recent memory. In Chester County, a large exurban and rural county west of Philadelphia, Democratic candidates swept row offices that Republicans had carried with an average 17-point margin of victory in 2015. School boards and township councils that had not had Democratic members in decades now did, sometimes, in the majority.[16] In Virginia, where all one hundred House of Delegates seats were up for election in fall 2017, Democratic candidates flipped fifteen seats to come within one vote of a majority.[17]

How did they do it? Relying organically on what social movement theorists call "relational organizing," the newly active volunteers mobilized existing social networks to pull in newcomers and needed expertise.[18] As they did so, they connected with organizations that had been at political work far longer, including organized labor (like the Service Employees International Union) in states where labor was strong, and progressive advocacy groups (including ones centered on immigrants' rights, race, or economic justice) in others. These partners shared with the new grassroots not just their organizing expertise but— critically—their hard-won semi-insider knowledge of their regions' political establishments and power centers.

Although mostly political novices, new grassroots group members brought a very useful array of transferrable skills to the table. The fact that professional women from mid-life to retirement years comprised the strong majority of new leaders and activists meant that even those with no prior experience in

politics had lifetimes of experience in working for change within existing systems. In contrast to some of the national voices embraced as spokespersons
of the "Resistance," the new hands-on grassroots were pervasively pragmatic.
These were individuals who had honed their skills in the "slow boring of hard
boards," to use Max Weber's definition of politics, over years of professional and
community life, and now brought those skills to bear full-strength on local political action.

Democratic Party officials seemed notably less sophisticated about how
organizing works. Nancy Reynolds, the retired librarian, labored throughout the
fall of 2017 alongside a tight network of women (their partnership forged on a
chartered bus to the January 2017 Women's March) to power phone canvassing
and door-knocking across Hampton Township. They elected three Democrats
to a five-person township council that had been all Republican as long as anyone
could remember. As Reynolds tried to explain to a party strategist aggrieved that
the party's online calling tools went unused, "My friends won't make calls for
you. They'll make calls for me." In this exchange, as in many others we witnessed,
the ones who seemed to need education in political organizing were the nominal
political professionals. The amateurs already understood what works.

Revitalizing the Local Democratic Party

With their communications networks reaching down to the local level and
laterally across districts, the new grassroots pop-up groups made it easy for
campaigns to connect with volunteers. Indeed, not infrequently it was already-
organized volunteers who showed up at the candidate's door demanding to
be helpful—or had recruited them to run in the first place.[19] Unsurprisingly,
candidates made eager use of these connections. In contrast, while in some
places local Democratic establishments welcomed the new grassroots, in others
they did not. As one group leader in Pennsylvania responded on a 2017 questionnaire, "Local Dems are not very interested in us. Believe it or not."

Although not all newly energized activists identify as Democrats, as noted
earlier, most do—and all of them represent an opportunity for enlarging
the party's ranks. But what exactly was there for them to join? In theory, the
Democratic Party recognizes the importance of sustained local relationships.
The "Precinct Committee Person Guide" distributed by the Pennsylvania
Democratic Party, for instance, suggests elected committeepersons should
greet families who move into their precinct and visit every Democrat in the
precinct regularly as well as before elections in particular.[20] But in recent years
such steps have only rarely been carried out. Indeed, in many places, elective
committeeperson slots remained empty year after year. Unlike the party officials

who simply shrug and move on when confronted with such gaps, the new grassroots groups—in place after place—set out to reanimate, or create, the local party capacities they found missing.

As we conducted interviews in 2017 and 2018, the Democratic Party insiders, political consultants, and national leaders we spoke to seemed strikingly uninterested in the evidence that a surge of hands-on, face-to-face *organizing*—not just "enthusiasm"—might have something to do with recent electoral victories, or could be relevant to future prospects. They still seemed focused on monetizing popular energy and hoarding contact lists, treating volunteers as interchangeable labor for last-minute door knocking. Each of us witnessed, or had related to us, numerous conversations between party officials and grassroots leaders in which the officials trumpeted new tools for digital "engagement" and then tuned out entirely when grassroots groups described their struggles to get even the most basic answers to simple logistical questions: like when local party committees meet, how decisions are made, and who can participate in an ongoing way. It was as if the insiders and consultants saw the interpersonal dimensions of political mobilization as a black box, about which nothing could be known or done.

This lack of curiosity from party insiders is mystifying, because organizations can do *lots* to help (or hinder) peer-to-peer bonds. Amway gets this. The National Rifle Association gets it. Academic sociology and political science recognize "relational organizing" and "social capital" as powerful drivers of political change.[21] Yet Democratic Party professionals seemed insistently unaware that structures facilitating sustained interpersonal engagement might matter for the short- and long-term success of their party and its candidates. In an era in which political consultants get big-ticket contracts to work with Big Data, as far as we can tell, as of 2019 the party was still not gathering even the most basic *small* data about local membership or the party efforts that could nurture or leverage ongoing participation.

Party leaders could fruitfully have asked: How many state party constitutions provide for ways of joining locally that can be scaled up beyond the finite number of elected committee slots? How many elected committeeperson seats are currently vacant? How many elected ward or township committees meet regularly? How many people attend? In the battleground state that is Pennsylvania—and in light of all the research confirming the importance of participatory mobilization—you might assume some party official would have been gathering and tracking such numbers, or at least worrying about how to start doing so. As far as we know, you would be wrong.

Indeed the private citizens we met seemed much more convinced than party leaders of the importance of local party structures. With remarkable regularity, new activists mentioned unbidden that one or more of their group members would be running or had just successfully run for their local party committee.

Once there, some worked to create further membership options, such as standing committees to which volunteers might be appointed. Although in some places women's and youth groups, chartered Democratic clubs, and "associate member" categories already existed to make expandable affiliation possible, in many others no such structures existed. Maintaining an artificial scarcity of membership slots—as happens when the elective committeeperson seats are the only option open—means that each new entrant into the party has to kick out someone already there. That's no way to build a movement.

Thus, across 2018, while national Democratic Party insiders were worrying about pledged delegate/superdelegate rules, grassroots people were obsessing instead about how to get empty seats filled on local committees: or how to pry open ironclad local machines that keep a lock on them. New York City saw particularly heated battles.[22] Yet far beyond blue metropoles, rural and rust belt counties with one-twentieth of the population of Queens or Brooklyn (even less than that if you count just Democrats), also saw cases of drama and insurgence around county committee leadership elections.[23] Grassroots activists had decided that a seat at the table was worth fighting for, even though the national party that put the tables out in the first place seemed not to think they mattered much at all.

Campaigns as Crossroads

The new grassroots helped propel upstart challengers to victory in suburban municipal elections and in Virginia and New Jersey's state legislative elections in November 2017, and in special elections like that of Doug Jones in Alabama in December 2017.[24] For municipal offices that had never seen active campaigns, much less full-on battle plans, they mapped precincts on whiteboards, begged access to the Democratic/progressive database VoteBuilder, and embraced door-to-door canvassing weekend after weekend. Whether knocking doors close to home or in an adopted district, some labor-of-love volunteers tended to veer off into the kind of deep conversations that "ground game" professionals find unjustifiable in terms of short-term payoff.[25] Grassroots group members were not only powering electoral campaigns forward but also being shaped by the experience.[26]

This dynamic was vivid in the special election held in March 2018 in Pennsylvania's eighteenth congressional district (PA 18), a Trump+20 mix of cosmopolitan suburbs, conservative exurbs, and former labor strongholds in southwestern Pennsylvania unexpectedly left vacant after Republican incumbent Tim Murphy's resigned amid scandal in October 2017. The campaign that would carry Democrat Conor Lamb to razor-thin victory there five months later was powered by two Democratic constituencies routinely portrayed as irreconcilable: college-educated suburban progressives and traditional blue-collar labor. They were not reconciled by some magic "messaging" that brought out the inner centrist in all: policy views among these different activist cores remained diverse and often divergent. It turned out, that didn't matter. As witnessed by those in the trenches, it was neither the message nor the messenger that made this congressional election different from the past. It was the organizations and conversations that surrounded them.

The movement to "Flip the 18th" was well underway before Lamb ever appeared. Grassroots democracy groups had been mobilizing in the suburbs south of Pittsburgh since the start of 2017, seeking a challenger to Murphy, who had run unopposed in 2014 and 2016.[27] Within the district, the new groups were thickest on the ground in PA 18's affluent Allegheny County suburbs, which had been trending more liberal for years. Yet even deep red Westmoreland County had the "Voice of Westmoreland," a grassroots group founded by three angry and inspired women in response to the same national events that drove such groups elsewhere. (The organizing core had come together on the frigid last weekend of January 2017. Driving through Greensburg, in despair over the "Muslim ban" just announced, nurse Angela Aldous was shocked to see a tiny cluster of protesters at the county courthouse in the snow. She pulled to the curb, jumped out, and joined them. The group has not let up since.)[28] In PA 18's center-west, the new independent Washington County Democrats club had powered up over the same months.[29]

An unusually diverse set of seven candidates—including two women and an African American psychologist and professor—stepped forward to run for Murphy's seat.[30] The nominating convention gathered all empaneled Democratic committeepersons in the congressional district. In a radical departure from previous inattention, the convention was streamed live on Facebook, while intent conversations on a half dozen closed grassroots Facebook groups tracked each round's vote totals, with real-time reports from those group members who had already gotten themselves appointed to vacant committee seats. Conor Lamb, young marine veteran and assistant US attorney from an established western Pennsylvania political family, had not necessarily been the top favorite among the grassroots women who had been protesting outside Tim Murphy's southern suburb office since January. Yet once Lamb was selected, they dived in to support him. As Lamb would herald with a grin at the start of his late-night nailbiter victory speech four months later, grassroots leaders reached out immediately after his selection, before any staff was even in place. " 'Print us something! Print anything, so we can get out there and start canvassing,' they said. 'Get *going*,' they said, 'or we're going without you.' Well, we went together."[31]

Organized labor stepped in as well. Emphasizing Lamb's strong support for organizing rights, pensions, and jobs, the Steelworkers, United Mine Workers of America, Service Employees International Union, and local Labor Councils began independent campaigns to reach union households across the district's steel and coal belts.[32]

In the abstract, the policy priorities of suburban moms and mineworkers might seem difficult to square. But politics do not happen in the abstract. Politics happen in carpools and smoke breaks and endless planning sessions. People make their choices about who to support and how much effort to give within a web of personal ties. In PA 18, those personal relationships had to mobilize again and again, as outside Republican groups, spending more than $10 million over the course of the campaign, sought to use gun control, fracking, and abortion as wedge issues to alienate the women in the suburbs or blue-collar men outside them, and dampen support for Lamb's campaign. Time after time, conversations with friends reeled people back when polarization loomed. In the wake of the Parkland shooting, Lamb sat down with local Moms Demand Action members and anguished grassroots leaders. Over the following days reassurance travelled from mouth to mouth, as Lamb's grassroots stalwarts worked through the nuance of his position, and reminded each other how much worse Saccone, with his NRA A+ rating, would be. Even last-minute stealth mailers by the NRA did not shake that resolve.[33]

Meanwhile, those of us canvassing in Washington County and Greene County heard echoes of a separate set of conversations—likewise carried along preexisting personal ties—among union members, as they reassured each other that this time, this Democrat shared the values that mattered most. "Me and the guys down at the shop were just talking about him!" "I walk with the Silver Sneakers every week, there are other veterans there too. We're pretty impressed with that young Marine." "A group of us retirees from the plant get together every week: One in leadership was talking about Lamb and pensions." "We'll spread the news down at the Fish Fry."

On Election Day, Conor Lamb outperformed Hillary Clinton by about 19 percentage points in Allegheny County, Westmoreland County, and Washington County, and by about 26 in Greene County. Tellingly, it was the elevated number of pro-Lamb absentee ballots from the Allegheny County suburbs that pushed him over the top: testimony to the months of micro-level interactions that had gotten an unusual number of kids off at college and folks traveling for work to power through Pennsylvania's cumbersome absentee vote process. The massive ground campaign that made Lamb's victory happen drew on relational ties and new organizational infrastructure. It pulled unfamiliar allies together and shaped their knowledge of each other as it did so. "Enthusiasm" doesn't get absentee ballot request forms into the hands of would-be voters on time to be cast and counted in an off-season election. Organization does. "Moderation" doesn't ensure suburban moms and retired mineworkers will discover the common ground they share. Conversations do. And ongoing local organizations can carry their insights forward.[34]

Infrastructural Boost, Not Ideological Swing

The new layers of connection and on-ramps to engagement that grassroots groups have generated through their diverse local initiatives have strengthened civic infrastructure and enriched regional political ecosystems. This had divergent results in different settings. The spring 2018 primaries saw grassroots groups in some Democratic strongholds (like New York) oust incumbents perceived as blocking the way to pro-democracy reform.[35] Meanwhile, those groups' counterparts in deep-red districts worked overtime just to get Democrats on the ballot to contest seats whose Republican incumbents were used to winning unopposed.[36] The grassroots organizers who carried red-district campaigns forward were in it for the long game, often supporting candidates they recognized as "right for the district" even when those candidates' positions or priorities differed from their own.

As a result, the ideological coordinates of candidates supported by post-Trump grassroots groups have varied widely, even while the underlying forces buoying them are consistent.[37] A generational inflection point had brought a mass of regular people into active political engagement, who became committed to fighting for better government up and down the ballot, right where they were, wherever that was.

In the spring of 2018, our first report on the findings presented here appeared online in the *Democracy Journal*. We heard from grassroots groups in Alabama, Arkansas, California, Illinois, Indiana, Iowa, Maryland, Massachusetts, Minnesota, Missouri, New York, North Carolina, Oregon, Vermont, Virginia, and Washington State. They reached out to say that they found their own experiences echoed in our words, sometimes for the first time in print.

By fall 2018, the role of new grassroots groups in channeling volunteers into midterm election campaigns had become fully visible.[38] By Election Day, canvassers for Democratic candidates up and down the ballot and allied progressive groups had knocked on 155 million doors nationwide: a 60 percent increase over the 2014 midterm year and fully 40 percent higher than in the presidential year of 2016.[39] Less visibly, the pop-up leaders and grassroots groups of 2017 had made significant strides towards repopulating the local layer of the Democratic Party in much of the country. That process (explored in more detail in chapter 13) has been smooth and cooperative in some places, conflictive or fraught in others. New grassroots energies have had the freest reign and found the easiest welcome outside the metropolitan cores where Democratic patronage structures still persist. Purple suburbs, big towns in red regions—these have been the unexpected epicenters of post-November 2016 political transformation. The cumulative result has impacted local-level Democratic leadership across the country, as the newcomers make the ranks of party "insiders" somewhat more progressive and much more female, although not much more socioeconomically diverse. The new arrivals have disparate ideological orientations and varied issue priorities. Where they coincide, consistently, is in their passion for procedural democracy: their determination to fight gerrymandering, regulate campaign activities and finance, and expand and guarantee voting rights for all.

This particular revolution fits no simple ideological formula. It is playing out to different effects in diverse districts across the country. Yet on the ground in most places, it looks a lot like retired librarians rolling their eyes, pushing up their sleeves, pulling out their calendars, and stepping in to get America's democracy back on course.

Notes

1. This chapter includes material originally published in an essay co-authored with Theda Skocpol, "Middle America Reboots Democracy," *Democracy: A Journal of Ideas*, Summer 2018, as well as a sole-authored piece, "Who Really Won PA 18?" *Democracy: A Journal of Ideas*, March 15, 2018. I am grateful to Skocpol and her collaborator Leah E. Gose for sharing key findings, and to *Democracy* for permission to adapt those articles here. My thanks also go to the many activists, candidates, and staff who took time from their urgent work to share insights with me. Jed Kolko, "How Suburban Are Big American Cities?" *FiveThirtyEight*, May 21, 2015.
2. "An Examination of the 2016 Electorate, Based on Validated Voters," Pew Research Center Report, August 9, 2018.
3. In addition to our own research, local reporting captured similar experiences across the country. See for example Will Bunch, "The 'Good Girls Revolt' Is the Untold Political Story of 2017," *Philadelphia Inquirer*, December 19, 2016; Elizabeth Flock, "A Women's Movement Grows in 'the Most Trumpian Place in America,'" *PBS Newshour*, May 30, 2017; Campbell Robertson, "These Women Mostly Ignored Politics. Now, Activism Is Their Job," *New York Times*, May 10, 2018; Nicholas Riccardi, "Resistance Makes Subtle Impact Even Where Trump Is Popular," Associated Press, May 26, 2018; and Judy Keen, "New Hyperlocal Political Force Emerges in Minnesota, Across U.S.," *Minneapolis Star Tribune*, July 21, 2018.
4. Leah E. Gose and Theda Skocpol, "Resist, Persist, and Transform: The Emergence and Impact of Grassroots Resistance Groups Opposing the Trump Presidency," *Mobilization: An International Journal* 24, no. 3 (2019): 293–317 Available at https://counties.gov.harvard.edu/publications/resist-persist-and-transform.
5. Further details on the methodology of this survey are found in Gose and Skocpol, "Resist, Persist, and Transform," 298–300.
6. Megan Brooker, "Indivisible: Invigorating and Redirecting the Grassroots," in *The Resistance: The Dawn of the Anti-Trump Opposition Movement*, ed. David S. Meyer and Sidney Tarrow (New York: Oxford University Press, 2018), 162–84; Hahrie Han and Michelle Oyakawa, "Constituency and Leadership in the Evolution of Resistance Organizations," in Meyer and Tarrow, *Resistance*, 230–45.
7. Gideon Lewis-Kraus, "How the 'Resistance' Helped Democrats Dominate Virginia," *New York Times*, November 13, 2017.
8. Interview with Christina Beam Proctor, March 15, 2018.

9. Nancy Solomon, "Trump Changed How These Suburbanites Feel About Politics," WNYC News, October 12, 2017.

10. *"Washington Post*–Kaiser Family Foundation Survey on Political Rallygoing and Activism, Jan. 24–Feb. 22, 2018," p. 12. Available at http://apps.washingtonpost.com/g/page/national/washington-post-kaiser-family-foundation-survey-on-political-rallygoing-and-activism-jan-24-feb-22-2018/2298/, as of June 11, 2019. For details on poll, see Mary Jordan and Scott Clement, "Rallying Nation: In Reaction to Trump, Millions of Americans Are Joining Protests and Getting Political," *Washington Post*, April 6, 2018.

11. On the synergies and overlap between protesting and organizing see Dana Fisher, "This Year's Women's Marchers Weren't Focused on the Leadership Controversy. They Were All About Local and National Political Organizing," *Monkey Cage*, January 22, 2019.

12. See Lara Putnam and Gabriel Perez-Putnam, "What Dollar Stores Tell Us about Electoral Politics," *Washington Monthly*, March 9, 2019.

13. Garance Franke-Ruta, "Women's Anger Transformed the 2017 Elections. Get Ready for 2018," *YAHOO! News*, November 14, 2017.

14. See Virginia Grassroots Coalition website, available at https://www.virginiagrassroots.org/vgr-organizations.php as of June 11, 2019; Pennsylvania Together website, available at http://www.patogether.org/ as of June 11, 2019; "Harnessing the Resistance: Building Grassroots Power Across Pennsylvania," America Votes blog post, *Medium*, October 30, 2018.

15. Hannah Burton Laurison, personal communication, November 20, 2017; Katie Meyer, "The Trump Resistance Works to Find Its Feet in Pa," WITF, May 15, 2017.

16. Marc Levy, "Pennsylvania Democrats See Anti-Trump Zeal in Election Wins," Associated Press, November 8, 2017.

17. Danny Hayes and Jennifer Lawless, "In Tuesday's Elections, Women Won Big. Here Are Three Things We Learned about Women in Politics," *Monkey Cage*, November 9, 2017.

18. See for example Michael Ganz, "Organizing Obama: Campaign, Organization, Movement," Proceedings of the American Sociological Association Annual Meeting, San Francisco, CA, August 8–11, 2009, permanent URL http://nrs.harvard.edu/urn-3:HUL.InstRepos:27306258. Available at https://dash.harvard.edu/bitstream/handle/1/27306258/Organizing-Obama-Final.pdf?sequence=1 as of June 11, 2019; Mark R. Warren, *Dry Bones Rattling: Community Building to Revitalize American Democracy* (Princeton, NJ: Princeton University Press, 2010).

19. For example, see Lewis-Kraus, "How the 'Resistance' Helped Democrats Dominate Virginia."

20. Pennsylvania Democratic Party, "Precinct Committee Person Guide & Resources," Version 2017.1.0. Available at http://beavercountydemocrats.com/wp-content/uploads/2017/10/Precinct-Person-Handbook-2017-2-2.pdf as of June 9, 2019.

21. Robert D. Putnam, *Bowling Alone: The Collapse and Revival of American Community* (New York: Simon & Schuster, 2000); Theda Skocpol, *Diminished Democracy: From Membership to Management in American Civic Life* (Norman: University of Oklahoma Press, 2003); Hahrie Han and Elizabeth McKenna, *Groundbreakers: How Obama's 2.2 Million Volunteers Transformed Campaigning in America* (New York: Oxford University Press, 2014).

22. Andy Newman and Tyler Pager, "How a Political Machine Works: Candidates Running for 21 Seats, All Unaware," *New York Times*, August 24, 2018; Martika Ornella and David Cruz, "Getting a Seat at the Bronx County Committee Table," *Norwood News*, June 26, 2018; Tyler Pager, "Democrats Turned Up in Record Numbers. But One Man Held All the Power," *New York Times*, September 30, 2018; Mark Chiusano, "'I Wouldn't Know Who to Ask': Trying to Join Queens County Committee," *AM NewYork*, September 4, 2018. Available at https://www.amny.com/opinion/columnists/mark-chiusano/example-headlines-1.20837818 as of June 12, 2019.

23. Melissa Klaris, "Mercer County Democrats Face Eviction from Headquarters over Unpaid Rent," [Shenango Valley] *Herald*, May 21, 2018. Available at https://www.sharonherald.com/news/local_news/mercer-county-democrats-face-eviction-from-headquarters-over-unpaid-rent/article_08a5b3d6-96a4-542b-a302-cb3420fb3165.html .

24. Charles Bethea, "How the Trump Resistance Went Pro in Alabama," *New Yorker*, December 15, 2017.

25. Joshua Kalla and David E. Broockman, "The Minimal Persuasive Effects of Campaign Contact in General Elections: Evidence from 49 Field Experiments," *American Political Science Review* 112, no. 1 (February 2018): 148–66; Betsy Sinclair, Margaret McConnell, and Melissa R. Michelson, "Local Canvassing: The Efficacy of Grassroots Voter Mobilization," *Journal of Political Communication* 30, no. 1 (2013): 42–57; and Maggie Koerth-Baker, "Why Politicians Don't Always Listen to Political Scientists," *FiveThirtyEight*, October 18, 2018.

26. Lara Putnam, "The Progressive Base Is More Pragmatic Than You Might Think," Vox, March 25, 2019.

27. Ryan Deto, "Since President Donald Trump's Election, a Grassroots Uprising Has Grown in All Corners of the Pittsburgh Region, and Women Are Leading the Charge," *Pittsburgh City Paper*, December 20, 2017; and Garance Franke-Ruta, "The Resistance is Organized and Ready in District Where Trump Is Visiting," *YAHOO! News*, January 18, 2018.

28. Interview with Angela Aldous, August 25, 2018.

29. One of the Washington County group's leaders' trajectory is quoted in note 8.

30. Chris Potter, "Democrats Choose Conor Lamb, a Former Federal Prosecutor, to Replace Tim Murphy," *Pittsburgh Post-Gazette*, November 19, 2017.

31. "Democrat Conor Lamb Declares Victory in PA Special Election," MSNBC, March 14, 2018. Video available at https://www.msnbc.com/brian-williams/watch/democrat-conor-lamb-declares-victory-in-pa-special-election-1185359427787.

32. Bridget Bowman, "Can Unions Push Conor Lamb to an Unlikely Victory in Pennsylvania?" *Roll Call*, March 8, 2018.

33. Emily Goodin, "NRA Drops Last-Minute Money for GOP Candidate into Pennsylvania Special Election," ABC News, March 13, 2018.

34. Sometimes groups very intentionally send insights forward to help others—for example, by writing them up and sharing, as in this document put together by canvassers from the Pittsburgh-based "Order of the Phoenix" in the wake of Lamb's special election: Elaine Kramer, Marie Norman, Sara Segel, Nathaniel Yap, "Key Takeaways from Our PA18 Experience by the Order of the Phoenix," unpublished document available at https://docs.google.com/document/d/1fYTL04F2sHZnkZFf3i4Eabei1AFzpmkTw77kUel9lAU/edit as of June 11, 2019. An example from the Virginia Grassroots Coalition is "Lessons Learned from the 2017 Virginia Elections 2.0: How the Grassroots Helped Flip VA Blue," March 2018, unpublished document available at http://virginiagrassroots.org/lessonslearned/Lessons-Learned-2017-Virginia-Elections-v2.pdf as of June 11, 2019.

35. Vivian Wang, "Democratic Insurgents Topple 6 New York Senate Incumbents," *New York Times*, September 13, 2018; and Masha Gessen, "A Triumphant Primary Night for Julia Salazar and the D.S.A. in Brooklyn," *New Yorker*, September 14, 2018.

36. Ryan Grim, "Real Resistance: A Grassroots Uprising in Amish Country Begins to Find Meaning in Politics," *The Intercept*, September 15, 2018; Brian Barth, "Sometimes It's Lonely Being Liberal," *American Prospect*, October 29, 2018; and Daniel Block, "The Democrats of Trump Country: How Liberals in the Reddest Parts of America Are Starting to Get Their Groove Back," *Washington Monthly*, November-December 2018.

37. Michelle Goldberg, "The Millennial Socialists Are Coming," *New York Times*, June 30, 2018; Michelle Goldberg, "Women Might Save America Yet," *New York Times*, July 2, 2018; Paul Rosenberg, "Beneath the Blue Wave in Orange County: Not Just about House Races in Longtime GOP Stronghold," *Salon*, August 26, 2018; and Nancy Solomon, "Meet the Women of the Suburban Resistance," *WNYC News*, October 17, 2018.

38. Charlotte Alter, "How the Anti-Trump Resistance Is Organizing Its Outrage," *Time*, October 18, 2018; Molly Hensley-Clancy, "Suburban Women Are Fed Up with the Republican Party and Could Drive a Blue Wave," BuzzFeed News, October 16, 2018; Michael Scherer and David Weigel, "'Blue Wave' or 'Left-Wing Mob'? Anti-Trump Fervor Fuels a New Movement Aimed Squarely at Winning Elections," *Washington Post*, October 15, 2018; Kate Zernike, "The Year of the Woman's Activism: Marches, Phone Banks, Postcards, More," *New York Times*, November 3, 2018; and Campbell Robertson, "'I Don't Even Know What to Think': The Whiplash of Watching the Election Results," *New York Times*, November 7, 2018.

39. Data provided by NGP VAN, personal communication, November 8, 2018.

9

Saving America Once Again, from the Tea Party to the Anti-Trump Resistance

LEAH E. GOSE, THEDA SKOCPOL, AND VANESSA WILLIAMSON

"We always voted, but being busy people, we just didn't keep as involved as maybe we should have. And now we're to the point where we're really worried about our country. I feel like we came out of retirement. We do Tea Party stuff to take the country back to where we think it should be."

—Arizona husband (age 69) and wife (age 67) who organized a Tea Party in April 2009

"I had always been a consistent . . . voter [and] . . . donated to my party . . . [but] I had not been super involved. I felt secure that we had reasonable and competent leadership in Washington. Even the ones I disagreed with . . . Then, the presidential campaign in 2016 became more and more ridiculous, and frightening— and . . . our very worst nightmare happened. My life changed overnight on November 8th. My peace of mind was robbed from me. I was called to action . . . I feel like a soldier in a war, trying to save this country, my children's future, the climate!"

—Wisconsin woman (age 55) who organized a resistance group soon after the 2016 election

Twice in the brief span of eight years, the United States witnessed massive protests and political organizing across much of the country. Professionally run advocacy groups mobilized both times, but—more remarkably—ordinary Americans voluntarily organized new local groups out of alarm about the nation's future. Their efforts are remaking US politics on both the right and left.

The first wave of "Tea Party" citizen organizing happened after the November 2008 election of Barack Obama and a large Democratic congressional majority. Elected with high levels of support from minorities and young people,

Leah E. Gose, *Theda Skocpol, and Vanessa Williamson, Saving America Once Again, from the Tea Party to the Anti-Trump Resistance* In: *Upending American Politics* Edited by: Theda Skocpol and Caroline Tervo, Oxford University Press (2020). © Oxford University Press
DOI: 10.1093/oso/9780190083526.003.0009

Barack Obama, a black man with an immigrant father and a history as a community organizer and liberal college professor, provoked fear and anger among many Republicans and other conservatives. They were worried that government efforts would soon move in liberal directions in areas ranging from economic recovery to heath care, immigration, and environmental regulation. Within months, grassroots conservatives went beyond attending protest rallies to organizing about a thousand locally meeting Tea Parties spread all over the United States.[1] In the 2010 midterm elections, Tea Partiers helped catalyze Republican victories that installed many like-minded politicians in the US Congress and state legislatures, well positioned to stymie Obama-era initiatives.

Another surge of activism, this time from the left, followed the November 2016 election to the presidency of a highly controversial GOP nominee, reality-TV star and real estate impresario Donald J. Trump. The incoming president promised draconian new restrictions on immigration and minority rights; and with Republican majorities in Congress poised to pass bills for his signature, it seemed a forgone conclusion that social safety net programs and environmental regulations would quickly be slashed, along with the taxes paid by the wealthy and corporations. Opponents started organizing at once, and the day after the inauguration, massive Women's Marches happened in Washington, DC, and hundreds of other places.[2] Even more remarkably, ordinary liberal-minded Americans followed scripts similar to those used by Tea Partiers eight years earlier to found thousands of new local resistance groups from late 2016 into 2017.

Making Sense of Two Electorally Sparked Movements

The authors of this chapter include two political scientists, Skocpol and Williamson, who, some years ago, did original research on the Tea Party, including interviews and field visits with local leaders and participants as well as examinations of national surveys and media coverage.[3] Now Skocpol and Williamson are working with sociologist Leah Gose to do similar research on the anti-Trump resistance, using evidence from online questionnaires gathered from dozens of resistance group organizers as well as insights from local field visits and national media and organizational sources. Drawing on these studies, this chapter uses the trajectory of the Tea Party to pose questions about today's anti-Trump resistance. The Tea Party showed that popular revulsion against a dreaded, newly installed US president and DC partisan order could give way to sustained, widely networked organizational efforts and growing clout on the far right. Are similar—or different—dynamics now afoot in the anti-Trump resistance?

Of particular interest are several critical issues. As anti-Trump efforts have moved beyond national protests and marches into sustained citizen-led organizing, who are the leaders and participants in such undertakings? Are their social backgrounds as well as their outlooks markedly different from earlier Tea Party citizen organizers? In addition, are local resistance efforts concentrated in liberal states or left-leaning enclaves, such as larger cities and college towns? Or have grassroots resistance organizations spread through all US states in ways that parallel the wide extent of Tea Party organizing starting in 2009?

We have been especially curious to learn whether today's grassroots resistance organizing efforts either reflect—and thus exacerbate—preexisting divides built into US political geography, or else cut against and to some degree soften such divides. Partisan sorting in the early twenty-first-century United States has left conservatives and Republicans dominating much of the interior and non-metropolitan parts of the country, while liberals and Democrats hold sway on the coasts and in the bigger cities.[4] Two successive waves of citizen organizing from the right and left could have the effect of simply deepening such geographically inscribed divisions. Yet that is not what our research shows is happening so far.

Grassroots anti-Trump organizing, we find, is just as widespread as earlier Tea Party organizing. In today's overall resistance to the Trump-GOP regime, national advocacy group efforts often do reflect metropolitan brands of progressivism, but many empirical indications suggest that grassroots resistance organizing crosses geopolitical divides and unites moderates, liberals, and progressives of many stripes. As a result, grassroots resistance efforts have tended to enhance citizen engagement in center-left politics without pushing the Democratic Party as much toward left extremes as Tea Party mobilizations pushed Republicans toward the far right.

Anti-Trump resistance efforts are still unfolding, of course, so we can only offer preliminary answers here about their ongoing effects. Even so, our past and current research allows us to offer fascinating comparisons of today's resistance groups and activities to those of the post-2008 Tea Party. We first focus on who organized, why, how, and where. Then we pinpoint important similarities and differences between these two movements, before finally considering their larger, ongoing political reverberations.

Who Has Organized—When, Why, and Where?

"Who organizes?" is almost invariably the first question posed by observers of social movements. Answers for the Tea Party and anti-Trump resistance are complicated by the fact that both include loosely coupled concatenations of mutually leveraging top-down and bottom-up organizations.[5] Professionally run donor and advocacy operations figured visibly in each endeavor, but the more interesting and unusual developments have happened in the form of voluntary citizen organizing at the grassroots level.

The Tea Party Reaction to Obama and Democrats

Initial conservative protests against the Obama administration started soon after the January 2009 inauguration, at first without any unifying symbolism. A mid-February rally in Seattle, for instance, decried "Porkulus" economic recovery spending, while signs spotted a few days later in Mesa, Arizona, complained of a "leftist power grab."[6] Then, on February 19, 2009, CNBC reporter Rick Santelli staged an outburst on live television against the new Obama administration's mortgage assistance policies. Lamenting that the government was "rewarding bad behavior," Santelli invited viewers—America's "capitalists"—to join a "Chicago Tea Party."[7] National conservative advocacy groups including FreedomWorks soon echoed this call; and Fox News and other conservative media outlets spread information about the time and place of planned rallies.[8] By Tax Day in mid-April 2009, between four hundred thousand and eight hundred thousand Americans staged protests in some 542 counties across the country.[9] Additional public protests happened periodically thereafter, including around the Fourth of July and during the Tea Party's first March on Washington in September 2009. By broadcasting "Tea Party" symbolism and actively encouraging participation in synchronized public rallies by their viewers and listeners, conservative media helped along much of this anti-Obama activism.

Nevertheless, ongoing local grassroots Tea Party activity from the spring of 2009 was *not* chiefly attributable to efforts by conservative media or professional advocacy organizations. Available evidence suggests that national conservative elites, not to mention Republican Party leaders looking to rebound after big losses in 2008, would have been content with recurrent spectacular, nationally publicized rallies and marches. Such events offered vivid visuals of older white Americans dressed in Colonial costumes and carrying signs angrily denouncing President Obama and Democratic policies as "fascist" or "socialist" threats to America. When such spectacles happened, conservative advocacy leaders or congressional Republicans could go on TV and claim that Tea Partiers supported whatever policies they were pushing at a given time—including measures like cuts to Social Security and Medicare that ordinary Tea Party sympathizers actually did not support. Right-wing elites, in short, would have been happy to use grassroots Tea Partiers as a passive backdrop.

At the grassroots, many conservative citizens were determined to do more than wave signs at occasional rallies. From the spring of 2009 on, like-minded conservative men and women sought each other out to found regularly meeting local Tea Party groups—groups that could keep grassroots opposition to Obama Democrats going month after month and give voice to popular priorities such as immigration restriction or laws outlawing abortion or restricting gay rights. In one place we studied, organizers of a local Tea Party got in touch with one another after a woman published an OpEd in the local newspaper, and a man searched for and found her address. In many other places, local Tea Party founders told us they had met at rallies or on buses to marches or when a driver of a car saw a few neighbors waving Tea Party signs stopped to introduce himself. Once would-be founders met, they tapped personal networks to recruit others, and used email or the internet application MeetUp to advertise and organize local Tea Party meetings.

Such Tea Party networking played out in many hundreds of places. Researchers at the *Washington Post* tallied up to 1,400 "possible" local Tea Parties in the fall of 2010 and managed to contact the organizers of about 650 of them.[10] In the spring of 2011, Skocpol and Williamson and their undergraduate research colleagues at Harvard University found a web presence or other evidence indicating current ongoing activities for more than 950 Tea Parties in all fifty states.[11] When the research team checked back a year later, at least two-thirds of these local Tea Parties were still meeting. Since 2012 Harvard researchers have used extensive web searches to uncover evidence of hundreds more local Tea Parties that met at one point or another—suggesting that a grand total of somewhere between 1,000 and 2,000 groups were organized and active for some stretch of time after 2009. Some Tea Party groups are still active today, close to a decade after their founding.

Most local Tea Parties convened at least once a month in rooms at public libraries, church basements, or the back rooms of friendly local restaurants. Older men and women often participated as couples; and curious newcomers might join regulars in publicly advertised meetings—which started with the Pledge of Allegiance and perhaps a prayer and typically featured invited speakers such as right-wing radio hosts or lecturers from regional or national conservative organizations. During parts of these gatherings, leaders usually notified participants about important upcoming decisions pending in local, state, and national governments; and often they organized teams of members to attend hearings or car pools to take members to lobby days or legislators' town hall meetings. National conservative organizations eventually offered grants to help local groups create websites or transport members to big marches. Nevertheless, funding for local Tea Parties was usually modest, raised from dues or small contributions or by selling baked goods or Tea Party pins and paraphernalia at meetings.

Who were the local organizers and members of Tea Parties? Using survey responses, studies by fellow scholars and information from our own field observations and interviews in New England, Virginia, and Arizona, we arrived at a clear picture.[12] Tea Party activists and general supporters alike were white, middle-class, relatively well-educated Americans, mostly older people in their mid-life to retirement years. Many were currently active in or retired from military careers, small business and construction firms, and white-collar occupations of many kinds. Like conservatives and Republicans overall, Tea Party supporters are disproportionately men, but women are more visible among activists. Many of the local groups we observed had women in their leadership teams and in the ranks of those who set up baked goods tables or organized car pools.

Beyond demographics, Tea Party activists and supporters were longtime conservative-minded citizens.[13] Pollsters were at first confused by the fact that many Tea Party people list their affiliations as "independent" rather than "Republican," but in practice these independents fall to the right of the GOP not in the middle of the US partisan spectrum. Some group leaders and members, the most active core of Tea Party sympathizers, were new to political activism beyond voting, but others had a history of participation in pro-life or other conservative cause groups.

The specific beliefs of Tea Party sympathizers and participants tend to lean in subtle but important ways in directions different even from the beliefs of most conservatives, as political scientists Christopher Parker and Matt Bareto documented.[14] Tea Partiers are more inclined to agree with negative stereotypes about African Americans, immigrants, and Muslims. In their field visits in 2011, Skocpol and Williamson found that Tea Party interviewees were consistently angry about illegal immigration into the United States, which they tended to overestimate. They especially focused their ire and fears on Hispanic newcomers, and frequently invoked disparaging stereotypes about African Americans and made hateful comments about Muslims.

Lastly, both national surveys and our own field interviews have documented another defining characteristic of Tea Party outlooks—an uncompromising approach to conservative politics. Tea Party members believe that many "establishment" or business-friendly Republicans have been too willing to compromise with liberals and Democrats, and they want an end to such squishiness. The very future of America is at stake, they believe, and they want hard-nosed conservatives in government and advocacy politics who will stand firm for such core goals as preventing illegal immigration, deporting undocumented immigrants, enforcing law and order, reinstating conservative Christian versions of family values, and slashing wasteful government welfare spending. Grassroots Tea Partiers vote for Republicans versus Democrats in general elections, but they have been equally determined to push GOP candidates and officeholders into ever more uncompromising stands on their core cultural and ethno-nationalist priorities.[15] Tea Partiers have regularly backed anti-establishment challengers in GOP primaries, and in the 2015-16 presidential election cycle, they were thrilled to get behind Donald Trump for president—setting the stage, as it eventually would turn out, for a new wave of citizen organizing from the left.

The Rise of the Anti-Trump Resistance

Feelings of dismay and disgust gripped millions of liberals and Democrats on the night of November 8, 2016, as Donald Trump claimed a presidential victory in the Electoral College. Hillary Clinton voters anticipated the first woman president, and her loss was a shock to many. In the run-up to the election, almost five million Hillary supporters joined "Pantsuit Nation" Facebook group founded by Libby Chamberlain, through which members could share words of encouragement and pictures of themselves voting for Clinton in pantsuits.[16] After Clinton's loss was evident, Pantsuit posts quickly turned to expressions of grief . . . and then to rallying calls. Participants set up local community-based Facebook pages for specific cities or districts and announced times and places for fellow Pantsuiters to meet.

On November 9, group member Theresa Shook suggested efforts that led to the massive Women's March on Washington held the day after Trump's inauguration, along with sister marches in more than six hundred additional large and small cities across America.[17] An estimated 4.2 million people participated in US and worldwide marches that day.[18] Additional national resistance initiatives were launched in late 2016 and early 2017.[19] But Pantsuit Nation lost relevance weeks after the 2016 election when the group's creator took the controversial step of signing a book deal and turning the organization into a nonprofit charity that could no longer engage in politics.[20] Emerging local resistance groups had to look elsewhere—and many found inspiration, support and connections in other regional or national frameworks. Those included regional coordinating bodies like Pennsylvania Together, national entities like the Action Together and Suit Up networks and, above all, a new coordinating effort started on December 14, 2016, when former Democratic congressional staffers led by Ezra Levin and Leah Greenberg publicly posted in Google Docs a manifesto called *Indivisible: A Practical Guide for Resisting the Trump Agenda.*[21]

Drawing from its organizers' understanding of what Tea Party activists had done to engage their base on the right eight years earlier, the *Indivisible Guide* spelled out exactly how anti-Trump resisters could organize locally to spread political messages, engage their neighbors, and contact the district offices of their members of Congress. Such pointers mattered to liberals who were used to turning directly to Washington, DC, and the White House. Levin and Greenberg

later told journalists that they were surprised at how quickly their guide went
viral on the internet and how many responses they suddenly received from concerned citizens across the nation excited to engage in political action.[22] Beyond
Facebook and Twitter, strong media support from left-leaning outlets including
the *Rachel Maddow Show* on MSNBC also helped spread the word to interested
individuals.[23] By March 2017, Indivisible set up shop as a Washington, DC–
based political organization with a growing paid staff and a curated website offering practical tools, ideas, and an interactive national map of local entities in
every state and congressional district.

As old and new liberal advocacy organizations turned to anti-Trump resistance
activities, still more significant developments were unfolding locally in cities,
suburbs, and towns all across the country. Both before and after the Women's
Marches in January 2017, and prior to the establishment of Indivisible's national
headquarters in March and the various public protests and marches staged periodically thereafter, Americans living and working in hundreds of places stepped
forward to launch what grew into thousands of grassroots resistance groups. Like
Tea Party activists years earlier, local organizers and the members they recruited
were determined to persist in challenging a dreaded presidency and unwanted
congressional and state-level initiatives. As a co-founder of one of the largest
Maine groups launched in January 2017 put it on one of our questionnaires,
"Many people . . . find common cause in resisting the Trump agenda. That is
the purpose of [our group]. Not to debate on which problem facing the country
today is 'the most important problem.' Not to hold a discussion group. Not to
host potlucks or book clubs. To organize action and take action that resists the
Trump agenda and those politicians who promote the Trump agenda."

Most scholarly research on the anti-Trump resistance so far has paralleled national media coverage in focusing on national advocacy organizations, including
pre-2016 groups (like MoveOn, the American Civil Liberties Union, Black
Lives Matter, and immigrant advocacy organizations) as well as on post-2016
creations like Indivisible, Swing Left, Sister District, and Run for Something.[24]
Social movement researchers have also done very creative studies of national
protest marches in the Trump era.[25] Our research, however, stands virtually alone
in its systematic efforts to document organizations and leaders and participants
in *local* anti-Trump resistance groups operating in many different places.[26] We
have been able to track in rich detail group activities and membership outlooks
for ten local resistance groups founded between late 2016 and early 2017 in
eight counties that voted in the majority for Trump in 2016, including two
counties apiece in North Carolina, Ohio, Pennsylvania, and Wisconsin. Within
each state, one county includes a medium-sized city, while the other is less populous and includes rural stretches surrounding a small city or several towns. To
track developments in a wider range of situations, we have also collected many

online questionnaires from resistance group leaders and members active in more than a hundred groups operating in various states—including an especially full set of responses from groups in metropolitan, suburban, exurban, and rural areas across the entire state of Pennsylvania. Using these unique data, we can offer clear findings about grassroots anti-Trump volunteer organizers, group participants, and group activities in 2017 and 2018.

The "who" of local anti-Trump organizing is very clear and may come as a surprise to some. Although national media outlets and researchers who have studied national resistance organizations often suggest that anti-Trump activities are spearheaded by young people and Americans from minority backgrounds, the vast majority of grassroots resistance group leaders and members are actually white, middle-class, college-educated women ranging in age from their thirties and forties to retirement years.[27] In the most conservative non-metropolitan places we have tracked, resistance organizers and participants are even whiter, more middle class and formally educated than their surrounding fellow residents; and we find no significant differences in the demographic profiles no matter where we look. Across all states and places we know, from two-thirds to 90 percent of volunteer resistance activists are female, white, and college-educated. Many of these women are retired from or currently employed in characteristic occupations—including educators in schools or colleges and professionals in health care delivery or management, nonprofit management, and small business. Men are certainly there, too—we know of no resistance group that has formally excluded them—yet from field observations we think most male participants are husbands, partners, or friends of the women involved.

We also have information on the political leanings of grassroots resistance activists and their motives for joining. Just as Tea Partiers were overwhelmingly either Republicans or independents situated to the right of the GOP, today's anti-Trump resisters are overwhelmingly self-identified Democrats, "progressives," or independents who lean to the left. Nine in ten of some 412 individual resistance participants who answered our 2017 online questionnaires identified as Democrats in some sense—including 252 who said they were "strong Democrats" while most of the rest, apart from a smattering who said they were straight-up "Independents" and "Republicans," said they "leaned" Democrats or were "Independent, near Democrat."[28] These results are hardly surprising, given that those who bothered to respond were likely very active in efforts that were born out of frustration at the 2016 Republican victories. This does not tell the entire story, however, because many of our field observations and questionnaire responses about group practices indicate that a high proportion of anti-Trump resistance groups were launched separately from local Democratic Parties and have chosen to maintain their independence, in order to welcome participants unwilling to call themselves Democrats. All in all, the evidence suggests that today's grassroots resistance groups and participants cover a relatively wide partisan span from centrist to far left, certainly a wider span than Tea Partiers who have consistently clustered at the right edge of the GOP.

We asked participants in grassroots resistance groups in various states to tell us why they became active, and coded up to four types of reasons cited in the 436 responses we received during the summer and fall of 2017. Figure 9.1 displays both percentages of all 765 reasons given by respondents, and the percentages of all respondents who gave each reason. Opposition to Trump was a motive mentioned by the highest percentage of respondents, more than two-fifths of them; and it also accounted for the biggest single category of all reasons given by all respondents. However, a desire to save or improve the country and American democracy was mentioned by almost as many respondents and made up the second-largest category of all reasons given. A heightened sense of civic purpose is evident among grassroots citizen activists on today's US center-left, perhaps because so many of these women and men are horrified at the self-serving narcissism they see in President Trump's character and actions. Many respondents also felt personally called to step up as active citizens; and people's desire to work cooperatively with others was evident in these responses. "Electing Democrats" was far from the top of the list of reasons for resistance activism, even though we

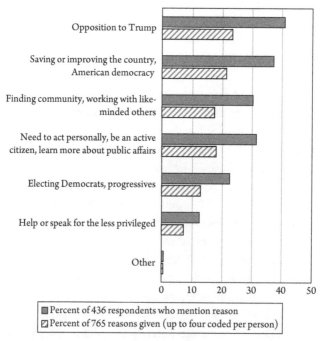

Figure 9.1 Reasons for Participation in Grassroots Resistance Groups.

know that, as the months passed leading into the 2018 elections, many resistance group members did get very involved in trying to do just that.

Beyond understanding the backgrounds and views of individual participants, we have been just as interested in learning how local groups took flight and operate as organizations.[29] Across founding stories, the scenarios have proved remarkably similar. Two to six organizers took the initiative, not necessarily people who knew each other before November 2016. Members of founding teams—mostly women, but also some men—very often met on Facebook right after the election or else on buses they took to attend January 2017 women's marches. They then tapped personal ties and existing organizational networks (for example in churches or work places or civic groups) to assemble a first meeting in a library or restaurant. After the group named itself and decided on some early activities—such as contacting their local congressional representative or writing letters to the editor at a local paper or mounting a public protest—members generally used Facebook and available lists (such as volunteer lists for local Hillary Clinton supporters) to add to their ranks. Through the early months of 2017, almost all the local resistance groups we knew about met regularly, at least once a month, before moving to less frequent meetings later. Unlike Tea Party meetings, the resistance group meetings we have attended as observers, or heard about from others, do not start with the Pledge of Allegiance or prayers. They usually involve a period of socializing, followed by a "let's get down to business" flavor characteristic of most secular civic gatherings.

Most local resistance groups supplement periodic face-to-face meetings with email communications and newsletters that reach many more adherents; and most have set up subcommittees or task forces. Subgroups may distribute volunteer opportunities according to functions—such as public outreach, member recruitment, lobbying Congress, and so forth—or according to issue areas of special interest to subsets of members. Saving ObamaCare from repeal was a universal priority during 2017 for all resistance groups we know about, as resisters took steps ranging from running community forums to visiting congressional offices every week to holding postcard writing parties. Beyond that, resistance group efforts have focused on issues like schools and education, climate change and environment, and immigration and refugees. Furthermore, almost all local resistance groups got engaged in the 2018 midterm elections, sometimes by generating new candidates from their ranks or endorsing candidates formally, and almost always by engaging in voter registration and canvassing activities.

American liberals are much more likely than conservatives to specialize in various ways, and this reality is reflected in the activities of Tea Parties versus resistance groups. Both kinds of citizen activists spend a lot of group time learning about the workings of government, deciphering gerrymandered election districts, and dispatching delegations to contact local or state or national officials.

But as Skocpol and Williamson learned in their 2011 research, Tea Partiers are eager to listen as entire groups to ideologically laden lectures, and encourage members to attend similarly ideological daylong workshops, for instance to go through the US Constitution line-by-line under the tutelage of some right-wing professor. Resisters, meanwhile, are more likely to want to educate themselves on specific policy issues or attend sessions to hone particular skills.

Indeed, this contrast also affects what local groups want from professional advocacy operations on their side of the partisan spectrum. We have pointed out that both the Tea Party and the resistance are far from any single hierarchy or organization. Each of these movements encompasses a wide variety of national, regional, and local organizations, loosely coupled with one another and all jostling to leverage resources from each other. A major dynamic in each movement has been the way local groups pick and choose resources on offer from national organizations that are trying to coordinate and even "speak for" the entire Tea Party or resistance. No one truly speaks for the whole, but national groups get advantages from telling their donors that they are offering valuable resources to volunteer citizen groups. In turn, leaders of local Tea Parties or anti-Trump resistance groups enjoy being able to choose the most useful resources offered from kindred professionals.

Local Tea Parties often invited lecturers from Second Amendment or anti-global warming groups or from federated operations like FreedomWorks or Americans for Prosperity. By contrast, grassroots resistance groups are more likely to take up offers from liberal advocacy organizations willing to send trainers to teach members how to write OpEds, or navigate voting laws, or gather petition signatures, or figure out the state budget, or encourage new people to run for office. Of course, these subtle but important differences in what right-leaning and left-leaning citizen activists want to hear go hand-in-hand with the different sets of middle-class occupations from which Tea Partiers and resisters usually hail. Resisters, in particular, are very likely to be from teaching and other professional backgrounds, where people take it for granted that training and skills are crucial.

Different Early Dynamics in Two Widespread Movements

Opposite political orientations aside, there were some revealing differences in the early dynamics of the Tea Party and the anti-Trump resistance movement. Although it took a month to six weeks following Barack Obama's inauguration on January 20, 2009, for Tea Party pushback to gain steam, widespread liberal resistance organizing started just hours to days after Donald Trump was declared the Electoral College winner on November 8, 2016. Both of these electorally sparked movements were unquestionably fast off the mark by any absolute standard, yet the anti-Trump resistance got going almost instantaneously, for several reasons.

By 2016, would-be resisters could take inspiration and borrow tactics from the earlier right-wing Tea Party activists.[30] As progressives and others excitedly engaged each other before the election through online sites such as Pantsuit Nation, the ties they created easily became the basis for post-election organizing, via both virtual and in-person means. What is more, Trump's 2016 win was unexpected by most observers and political leaders, compared to Obama's more widely anticipated 2008 victory. The sheer shock effect of November 8, 2016 spurred many Americans on the losing side to quicker responses—including to local resistance organizing that, thanks to the *Indivisible Guide*, could borrow models from earlier Tea Party building tactics. Back in 2009, local citizen activists took a bit more time to make contacts with one another and devise local organizing strategies.

The eight years between the genesis of the Tea Party and the anti-Trump grassroots resistance also brought changes in electronic media tools relevant to civic organizing. Tea Parties were formed by self-appointed organizers who met by local happenstance, at rallies, or on buses to marches, after which they recruited members through personal networks and used MeetUp websites and email to make their fledgling groups visible and keep in touch with adherents. Arguably, too, many would-be local Tea Party organizers needed the encouragement and practical tips propagated by conservative media and on certain advocacy organization websites in early 2009. Unlike later resistance organizers, Tea Party organizers could not just appropriate recent analogous models—and they were not already Facebook adepts.

Years later, many local anti-Trump resistance organizers also first met in-person on the way to marches; and some no doubt learned about the *Indivisible Guide* from left-leaning media sources that did cheerleading for resistance organizing just as conservative media urged organizing on the right in 2009. Nevertheless, our investigations of the origins of many resistance groups reveal that people in local organizing teams often connected quickly through Pantsuit Nation's location-finding mechanisms and got down to work within days of the November election. Furthermore, even after emerging local resistance groups and networks shifted to new coordinating frameworks like Indivisible or Action Together, they continued to use the Facebook platform for group communications. From late 2016 on, Facebook played a major role in facilitating quick and widespread connections among grassroots resisters, not just because of that platform's inherent technical capacities but also because most of the older white middle-class women and men who organized the grassroots resistance already understood how to use this kind of social media.

Recognizing the speed and ease with which so many local resistance groups got started in late 2016 and early 2017 brings us to evidence about this movement's lightning fast spread across states and the country as a whole. Remarkably, even though Democratic voters these days are packed into big cities and a few other "blue" locales, resistance organizing has not been similarly circumscribed. Grassroots anti-Trump groups have been created at least as extensively across the federated American political geography as local Tea Parties were in earlier years.

For related projects, our research associate Caroline Tervo has used all available sources, including websites and past research results along with the internet Wayback Machine, to assemble maps of North Carolina and Pennsylvania showing the counties that have, at any point since 2009, had one or more local Tea Parties, one or more local resistance groups, neither type of group, or both types. These maps reproduced in Figure 9.2 show that the majority of counties in both states (and especially Pennsylvania where counties are larger) have had both types of local movement organizations. In addition, more counties show indications of recently formed local resistance groups than show evidence of Tea Parties at any point. This is a very important—and telling—finding. From all indications, grassroots organizing in the current anti-Trump resistance has not been restricted to "blue enclaves" where voters mostly support Democrats. Even in places where Democrats or liberals are the beleaguered minority, women and men stepped forward after November 2016 to speak out and band together in resistance groups, gaining some visibility in local media in the process.[31]

Indeed, our field visits, interviews, and questionnaire responses offer some hints that organizing a local group may have been especially important in relatively conservative communities. Non-conservatives in those places who were frustrated or horrified by the election of Donald Trump may have felt an even stronger need to come together than their counterparts in liberal-leaning areas. "In the community I live, especially" said one resident of a conservative Ohio county on our questionnaire, "I hoped to share some thoughts with like-minded people—to feel a local connection." In the smallest, most conservative counties we have visited repeatedly since 2017, local resistance group members have taken increasing pride in mounting public displays of their values—by supporting new candidates for public office, marching in Fourth of July parades, setting up booths at local fairs, and demonstrating in town centers about issues ranging from the Charlottesville killing to the separation of immigrant children from their parents at the southern US border.[32]

Obviously, our most detailed data refer only to eight non–big city counties in four states plus the entire state of Pennsylvania. Could these be unusually well-organized places? Although we cannot say for sure, there are good reasons to believe that our states and areas are not unusual, that similar grassroots resistance

Figure 9.2 Resistance Groups and Tea Parties in North Carolina and Pennsylvania.

groups emerged all over the United States. For one, the interactive US map on the national Indivisible website has, since early 2017, consistently listed and linked to five to six thousand local entities. Many of them are not actual groups founded since 2016, but we estimate that about one third of them are, adding up to about two thousand spread across all US states.[33] Indivisible's national leaders say they are in touch with at least one group in every congressional district, and they have moved to deploy state and regional organizers across the country. We also know from our detailed work on groups in Pennsylvania counties that additional local resistance groups can be found that are not affiliated with Indivisible or linked to that organization's website map. Similarly, across the vast state of Maine, local resistance groups have been organized everywhere, from the southern coast and relatively populous cities to the western parts of the state and the upper reaches of Washington and Piscataquis Counties.[34] Maine groups include both stand-alone organizations and some two dozen groups that have been at some point formally linked to the national Indivisible network. Available data, moreover, suggest that the anti-Trump resistance launched in late 2016 and early 2017 has spawned many more local citizen-run groups than the Tea Party did after 2008.[35]

Reverberations in Elections and Party Politics

By early 2018, leaders of national resistance efforts—including the leaders of national Indivisible and organizers of the 2018 Women's March—were calling for local groups to focus on upcoming primary and general elections. This meant nominating and supporting candidates for government offices at all levels, registering voters, and ultimately getting out the vote for Democrats.[36] However, evidence from our research and other sources suggests that most grassroots resistance groups had already incorporated such electoral activities into their repertoires. Indeed, in special elections or state-level contests in 2017 and early 2018, newly created local resistance groups, mostly led by women, played major roles in fueling Democratic victories or greatly improving the vote shares of Democratic candidates all over the United States.[37]

Like the local Tea Parties starting in 2009, today's grassroots anti-Trump resistance groups take a "do everything" view of politics. To be sure, they stress policy campaigns such as defending health reform or pushing against Trump rollbacks of environmental regulations. Yet from early in their existence many local anti-Trump groups have also looked ahead to the next rounds of elections. Initially, explained one Pennsylvania leader, her group primarily agitated against Trump era policies, but eventually "we had so many people running for local offices we switched to an *offense* versus *defense* approach where people could choose if they wanted to focus on *resistance* throughout the week or focusing on trying to help get [Democrats] elected." Early on, agreed another Pennsylvania group leader, it became clear that her "group would not just be resistance but that to make policy we had to govern and to govern we had to *win elections*. So, since we live in a very Democratic area, we are partnering with Red districts. We have 'adopted' a PA House race . . . to unseat the Republican as part of Turn PA Blue . . . We are also supporting Wolf and Casey with fundraisers etc." In a more conservative area of North Carolina, meanwhile, members of the local resistance group mounted early and persistent efforts on behalf of a local doctor running to unseat the incumbent Republican representative in the US Congress. A group in Ohio decided to prioritize collecting signatures on petitions to get an anti-gerrymandering referendum on the November 2018 ballot. Virtually everywhere, members of resistance groups attended workshops to learn about voter registration and canvassing procedures in anticipation of mounting such outreach for future elections.

Have local resistance groups functioned, simply, as local arms of the Democratic Party? This is an obvious question, given that (as we have seen) the vast majority of their active participants identify (more or less strongly) as Democrats. Here, too, we can wonder about parallels with the Tea Party participants eight years before.[38] As individuals, Tea Party participants virtually all voted for Republicans, although some labeled themselves Independents or Libertarians. Nevertheless, the Tea Partiers were wary of the institutional Republican Party at all levels. They voted for GOP candidates in general elections versus Democrats, but in primary elections often backed newcomer challengers to incumbent Republican officeholders. What is more, despite participation by some GOP officeholders, local Tea Parties were not launched or formalized as parts of county Republican Parties, and in many places the early Tea Parties were at odds with party officials. To this day, as our field research indicates, local Tea Parties that still meet on their own may do so in part to mount opposition to the local Republican "establishment." In other places, the Tea Partiers of yore have simply taken over local and state GOP institutions. With these earlier patterns in mind, our examination of today's grassroots anti-Trump resistance groups is probing the nature of their formal and informal ties to the Democratic Party. We collected some interview and questionnaire evidence on these ties in 2017 and 2018, and again in questionnaires we collected from groups across Pennsylvania in early 2019.

It is too early to tell whether parallels to the Tea Party-GOP dynamics will unfold on the US left, but there are early indications of both similar and different tendencies. For starters, just as most Tea Parties emerged outside the GOP, local anti-Trump resistance groups mostly formed outside of formal Democratic Party channels. In several of the localities we have studied, county-level Democratic Party women's groups lent early support and participants to resistance groups and sometimes convened the first meetings. This happened in a few places where local Democrats already had some organizational heft, and especially where there were strong Democratic women's associations. Yet in many places, local Democratic Party organizations were moribund, so resistance groups had to get started entirely on their own. In some places, moreover, local Democratic Party leaders were downright hostile to the idea of new, independent political groups forming in their orbit.

Even resistance groups that formed with some party help still adopted their own names and identities. Everywhere we have looked, local resistance leaders have told us that they see advantages in standing somewhat apart from the formal Democratic Party—either because this gives them greater freedom of political action or because their groups include some members who do not consider themselves "Democrats." Especially in GOP-dominated, conservative areas, resistance groups also see real advantages in being able to speak up as "concerned citizens," reaching out to neighbors, friends, and co-workers who share worries about Trump and current US policy directions but do not feel comfortable participating in an openly partisan "Democratic Party" venture.

This desire of many current resistance groups to organize and act somewhat apart from party structures resembles earlier Tea Party stances toward the GOP. Nevertheless, there may be a key difference. During the Obama presidency, grassroots Tea Partiers positioned themselves, both individually and as groups, at or beyond the right edge of the Republican Party. They saw themselves as stronger, truer "conservatives" pushing for a purer GOP whose candidates and officials would refuse to compromise with President Obama or Democrats. But today's grassroots anti-Trump groups and participants span a wider range from centrist to far-left; and the outreach practiced by some of today's resistance groups is directed toward middle-of-the-road fellow citizens, even toward disaffected Republicans, not only toward fellow liberals or progressives. In contrast to constant Tea Party pressure on the GOP to refuse any and all governing compromises, we do not see much evidence that grassroots resistance groups, especially outside of larger urban centers, are advocating far-left policy stands or insisting that Democratic officeholders and candidates shun all forms of moderation or compromise. In certain 2017 special elections, resistance group members were among those knocking on doors to help elect very moderate Democrats— including Connor Lamb in Pennsylvania's eighteenth congressional district and Doug Jones in the Alabama Senate contest.[39] By way of contrast, Tea Partiers have often refused to support moderate Republicans. Tea Party insistence on uncompromising right-wing purity has contributed to general election defeats for GOP candidates, as it did in the 2012 Senate races in Missouri and Indiana.

In 2010 and again in 2018, non-presidential midterm elections offered Tea Parties and anti-Trump resistance groups, respectively, their first chances to boost electoral outcomes for their favored party and, in the process, push back against the incumbent president (Obama or Trump) they strongly opposed. In both election cycles, there were surges of new candidates for the movement-aligned party—for Republicans in 2010 and Democrats in 2018. The sheer totals of GOPers running for the US House of Representatives attained a sharp peak in 2010 and even more Democrats ran for the House in 2018.[40] Many of those new candidates came from movement ranks or had support from the Tea Party in 2010 and from the resistance in 2018. At state as well as national levels, moreover, 2018 was not only a "blue wave" election, but it also brought victories for an extraordinary number of female Democrats—in a year when female-led anti-Trump resistance groups dotted the land.[41]

Tellingly, though, most Democratic victories in 2018 were secured by moderately liberal candidates running in suburban districts with high proportions of college-educated voters.[42] This contrasts with the disproportionate gains made by very conservative Republicans in the Tea Party-fueled election of 2010. Congress and many state legislatures moved markedly to the right after 2010—not only because Republicans defeated so many Democrats, but also because the kinds of GOP candidates who were nominated and won office were well to the right of earlier Republican officeholders and candidates.[43] The same is not true for the Democratic majorities newly installed in 2018. Progressive Democrats won office in many places, to be sure, but moderate liberals secured most of the victories in that election.

Even if more moderates won, both moderately liberal and left-progressive Democratic candidates running in 2018 for local, state and national offices usually enjoyed energetic support from newly engaged citizens in the grassroots resistance. Time will tell if such "big tent" dynamics continue into the future, but in the critical 2018 midterm election the effect of the grassroots resistance was to boost and energize Democrats of many stripes. The Tea Party's impact on Republicans has arguably substantially sharpened partisan and ideological divides in the United States, but there is a good chance that the anti-Trump resistance—as it has unfolded at the grassroots in so many different locales—will revitalize the Democratic Party and boost many of its candidates across the board, without increasing polarization in the process.

Notes

1. Theda Skocpol and Vanessa Williamson, *The Tea Party and the Remaking of Republican Conservatism* (New York: Oxford University Press), 90–92.
2. Overviews appear in David S. Meyer and Sidney Tarrow, eds., *The Resistance: The Emergence of the Movement against President Donald Trump* (New York: Oxford University Press, 2018).
3. Skocpol and Williamson, *The Tea Party and the Remaking of Republican Conservatism*. We draw on evidence gathered for this book throughout this chapter.
4. David A. Hopkins, *Red Fighting Blue: How Geography and Electoral Rules Polarize American Politics* (New York: Cambridge University Press, 2017).
5. See chapter 3 of Skocpol and Williamson, *The Tea Party and the Remaking of Republican Conservatism* for a discussion of the various kinds of organizations that made up the entire Tea Party universe.
6. Michelle Malkin, "Taxpayer Revolt: Porkulus Protest in Seattle, Obama to Sign Theft Act in Denver," MichelleMalkin.com, February 15, 2009; and P. J. Standlee, "Obama Protesters Leave Signs Near Dobson High School in Mesa," *Phoenix New Times*, February 18, 2009.
7. Video of Rick Santelli's "rant" can be found at CNBC's website, available at https://www.cnbc.com/video/2016/03/02/santellis-rant-heard-round-the-world.html as of April 14, 2019.
8. The cheerleading role of right-wing media is documented in chapter 4 of Skocpol and Williamson, *The Tea Party and the Remaking of Republican Conservatism*.
9. Andreas Madestam, Daniel Shoag, Stan Veuger, and David Yanagaizawa-Drott, "Do Political Protests Matter? Evidence from the Tea Party Movement," *Quarterly Journal of Economics* 128, no. 4 (November 2013): 1633–85.
10. Amy Gardner, "Gauging the Scope of the Tea Party Movement in America," *Washington Post*, October 24, 2010.

11. Skocpol and Williamson, *The Tea Party and the Remaking of Republican Conservatism*, Figure 3.1, 91.

12. Further details and references appear in chapter 1 of Skocpol and Williamson, *The Tea Party and the Remaking of Republican Conservatism*.

13. For further discussion and references, see chapter 2 of Skocpol and Williamson, *The Tea Party and the Remaking of Republican Conservatism*.

14. Christopher S. Parker and Matthew A. Barreto, *Change They Can't Believe In: The Tea Party and Reactionary Politics in America* (Princeton, NJ: Princeton University Press, 2014).

15. See the excellent tracking of Tea Partiers' attitudes compared to other Republican identifiers in Pew Research Center, "Trump's Staunch GOP Supporters Have Roots in the Tea Party," report issued May 2019.

16. Annie Correal, "Pantsuit Nation, a 'Secret' Facebook Hub, Celebrates Clinton," *New York Times*, November 8, 2016; and Abby Ohlheiser, "Inside the Huge, 'Secret' Facebook Group for Hillary Clinton's Biggest Fans," *Washington Post*, November 7, 2016.

17. The Women's March on Washington became a formalized nonprofit organization through the work of Bob Bland, Tamika Mallory, Carmen Perez, and Linda Sarsour. See Laila Kearney, Laila, "Hawaii Grandma's Plea Launches Women's March on Washington," *Reuters*, December 5, 2016.

18. The 2017 marches constituted the largest mass demonstration in US history, according to Erica Chenoweth and Jeremy Pressman, "One Year after the Women's March on Washington, People Are Still Protesting en Masse. A Lot. We've Counted," *Monkey Cage*, January 21, 2018. For a map of first women's marches, see Sarah Frostenson, "The Women's Marches May Have Been the Largest Demonstration in US History," Vox, updated January 31, 2017.

19. Many protest and advocacy initiatives are described in the various chapters of *The Resistance*, edited by Meyer and Tarrow, and in Dana Fisher, *American Resistance* (New York: Columbia University Press, 2019).

20. Correal, "Pantsuit Nation"; Kaitlyn Tiffany, "The Organizer of a Massive Pro-Clinton Facebook Group Has Landed a Book Deal," The Verge, December 20, 2016; and Bill Trotter, "Pantsuit Nation Founder Defends Controversial Book Deal," *Bangor Daily News*, December 22, 2016.

21. Ezra Levin Leah Greenberg, and Angel Padilla, *Indivisible: A Practical Guide for Resisting the Trump Agenda*. Initially posted as a Google doc, December 14, 2016; Charles Bethea, "How the Trump Resistance Went Pro in Alabama," *New Yorker*, December 15, 2017; Doug Criss, "What Is Indivisible? Political Group Hopes to be Flip Side of Tea Party," CNN, March 13, 2017; and Ezra Levin, Leah Greenberg, and Angel Padilla, "To Stop Trump, Democrats Can Learn from the Tea Party," *New York Times*, January 31, 2017.

22. Casey Tolan, "Meet the Husband-Wife Duo Who Are Sparking a Liberal Tea Party Movement," MercuryNews.com, May 13, 2017 (updated May 17). See also Megan Brooker, "Indivisible: Invigorating and Redirecting the Grassroots," in *The Resistance*, edited by Meyer and Tarrow.

23. MSNBC, "Online Guide Helps Focus Anti-Donald Trump Movement—Rachel Maddow—MSNBC," January 5, 2017. Available on YouTube https://www.youtube.com/watch?v=1JwOLRWaGX4.

24. Many initiatives sponsored by old and new organizations are described in *The Resistance*, edited by Meyer and Tarrow. See also *Democracy Alliance Resistance Efforts*, a pamphlet listing old and new groups seeking support from liberal donors (Washington, DC: Democracy Alliance, 2017); Jordan James-Harvill, "19 Resistance Organizations at the Forefront of the Anti-Trump Movement," Organizer.com, posted July 28, 2017; and Kenneth P. Vogel, "'The Resistance,' Raising Big Money, Upends Liberal Politics," *New York Times*, October 7, 2017.

25. See especially Fisher, *American Resistance*.

26. Leah E. Gose and Theda Skocpol, "Resist, Persist, and Transform: The Emergence and Impact of Grassroots Resistance Groups Opposing the Trump Presidency," *Mobilization: An International Journal* 24, no. 3 (2019): 293–317.

27. In addition to findings reported in Gose and Skocpol, "Resist, Persist, and Transform," see Lara Putnam and Theda Skocpol, "Middle America Reboots Democracy," *Democracy: A Journal of Ideas*, February 20, 2018; and Hahrie Han and Michelle Oyakawa, "Constituency

and Leadership in the Evolution of Resistance Organizations," in *The Resistance*, ed. Meyer and Tarrow, 237.

28. Gose and Skocpol, "Resist, Persist, and Transform."

29. The following claims summarize evidence from our field visits and online questionnaires asking organizers to recount details of the founding of local groups, including exactly how and when members of the organizing team met one another. Details are spelled out in Gose and Skocpol, "Resist, Persist, and Transform."

30. Kaya Axelsson, "Do Protests Matter? What the Tea Party Movement Can Teach the Trump Resistance," *YES Magazine*, January 30, 2018.

31. For examples from conservative areas we have tracked in North Carolina, Wisconsin, and Pennsylvania, see Kevin Griffin, "Indivisible Citizens to Host Demonstrations at Rep. McHenry's Office Saturday," *Hickory Record*, February 10, 2017; Steve Rundio, "Indivisible Organizes in Tomah," *Tomah Journal*, March 1, 2017; and Scott Shindledecker, "'Indivisible We Rise West Central PA' Organizes in Clarion," ExploreClarion.com, April 19, 2017.

32. As recounted in our field interviews and reported, for example, in John Bailey, "Facing the Hate: Community Groups Host Candlelight Vigil in Downtown Hickory," *Hickory Record*, August 13, 2017; and Ron Wilshire, "Clarion Peace Walk: 'Love, Not Hate, Makes America Great,'" ExploreClarion.com, September 23, 2017.

33. Careful work by our research colleagues Caroline Tervo and Lara Putnam informs this conclusion.

34. Our discussion of Maine resistance groups relies on current and retrospective compilations of organizations and descriptions of their activities prepared by Bill Skocpol in the spring of 2019, drawing on Maine Facebook pages and the national Indivisible map.

35. In 2011 and 2012, Skocpol and Williamson identified four Maine Tea Party groups. Even if this is an underestimate and there were actually six to eight at one point or another, the number of Maine Tea Parties is substantially lower than the two dozen or more local anti-Trump resistance groups identified as operating since 2016.

36. Charlotte Alter, "The Pink Wave," *Time*, January 29, 2018; Lege King, Jinizail Hernandez, and Trevor Hughes, "'Grab Him by the Mid-Terms': Women's Marches Push Power of the Vote," *USA Today*, January 21, 2018; and Anna North, "How the Women's March Made Itself Indispensable," Vox, January 19, 2018.

37. Bethea, "How the Trump Resistance Went Pro in Alabama"; Danny Hayes and Jennifer L. Lawless, "In Tuesday's Elections, Women Won Big . . . ," *Monkey Cage*, November 9, 2017; Gideon Lewis-Kraus, "How the Resistance Helped Democrats Dominate Virginia," *New York Times*, November 13, 2017; and Putnam and Skocpol, "Middle America Reboots Democracy."

38. Our discussion of Tea Partiers' relations with Republicans draws on Skocpol and Williamson, *The Tea Party and the Remaking of Republican Conservatism*, as well as from more recent field interviews and observations, including reports from state and county Republican Party leaders and the leaders of two Tea Parties that are still meeting regularly in two of the eight counties we have visited since 2016.

39. Garance Franke-Ruta, "The Resistance Is Organized and Ready in District Where Trump Is Visiting," Yahoo News, January 18, 2018; Lara Putnam, "Who Really Won PA 18?" *Democracy: A Journal of Ideas*, March 15, 2018; and Bethea, "How the Trump Resistance Went Pro in Alabama."

40. Jonathan Martin and Denise Lu, "Democrats' Best Recruitment Tool? President Trump," *New York Times*, April 6, 2018.

41. Meredith Conroy, "At Least 123 Women Will Be in the Next Congress. Just 19 are Republicans," *FiveThirtyEight*, November 16, 2018; and Geoff Mulvill, "Women Elected in Record Numbers in State Legislative Races," Associated Press, November 15, 2018.

42. Ella Nilsen, "Progressive Democrats Running in Competitive House Districts Had a Bad Night on Tuesday," Vox, November 7, 2018; and Geoffrey Skelley, "The House Will Have Just as Many Moderate Democrats as Progressives Next Year," *FiveThirtyEight*, December 20, 2018.

43. See discussion and references for chapter 5, Skocpol and Williamson, *The Tea Party and the Remaking of Republican Conservatism*, including Figure 5.1, 169.

10

The Surprising Advance of Gun Control Politics after Parkland

SOPHIA YOUNG

On April 20, 1999, two students shot and killed thirteen people and injured twenty-one others at Columbine High School in Jefferson County, Colorado. At the time, it was the deadliest school shooting on record. In the aftermath, millions of horrified Americans tuned in on live television to watch the scene unfold.[1] Nobody could explain why two teenagers would commit such a senseless act— and soon there were calls for corrective actions. That July, Colorado high school students traveled to Washington, DC, and met with President Bill Clinton to advocate for reasonable gun regulations. Clinton urged legislators to pass regulations that would prevent a massacre like Columbine from ever happening again.

Ultimately, however, the Columbine survivors and other high school students from Colorado were unable to convince the House of Representatives to take any action on gun control. Years passed, bringing many additional mass shootings—the most notable at Virginia Tech in 2007, Sandy Hook Elementary School in 2012, a Las Vegas music festival in 2017, and a church in Sutherland Springs, Texas in 2017. Even though such murderous shootings increased in frequency, they had little effect on legislation or activism to further gun control.

Then, almost two decades later, the narrative changed. On February 14, 2018, a nineteen-year-old gunman killed seventeen people and wounded seventeen more in a shooting spree at Marjory Stoneman Douglas High School in Parkland, Florida. Once again, students from the victimized school and beyond mobilized to demand action. Unlike President Clinton in 1999, President Donald Trump (after paying a bit of lip service to the need for reforms) did not urge Congress to take any immediate action. In his statement to the nation after the Parkland shooting, Trump did not even identify the ready accessibility of guns in the United States as a problem; instead, he focused on mental

Sophia Young, *The Surprising Advance of Gun Control Politics after Parkland* In: *Upending American Politics* Edited by: Theda Skocpol and Caroline Tervo, Oxford University Press (2020). © Oxford University Press DOI: 10.1093/oso/9780190083526.003.0010 instability as the cause of senseless shootings and suggested that violence could be contained by arming teachers and other law-abiding citizens. This tepid response from President Trump appeared to set the stage for another chapter of the same old story of America's non-responsiveness to mass shootings. But this time, events took another turn. Urged on by protesting students and parents, the State of Florida soon passed legislation that raised the age to buy a rifle to twenty-one years, mandated a three-day waiting period for gun purchases, and banned the sale of bump stocks.

Even more remarkably, changes happened across the United States, as students organized a Washington, DC, march and other protests in favor of gun control. By the end of 2018, state legislatures passed sixty-nine gun control laws.[2] In the months after the Parkland shooting leading into the 2018 midterm elections, more and more candidates for Congress and other offices spoke up about the need for new gun safety measures; and after Democrats gained forty seats and took control of the House of Representatives, they passed the Bipartisan Background Checks Act on February 27, 2019, to mandate background checks for all gun purchases.[3] Although this bill faces significant hurdles in the Republican-controlled Senate, it represents a breakthrough as the most significant gun control legislation passed in over two decades.

Why Different Political Dynamics Two Decades Apart?

The United States experiences regular, horrific mass shootings not seen at a similar rate in any other country in the world. Over the past two decades, mass shootings have received saturated national media coverage and, following each episode, activists and legislators call for new public engagement supporting legislative gun regulations. Yet such efforts have rarely led to changes in directions gun control advocates want—until the aftermath of the early 2018 event at Marjory Stoneman Douglas High School brought important shifts in public opinion along with some new accomplishments for gun control legislation and openings for candidates willing to champion gun safety issues.

Why have political aftereffects of mass shootings unfolded as they have— and, in particular, why has the Parkland shooting spurred much more political change than earlier mass shootings in the United States, including those with many more victims or more heart-rending victims such as the small children killed at Sandy Hook Elementary School? In order to attempt to answer this question, as well as understand the political reverberations of mass shootings in the contemporary United States, I examine the political aftereffects of six mass shootings that occurred from 1999 to 2018:

- **Columbine:** In April 1999, two high school students killed thirteen of their peers at Columbine High School in Colorado, after obtaining two shotguns from a private seller at a gun show. While this prompted calls to increase restrictions on firearm purchases, then-president Clinton urged Congress to take action to no avail. In 2001, the State of Colorado managed to pass new gun control laws through a ballot provision, ultimately requiring background checks for all gun show firearm sales.

- **Virginia Tech:** In April 2007, a student killed thirty-two people on the Virginia Tech campus, after purchasing handguns and clearing a criminal background check. Since the shooter had previously been ordered by a judge to attend treatment for his psychological health, legislators pushed for regulations that could include information about individual's mental illness in the database for firearm background checks. By the end of the year, Congress passed legislation to make it easier to flag gun purchasers who have mental health issues. Almost a year later, Virginia state legislators enacted a similar law to increase the ability for institutions to communicate concerns about mental illness to gun sellers. Nevertheless, much of the controversy after the shooting surrounded the flaws in the university's response, with many parents filing wrongful death suits.

- **Sandy Hook:** In December 2012, a twenty-year-old man killed twenty-six people at an elementary school in Connecticut, after shooting his mother with her own semi-automatic firearms. This prompted then-president Barack Obama to call for action to prevent future shootings. Within a year of the massacre in Connecticut, the Democrat-controlled state legislature passed thirteen new gun control laws. However, no new federal gun control law was passed.

- **Las Vegas:** In October 2017, a gunman killed fifty-eight people and injured 851 others at a country music festival in Las Vegas, Nevada. This shooting prompted a conversation about banning bump stocks, the firearm accessory that enables a semi-automatic rifle to function like an automatic machine gun, which the gunman used in Las Vegas. As a result, multiple states introduced legislation banning the accessory.

- **Sutherland Springs:** In November 2017, a man shot and killed twenty-six people in a church in Sutherland Springs, Texas, and was then shot by an armed civilian present near the shooting before fleeing the scene.

- **Marjory Stoneman Douglas:** In February 2018, seventeen people were killed and seventeen more were wounded during a mass shooting at Marjory Stoneman Douglas High School in Parkland, Florida. Student activists from Parkland traveled to Tallahassee in an attempt to persuade legislators to pass gun control reforms. A month later, the Republican-controlled state legislature in Florida passed legislation that raised the age to buy a rifle to twenty-one years, mandated a three-day waiting period for gun purchases, banned the sale of bump stocks, and included a measure to train and arm some school employees.

It is appropriate to compare these six incidents specifically because they involved the largest number of fatalities in the last twenty years, were not considered terrorist attacks, and generated significant media attention. In these six shootings, the presence or absence of certain factors could have led (or not led) to gun control legislation or political activism in the year following the event. Across the six cases, I consider a range of factors that influenced ensuing political events, such as the number of deaths and injuries, the demographics of the affected population, the location, and the perpetrator's age and mental health history. I also examine which political parties were in power in the state legislature at the time of the event, the political party controlling Congress, the political party affiliation of the president of the United States in office at the time, and the president's prioritization of gun control.[4] In addition, I consider public opinion polls on issues of gun ownership and gun restrictions.[5] Using these data, I evaluate the extent to which these factors shaped differences in the gun legislation that was passed at the state and federal level in the twelve months following a specific shooting and whether the legislation strengthened or loosened existing gun laws.[6] Articles from national and local newspapers helped me determine which resources were available to gun control advocates at the time of the shooting and the breadth of activism that followed, including the size of protests, the demographics of protest participants, when and where the activism occurred, and the organizations involved, as well as the objectives of activists.

Ultimately, my findings suggest that the aftermath of the shooting in Parkland, Florida, has been different for two key reasons. The expansive, present-day social media environment helped student activists promptly gain nationwide attention, giving them access to key resources from newly developed gun control organizations. In addition, preexisting citizen organizing networks, formed in the early Trump presidency, provided political opportunity structures that helped students across many locations create a nationwide movement to pressure legislators and shift the political agenda in a critical election year.

Why Gun Control Efforts Stalled after Recurrent Mass Shootings

Although gun control laws and political advocacy on behalf of gun safety made only halting progress in the late twentieth century United States, an objective observer might have expected that the increasing frequency of mass shootings would have shifted the balance of forces in favor of gun controls.

New openings for gun control advocates might have happened for a number of reasons. Because mass shootings receive extensive media coverage and spark national-level conversations about gun control, they might shift public attitudes in favor of remedial laws. Mass shootings could also spur sustained protest movements—boosting the resources available to advocates demanding changes in gun regulations. In turn, either shifts in public attitudes or protest movements could have created new incentives for officials and candidates to sponsor further gun control legislation or administrative measures. Until recently, however, such factors have not tipped the balance in favor of America's gun control movement.

Mass Shootings and Public Opinion

The issue of gun control has become increasingly contentious over the past twenty years. Trends in public opinion by party affiliation on the issue of gun control mirror the political polarization of Congress in general, making it difficult as ever to pass federal legislation that could reduce gun violence in the United States. Although shifts in public opinion could have driven politicians to be more willing to enact these kinds of policies, the increasing frequency of mass shootings failed for years to propel public opinion in favor of gun control regulations.

During the past ten years, in fact, there has been a gradual decline in support for gun control, largely driven by a plunge in support for gun control among US Republicans.[7] This decline began in 2008, after the Supreme Court ruled in *District of Columbia v. Heller* that the Second Amendment protects the rights of individuals to possess a firearm unconnected with service in a militia.[8] The *Heller* ruling cemented the partisan difference in public support of gun control between the Democratic and Republican Parties: from 2007 to 2009, public support for gun rights in the United States increased by 13 percentage points, with 45 percent of the population supporting the protection of gun rights.[9] Although the support for gun rights among Democrats has remained stable, around 20 to 25 percent since 2008, it increased significantly among Republicans from 50 percent in 2007 to 79 percent in 2017.

Increasing Republican support for gun rights can be explained by research that demonstrates how exposure to mass shootings in the media tends to reinforce individuals' predisposed attitudes toward gun policies, rather than shifting public opinion towards favoring gun control.[10] In addition, public opinion polls from Pew Research Center and Gallup indicate that public opinion on gun control is solidly aligned with party identification, and that Americans largely interpret the issue of gun policy as a partisan issue.[11] Together, these two findings help explain why public opinion does not tend to shift in favor of gun control as mass shootings become more frequent. Essentially, mass shootings tend to reinforce the attitudes and policy preferences people already had before the mass shooting took place.

Resources, Strategies, and Political Leadership

If mass shootings do not necessarily move public opinion toward reform, they might still lead to a shift in the balance of resources available to gun control and gun rights interest groups—a shift that would, in turn, affect their capacity for political influence. Interest groups' capacities to influence politics and public policymaking depend on the size of their memberships, the availability of financial resources, and the strategies groups devise. In addition, the effectiveness of interest groups is influenced by whether or not their members are an influential bloc of voters that mobilize for elections and protests.

When the Columbine shooting happened in 1999, the gun control movement was deficient in each of these areas, and at a clear disadvantage to the NRA. Political scientist Kristin Goss has explored this comparison in depth in her book, *Disarmed, America's Missing Popular Movement for Gun Control.*[12] Until very recently, gun control advocates have had a small membership, minimal financial resources, and a weak political strategy. In the past, the gun control movement typically focused on high-impact solutions to gun violence at the federal level instead of attempting to introduce policies incrementally by beginning at local and state levels—where law enforcement is more effective at implementing regulations—and moving progressively to the national level. In contrast, gun rights advocates and gun rights organizations like the NRA are extremely well organized at the local, state, and federal levels, and have access to significantly more financial resources than gun control groups. Moreover, gun rights advocates utilize language about patriotism, countering liberals, and protecting freedom that helps to mobilize gun rights supporters to fight for their Second Amendment rights and vote accordingly. On the other hand, gun control advocates have historically struggled to generate language that inspires supporters to take action with the same intensity.[13] Gun control advocates have thus had difficulty winning battles with large pro-gun organizations such as the NRA that have wide citizen followings moved by intense messages about the right to bear arms.

This unpropitious environment for gun control arguments in the United States persisted until recent changes in media modalities created a new possibilities (very different from those in the Columbine era) for gun control advocates to quickly communicate a far-reaching, unified message after a mass shooting. Today, the increase in social media usage, including the proliferation of popular social networking platforms like Facebook and Twitter, enables survivors of gun violence to participate directly in the national conversation. They can bring continual focus to mass shootings, communicate with one another, and call politicians to action in ways that were not possible just twenty years ago.[14]

However, even if mass shootings push political leaders to act, they might not act in favor of gun control. The party affiliations of state legislatures and the sitting president's position on gun control are both factors that can affect whether legislation passed in the wake of a mass shooting restricts or expands access to guns. Between 1989 and 2014 in states with Republican-controlled legislatures, enactments of new laws that loosened gun restrictions increased after mass shootings by 75 percent, while shootings had no significant effect on laws enacted in states with Democratic-controlled legislatures.[15] Moreover, in Republican-controlled states, gun policies that restrict firearm access are not proposed as often as they are in Democratic-controlled states.[16] The evidence suggests that lawmakers regard mass shootings as an opportunity to introduce legislation in line with their party's platform. Republicans have long argued that looser gun restrictions will allow law-abiding citizens to defend themselves in dangerous situations, so they have tended to use mass shootings to justify loosening restrictions on gun ownership. This trend persisted for years—until the aftermath of the Parkland shooting.

Political Opportunity Structure as a New Perspective on Outcomes

It appears that no single factor by itself can account for the varying political outcomes after mass shootings. Instead, it might be that a combination of resources, political leadership, strategies among activists, and shifts in public opinion can tip the balance in favor of certain gun control measures. Each of the pre-Parkland mass shootings occurred in "political opportunity structures" that were relatively unfavorable to gun safety reforms. Such structures include "specific configurations of resources, institutional arrangements, and historical precedents for social mobilization, which facilitate[d] the development of protest movements in some cases and constrain them in others."[17] Although these various political elements cannot definitively determine the course of social movements, they act as ingredients that, when mixed together in certain ways, can produce very different results. No single ingredient is the most essential, but the combination of factors in political opportunity structures can be critical to explaining the variability in outcomes of social movements that have similar demands.

Political opportunity structures have the potential to either facilitate or impede social movements in several ways.[18] First, political opportunity structures determine what sources of information and financial support are available to activists and the extent to which activists can mobilize effectively and disseminate their message. In addition, current electoral laws and institutional rules can assist, impede, or shape the demands of social movements as they determine how political decision makers and interest groups interact with one another. Finally—and this factor is especially important for understanding US gun politics since Parkland—the mobilization of one social movement can boost additional movements by creating new opportunities and combining forces. A previously struggling movement can benefit from new tools and additional resources to tip the balance of public debate and incentives for policy changes.

I use the concept of political opportunity structure to help decipher differences in the effectiveness of gun safety activism and the kinds of legislation introduced after mass shootings. The political opportunity structure at the time of the 2018 Parkland shooting was more favorable to gun reformers than previous political opportunity structures had been, not because a friendly president was in office, but because there were already nationwide social protest movements willing to help the Parkland organizers and because contentious midterm elections loomed with many legislative seats apparently at stake.

What Made Parkland Different

"Welcome to the Revolution," proclaimed seventeen-year-old Cameron Kasky in front of hundreds of thousands of demonstrators gathered on Pennsylvania Avenue in Washington, DC.[19] It was March 24, 2018, and in eight hundred cities across the United States, gun safety activists took to the streets to demand gun control reform. More than one month had passed since February 14, 2018, when seventeen people were killed and seventeen more were wounded during a mass shooting at Marjory Stoneman Douglas High School in Parkland, Florida, and the high school students who survived the tragedy jolted the country into action. Students emphasized how they might turn the protest into actionable change through the upcoming elections: "Who here is going to vote in the 2018 election? If you listen real close, you can hear the people in power shaking."[20] For the first time since the Million Mom March in 2000, gun control activists took to the streets in monumental numbers, effectively putting pressure on politicians to take action on gun control.

On March 9, 2018, Florida passed Senate Bill 7026, a gun control law called the Marjory Stoneman Douglas High School Public Safety Act. This law raises the age to buy a rifle to twenty-one years, mandates a three-day waiting period for gun purchases, bans the sale of bump stocks, and includes a measure to train and arm some school employees.[21] The bill also appropriates $69 million for mental health purposes in schools, and $98 million for increasing security of school buildings.[22] Even with the provision to train and arm teachers (a provision that gun safety advocates mostly oppose), Senate Bill 7026 largely restricts gun rights for law-abiding citizens in the state of Florida. As a consequence, the NRA quickly responded by filing a federal lawsuit against the state, claiming that the provision that raised the minimum age required to purchase a rifle from eighteen to twenty-one was in violation of the Second Amendment of the US Constitution.[23]

Until the shooting in Parkland in 2018, the majority of gun laws approved at the state level after mass shootings tended to reflect the ideology of the party in power in the state. When former president Barack Obama made it a goal of his second term to call for more gun control after the Sandy Hook shooting, state legislatures only passed thirty-nine laws tightening and seventy laws loosening gun restrictions. However, when President Donald Trump did almost nothing to push for changes in gun policies in the United States after the 2018 Parkland shooting, sixty-nine gun control laws passed at state level, and only nine laws passed that loosened restrictions on gun ownership.[24] What caused such different outcomes? One contributor was unusually sustained activism by student protestors in the wake of the Parkland shooting.

A Boost from Recently Established Liberal Organizations

The Parkland students' ability to mobilize large numbers of protestors in the wake of the shooting was due, in part, to organizational networks that had already been set up by the Women's March in January of 2017. Shortly after the Parkland shooting, Women's March organizers called for students, teachers, and allies to participate in a National School Walkout on March 14, 2018, in an effort to put pressure on legislators in Congress to pass gun control reform.[25] Similar to the Women's March, the National School Walkout on March 14 began as a single Facebook event that quickly grew to include schools across the United States.[26] Upwards of three thousand schools across the country participated in the ENOUGH National School Walkout.[27]

On March 24, 2018, the March for Our Lives drew at least 1.2 million people onto the streets to protest gun violence in 450 marches across the United States.[28] Although students largely led the March for Our Lives protests, they received the help of organizational skills and resources from gun control advocacy groups and celebrities.[29] Importantly, students began the March for Our Lives Action Fund, collecting donations to push for gun safety legislation at the local, state, and federal level. Funding is critical for continuing activism, maintaining the salience of gun control as a policy issue, and keeping pressure on politicians to introduce legislation.

Indivisible is a widespread network of local progressive groups working to resist the Trump agenda, and this nationwide network helped organize protests against gun violence after the shooting in Parkland.[30] National Indivisible, a professional advocacy organization headquartered in Washington, DC, worked to make gun control a highly relevant issue by backing a National School Walkout on April 20, 2018, initiated by Lane Murdock, a high school student in Connecticut.[31] The organization played a large role in amplifying this National Walkout, assisting individuals in registering their own school walkouts on the Indivisible website or finding local school walkouts in communities around the United States.[32] Local, volunteer-led Indivisible-affiliated groups also organized many local anti-gun violence marches, in places ranging from Seattle to Charlottesville.[33] Indivisible Evanston set up voter registration booths in Chicago to help the student organizers during the March for Our Lives to register young voters.[34] Since the early marches, Indivisible groups have continued to encourage dialogue within communities about gun policy.[35]

In other words, by the time of the Parkland shooting, organizational networks and institutions that were set up in response to Donald Trump's 2016 election were in place to help students at Marjory Stoneman Douglas High School spark and spread large-scale protests and provoke legislative responses in states around the country. Because the Women's March organizers, as well as liberal groups like Indivisible, had mobilized after the election of Donald Trump, they were already active and able to share organizational skills and resources to boost new young activists in early 2018. In short, to understand why gun control calls did better after Parkland, by mobilizing thousands of people to protest of gun violence and ratcheting up political pressure on politicians to respond, we must situate the Parkland case in the broader political context of backlash and protest against President Trump and his political agenda.

Ultimately, the broad scope of protest after the shooting in Parkland, Florida shows how emerging movements can gain momentum from other social movements already under way. The March for Our Lives that took place in cities across the nation is a clear example of this convergence and cross-feeding of movements prepared to push together for a particular cause.

A Significant Shift in Public Opinion

According to a CNN poll conducted by SSRS after the shooting at Marjory Stoneman Douglas High School, American public support for stricter gun control legislation in February 2018 was at the highest level (70 percent) since 1993, when the Brady Bill was passed.[36] Although there are always upticks in support for gun control after mass shootings, the Parkland shooting created an unusually large shift in public support for stricter gun laws. A February 2018 *Politico/Morning Consult* poll showed support for stricter gun laws around 68 percent, a high-water mark in the percentage of Americans who want more restrictive gun laws since *Politico* starting measuring views two years prior. Previously, *Politico* had found that 58 percent of Americans supported stricter gun laws after the 2016 Pulse nightclub shooting that left forty-nine people dead, 64 percent supported such reforms after the 2017 Las Vegas music festival that left fifty-eight dead, and 60 percent supported reforms after the 2017 Sutherland Springs church shooting that left twenty-six people dead. Analysts claimed that something was different about the post-Parkland shooting, noting that support for gun control legislation was higher than after any of the other preceding mass shootings.[37]

Most interesting is the increase in support for stricter laws on gun sales among Independents and Republicans. According to Gallup polls, in November 2016, support for stricter laws on gun sales was 78 percent among Democrats, 51 percent among Independents, and 33 percent among Republicans.[38] After the Las Vegas shooting, support for stricter gun laws increased among Democrats to 90 percent and 56 percent among Independents, but remained the same for Republicans at 33 percent. However, the Parkland shooting created a remarkable shift in public opinion. In March 2018, support among Democrats remained the same at 90 percent, but support among Independents increased by 9 percentage points to 65 percent and support among Republicans increased by 8 percentage points to 41 percent.

An important new development since the Parkland tragedy is that young voters seem to be more willing to vote for candidates that favor gun control, putting additional pressure on politicians who run for office. One of the survivors of the Parkland shooting argued that the March for Our Lives movement demonstrated to politicians that young people were going to be a much more organized force than in the past.[39] Moreover, she claimed that the issue of gun control in particular would motivate their voting patterns, making gun laws a "central issue" in the midterm elections in November 2018 and in the future.

The language used by the high school students who gave speeches at the march in Washington, DC, echoed and encouraged this sentiment, especially the speech by Parkland shooting survivor Cameron Kasky. He pointed to his generation's unique position, as individuals who have grown up in a society where mass shootings are frequent. He called the #NeverAgain movement for gun control "the revolution" and he emphasized that it is "by and for the young people of this country."[40] Importantly, Kasky's speech underlined the power of young citizens' voices and votes, and he called on politicians to "either represent the people or get out." In light of the virtually exclusive use of semi-automatic assault firearms in mass shootings, his message was further stressed in his concluding remark: "The people demand a law banning the sale of assault weapons. The people demand we prohibit the sale of high-capacity magazines. The people demand universal background checks. Stand for us or beware: the voters are coming."

Changing the Narrative and Expanding the Rhetoric

In the past, after many US mass shootings prior to Parkland, the gun control movement struggled to communicate a compelling and convincing narrative about restricting gun rights.[41] In the wake of high-profile mass shootings, legislation that restricted gun rights tended to fail because gun rights advocates are quick to claim that the underlying causes of mass shootings are difficult to pinpoint. They argue against broad proposals to restrict gun rights such as a ban on assault weapons by asserting that these measures would not have prevented the specific mass shooting that just occurred.[42] And they focus on pinpointing specific problems that may have led to each specific shooting. In the case of Virginia Tech, Sandy Hook and Marjory Stoneman Douglas, gun rights advocates argued that there were gaps in mental health reporting.[43] After the Las Vegas shooting, they focused on banning bump fire stocks, a mechanism that turned the semi-automatic weapons the shooter was using into virtually automatic firearms. In Sutherland Springs, the fact that a law-abiding bystander was able to use his own gun to stop the church shooter encouraged pro-gun advocates to push for new rules allowing guns in churches. These examples demonstrate how debates surrounding mass shootings can become narrowly focused on creating legislation that follows partisan lines and addresses indirect or secondary causes of the shooting rather than tackling the overall issue of easy access to guns and ammunition.

The students in Parkland, Florida, made headway at shifting the public conversation in part because they built on other movements underway, and in part because they took heart from the liberal tendencies of their immediate local community. But the Parkland students also moved quickly to build national alliances, to include students and families in many other places who are exposed to gun violence on a daily basis. The Parkland students intentionally met with other students from schools in Chicago's inner city and spoke with them about the effects that a very different kind of gun violence has had in their communities. The meeting was organized by the former Chicago Public Schools CEO and US secretary of education, Arne Duncan, and held at the home of Emma Gonzalez in Florida.[44] The dialogue between these two groups of students—both in person and ongoing via social media—demonstrates how the issue of gun violence is now being reframed. At the March for Our Lives rally in Washington, multiple speakers of color called attention to the daily burden of gun violence in America's inner cities. Through this inclusion, the #NeverAgain Movement opened the doors to a debate that gets outside of the usual rhetoric about preventing mass shootings by specifically closing "loopholes" in the laws that enable mentally ill individuals to access guns. Instead, the movement turned the focus to a multiracial issue, seeking to address the everyday gun violence experienced by students living in cities with high homicide rates such as Washington, DC, Los Angeles, and Chicago.

Students from Marjory Stoneman Douglas High School have been actively including these students' voices in their rallies, acknowledging that the media tends to focus on suburban school shootings in white, privileged communities.[45] Emma Gonzalez, a Parkland survivor and a leading figure of the #NeverAgain Movement, stresses that "the platform us Parkland students have established is to be shared with every person, black or white, gay or straight, religious or not, who has experienced gun violence."[46] This shift in the way the gun violence debate is framed in the aftermath of the mass shooting in Florida was absolutely vital to the capacity of the gun control movement to expand the political base of individuals pushing for changes in gun control legislation. Furthermore, this language helped ensure that solutions proposed by legislators are not simply small changes to specific legislation gaps that facilitated a single shooter's access to guns. The Parkland students were able to appeal to more broadly shared positions about the problems of everyday gun violence in America, improving the gun control movement's ability to mobilize advocates for its cause.

Rising Pressure on Politicians

In addition to cultivating a broad base of advocates, the efficacy of social movements depends on the institutional rules that affect how politicians, the public, and interest groups interact with one another. These arrangements can assist, respond to, or shape the demands of social movements.[47]

One underappreciated institutional factor in the political aftermath of the Parkland shooting was the fact that the Florida State legislature was in the midst of their two-month session when the shooting occurred. This circumstance enabled a powerful member of the Florida senate, Democrat Lauren Book, to persuade the Republican senate president, the incoming Republican senate president, the House Speaker, and all his deputies to come to Parkland High School before they cleaned up the scene of the shooting.[48] The visual aspect of the bloody aftermath inside the school affected Republican legislators aligned with the NRA immensely, and they felt that kids like the seventeen-year-old Parkland shooter should be prevented from gaining access to a gun. Lauren Book also helped organize the students' trip to Tallahassee to advocate for stricter gun laws in the state legislature. Neither of these outcomes would have happened had the legislature not been in the middle of its two-month session.

At the national level, both Republican and Democratic legislators focused on the issue of gun control as the 2018 midterm elections approached, a clear result of the aftermath of the Parkland shooting. The increasing salience of gun control advocacy is a clear rallying point for voters opposed to Donald Trump, and local Democratic Parties across the country used the March for Our Lives to register voters in their state. In Virginia, Democrats went to the area where buses were leaving to bring protesters to Washington and registered voters at this site.[49] In addition, gun control organizations such as Everytown for Gun Safety and Giffords began voter-registration initiatives at high schools in swing states. The executive director of Giffords explained that "you either change the composition of the electorate or you change people's minds who are already voting, and I think the post-Parkland movement will be helpful on both fronts."[50]

During 2018, Republicans also showed movement on the issue of gun control in the face of the upcoming elections. John Kasich, the Republican governor of Ohio, argued that lawmakers should be held accountable in the 2018 midterm elections due to their inaction in implementing gun laws that are supported by the majority of the electorate.[51] Major donors to the Republican Party claimed they would no longer support candidates who do not want a military-style weapons ban.[52] Some Republican strategists stressed that the gun issue would deepen the party's problems in moderate suburban areas, and that the Republicans must defy the NRA or risk driving away these voters.[53]

The stands taken by many 2018 candidates on gun control demonstrate how the NRA had lost some of its grip on gun politics.[54] In the wake of the Parkland shooting, Democrats in rural areas openly defied the NRA.[55] For example, a Democratic representative of Kentucky called for gun control on the House floor, claiming he was "surrendering" his NRA rating. In addition, some Democratic candidates in Montana, who were silent on the issue before the Parkland shooting, quickly modified their platforms after—some calling for new gun laws to ban bump stocks, outlaw the AR-15, or eliminate the loopholes for purchases made at private gun shows. Candidate Kathleen Williams, a Democratic politician, claimed that "if the NRA wants to give me an F for that, then I will proudly stand with all of you and say that F means fearless."[56] These Democrats pointed to growing dissatisfaction with the NRA and increasing support for universal background checks among voters as reason for testing the rules of election success in rural America.

Ultimately, representatives and candidates of both parties were paying attention to the significant shifts in public opinion after the Parkland shooting, and some were definitely focusing in on the issue of gun control in the 2018 midterm elections. Along with the support gun control causes received from coterminous resistance movements that emerged after the election of President Trump, the proximity in time of the February 2018 Parkland shooting to the November 2018 midterm elections clearly encouraged increased attention to gun control from candidates in both parties.

After the Parkland shooting, the convergence of multiple factors affected the legislative response and outcome in the state of Florida. These factors include a substantial shift in public opinion, possibly resulting from the recent high frequency of shootings with large numbers of victims, the activism embraced by the students of Stoneman Douglas High School, the organization and mobilization of large groups of people in attention-grabbing marches nationwide, and the use of social media to communicate a concrete and compelling message to encourage young people to vote specifically with gun control in mind in the November 2018 midterm election. This protest against gun violence played out against a backdrop of significant protest against Donald Trump's political agenda, enabling students across the country to utilize preexisting liberal organizational networks to spread their message and movement. In previous shootings during the Trump presidency, the victims were not connected in a close-knit liberal community such as the one in South Florida. The Parkland survivors enjoyed a sense of cohesion—and they were teenagers who could tap into allies beyond their high school to spread a unified message on a national scale. As a consequence of this survivor advocacy in aftermath of the Parkland shooting, public discussions of gun violence, its costs and remedies, broadened rather than narrowed and grew rather than fizzled out as they did after earlier mass shootings. The fusion of the post-Parkland activism into the broader political currents and social movements roiling in 2018 in turn put tremendous pressure on politicians in many states to respond with gun control debates and some actual reforms. Crucially, the post-Parkland gun control movement also expanded debates to include the voices of victims of everyday gun violence rather than just mass shootings.

Organization and Protest from 1999 to 2018

In the big picture, clear differences between 1999 and 2018 enabled the Marjory Stoneman Douglas students in Florida to organize extensive protests in ways that Columbine students could not, despite the fact that both shootings had similar profiles: young shooters, more than ten deaths, and a cohesive high school community. The extent of social media usage in society by 2018 allowed activists to communicate with large numbers of people very quickly. In addition, the resources available to gun control organizations had grown in number, especially in the years after the Sandy Hook shooting. Moreover, the specific juncture in the Florida State legislature created a unique opportunity for students to influence state legislators.

In the political aftermath of the Parkland shooting, the affected surviving students mobilized massive protests across the country in a relatively short amount of time, gained funding and resources from prominent figures, and created a compelling narrative about the role that the younger generation could have in voting politicians out of office in the 2018 midterm elections. In the aftermath of the Columbine mass shooting, students and their supporters also mobilized; for instance, the Colorado Coalition Against Gun Violence organized the May 2, 1999, demonstration against the NRA's decision to hold its convention in Denver two weeks after the shooting at Columbine High School, and seven thousand people marched in protest.[57] In addition, the father of one Columbine shooting victim launched a gun control organization and political action group called Sane Alternatives to the Firearms Epidemic (SAFE) to advocate for reform to gun regulations.[58] On July 15, 1999, ninety students representing SAFE Colorado traveled to Washington, DC, and met with then-president Clinton and members of Congress to advocate for reasonable gun regulations and close the gun-show loophole that had enabled the perpetrators of the Columbine massacre to obtain firearms. But the Columbine survivors were not successful in the nation's capital, and when they returned to Colorado they shifted toward trying to get gun limits through the state legislature.[59] However, unlike the students in Parkland nineteen years later, Columbine students were not able to provoke action from the Republican-controlled state legislature.

While the legislative outcomes were significantly different, the Columbine shooting and the Marjory Stoneman Douglas shooting had factors in common that allow us to pinpoint what ultimately changed by 2018. In both of these cases, students were able to band together and advocate for gun control in ways that the affected populations in other mass shootings could not—because the affected population was either too young (Sandy Hook), or too disconnected from one another (Las Vegas). Similarly, the college students at Virginia Tech came from various parts of the country and the student body as a whole likely held dissimilar political ideologies. As high school students from small communities, the survivors of Columbine and Parkland were better equipped to promote a unified message about gun violence and gun control after the shootings at their schools.

By 2018, however, the Parkland students were able to take advantage of widely used social media platforms like Facebook, Twitter, and Snapchat to spread and control their own message rapidly in the days after the shooting— and this, in turn, helped them connect to other ongoing social movements.[60]

Within forty-eight hours of the shooting, the student protestors, led by a group from the drama club and debate team who were comfortable with public speaking, began their #NeverAgain movement. During these initial stages of the protest, the students gained enough traction on social media to get the attention of Women's March organizers, who connected with students to provide the organizational structure and the channels for the #NeverAgain movement to arrange a march on Washington. This connection with the Women's March organizers was particularly important in amplifying their message nationwide and in achieving the broad impact of the Parkland student activism.

The clever use of social media was vital for the Parkland students to gain attention from mainstream news outlets, prominent politicians, and other gun control activists. However, their momentum depended on other crucial factors: the availability of resources and, ironically, the lack of presidential support for gun control. The importance of these factors is apparent when compared to the political aftermath of the Sandy Hook Elementary School shooting. Both the Sandy Hook shooting and the Parkland shooting took place in a school setting during a time when social media allowed for quick online communication. However, the children at Sandy Hook, mostly ages six and seven, were too young to promote a cohesive political message like the high school students at Parkland. The parents of the victims, rather than the students who witnessed their classmates murdered, wound up carrying the mantle as the main voices in the ensuing gun control debates—and they quickly reached out to President Obama, who made a major push for federal legislation that restricted access to guns. Sandy Hook gun control advocates felt that the president was working to promote their agenda and that they would likely come out victorious. Ironically, this may have undercut immediate incentives for them to continue their own vehement protests—in a way that post-Parkland advocates always knew they had to do with Republican officials in control both in Washington, DC, and their own state. The post–Sandy Hook efforts followed the trajectory of previous mass shootings, in that they subsided short of sustained gains. Nevertheless, the gruesome massacre of small children at Sandy Hook and its extreme emotional impact prompted supporters of gun control such as Shannon Watts and Michael Bloomberg to create new gun control advocacy organizations, respectively Moms Demand Action and Everytown for Gun Safety, that some years later became critical to the effectiveness of the gun control movement after the Parkland shooting. The Sandy Hook shooting demonstrated that it was not enough to have the president of the United States advocating for and pressuring Congress to act on gun control. In fact, it would later turn out that resources and organizational capacity of the individuals affected by the shooting and their capacities to connect to nationwide allies would be much more pivotal.

The Future of US Gun Control Politics

Although a majority of voters in the United States support gun control policies such as universal background checks, the individuals who oppose gun control laws have long been much more likely to call their congressional representatives about the issue of gun rights protection and make it the determinant factor of how they vote in elections.[61] The 2018 midterm elections marked a shift in this pattern. Democratic politicians became much more willing to include gun control in their platform.[62] The majority of Democrats on the "red to blue" list, which is a list of candidates who were competing in districts held by Republicans that the Democratic Party aimed to flip, advocated for gun regulation and included gun control on their election platforms. This expanded campaign focus on gun control represented a tremendous increase from 2016, when only four of the thirty-six candidates on the list included gun control in their platforms.[63] Shannon Watts, founder of Moms Demand Action for Gun Sense in America, explained how "so many candidates for Congress, particularly women, are running on this issue—not just making it part of their platform and not just supporting it, but actually running on it."[64]

The 2018 midterm elections marked the first time that the NRA was outspent by gun control groups under current finance laws. The NRA spent $10 million during this election, and gun control groups spent $2.4 million more.[65] According to the Center for Responsive Politics, Everytown for Gun Safety and Giffords Law Center spent millions of dollars on the campaigns for Lucy McBath and Jason Crow.[66] A gun safety advocate and national spokeswoman for Everytown, McBath upset the incumbent Republican in Georgia's sixth congressional district, Karen Handel.[67] Democrat Jason Crow in Colorado, who spoke about the disproportionate impact that gun violence has had on his community and the need to fund the Center for Disease Control to look into this "public health crisis," beat incumbent Republican Mike Coffman, who had an A rating from the NRA.[68] Crow ran on a platform explicitly in favor of gun control, advocating for banning assault weapons and restricting high-capacity magazines.[69] In the 2014 midterm elections, the NRA spent upwards of $25 million on congressional campaigns, and $55 million in the 2016 elections, more than half of which was utilized for Donald Trump's election.[70] The amount spent in 2018 presents a significant decrease in the amount of political spending from the NRA. Overall, Democrats with an F rating from the NRA, who made gun control a part of their campaign, prevailed in swing states such as Virginia, Nevada, Wisconsin and Colorado and in conservative states such as South Carolina and Kansas. In addition to these candidate electoral outcomes, the State of Washington passed a referendum called Initiative 1639, "Safe Schools, Safe Communities."[71] This initiative raises the legal age to purchase semi-automatic rifles to twenty-one years, implements a ten-day waiting period, requires gun owners to store their guns properly or face criminal charges, and mandates that purchasers pass an "enhanced background check" and take a firearm safety class before obtaining a gun.[72]

The political aftermath of the Marjory Stoneman Douglas High School shooting diverges significantly from the political responses to other high-profile mass shootings in multiple ways. First, the students defied previous partisan legislative responses to shootings by provoking the Republican-controlled Florida legislature to pass the state's first serious gun restrictions in decades.[73] Second, students across the United States organized nation-wide protests in favor of gun control, overcoming historic and significant barriers to such widespread activism. This activism culminated in a massive Washington, DC, march, as well as in demonstrations across countless other cities, paralleling the Women's March in January of 2017. Third, by the end of 2018, state legislatures passed sixty-nine gun control laws, and rejected 90 percent of state-level measures backed by the NRA, a significant difference from the aftermath of Sandy Hook, when state gun control measures roughly equalled numbers of pro-gun rights measures.[74]

The political opportunity structure perspective provides a useful framework for understanding differences in the political outcomes of mass shootings. Each shooting took place within a specific configuration of resources, precedent for mobilization, institutional arrangement, and political leadership strategy. These factors all contribute to either constraining the gun control movement or enhancing the ability of gun control activists to promote change. Considered together, they explain why some shootings led to almost no new legislation on gun control, while others, like the Parkland shooting, furthered widespread movements to influence policy and election cycles.

Parkland students were successful in organizing quickly because they first captured and held the public's attention through their clever use of social media, enabling them to gain strong political momentum at the state level and bring the issue to national attention. Then, students in various states capitalized on preexisting liberal organizational networks and gun control organizations, created or expanded after the Sandy Hook shooting, to further structure and expand their influence and create a nationwide protest movement. This translated into the ability to raise significant funding to further advocate for comprehensive gun control reform and made gun control a salient issue during the 2018 midterm election. Preexisting gun control organizational networks such as Brady, Everytown, and Giffords, as well as Women's March leaders provided resources and expanded the organizational capacity of the Parkland students. In addition, the looming 2018 midterms put increasing pressure on politicians and enabled activists to make gun control a highly visible election issue.

America's responses to future deadly violence will heavily depend on the ability of gun control advocates to organize effectively, maintain pressure on state legislators, and influence politicians' positions in such a way that gun control becomes a critical focus of future policy agendas. Gun control in the United States will continue to be a contentious issue, and gun control legislation proposed at the federal level may or may not not be signed into law in the near feature. The politics of gun control in the United States is about much more than which political party has control in state legislatures and the federal government. It is about more than political polarization. In order for legislation on gun policy to change, the gun control movement needs immense resources, nationwide connections and organizational capabilities among its proponents, and the ability to put sustained pressure on politicians.

Was the shooting in Parkland, Florida, a tipping point toward more significant progress in fights for gun control legislation? So far, the answer appears to be yes. The Parkland shooting happened when many of the cofactors necessary to facilitate a significant step forward by the appropriate activism were available. Although no individual shooting can completely tip the scale so drastically toward very strict gun control in this country, each successive shooting in the past twenty years has contributed to slight changes in the political opportunity structure, pushing the scale slightly farther in support of new gun control policies. The activism among gun control advocates during 2018 carried the Bipartisan Background Checks Act of 2019 through the House of Representatives and onwards to the Senate. As a result of this momentum—and given the obvious reality that mass shootings continue as they horrifically did through the summer of 2019—the Democratic Party's 2020 presidential candidates are making gun reform a top priority in their campaigns. These are clear signs that gun control advocates accomplished something incredibly important in 2018: they maintained the relevance of gun violence prevention and kept the country focused on possibilities for gun control legislation long after the Parkland shooting itself receded from America's television screens.

Notes

1. Maggie Astor, "Columbine Shocked the Nation. Now, Mass Shootings Are Less Surprising," *New York Times*, November 10, 2017.
2. Maggie Astor and Karl Russell, "After Parkland, a New Surge in State Gun Control Laws," *New York Times*, December 14, 2018.
3. Bipartisan Background Checks Act of 2019, H.R. 8, 116 Cong. (2019).
4. Data on the composition of state legislatures was taken from the National Conference of State Legislatures, Washington, DC, 2018.
5. "America's Complex Relationship with Guns," Pew Research Center, June 22, 2017. Available at http://www.pewsocialtrends.org/2017/06/22/americas-complex-relationship-with-

guns/#ideology; "Public Views About Guns," Pew Research Center, June 22, 2017; and "2012 Frank Luntz National Poll of Gun Owners and NRA Members," Everytown for Gun Safety, New York, October 20, 2012.

6. Michael Siegel, "State Firearm Laws," Boston University School of Public Health, available at http://www.statefirearmlaws.org as of March 11, 2019.

7. S. Mo Jang, "Mass Shootings Backfire: The Boomerang Effects of Death Concerns on Policy Attitudes," *Media Psychology* 22, no. 2 (2019): 298–322.

8. Robert Longley, "See a Timeline of Gun Control in the United States," ThoughtCo., February 22, 2018, available at https://www.thoughtco.com/us-gun-control-timeline-3963620, as of March 13, 2019.

9. "Public Views About Guns," Pew Research Center.

10. Jang, "Mass Shootings Backfire."

11. Jang, "Mass Shootings Backfire."

12. Kristin Goss, *Disarmed, America's Missing Popular Movement for Gun Control* (Princeton, NJ: Princeton University Press, 2006).

13. Kristen Goss, "Ep. 51, The Missing Gun Control Movement," interview by Kelly Brownell, *Policy 360 Podcast*, Sanford School of Public Policy, October 5, 2017, audio, available at https://sites.duke.edu/policy360/2017/10/05/ep-51-the-missing-gun-control-movement.

14. These observations are informed by email exchanges with Kristin Goss.

15. Michael Luca, Deepak Malhotra, and Christopher Poliquin, "The Impact of Mass Shootings on Gun Policy," Harvard Business School NOM Unit Working Paper No. 16-126, October 2016. Available at https://www.hbs.edu/faculty/Pages/item.aspx?num=51060.

16. Katie Park, Nate Rott, Jeff Landa, and Alyson Hurt, "After Mass Shootings, Action on Gun Legislation Soars at State Level," NPR, July 12, 2016.

17. Herbert Kitschelt, "Political Opportunity Structures and Political Protest: Anti-Nuclear Movements in Four Democracies," *British Journal of Political Science* 16, no. 1 (January 1986): 57–85.

18. This paragraph draws from Kitschelt, "Political Opportunity Structures and Political Protest," 61–62.

19. Annie Correal, Caitlin Dickerson, Jacey Fortin, Jonathan Wolfe, and Louis Lucero II, "March for Our Lives Highlights: Students Protesting Guns Say 'Enough is Enough,'" *New York Times*, March 24, 2018.

20. Correal, Dickerson, Fortin, Wolfe, and Lucero II, "March for Our Lives Highlights."

21. Meghan Keneally, "How Gun Laws Have Changed in 4 States Since the Parkland Shooting," ABC News, March 22, 2018.

22. Ray Sanchez and Holly Yan, "Florida Gov. Rick Scott Signs Gun Bill," CNN, March 9, 2018.

23. Steve Almasy, "NRA Sues Florida to Block Part of New Gun Law," CNN, March 9, 2018.

24. Astor and Russell, "After Parkland, a New Surge in State Gun Control Laws."

25. Isabella Gomez and Amanda Jackson, "Women's March Organizers Are Planning a National Student Walkout to Protest Gun Violence," CNN, February 18, 2018.

26. Gomez and Jackson, "Women's March Organizers."

27. Jack Crow, "School Walkout Organizers Can't Decide What They're Protesting," *National Review*, March 14, 2018.

28. German Lopez, "It's Official: March for Our Lives Was One of the Biggest Youth Protests Since the Vietnam War," Vox, March 26, 2018.

29. Alan Blinder, Jess Bidgood, and Vivian Wang, "In Gun Control Marches, Students Led but Adults Provided Key Resources," *New York Times*, March 25, 2018; and Sarah Gray, "The March for Our Lives Protest Is This Saturday. Here's Everything to Know," *Time*, March 23, 2018.

30. Information on the Indivisible Project comes from its website: https://indivisible.org/ as of May 2019.

31. Jen Kirby, "The March for Our Lives, Explained," Vox, March 24, 2019.

32. Information on Indivisible activities supporting the National School Walkout is available at https://act.indivisible.org/event/national-school-walkout/create, as of May 7, 2018.

33. Melissa Hellmann, "Students against Gun Violence Speak Out at March for Our Lives," *Seattle Weekly*, March 25, 2018; and Daily Progress Staff Reports, "Local Anti-Gun Violence

March Set for Saturday," *Daily Process*, available at http://www.dailyprogress.com/news/local/local-anti-gun-violence-march-set-for-saturday/article_559a1e1e-2ef2-   11e8-8d5d-6744b3d6b657.html, as of March 13, 2019.

34. Syd Stone, "Evanston, North Shore Residents Protest Gun Violence at March for Our Lives," *Daily Northwestern*, April 3, 2018.
35. For example, Jaime Cook, "Indivisible Lowville to Host Second Gun Forum," *Watertown Daily Times*, May 1, 2018.
36. SSRS Solutions Study, *CNN*, February 25, 2018.
37. Steven Shepard, "Gun Control Support Surges in Polls," *Politico*, February 28, 2018.
38. "U.S. Preference for Stricter Gun Laws Highest Since 1993," Gallup, Washington, DC, March 14, 2018.
39. Alexander Burns and Julie Turkewitz, "Beyond Gun Control, Student Marches Aim to Upend Elections," *New York Times*, March 22, 2018.
40. Kayla Epstein and Teddy Amenabar, "The 6 Most Memorable Speeches at the March for Our Lives in D.C.," *Washington Post*, March 24, 2018.
41. Goss, "Disarmed."
42. Bowes, "Va. Tech Tragedy Had Little Impact."
43. Bowes, "Va. Tech Tragedy Had Little Impact."
44. Matt Masterson, "Chicago Students Talk Gun Violence with Parkland Shooting Survivors," *Chicago Tonight*, March 6, 2018.
45. George Zornick, "How the #NeverAgain Movement Is Disrupting Gun Politics," *The Nation*, April 3, 2018.
46. Masterson, "Chicago Students Talk Gun Violence."
47. Kitschelt, "Political Opportunity Structures and Political Protest," 62.
48. This account comes from an interview by the author with Mary Ellen Klas, capital bureau chief for the *Miami Herald*, November 20, 2018.
49. Alexander Burns and Jonathan Martin, "Gun Marches Keep Republicans on Defense in Midterm Elections," *New York Times*, March 25, 2018.
50. Amber Phillips, "How to Tell If the Gun-Control Movement Is Going to Be a Major Player in November," *Washington Post*, April 20, 2018.
51. Devan Cole, "Kasich: Politicians 'Should Be Held Absolutely Accountable at the Ballot Box,'" CNN, March 25, 2018.
52. Al Hoffman Jr., "Republican Donor Breaks with Party over Gun Legislation," interview by Rachel Martin, NPR, February 23, 2018.
53. Burns and Martin, "Gun Marches Keep Republicans on Defense."
54. Nicole Hong and Reid J. Epstein, "After the 'March for Our Lives,' Student Activists Focus on Midterm Elections," *Wall Street Journal*, March 25, 2018.
55. Alan Blinder, "In Red-State Races, Democrats Seek an Edge by Defying the N.R.A.," *New York Times*, April 11, 2018.
56. Blinder, "In Red-State Races."
57. Katherine Seelye and James Brooke, "Terror in Littleton: The Gun Lobby; Protest Greets N.R.A. Meeting in Denver," *New York Times*, May 2, 1999.
58. Jeremy Schulman, "19 Years Before Parkland, Columbine Students Tried to Fix America's Gun Problem," *Mother Jones*, March 23, 2018.
59. "President Clinton and Vice President Gore: Working to Protect Children from Gun Violence," White House, July 15, 1999, https://clintonwhitehouse4.archives.gov/WH/Work/071599.html; Schulman, "19 Years Before Parkland."
60. "5 Facts About Americans and Facebook," Gallup, Washington, DC, April 10, 2018.
61. German Lopez, "The 2018 Midterm Elections May Have Exposed a Shift on Gun Control," Vox, November 7, 2018.
62. Jason Le Miere, "Gun Control Laws 2018: Midterm Elections Measures and How Vote Could Impact Legislation," *Newsweek*, November 6, 2018.
63. Le Miere, "Gun Control Laws 2018."
64. Quoted in Le Miere, "Gun Control Laws 2018."
65. Erin Corbett, "Gun Control Groups Spent $2.4 Million More than the NRA in Midterm Elections," *Fortune*, November 13, 2018.

66. Lois Beckett, "Gun Control Groups Outspent NRA in Midterm Elections," *The Guardian*, November 11, 2018.
67. Timothy L. O'Brien, "A Step Forward in the Fight Against Gun Violence," *Bloomberg*, November 9, 2018.
68. Corbett, "Gun Control Groups."
69. Maggie Astor, "Bearing F's from the N.R.A., Some Democrats Are Campaigning Openly on Guns," *New York Times*, November 4, 2018.
70. Beckett, "Gun Control Groups Outspent NRA."
71. Le Miere, "Gun Control Laws 2018."
72. O'Brien, "A Step Forward in the Fight."
73. "2018 State and Legislative Partisan Composition," National Conference of State Legislatures, Washington, DC, 2018. Available at http://www.ncsl.org/Portals/1/Documents/Elections/Legis_Control_011018_26973.pdf as of March 13, 2019.
74. Astor and Russell, "After Parkland, a New Surge in State Gun Control Laws."

11

The Texas-Sized Impact of Beto O'Rourke's 2018 Senate Campaign

ELIZA OEHMLER AND MICHAEL ZOOROB

Texas has not elected a Democrat statewide since 1994, the longest partisan shutout seen in any state. That did not change in 2018, when El Paso Democratic Representative Robert O'Rourke—popularly known as "Beto"—ran against Ted Cruz, an incumbent GOP senator. Although Cruz survived, Beto's surprisingly strong challenge upended Texas politics by garnering 48 percent of the vote in a state Republicans usually win by landslide margins. Beto's energetic campaign made inroads into suburban districts and developed a robust campaign network of volunteers, offices, and staff that sparked a massive Democratic turnout in November 2018, when O'Rourke's more than four million votes exceeded Hillary Clinton's 2016 total by two hundred thousand. The 2018 election suggests that gigantic Texas is fast turning into a competitive state—a development that amounts to an earthquake in national politics.

What made Beto's remarkable Senate campaign possible, and how exactly has it contributed to shifts in Texas politics? Why was 2018 the year that Texas became a battleground? Although much ink has been spilled on O'Rourke's personality and charisma, we chart a different path to address these questions by examining the organizational precursors and products of his campaign. We begin by tracing changes in the partisan landscape since the civil rights movement, including the long decline in Democratic Party strength in Texas and its increasing confinement to major cities and Hispanic areas of the Rio Grande Valley. We survey recent efforts by organized groups like Battleground Texas and the Texas Organizing Project to revive political competition in the state, and then probe two important organizational elements in O'Rourke's 2018 campaign. First, we examine Beto's "254 Strategy," his project to visit each of the 254 counties in Texas between March 2017 and June 2018 to contact voters missed

Eliza Oehmler and Michael Zoorob, *The Texas-Sized Impact of Beto O'Rourke's 2018 Senate Campaign* In: *Upending American Politics* Edited by: Theda Skocpol and Caroline Tervo, Oxford University Press (2020). © Oxford University Press
DOI: 10.1093/oso/9780190083526.003.0011

by Democrats for a generation. Although this effort likely helped O'Rourke boost his credibility and name recognition and cultivate an amiable reputation, it did not win new votes in rural Texas. In the final six months before November 2018, Beto's campaign focus shifted dramatically towards large metropolitan areas and involved opening more than seven hundred Grassroots HQs (headquarters) and "Pop-Up Offices" where staff and volunteers coordinated to turn out the vote. Coincident with the Beto campaign, many Indivisible grassroots resistance groups also took to the field. Focusing on these efforts, the second part of our analysis uses statistical models to estimate the electoral effects of the O'Rourke campaign infrastructure and the presence of Indivisible affiliates. Controlling for past election results and a battery of socioeconomic and demographic covariates, we find evidence of meaningful, if modest, effects from these organizational networks.

As we spell out in this chapter, even though Beto O'Rourke ultimately did not unseat Ted Cruz, his strong performance mattered in several ways. By the night of the election, Beto's coattails contributed to down-ballot Democratic successes in unseating two incumbent Republican members of Congress and winning fourteen state legislative seats and dozens of local contests. The earlier unfolding of his campaign may have accelerated the rebuilding of statewide Democratic Party infrastructure by developing new connections, experience, data, and organizing skills to pass forward into future campaigns. Not least important, O'Rourke's surprisingly strong 2018 performance has also prompted ongoing efforts from the national Democratic Party to invest new field offices and staff in Texas—with an eye to competing hard for new legislative seats and even the presidency in 2020 and beyond.

The Prior Organizational Landscape

Beto's 2018 campaign emerged in the context of long-term decline and failure for Democrats in Texas, yet the campaign's efforts also built on and benefited from large-scale liberal organizing efforts that had been under way there for many years. Since 2010, groups associated in the Texas Organizing Project had focused on local issues to expand the electorate and boost Democratic prospects in the most populous counties. In 2013, the "Battleground Texas" project entered the scene, holding voter drives and training volunteers to conduct their own mobilization efforts. Finally, around the same time that the Beto campaign got going various anti-Trump resistance groups like those in the national Indivisible and Swing Left networks entered the scene. While Texas remained staunchly red, all of these organizing efforts helped shape the context in which the O'Rourke campaign operated, laying the groundwork for a robust statewide Democratic campaign.

The Decline of Texas Democrats

Like much of the South, Texas was a one-party Democratic stronghold for the bulk of the twentieth century. However, the civil rights movement and rapid population growth weakened the Democratic stranglehold on the levers of power, and two-party competition emerged in Texas. Compared to other parts of the South, this process occurred relatively earlier in Texas, where massive growth of cities and suburbs brought outsiders without peculiarly southern partisan loyalty to the Democratic Party. At the national level, Eisenhower won the state twice in 1952 and 1956, and no Democratic presidential candidate has carried the state since 1976. In 1961, Republican John G. Tower won a special election to the Senate with 50.6 percent of votes, filling the Senate seat vacated by incumbent Lyndon B. Johnson, who had become vice president. This victory brought to power the first statewide Republican in Texas since Reconstruction (Tower was also the first modern Republican senator in the entire former Confederacy). Capitalizing further on these gains, and Texans' frustrations with the Kennedy administration and its push for civil rights legislation, the Republicans won two additional congressional seats in 1962. By 1978, Republicans won their first victory in a governor's race in a century, an event described as demarcating an "entirely new type of politics in the state, establishing a viable Republican Party and a shaken and weakening Democratic Party for the next generation of Texas politicians."[1]

In a few decades, the narrative changed from "first Republicans to win statewide" to "the last Democrats to win." In 1988, Texas reelected Democratic Senator Lloyd Bentsen, the last Democratic senator to win in Texas. In 1994, George W. Bush unseated incumbent governor Ann Richards, the last Texas Democrat to serve as governor. That same year was the last time Democrats won any statewide office: incumbent Democrats held onto their posts on down-ballot executive offices like lieutenant governor, attorney general, and land commissioner (indeed, Lieutenant Governor Bob Bullock handily won reelection with 60 percent of the vote). But none of these officeholders ran for reelection in 1998, and all were replaced by Republicans. Since then, no Democrat has won statewide in Texas, and long-standing majorities in the state Congress and the state's congressional delegation had vanished by the early 2000s. The small minority of Democrats in elected office have been relegated to the big cities and the heavily Hispanic parts of southern Texas.

One consequence of declining Democratic Party strength in Texas has been the exodus of skilled staffers able to run campaigns. A drought of statewide officials and other officeholders left party staffers without full-time work between election cycles, prompting them to leave Texas. The absence of such talent imposes barriers on candidates seeking to challenge Republicans. In 2018,

Democratic candidates for state legislature were unable to hire and relied on in-experienced volunteers.[2] These organizational hurdles create a negative feed-back loop that hinders Democratic electoral success, as strong candidates are discouraged from running, in turn further eroding the pool of trained staff and further reducing turnout and electoral wins.[3] This dynamic of weak candidates and low turnout produces a "perpetual downward spiral."[4]

The degradation of Texas Democrats also had an effect on the state party organization. State party fundraising has become anemic. In 2002, the state party raised nearly $20 million; in the most recent cycle—2018—it raised just $1.5 million.[5] Although the 2002 numbers were atypical for the party, the Texas Democratic Party has consistently raised about $5 million or just under in competitive election years. Since 2010, the figures have always been less than $3 million—with the past midterm and presidential cycle well under $2 million. County-level organization appears to have dwindled as well. Between 2013 and 2018, Texas Democratic county parties regressed on several metrics of infrastructure. The percentage of counties with a Democratic office available by either email, phone, or county chair dropped over these five years.[6] In 2013, almost all Texas counties had a Democratic presence available by phone, but by 2018 that number had dropped to 80 percent.

Despite long-standing electoral losses, a persistent source of optimism for Texas Democrats is favorable demographic change. The backbone of the Texas Democratic Party was once rural whites, and Republican gains in the twentieth century came from growing urban centers like Dallas. The contemporary electoral geography is reversed: Democratic success is centered in the cities and majority-Latino places in the Rio Grande.[7] In a mirror image of the previous realignment, growth in the cities and especially suburbs, as well as soaring immigration, have portended possible Democratic successes. If Democrats could activate these constituencies, they could win in Texas.

The Texas Organizing Project and Battleground Texas

In recent years, in fact, much liberal organizing in Texas has centered on engaging, registering, and mobilizing low-income, Latino, and black voters. Founded in 2010 by alumni of ACORN, a now-defunct national consortium of community-organizing groups, the Texas Organizing Project—dubbed "TOP" for short—has focused on mobilizing such citizens in the Lone Star State's big cities of Houston, Dallas, and San Antonio. To convince voters that participating in politics matters, TOP groups have emphasized local issues like disaster aid, bail reform, and public works. TOP has scored major wins on local issues like paid-sick leave for city workers, and it has boosted progressive candidates in local elections for district attorney and sheriff. In addition to year-round organizing on local issues, TOP runs voter mobilization campaigns targeting irregular voters and the group hopes to register 850,000 new voters by 2022.[8] TOP is not alone in its efforts to mobilize irregular voters. Other groups like Jolt and the Latino Vote Project focus on potential Latino voters, who have lower rates of participation than both blacks and whites.

By 2013, Texas organizing efforts ramped up even further. Led by Jeremy Bird, the Obama 2012 national field director, a cadre of former Obama campaign staffers set-up shop in Texas. Aiming to make the Lone Star State truly competitive, they formed Battleground Texas, whose operating philosophy was to "make Texas a battleground state by treating it as one"—specifically by investing in candidate recruitment, voter registration, and mobilization, the same sorts of resources cultivated in traditional swing states.[9] Pointing out that Texas has had dismal levels of voter participation, Battleground Texas operatives argued that "Texas is not a Republican state—it's a nonvoting state," a slogan later repeated by the O'Rourke campaign. Indeed, GOPer Rick Perry won the 2010 governor's race with support from just 18 percent of the voting-age population.[10] Draconian GOP-installed voter registration laws require official appointments for voter registration volunteers in each county and make minor mistakes a misdemeanor offense. Along with widespread apathy after many uncompetitive election cycles, such laws had impeded the expansion of the electorate.

The 2014 election provided the first opportunity to assess the impact of Battleground Texas—and that contest went quite poorly for Texas Democrats. Despite a lot of national donor enthusiasm, Democratic gubernatorial candidate Wendy Davis garnered only 38 percent of the vote, losing ground compared to the 2010 Democratic candidate Bill White. Still, Battleground Texas credited itself with building infrastructure in the state, including registering about one hundred thousand new voters, training twenty-five thousand volunteers, and developing new data banks. Those achievements could help Democrats in the future. As one candidate for the state house explained, "I didn't win, but Battleground Texas helped me increase turnout significantly. And because we cleaned up the data file . . . [and] now have a solid network of volunteers in the district, the next person who runs for that seat will start at a considerable advantage over me."[11] After the 2014 election, Battleground Texas centered its efforts on voter registration, expanding the electorate with targeted outreach toward Latinos and young voters. These efforts paid dividends. Operatives affiliated with Republican governor Greg Abbott's 2018 campaign hold Battleground Texas responsible for the increasing Democratic lean of Harris County, Texas's most populous.[12]

A final wave of local organizing by Indivisible-connected and other kinds of grassroots resistance groups erupted in Texas after the election and inauguration of President Donald Trump—along the same lines as groups discussed in many other chapters of this volume. Unlike TOP or Jolt, which focus on low-income and minority citizens in cities, Indivisible groups dominate in college-educated suburbs and are typically led by middle-aged or older white women. Anecdotally, a large number of activists and volunteers for the O'Rourke campaign were also active members of Indivisible groups, including many of the five hundred mostly female "Beto Ambassadors" who comprised his most dedicated volunteers.[13] Indivisible groups have played a big role in registering new voters as well. Julie Gilberg, an Indivisible organizer, local Democratic party leader, and activist in the O'Rourke campaign, explained that, besides gerrymandering, the reason why Texas is a non-voting state—and thus a red state—is because it "hasn't had the canvassing infrastructure, people haven't been going out, knocking on doors."[14] Erin Zwiner, in Hays County outside of Austin, became an activist with Indivisible and a successful candidate for state house, where her campaign divided up canvassing efforts with the local Indivisible activists. The county has added twenty thousand new voters since the 2016 election, partially due to registration efforts by the Indivisible group.[15]

Beto's First Phase: The 254-County Strategy

Beto O'Rourke launched his campaign officially on an El Paso rooftop on March 31, 2017– and a persistent early campaign theme was reaching out to Texas voters who had long been overlooked. Thus O'Rourke proclaimed a plan to visit all 254 counties in Texas, a plan that got outsized media coverage for a time, even though various (always unsuccessful) Texas Democratic statewide candidates over the years have visited every county since the 1980s. How did Beto's "254-county strategy" actually play out in the Senate campaign and for the Texas Democratic Party more generally?

New Twists in a Long-Standing 254-County Strategy

In Austin, just one day after he launched his 2018 campaign, O'Rourke proclaimed "I'm gonna work my heart out. I'm gonna walk my shoes off. I'm gonna be in every one of these 254 counties working for you, making sure that when 2018 comes we have something to celebrate for Texas and for this country."[16] As noted in an *Austin Statesman* article, the idea for visiting all counties in Texas came from former Texas governor Mark White. "I called your dad" O'Rourke recalled in speaking with White's son, and he said "Don't forget it's a 254-county race."[17] As a matter of fact, traveling to all 254 counties has a history among Texas Democrats. In the late 1980s, John Odam, a Democratic candidate for attorney general who ended up losing by 8 points, visited every county courthouse in the state, as he later recounted in a book called *Courtin Texas*.[18] In 1996, Victor Morales visited each county in an eccentric challenge to incumbent Senator Phil Gramm. Morales had no staff, decided to run on a dare and drove across the state in a white pickup truck, drawing comparisons to Lyndon B. Johnson's strategy of flying to events in a helicopter.[19] Although Morales claims the strategy won him votes, he picked up just a 44 percent share.[20] Again in 2012, the Democratic Senate candidate Paul Sadler visited every county as he lost to Cruz; however, news coverage called Sadler the "unequivocal underdog" and did not mention his visiting any county, much less 254 of them.[21]

Following in the footsteps of earlier Democrats, O'Rourke embarked on a fifteen-month 254 county voyage across Texas—but unlike his predecessors, O'Rourke gained a concrete uptick in name recognition and a reputation as a serious candidate. This time, both traditional media and social media amplified the Democratic candidate's efforts across Texas, projecting his travels to the country as a whole. For the Beto campaign, this strategy was not just about travel. It was choreographed to boost O'Rourke's reputation as an earnest and energetic campaigner, and his first campaign ad, called "Showing Up," was filmed on an iPhone and opened with a voiceover from O'Rourke saying "The only way for me to be able to deliver for the people of Texas is to show up in every community, in every county."[22] O'Rourke linked the physical act of visiting every county— usually driving himself for hours on end —with his commitment to speak for voters who had been overlooked. "Writing no person off. Taking no person for granted" was the oft-repeated mantra as Beto's campaign touted the 254-county commitment as a concrete example of his listening skills and ability.[23]

This adept and persistent social-media livestreaming of O'Rourke's travels marked a significant departure from analogous previous efforts—amplifying his reach and overcoming the inefficiencies of campaigning in counties with tiny populations dwarfed by single neighborhoods of some larger counties. Even though O'Rourke met with just two or three voters out of 150 residents of Loving County, for example, his livestreams driving around West Texas reached several thousand people watching online.[24] While physically present in small town Texas, O'Rourke was speaking to a statewide—and even nationwide— audience of politicos, activists, and donors. In addition, local and sometimes even national media picked up his visits. Features or interviews mentioning O'Rourke's 254-county strategy appeared on CNN and on a local Fox 24 station and on High Plains Public Radio, as well as in *The Guardian, New York Times, Texas Tribune, El-Paso Times, Austin-American Statesman, Esquire, North Texas Daily,* and *Dallas News,* among many others. Visiting every county showcased O'Rourke's outreach to small town Texas and built his reputation for a nationwide audience.

What Did the Strategy Look Like on the Ground?

Analyzing a subset of county visits reveals the strategic underpinnings of in-dividual stops along the 254-county tour. To identify how campaign events changed across time and between geographies, we collected and coded the location and type of all 391 campaign events advertised on O'Rourke's social media and campaign website from April 2017, December 2017, and January through November 2018. We coded April 2017 events to register the start of the campaign, and December 2017 through November 2018 events to grasp key moments of the campaign's development leading up to Election Day. December 2017 and the subsequent year include the bulk of the campaign's efforts. We used these data to piece together how visits around the state played out in different areas and how his campaign style varied during and after O'Rourke completed his tour of all the state's counties in June 2018.

Although O'Rourke's county stops took many different forms, the most common events he advertised were town halls, rallies, meet and greets, and happy hours and events with bands. Some events were more creative—like a February 10, 2018, town hall held in a movie theater with a bowling alley in Bay City, which has a population of less than twenty thousand people. Other events seemed born out of convenience or necessity—like a donut stop in Sonora on the way to Eldorado from Rocksprings in April 2018. When he could, O'Rourke would cram as many events as possible in twelve hours, sometimes up to seven events throughout the day in seven separate locations. Many of these events cen-tered on young voters or in Democratic-leaning areas. He held several events at Texas colleges and hosted concerts as campaign stops—with headliners ranging from Willie Nelson to a local mariachi band.

What O'Rourke did during these visits varied between urban and rural places.[25] In our sample of events, he hosted 104 town halls in rural counties (out of the 176 town halls he hosted from the total sample), nineteen rallies, six voting events, and eight events of other types (including donut stops, marches, and bowling). At these rural stops O'Rourke spent his time in local bars, restaurants, and cafes, as well as locations like libraries, schools, and personal residences. In contrast, suburban and urban county visits were usually larger and less inti-mate; the campaign most often visited parks, universities, and local eateries. In all types of counties he hosted events in spaces such as concert halls, ballrooms, hotels, and theaters. In total, roughly 7 percent of O'Rourke's visits were at local universities, 26 percent were at local bars, restaurants, or cafes, 27 percent were held at event or entertainment venues, 19 percent took place at parks, and 18 percent were held at other types of locations.

In the most sparsely populated counties, O'Rourke's visits took the form of a listening tour. Coverage of O'Rourke's stop in Loving County (home to fewer than two hundred residents) shows that he knocked on doors and conversed with anyone willing to engage. When a resident introduced himself to O'Rourke as a Republican, the candidate responded with, "That's okay, you don't have to vote for us," before engaging in a discussion about the political issues weighing on the man's mind.[26] O'Rourke even hosted an early morning breakfast town hall at a Sonic drive-in in Ozona, population just above three thousand, along with similar events in places with populations of less than five hundred people.[27] These events were not in vain. In Lubbock, Texas, a medium-sized city which went to Trump by over 60 percent, Beto's visits began with a couple dozen people coming out to hear him speak at a local barbecue joint; but by the end of the campaign over nine hundred people attended an event in Lubbock.[28]

Only rarely did O'Rourke hold events implying coordination with local organizations. In our sample, a total of only seventeen events were held at the meeting spaces of local organizations. The most common of these were veterans' groups (six events), union groups (five events), or local government (five events). Beto would speak or host a roundtable at the county judge's office, the local sheriff's haunt, or the city hall. In January 2018, he hosted a town hall at Missouri City's Justice of the Peace Precinct Two Courtroom. Most collaboration with local organizations occurred in rural counties. Ten of the seventeen events held with local organizations were hosted in counties with fewer than fifty-five thousand people—oftentimes fewer than twenty thousand people—as were four of the six veterans group visits. Perhaps the O'Rourke campaign had to grapple with the reality that redder, less dense counties may not be suitable for rallies and so opted instead to host a roundtable or town hall. Hosting events with locally rooted civic associations could also have been a product of necessity given available venue space in sparsely populated areas.

Where the O'Rourke campaign hosted events also speaks to its relations (or lack thereof) with other candidates and the Texas Democratic Party organization. In 2018 the only O'Rourke campaign event sponsored at an official Democratic Party space featuring Beto himself or a surrogate was a September 14 meet and greet with his mother and sister in the Ellis County Democratic headquarters.[29] O'Rourke rarely, if ever, hosted events or coordinated with organizations in a manner that implied a broader partnership with Texas Democrats. Most of O'Rourke's events were solely focused on his candidacy; he only occasionally co-campaigned with other candidates like Colin Allred from Dallas, or local Texas figures like the Castro brothers, Julián and Joaquin. This singular campaigning style created friction with other Democratic candidates at times. He refused to endorse Democratic challenger Gina Ortiz Jones against Republican congressman Will Hurd in a district near El Paso, and she narrowly lost the race by 926 votes.[30] An Indivisible organizer in the area said "All I kept

thinking was, wait, Beto is supposed to be helping us because he's a Democrat . . .
I really felt like Beto was just getting in my way."[31]

Still, O'Rourke and other Democratic candidates and party organizations
cooperated in some important ways. The O'Rourke campaign had access to the
Texas Democrats' voter information, which they used to target up to 5.5 million
potential voters from cell and landline phone numbers and home addresses.[32]
O'Rourke's campaign returned the favor and shared its own voter database with
other Democratic candidates, as well as allowed them to use its campaign space
and speak at events.[33] Undoubtedly, Democrats up and down the ticket tried to
hang onto O'Rourke's coattails and leverage the unprecedented excitement he
was creating for Democrats in the state.

Beto's Second Phase: The Metropolitan Shift

O'Rourke's campaign strategy shifted significantly towards metropolitan areas
after the end of the 254-county tour. He spent more of his time in suburban
and urban counties, using the last few months to bolster support in areas with
favorable demographics. In suburban counties with more than fifty-six thousand people, O'Rourke hosted seventy-two town halls, fifty-one rallies, forty-
three events for voting purposes, twenty meet and greets, eighteen concerts or
events with music, fourteen happy hours, eleven runs, and thirty-seven other
events—such as an August Dallas campaign office opening and a December
"Tacos with Beto" event in Fort Worth. These events often drew crowds in the
thousands—fifty-five thousand people showed up for a September 29, 2018,
rally with country star Willie Nelson.[34] There were also more intimate events,
like the San Antonio blockwalk on August 16, when over a dozen people
attended, and events somewhere in between—like the San Angelo "Beers
with Beto" event at the Concho Pearl Icehouse for two hundred to six hundred people.[35] Although event attendance varied based on event size and event
type, one thing is certain: demand for Beto was high and the campaign did its
best to deliver.

The Final Push in Urban and Suburban Texas

Total in our sample, O'Rourke visited rural counties 138 times, suburban
counties 95 times, and urban counties 158 times. Before completing visits to
every Texas county, he spent substantial time across the entire state, including
more Republican-leaning, less populous counties. During the 254-county
tour period, less than 30 percent of events were in urban counties and about

46 percent were in rural counties. But after completing his visits of 254 counties in June 2018, O'Rourke mainly focused his efforts revisiting the largest ones. During this period, about half of his events were in urban counties and just 25 percent were in rural ones. In total, he visited the counties containing San Antonio, Dallas, Fort Worth, Austin, and Houston at least fifteen times each, while other counties received just one visit, oftentimes not even publicized on social media. The O'Rourke campaign valued its time in urban and suburban areas the most—using the rural counties as stops along the way to 254. After achieving this target, he stopped visiting counties off-the-beaten trail, but still made stops in some rural counties and in small cities on the way between bigger cities.

O'Rourke acknowledged that his campaign would spend the majority of the last six months before November working in the larger areas with more likely Beto voters.[36] In the last month before the election, the campaign focused on "get out the vote" efforts in big cities, and kept the congressman bouncing among Austin, Houston, and Dallas for the month of October. In the last twelve days alone, O'Rourke made twenty-five stops along I-35 corridor, which runs from Laredo in South Texas up to Dallas and the Oklahoma border, trying to get out the vote in this area.[37]

Organizing to Reach Voters

In addition to O'Rourke's personal outreach, the campaign launched a massive get-out-the-vote operation, including more than seven hundred Pop-Up Offices and Grassroots HQs. Pop-Up Offices were volunteer-run spaces like homes, offices, and restaurants which served as hubs for reaching unlikely voters. Paid-staff provided informational training, campaign literature and other support to multiple Pop-Ups, creating hubs where senior volunteers trained other volunteers to canvass nearby neighborhoods and precincts in order to meet widely shared campaign door-knocking targets. This "distributed-organizing" model—sometimes dubbed "Uber for organizing"—was developed during the 2016 Bernie Sanders campaign and has been touted as a model for future Democratic organizing. David Wysong, a senior O'Rourke aide and campaign strategist who hired the architects of the 2016 Sanders campaign to O'Rourke's camp, attributed the campaign's overperformance of the polls to its robust fieldwork. In total, the campaign knocked on a staggering 2.8 million doors and made twenty million phone calls.[38]

To study the effects of this campaign organizing systematically, we obtained the addresses of the Grassroots HQs and Pop-Up Offices by scraping all events listed on the O'Rourke campaign's website and identifying these field offices by string searches. After standardizing and cleaning these hand-entered addresses and geocoding addresses using Esri's ArcMap, 734 campaign offices matched to the street or address level and were included in the analysis. As Figure 11.1 shows, campaign offices were concentrated in major metropolitan areas and suburbs, though a handful dot some of the less populated counties of Texas. Just seventy-six counties (29.9 percent) had at least one campaign office, but these counties comprise about 90 percent of the state's population. Dallas County and Harris County had the most offices, with 103 and 168, respectively.

Along with these campaign offices, anti-Trump resistance or Indivisible-affiliated groups which proliferated in the months following Trump's inauguration and the Women's March played a major role in 2018 Texas outreach. As mentioned earlier, there is some crossover between local Indivisible activists and the most dedicated O'Rourke volunteers. Independent of the campaign, however, Indivisible-affiliated groups worked to register and mobilize voters. To study this systematically, we obtained the locations of Indivisible contacts from an August 2017 web-scrape of the Indivisible website, generously provided by Vanessa Williamson. There were 270 Indivisible contacts in Texas included in the analysis, mostly found in major metropolitan areas and suburbs, as indicated in Figure 11.1. Seventy-two (28.4 percent) counties had at least one Indivisible contact; Harris County and Travis County had thirty-eight and forty contacts, respectively.

Figure 11.1 Locations of O'Rourke Campaign Offices and Texas Indivisible Contacts.

Notes: The map shows, across Texas counties, the locations of Beto Pop-Up Offices and Grassroots Headquarters (dots) and Indivisible contacts (indicated by X's). Although most counties do not have a campaign office or Indivisible contact, the state's population centers and suburbs feature multiples of each.

Analyzing the Electoral Results

To assess the success of the 254 strategy and the subsequent push in metropolitan places, we now analyze the electoral geography of the 2018 Senate race. O'Rourke received an impressive 48 percent of votes in his 2018 Senate bid, a higher vote share than any statewide Democratic candidate in Texas in recent memory. His four million votes also constituted the most votes ever cast for a Democrat in Texas, exceeding Hillary Clinton's total by about two hundred thousand. This is especially remarkable given that electoral trends in Texas had been getting worse for Democrats, rather than better, as Figure 11.2 shows. Since 1994, no Texas Democrat has won statewide office, and the share of votes accruing to Democratic candidates steadily declined over the following twenty years. In 2014, despite high hopes and considerable outside fundraising, Democrats scored new lows on statewide ballots, with gubernatorial candidate Wendy Davis receiving less than 40 percent of the vote and Senate candidate David Alameel receiving just 34 percent of the vote. O'Rourke reversed this long-standing decline, gaining 14 percentage points over his predecessor running for Senate.

O'Rourke's 48 percent also topped the Democratic ticket, though only barely, with state candidates for attorney general and lieutenant governor receiving 47 percent of the vote, and gubernatorial candidate Lupe Valdez receiving about 43 percent. His gains were made alongside massive advances in Democratic turnout, particularly among young voters. Where did his support come from?

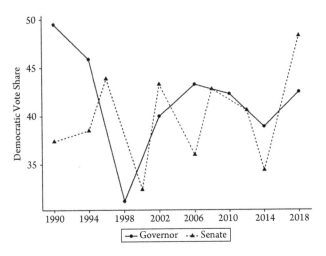

Figure 11.2 Texas Statewide Democratic Vote Share 1990–2018, by Office.

Notes: Democratic votes for Senate (dashed) and Governor (solid) from 1990 to 2018. O'Rourke's Senate performance reverses long-standing declines.

Did Beto's outreach to far-flung counties in Texas persuade rural voters to support him? Or were his gains made primarily in the more densely populated parts of Texas?

The geography of O'Rourke's electoral performance sheds light on this question. As Figure 11.3 illustrates, O'Rourke's support was concentrated in the state's more populous counties and suburbs. O'Rourke visited all 254 Texas counties, but he won just thirty-two of them. Indeed, more than half of his votes came from just five counties, and more than 75 percent came from just eleven counties. Although the skewed population of Texas counties drives much of this unequal distribution in votes, support for Cruz was somewhat more diffuse than for O'Rourke. Cruz received half of his vote from eleven counties (compared to O'Rourke's five) and 75 percent of his votes from thirty-nine counties (compared to eleven for O'Rourke).

Garnering about 25 percent of rural votes, O'Rourke slightly outperformed Hillary Clinton among rural voters, but only by 2 percentage points. But he vastly underperformed among rural voters relative to some other recent Democrats. In

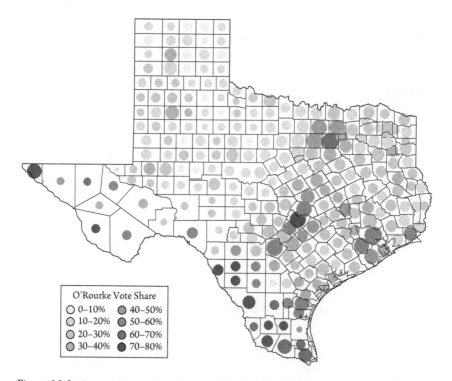

Figure 11.3 Electoral Geography of the 2018 Texas US Senate Race.

Notes: The plot shows, for each county, support for O'Rourke (darker shades imply more support) and the total number of votes (on a logarithmic scale). O'Rourke performed well in major metropolitan areas and in the heavily Latino counties of southern Texas.

2002, the Democratic candidate for Senate received 40 percent of the rural vote.[39] O'Rourke received a smaller vote share than Paul Sadler, Cruz's Democratic opponent in 2012, in 185 counties (although O'Rourke did much better overall).[40] He also underperformed in rural counties relative to some other statewide Democratic candidates. Mike Collier, a moderate Democrat and ex-Republican, focused on bread-and-butter issues like public education funding and property taxes in his campaign for lieutenant governor. Collier contrasted his pragmatism with the extremism of the Tea Party-connected incumbent Dan Patrick. His campaign manager described Collier as a "gateway Democrat" for Republicans "who want someone they can hold their nose for."[41] Although Collier lacked the fundraising and campaign apparatus of O'Rourke, he outperformed O'Rourke in 171 of the 254 counties in Texas.[42] Garnering 47 percent of votes, Collier's skeleton campaign performed neck-and-neck with O'Rourke, though he tended to perform better than O'Rourke in traditionally Republican and rural counties and worse in big cities and suburbs (of course, Collier probably benefited from pro-O'Rourke and anti-Trump sentiment which brought out straight-ticket Democratic votes).

Why did O'Rourke's outreach to these rural places fail to swing over many votes? One important barrier comes from nationalized politics, with strong partisanship acting as a firewall against Democratic inroads in rural Texas. Even though many rural voters came out to hear what Beto had to say, he was still a Democrat running for Senate. It did not help his cause that O'Rourke took progressive stances to rural Texas where President Trump is extremely popular.

O'Rourke prided himself on his "authenticity" and transparency, meaning that liberal Dallas County got the same message as conservative Borden—which voted for Donald Trump by more than 90 percent.[43] Across the state, O'Rourke expressed his support for universal health care, impeaching President Trump, and kneeling during the national anthem to protest police brutality against African Africans, messages likely out-of-step with rural conservative Texas. O'Rourke ran as a staunch liberal even though his congressional voting record shows he was 77 percent more conservative than other Democrats.[44] In emphasizing progressive stances in rural counties rather than his moderate voting record, he might have missed an opportunity to grab votes. Mark White, a son of Texas Democratic governor Bill White, argued that O'Rourke "literally" campaigned in all counties, but did not sincerely reach out to moderate Texas voters. A resident of San Saba County, where O'Rourke got a mere 11.9 percent of the vote, described it like this: "People came out and listened to him but then decided not to vote for him. Free education. Free health care. Open borders. Anybody can come in."[45]

However, this consistent progressive messaging did not preclude O'Rourke from making material gains over previous Texas Democrats or from topping the ticket in non-rural areas. He made new-inroads into suburban areas, as did Democrats nationwide in 2018, and benefited from supercharged turnout among urban counties and Democratic-leaning constituencies. A whopping 53 percent of registered voters turned out in the 2018 midterms, compared to 33.7 percent in 2014 and youth turnout rates more than doubled compared to the 2014 midterms.[46] Democratic gains were especially noteworthy in the urban and suburban counties comprising the I-35 corridor. These counties saw a massive swing to Democrats between 2014 and 2018—about 800,000 votes— resulting in ten Democratic flips in the state house (of twelve total) and both of the flips Democrats made in the state senate.[47] In 2018, Tarrant County, which includes Fort Worth, went blue by 3,869 votes—or just under 1 percent—and Williamson County and Hays County outside Austin also went blue—Hays by 12,186 votes and Williamson by 5,773 votes.[48] Smaller cities like Corpus Christi helped turn Nueces County blue, despite voting Republican in the last few cycles. Both population growth and increases in turnout have happened mostly in the urban and suburban parts of Texas where O'Rourke improved on his predecessors. In contrast, the rural counties which held steadfast for Ted Cruz are not growing and thus comprise a decreasing portion of the electorate. As Kirk Goldsberry of FiveThirtyEight points out, "Those areas may be staunchly red, but they're also staunchly stagnant too."[49] Indeed, by pitching a consistent progressive message, even in rural Texas, Beto energized liberals across the state and nationwide, cultivating a huge following among donors and activists. This excitement and fundraising, in turn, galvanized an unprecedented ground game, the effects of which we now turn to study.

To estimate the electoral effect of these mobilization efforts, we aggregated campaign offices and Indivisible contacts to the county-level and calculated the density per ten thousand people for each of these organizations to proxy for levels of organizational capacity. Next, using a population-weighted least-squares regression model, we estimated the association between the two treatment variables—campaign office density and resistance group density—and the dependent variable, Democratic votes as a proportion of registered voters in the county in November 2018. This dependent variable increases both as a function of voter persuasion (O'Rourke receiving a larger proportion of votes cast) and mobilization (a larger number of voters turning out for O'Rourke, rather than abstaining from voting), so it provides a comprehensive measure of political support. To reduce the risk of confounding, we control for past Democratic support (a lagged dependent variable from the 2016 election) as well as a variety of socioeconomic, demographic variables obtained from the Texas Association of Counties website. The control variables are county percentage Hispanic, percentage black, percentage rural, percentage college educated, median income, population density, median age, and a dummy for El Paso County, O'Rourke's home county. Adjusting for these potential confounders gives more confidence that we are capturing the independent effect of organizational density on Democratic support.

Controlling for these other factors, the density of campaign Pop-Up Offices per ten thousand people had a positive and statistically significant association with Democratic support ($\beta = 2.7$; $p < 0.05$). Similarly, the density of Indivisible contacts had a positive and statistically significant relationship ($\beta = 2.2$; $p < 0.01$). To get a sense of the substantive magnitude of these effects, we used these model coefficients, and each county's level of organizational capacity and vote totals, to provide a back-of-the-envelope estimate of the number of O'Rourke votes attributable to these groups. To do this, we calculated each county's counterfactual share of Democratic votes as a proportion of registered voters if there were zero Indivisible contacts and zero campaign offices in the county and compared this share with the actual amounts. We did this by subtracting each county's actual level of Democratic support by its levels of organizational density multiplied by the organization's estimated marginal effect on votes. Then we multiplied this difference by the county's number of registered voters to calculate each county's number of votes attributable to campaign offices and Indivisible contacts and summed this number over all counties to produce a statewide estimate. This exercise provides evidence of a meaningful, though modest, electoral effect of these groups. About 32,400 O'Rourke votes were attributable to the density of campaign offices and about 9,200 votes were attributable to Indivisible contact presence. Although the 2018 midterm election was widely seen as a referendum on the president, local organizing still played an important role. And Indivisible contacts, despite their overlap with O'Rourke's volunteer network, still had an independent effect on votes. Collectively, these two organized efforts added about half a percentage point to O'Rourke's vote share.

Legacies of O'Rourke's 2018 Campaign

O'Rourke's impressive performance marked an important turn in Texas politics. In 2013, Battleground Texas promised to make Texas politically competitive by treating it like it already was—investing the time and resources into candidate recruitment, registration, and mobilization efforts that the party organization does in other competitive places. After Democratic setbacks in 2014, including the hugely underwhelming 2014 Democratic gubernatorial election, hopes of realizing battleground status in Texas seemed bleak.

Yet just four years later, O'Rourke's 2018 Senate campaign seems to have reignited hopes for a Democratic revival in the Lone Star State. This may ultimately bode well for the future success of Democratic candidates in Texas.

Cruz's narrow margin of victory—about 215,000 votes—falls well within the reach of an expanding electorate. Oscar Silva of Battleground Texas noted that four hundred thousand people registered to vote in the state between March and October 2018, and three hundred thousand high school students here turn eighteen each year: "We can register that [partisan] gap."[50] O'Rourke's strong performance may help convert these favorable demographic trends into political gains for Democrats by building organizational capacity in Texas—strong candidates and trained staff—to mobilize these new voters. Because O'Rourke poured his massive fundraising hauls into hiring staff, his campaign apparatus was enormous—with more than eight hundred people on payroll and twenty-five thousand volunteers—compared to eighteen people on staff for Ted Cruz, who relied on Greg Abbott's large organization of staff and volunteers.[51] The campaign leaves behind this infrastructure and network of activists, many of whom first became politically involved with O'Rourke's campaign.[52]

Down the ballot, Democrats made gains in the state's major metropolitan areas. Democrats flipped twelve state house seats and two state senate seats, mostly in Dallas, Austin, and Houston.[53] Democrats also flipped two congressional seats. Colin Allred unseated incumbent Peter Sessions in a Dallas area seat by just under eighteen thousand votes in a race where he received 52.3 percent of the vote. Lizzie Fletcher of the Houston area unseated incumbent John Culberson with 52.5 percent of the vote, a lead of just over twelve thousand votes in a longtime Republican seat previously held by George H. W. Bush.[54] Democrats also made gains in county offices in the state's major cities and suburbs. In Harris County, Democrats flipped more than fifty judgeships from Republican incumbents; seventeen of those successful challengers were black women.[55]

Even though anti-Trump sentiment helped Democrats everywhere, the O'Rourke campaign also shares some credit in these down-ballot successes. As a Democratic candidate for county clerk noted, "My race of course is at the bottom of a very long ballot, so this excitement that [Beto] generates . . . is turning into voter engagement. And that has resulted in more people being interested in all levels of government." The founder of a Democratic communications firm said in October before the election, "The fact that Beto has run a good campaign, he's remained competitive, and he's communicated through the end, that has helped all Democrats." A candidate for state house spoke about the campaign's willingness to help smaller campaigns. "They've been very gracious about sharing the stage with . . . people who get little to no exposure."[56]

Because so many first time Democrats won their races in 2018, O'Rourke's campaign may have boosted the qualifications of future Democratic candidates in Texas; in his concession speech, O'Rourke himself declared that "there are so many great candidates who are going to come out of this campaign whose work I look forward to supporting and following and cheering on." Fielding candidates with previous experience in elected office is important because such candidates tend to cultivate more votes and fundraise more effectively.[57] The absence of high-quality candidates for many decades impeded Republican realignment in the American South.[58] Since Republicans have gained control, Texas Democrats have suffered from relatively lackluster candidates running for statewide office: "whoever was willing to run"—and for many local races no Democrat would run at all.[59] The *Dallas Morning News* wrote that the competitive 2020 Democratic primary to challenge Senator Cornyn "signals that Democrats are entering a new era in Texas politics. They don't have to find sacrificial lambs to fill out candidate slates."[60] By helping to elect dozens of down-ballot candidates to office on his coattails, and by restoring the hope that victory in statewide office is a reasonable possibility, O'Rourke may have left a legacy of higher-quality Democratic candidates going forward.

All these encouraging signs for Democrats—a massive increase in turnout, narrow defeat in a statewide race for the US Senate, wins in numerous local and state legislative contests, and competitive performances in several congressional races—have encouraged the national Democratic Party to renew its efforts in Texas, eyeing in particular the six Republican incumbents who held onto their congressional seats by less than 5 percent of the vote. Starting just a few months after the 2018 election, the Democratic Congressional Campaign Committee (DCCC) made new investments to develop Democratic strength in Texas. In March 2019, the DCCC announced that field organizers would set-up shop in the suburbs of San Antonio, Austin, Houston, and Dallas. In April, the group opened a new satellite office in Austin with eight full-time staffers, trying to replicate in 2020 the Democratic sweep of congressional seats in California's Orange County in 2018. Three of the six Republicans eyed by Democrats in 2020 have districts in metropolitan Austin. Cheri Bustos, chairwoman of the DCCC, explained: "When it comes to places where House Democrats can go on offense, it doesn't get any bigger than Texas."[61] Republicans are taking these Democratic challenges seriously by recruiting candidates to run against new Democratic incumbents and using the threat of new Democratic outreach as a fundraising tool.

O'Rourke's performance also portends a more competitive 2020 presidential election in Texas. Early surveys of the Texas electorate suggest that certain 2020 Democratic presidential aspirants—including Biden and O'Rourke—could compete with Trump for the state's thirty-eight electoral votes.[62] Texas is also becoming competitive grounds within the Democratic presidential primary. In one May weekend, five "high-profile Democrats" and presidential candidates visited in an attempt to raise money and gain support from the state.[63] In an interview with Rachel Maddow O'Rourke argued, "Texas and its thirty-eight

Electoral College votes have been unlocked. They are in contention, and we will have a seat at the table."[64]

O'Rourke's 254-county campaign strategy was an important feature of his bid, but its merits were not in persuading rural voters. His performance among those constituencies was worse than that of other statewide Democrats—such as lieutenant governor candidate Mike Collier—and much worse than less successful Democrats of recent memory. Instead, this strategy helped O'Rourke establish his credibility as a candidate, cultivate a likeable and energetic persona, and attract a deluge of press coverage. His listening tours in small-town Texas, broadcast nationwide through constant livestreams on social media, showcased O'Rourke's authenticity and earnest outreach to audiences both in Texas and around the country. The campaign was thus both quintessentially local and national, as were its consequences: impacting down-ballot races for state house and Congress, reviving political competition in statewide Texas races, and setting the stage for O'Rourke's presidential ambitions.

However, O'Rourke's performance did not come out of a vacuum. He benefited from the intense efforts of organizations and individuals working to expand and mobilize a sleepy electorate in Texas; indeed, Texas had been trending Democratic in presidential elections in recent cycles, and by 2016 the vote in Texas was as close as in traditional swing states like Iowa and Ohio. Many years of organizing by groups like Battleground Texas and the Texas Organizing Project had helped set the stage for his rise through registration and activation of low-income and minority citizens. More recently, the sharp reaction to Trump, including the rise of Indivisible and other resistance groups, also helped spur Democratic votes in 2018 and boost O'Rourke's fundraising. O'Rourke in turn poured these monies into a massive campaign apparatus, helping deepen political activism and experience in Texas. Beto O'Rourke was undoubtedly an unusually charismatic candidate. But the organizational analyses employed here show that efforts to make Texas competitive both preceded his 2018 campaign and promise to outlast it.

Notes

1. Kenneth Bridges, *Twilight of the Texas Democrats: The 1978 Governor's Race* (College Station: Texas A&M University Press), chapter 1.
2. David Yaffe-Bellany, "Surge of Candidates Leaves Texas Democrats Struggling to Recruit Qualified Staffers," *Texas Tribune*, July 19, 2018.
3. Don Gonyea, "Obama Campaigners Try to Get Texas Fired Up for Democrats," NPR, July 2, 2013.
4. Mimi Swartz, "How to Win Texas," *Politico*, November 2, 2018.
5. Texas Democratic Party fundraising records accessed via the National Institute on Money in Politics, Campaign Finance Institute, available at FollowTheMoney.org as of 2019.

6. Authors' original research of current and archived versions of state and county party websites.
7. A. S. Myers, "Secular Geographical Polarization in the American South: The Case of Texas, 1996–2010," *Electoral Studies* 32, no. 1, (2013): 48–62.
8. Christopher Connelly, "How One Texas Progressive Group Is Mobilizing Unlikely Black And Latino Voters," *Kera News*, Oct. 31, 2018.
9. Gregory Wallace, "Could Texas Be a Battleground State?" CNN, February 26, 2013.
10. Jenn Brown, "Texas Is Not Innately Conservative," *Dallas Morning News*, August 2, 2013.
11. Brian Sweaney and Robert Draper, "The Future of Battleground Texas," *Texas Monthly*, February 26, 2015.
12. Jeremy Wallace, "Republicans in Texas Scoff at 'Blue Wave' Even as They Brace for It," *Houston Chronicle*, June 16, 2018.
13. Anne Helen Petersen, "Women Built the Beto Campaign in Texas—So Where Are the Men?" BuzzFeed News, November 6, 2018.
14. Emily Witt, "Calling for Beto O'Rourke in Texas," *New Yorker*, November 5, 2018.
15. Tim Murphy, "Beto O'Rourke Was Just the Beginning," *Mother Jones*, November 2018.
16. Beto O'Rourke Facebook video, April 1, 2017, 00:20:58.
17. Jonathan Tilove, "Why Beto O'Rourke's 254-County Strategy Flopped," *Austin-American Statesman*, December 31, 2019.
18. David Yaffe-Bellany, "Texas Has 254 Counties. Beto O'Rourke Has Campaigned Against Ted Cruz in Each of Them," *Texas Tribune*, June 9, 2018.
19. Sam Howe Verhovek, "Running on Dare, Teacher Wins Senate Primary," *New York Times*, April 11, 1996.
20. Katie Leslie, "Beto O'Rourke Checks off Last of 254 Texas Counties," *Dallas News*, June, 2018.
21. Aman Batheja, "Once a Powerhouse, Sadler Works to Remind Voters of Past Status," *Texas Tribune*, September 16, 2012.
22. @BetoORourke tweet, July 26, 2018, 9:01 a.m., available at https://twitter.com/BetoORourke/status/1022466953288593409.
23. @BetoORourke tweet, February 23, 2018, 1:40 p.m., available at https://twitter.com/BetoORourke/status/967106868979093505.
24. Robert Moore, "The Texas Democrat Hoping to Unseat Ted Cruz, One County at a Time," *The Guardian*, June 4, 2018.
25. For this analysis, we considered counties "urban" if they are home to more than two hundred thousand people, suburban if home to between fifty-six thousand and two hundred thousand people, and rural if home to fewer than fifty-five thousand people.
26. Moore, "The Texas Democrat Hoping to Unseat Ted Cruz."
27. Christopher Hooks, "On the Road with Beto: Is O'Rourke's Personality-Driven Campaign Reaching the Right Voters?" *Texas Observer*, July 10, 2018.
28. Moore, "The Texas Democrat Hoping to Unseat Ted Cruz."
29. Authors' review of campaign social media.
30. "Texas Election Results 2018," *Politico*, September 7, 2019, available at https://www.politico.com/election-results/2018/texas/ as of September 7, 2019.
31. Matt Flegenheimer and Alexander Burns, "As Beto O'Rourke Weighs 2020 Run, Democrats Chafe at His Go-It-Alone Style," *New York Times*, January 19, 2019.
32. Beto for Senate, "The Plan to Win," November 5, 2018, available at http://web.archive.org/web/20190308060128/https://betoorourke.com/plan/.
33. Flegenheimer and Burns, "Democrats Chafe at His Go-It-Alone Style."
34. Madlin Mekelburg, "Beto O'Rourke-Willie Nelson Fans Pack Turn Out for Texas rally in Austin," *El Paso Times*, September, 29, 2018.
35. Event estimate from Facebook RSVPs: sixteen people responded "going" to the August 16 blockwalk while ninety-six marked interested. The Concho Icehouse Facebook event marked 198 as going, 539 as interested.
36. Moore, "The Texas Democrat Hoping to Unseat Ted Cruz."
37. Jeremy Wallace, "O'Rourke Exposed a Blue Spine Across the Middle of Red Texas," *San Antonio Express News*, November 23, 2018.

38. Justin Miller, "How Beto Built His Texas-Sized Grassroots Machine," *Texas Observer*, December 3, 2018.

39. Tilove, "Why Beto O'Rourke's 254-county strategy flopped."

40. Texas Election Source, "By the Numbers: Beto's 254-County Strategy," TXElects, February 24, 2019.

41. Jasper Scherer, "Republicans Scoff as Moderate Democrat Mike Collier Campaigns for Lieutenant Governor," *Houston Chronicle*, October 26, 2018.

42. Ross Ramsey, "Analysis: Mike Collier Lost, But Outdid Beto O'Rourke in Most Texas Counties," *Texas Tribune*, December 19, 2018.

43. "Texas Election Results 2018," *Politico*.

44. Matthew Yglesias, "Beto O'Rourke's Voting Record Is More Conservative than the Average Democrat's," Vox, December, 21, 2018.

45. Tilove, "Why Beto O'Rourke's 254-County Strategy Flopped."

46. Texas Secretary of State, "Turnout and Voter Registration Figures," available at https://www.sos.state.tx.us/elections/historical/70-92.shtml as of September 7, 2019; Amanda Seitz and Will Weissert, "AP FACT CHECK: Did Beto O'Rourke Boost Texas Voter Turnout?" NBC News 9 KTSM.com, April 2, 2019.

47. Wallace, "O'Rourke Exposed a Blue Spine Across the Middle of Red Texas."

48. "Texas Election Results," *New York Times*, May 15, 2019.

49. Kirk Goldsberry, "What Really Happened in Texas," *FiveThirtyEight*, November 14, 2018.

50. Jeremy Wallace, "Ted Cruz's Margin of Victory over Beto O'Rourke Was Even Slimmer than We Thought," *San Antonio Express News*, December 8, 2018.

51. Patrick Svitek, "In Getting Out the Vote, Cruz Turns to Abbott's Infrastructure while O'Rourke Builds His Own," *Texas Tribune*, November 1, 2018.

52. Andrew Rice, "Beto O'Rourke and the Limits of Charisma," *New Yorker*, November 7, 2018.

53. James Barragan, "Democratic 'Blue Wave' Makes Landfall in Texas House, Flipping 12 Red Seats Across the State," *Dallas News*, November 7, 2018.

54. "Texas Election Results 2018," *Politico*.

55. Adeel Hassan, "17 Black Women Sweep to Judgeships in Texas County," *New York Times*, November 9, 2018.

56. Lissandra Villa, "Democrats in Texas Are Going to Huge Lengths to Try to Ride the Beto Wave," BuzzFeed News, October 31, 2018.

57. M G. Hall and C. W. Bonneau, "Does Quality Matter? Challengers in State Supreme Court Elections," *American Journal of Political Science* 50, no. 1 (2006): 20–33; Daniel Lublin, "Quality, Not Quantity: Strategic Politicians in US Senate Elections, 1952–1990," *Journal of Politics* 56, no. 1 (1994): 228–41.

58. David Lublin, *The Republican South: Democratization and Partisan Change* (Princeton, NJ: Princeton University Press, 1994).

59. Edgar Walters and Ryan Murphy, "While Beto O'Rourke Rakes in Cash, Big Donors Ignore the Democratic Statewide Ticket," *Texas Tribune*, November 1, 2018.

60. Gromer Jeffers Jr., "Will Dallas' Royce West Challenge MJ Hegar for the Chance to Unseat Senate Incumbent John Cornyn?" *Dallas Morning News*, June 17, 2019.

61. Abby Livingston, "U.S. House Democratic Campaign Arm to Open Austin Office, Boosting Focus on Texas in 2020," *Texas Tribune*, April 9, 2019; DCCC Chairwoman Cheri Bustos announces DCCC: Texas Headquarters." DCCC, April 9, 2019, available at https://dccc.org/dccc-chairwoman-cheri-bustos-announces-dccctexas-headquarters/.

62. Jonathan Tilove, "Presidential Poll Suggests 2020 Texas Battleground," *Austin-American Statesman*, April 29, 2019.

63. Patrick Svitek, "Five High-Profile Democrats Descend on Texas as 2020 Spotlight on State Grows," *Texas Tribune*, May 4, 2019.

64. Jonathan Martin, "'I Recognize That I Can Do a Better Job,' Beto O'Rourke Says," *New York Times*, May 13, 2019.

12

How Grassroots Resistance Networks Boosted Pennsylvania Democrats in 2018

MAXIMILIAN FRANK

Seventy-five hours before polls closed on Election Day 2018, Pennsylvania State Senate candidate Katie Muth addressed supporters in the Thomas Paine Unitarian Universalist Fellowship in Collegeville, Pennsylvania. Three rows of folding chairs hugged the stage, but most of the rally's three hundred attendees occupied the loosely packed standing area in the back half of the church. Alongside Muth were fellow Democratic state senate candidates Linda Fields and Vincent Hughes and state house candidate Joe Ciresi. Governor Tom Wolf and US Senator Bob Casey, both campaigning for reelection, would arrive soon.

"It's a pleasure to be here with the people who started this campaign," Muth said to applause. "Since we started our Indivisible group in 2016, we've grown into a massive army of not just protesters, but people that are actually out in every single community . . . having conversations with voters of all parties about how government can be truly for the people!"[1] Cheers broke out over the crowd as friends and volunteers dressed in "Muth for Senate" apparel waved supportive homemade signs. Behind them, sleep-deprived field organizers with full clipboards conferred in hushed tones along the back wall.

An observer of this event might well have confused the Muth campaign for just another state senate election effort. But Muth was not a typical candidate. A thirty-four-year-old former athletic trainer and adjunct professor of kinesiology, Muth had never run for elected office before. Her 2018 opponent in the forty-fourth state senate district was John Rafferty, a Republican who had been in office since 2003 and who won his last reelection campaign by eighteen thousand votes. There was, nevertheless, one advantage that Muth enjoyed: the unconditional support of Indivisible MontCo, the grassroots progressive political group

Maximilian Frank, *How Grassroots Resistance Networks Boosted Pennsylvania Democrats in 2018* In: *Upending American Politics* Edited by: Theda Skocpol and Caroline Tervo, Oxford University Press (2020). © Oxford University Press DOI: 10.1093/oso/9780190083526.003.0012 she founded in 2017. With hundreds of members throughout Montgomery County, many of whom were in attendance at that rally, this grassroots group could make the difference for Muth on Election Day.

A hotly contested swing state, Pennsylvania is accustomed to vigorous political campaigns but—as this scene suggests—2018 was different. Katie Muth and her campaign were part of a post-2016 phenomenon unfolding across large swathes of Pennsylvania and much of the United States, exemplary of the broad mobilization of key Democratic Party constituencies in local, federal, and statewide elections. Fueled by the rapid formation of potent grassroots political groups, this movement coalesced around a common label: the Trump resistance.

Both academics and the national media have used the resistance label to describe the left-leaning political movement formed in opposition to the presidency of Donald J. Trump. By late 2017, this movement, although amorphous and poorly understood, was making headlines by disrupting congressional town halls, sending large amounts of money to progressive candidates and existing progressive political groups, and organizing around special elections.[2] Political action committees and nonprofit organizations soon emerged to coordinate this activist energy in order to elect progressives to office and advocate for progressive approaches to health care and immigration policy. This coalition of grassroots groups and national organizations brought together newly mobilized activists and political veterans determined to influence community, state, and national affairs from Pennsylvania to California.

Despite its many visible manifestations, the resistance has been hard to study, due in part to its decentralization. Unlike a traditional political party, there is no unified organizational network or hierarchy in the resistance. There are obvious signs of heightened activity on the political left, including increased fundraising efforts and numbers of Democratic candidates running for office, but the precise nature and impact of resistance organizations has remained unclear.

To be sure, anecdotal evidence suggests significant effects. Flippable, a group formed in early 2017 to steer contributions to progressive candidates, claims it has raised over $2 million for its candidates and spent 2017 targeting special elections in state legislatures around the country.[3] Indivisible, an umbrella organization with hundreds of affiliated grassroots groups that emerged out of an organizing guide published by former Democratic congressional staffers called the *Indivisible Guide*, was credited with playing a major role in the failure of congressional Republicans' attempt to repeal the Affordable Care Act in early 2017.[4] Most notably, future leaders of the resistance helped organize the 2017 Women's March, the largest single-day demonstration in United States history.

This chapter moves beyond these highly visible examples of resistance activity to examine how grassroots resistance groups operate at the most granular level. Through close study of the resistance groups of south-eastern Pennsylvania, it seeks more complete answers to two fundamental questions: how did the resistance emerge and grow after the November 2016 election? And what role did grassroots groups in this movement play in the 2018 midterm elections?

To answer these questions, this chapter reports on research conducted in six contiguous counties in southeastern Pennsylvania: Chester, Berks, Montgomery, Bucks, Lehigh, and Northampton. Collectively known as the "collar counties" and Lehigh Valley, these counties provide a unique opportunity for compara-tive analysis. They are located in a region long reputed to determine the out-come of statewide elections in Pennsylvania, where core metropolitan areas vote Democratic and rural areas vote Republican.[5] Four competitive congres-sional districts in this area straddle the borders of the counties studied here, providing an opportunity to assess the interactions between county Democratic Parties and campaigns across district and county lines.[6] With high numbers of relatively moderate and independent voters, these counties were split in their support for Trump versus Clinton in 2016.[7] What is more, these counties have also seen heightened political mobilization since 2016, measured by the number of grassroots groups listed on the national Indivisible website and growth in Democratic voter registration and turnout between 2014 and 2018. To under-stand the role southeastern Pennsylvania's grassroots resistance groups played in these counties during the 2018 midterm elections, interviews were conducted with the leaders or founders of all groups that responded to email outreach, as well as with activists, local Democratic Party officials, local officeholders, and campaign representatives.[8] Data gathered from these interviews were then assessed alongside publicly available election results, candidate records, and voter registration data.[9]

This chapter identifies three principal ways in which the grassroots resistance groups of the collar counties and Lehigh Valley have dramatically and conse-quentially altered their political environments. First, in their early stages, these groups mobilized new waves of activists to pursue political efforts ranging from issue advocacy to the election of Democrats to local office. Second, their efforts strengthened the Democratic Party in suburban and rural areas by increasing the number of Democratic precinct representatives and registering substantial num-bers of new Democratic voters. Finally, and most significantly, the grassroots groups contributed to the election of a new cohort of public officeholders: they generated many new volunteers committed to electing progressive candidates, and they provided their own members with the networks, connections, and re-sources to run for office at both the local and federal level. This chapter describes each of these effects in detail before concluding with an assessment of these re-sistance groups' implications for future regional political developments.

Pennsylvanians Resisting Trump Shake Up
Local Politics

The grassroots resistance groups that first emerged in the collar counties and Lehigh Valley in the wake of President Trump's election began as small meetings of friends and neighbors discussing the election outcome, which for many future activists was a moment of sadness and reckoning. These small meetings, held in diners and living rooms throughout the region, grew to gatherings of up to two hundred individuals in church basements and community centers within only a few weeks. The new groups quickly formalized their structures, elected leadership, and decided upon organizational priorities. Members and leaders alike began to pay attention to resources like the *Indivisible Guide* and implement its tactics: within weeks, group members were writing postcards to legislators, calling legislative offices, and attending congressional town halls.

Throughout 2017 and 2018, these grassroots groups averaged approximately one hundred core volunteers each, and many of these volunteers lacked substantial prior political experience. Demographically, almost all of the groups were skewed towards older, affluent women: some groups, like Lehigh Valley Rally of America's Resistance (ROAR), were made up almost entirely of late-career or retired women from professional backgrounds and advocated almost exclusively for female candidates.[10] Most groups also communicated in similar ways, relying on social media networks and email lists in addition to their in-person meetings. Many took inspiration from the popular Facebook group Pantsuit Nation to form social media pages on which their members discussed policy matters and raised awareness of political events in the region.

But despite their similar origin stories and common opposition to the incoming administration, these resistance groups varied significantly in their stated purposes. Some, like the Tri-County Democrats of Pottstown, Pennsylvania, focused on electing Democrats to local office and supporting local branches of the Democratic Party. Others, like Indivisible Berks in Berks County, were more wary of party politics and focused on building "sustainable progressive infrastructure" in their historically conservative suburban and rural communities. Yet others found a middle ground, recruiting and training their own candidates for political office while simultaneously directing their members towards the local Democratic Party in support of existing Democratic initiatives.

To enact their agendas, the leaders and members of resistance groups deliberately followed examples set by previous grassroots movements like the conservative Tea Party. Flippable, a national resistance group started by former staffers of the Clinton presidential campaign, sought to emulate the success of the Republican Party in down-ballot elections. Flippable co-founder Chris Walsh explained that his group "decided to think about politics the way Republicans have for years . . . People woke up on November ninth with a desire to do something; they had been totally caught off guard. We thought that it's about time Democrats start paying attention to down-ballot races, so we started this project to flip state houses across the country."[11] The *Indivisible Guide* authors recommended similar tactics to their followers, writing that "we saw [the Tea Party] organize locally and convince their own MoCs [members of Congress] to reject President Obama's agenda. Their ideas were wrong, cruel, and tinged with racism—and they won."[12] The guide goes on to highlight the congressional town hall as a particularly powerful organizational tactic, advice that grassroots resistance groups acted on in their attempts to thwart the Republican Party's efforts to repeal the Affordable Care Act in early 2017.

As the grassroots resistance groups of the collar counties and Lehigh Valley began to make noise in the region, local news outlets took notice of their popularity, effectiveness, and electoral ambitions.[13] As Pennsylvania's Democrats began to look ahead to the 2018 midterm elections, the wide coverage and quick mobilization of grassroots resistance groups raised a novel question within the political arena: how would these groups engage with the region's existing political institutions?

Disrupting the Democratic Party

Following their rapid growth in early 2017, southeastern Pennsylvania's resistance groups found themselves in one of the most contested political areas in the United States, and as a result, their activities often led them to engage with local branches of the Democratic Party. Pennsylvania's Democratic Party is organized on both the state and the county level, with county committees comprised of elected representatives from each voting precinct in the county. These county committees and their elected leadership serve as the Democratic Party's closest direct connection to voters, and as such, their political power and influence can affect the success of Democrats at every level of government. Despite their significance, these organizations rarely get the same attention as statewide parties, the national party, or individual campaigns, and therefore they can lapse into inactivity. When the grassroots resistance groups of the collar counties and Lehigh Valley emerged in early 2017, they were forced to contend with these organizations as they sought to influence their immediate political environment.

The nature and scale of cooperation between grassroots groups and county parties varied across the region and was shaped by the parties' level of openness to newcomers, as well as the specific goals of each grassroots group. Some groups' relationships with county committees were shaped by their lack of familiarity with the role of local Democratic organizations: Jamie Perrapato, founder of Turn PA Blue, recalled, "People started to look at these [party] organizations and ask, 'how come didn't I know about this? How come no one told me?' "[14] Activists' lack of awareness of local party organizations led them to pursue alternative, independent forms of activity through their grassroots groups.

In addition, party committees were caught unprepared for the initial wave of activism that took place in early 2017, which limited their ability to absorb new activists and contributed to the formation of independent groups. Perkiomen Valley Women founder Marla Hexter tried to reach out to the Montgomery County Democratic Party while she was forming her group in western Montgomery County, a rural area. At the time, she was considering running for Supervisor in her township. "They just seemed to be not very well organized, not really having their fingers on the pulse," she said of the county committee. "The local party kind of looked at us like, 'Okay, well, this area has always been Republican, we're going to focus our resources elsewhere.' "[15] This relative lack of support from the Democratic Party required Hexter to run a campaign that relied on the support of her own grassroots group, rather than on the party.

Activists were also concerned that the official party apparatus remained inactive between elections and was not equipped to build robust, year-round progressive infrastructure. This was the case for the leaders of Indivisible Berks, who acknowledged the relative conservatism of their surrounding area by "not canvassing as Democrats, or even progressives, but just as neighbors advocating for government that works for everyone, not just the privileged few."[16] Founder and President Jane Palmer further described how the group "bent over backwards not to be the [Democratic] Party" in order to "build a local organization that goes forward, that doesn't rise and fall with the fortunes of the Democrats, that is active 12 months out of the year."

Committee Cooperation

Despite the apprehension that some resistance leaders felt about engaging with the Democratic Party, many groups cooperated with party committees even as they pursued their own agendas. No group better demonstrated this fluidity than the East Penn Democratic Club of Lehigh County (EPDC). Originally founded during the 2008 campaign season as result of grassroots support for candidate Barack Obama, the club represented the growing impact of the Democratic Party in the suburban areas west of Allentown. During the early period of resistance mobilization, activist Naomi Winch took on the task of revitalizing the EPDC, which had become dormant since President Obama's 2012 reelection. To her dismay, Winch found that "the local county party was all but inactive, and there was very much establishment kind of Democrats running it." She nevertheless sought opportunities to get involved in order to "give people a pro-gressive outlet" and soon learned that the EPDC was nominally operating in her hometown of Emmaus. There was, however, a problem: "It was 100 percent inactive," recalled Winch: "There wasn't even an email that had been sent out to the group in two years."[17]

By the time of the 2016 general election, Winch had become president of the group and refocused its purpose. She brought in new members, most of whom had been independently active in the Democratic primary. Members of the revitalized EPDC began designing and printing their own campaign flyers in sup-port of local Democrats and canvassing their area to identify Democratic voters, notably without the participation of the Lehigh County Democratic Party. The EPDC felt it necessary to proceed with these independent efforts because "there was no GOTV [Get Out The Vote initiatives] going on, and, as a matter of fact, we got screamed at for doing GOTV by the county party!" Despite such occa-sional sources of tension with the Lehigh County Democratic Party, the EPDC fully committed itself to strengthening the party's presence in the county and making it more open to progressive activists like Winch. It actively recruited individuals to serve as precinct representatives on the county Democratic com-mittee itself, thereby increasing the party's footprint in communities around the area. "The local party may try to recruit a few [precinct committee people] in a given cycle . . . this past election, we recruited 120 of them," claimed Winch.[18]

The East Penn Democratic Club was not the only grassroots group that worked to increase participation in county committees. In the May 2018 Democratic Party primary, five of the six county parties studied here experi-enced a significant increase in the number of their elected precinct committee people, and the region overall experienced a 33 percent increase in the number of candidates running for committee positions. Northampton County, which has 155 precincts and 310 allocated precinct committee positions, elected 206 committee members, a 54 percent increase since 2010. Bucks County elected seventy-eight more Democratic committee representatives in 2018 than in 2014, a 28 percent increase. Lehigh County elected 282 county committee members in 2018, a 25 percent increase since 2014.[19]

In all of these cases, interviews with resistance leaders and Democratic officials suggest that grassroots groups positively contributed to these changes by both recruiting new committee members and increasing the commitment of those already elected to the body. For example, a leading member of the Tri-County Democrats also became a regional organizer for the Chester County Democratic Party prior to the 2016 election. After 2016, he continued to serve as a regional party organizer, overseeing sixteen precincts and an associated thirty-two county committee seats. As a member of both a resistance group and his county party, this activist began bridging the gap between his grassroots network and county party after the 2016 election by recruiting members of the Tri-County Democrats to serve on the Chester County Democratic Committee. "At the time of the 2016 election, only five of my thirty-two county committee slots had representation on the committee," he remarked. By late 2018, this had changed: "Now, every precinct in Zone 1 is represented."[20] A new county committee member also affiliated with the Tri-County Democrats described attending her first meeting of the county committee as "incredible . . . when they asked new committee members to stand, half the room stood up. . . I felt like my voice would now be heard by the Democratic Party."[21] The member had transitioned from the Tri-County Democrats into the county committee in search of a "more permanent" form of political activism.

Turn PA Blue, a regional group active throughout the collar counties and Lehigh Valley, actively directed its followers towards the Democratic county committees as well. Its founder Jamie Perrapato noted that "for grassroots groups to succeed, they need to be partnered with the county committees . . . they need the help and we need the institutional knowledge."[22] When the organization's followers expressed confusion about the state of the local committees, Turn PA Blue would facilitate communication with the county party about available vacancies. "Often, the response was, 'I'll do it. I didn't know this was a thing, that you need it and why you need it and why it's important.' "[23]

In some cases, the county parties explicitly reached out to grassroots groups in an attempt to recruit county committee representatives. In Northampton County, county chair Matt Munsey asked grassroots leaders to help recruit people for the committee.[24] One of those groups was FIERCE Lehigh Valley, a Facebook-based group inspired by Pantsuit Nation that formed in 2016. According to founder Vanessa Williams, these recruitment efforts paid off. Conducted almost entirely through information sharing on the group's Facebook page, the drive to increase party participation showed results: "A lot of the people in FIERCE are now Democratic committee members, whether that be on the state committee, a local official, or a precinct committee person."[25]

Data taken from counties' boards of election confirm that interest in precinct committee positions increased between the 2014 and 2018 party elections. Four of the six counties studied here saw large increases in the number of candidates running for such positions. The largest increase in candidate enthusiasm took place in Lehigh County, home of the EPDC, in which 84 percent more candidates ran for precinct committee positions in 2018 than in 2014. The only county in which the number of candidates on the ballot decreased was Berks County—interestingly, the only county in which the largest grassroots group,

Indivisible Berks, deliberately chose not to engage with the county committee as described earlier. This further suggests that grassroots groups played a significant role in the change in committee participation.

County committee participation data thus appear to affirm that the recruitment efforts of grassroots groups bore fruit in the 2018 party elections. However, these changes were not the only consequence of grassroots mobilization in the collar counties and Lehigh Valley. The increased mobilization around Democratic Party institutions also advanced the grassroots groups' ultimate goal of contesting regional elections and electing their members to offices ranging from local school boards to the US House of Representatives.

How Resistance Networks Influenced Elections

On the evening before Election Day, congressional candidate Susan Wild sent a text to Shirley Morganelli, the founder of Lehigh Valley ROAR. "She texted me that night and said, 'If I win this thing, it'll be because ROAR gave me my start,'" recalled Morganelli.[26] Wild's tribute to the resistance group that had launched her campaign was justified. Shortly after Republican incumbent Charlie Dent announced his intent to retire from Congress, Wild began strategizing with Morganelli and others in ROAR. A grassroots campaign from the start, Wild's election efforts began with a speech at a monthly meeting of ROAR, hosted in Morganelli's house, to forty of the group's members. "All of a sudden after that, it kind of took a life of its own. Then other members hosted meet and greets, and then they would fan out with their friends, so there would be an entire new group of people meeting her," recalled Barbara Burkhardt, another member of ROAR. The group's membership hosted fundraisers, took time off to knock on doors, and kept the Wild campaign fully tethered to the local community. The activists knew whom to talk to and what to say. They formed bonds with other groups like Lehigh Valley for All and the East Penn Democratic Club, all of whom began sending volunteers to her campaign. Wild truly did have reason to be grateful.

The story of Lehigh Valley ROAR is not unique, and many grassroots resistance groups active in the collar counties and Lehigh Valley undertook similar activities on behalf of candidates they supported, either those who were already running or candidates recruited from within the groups' own membership and extended networks. Cumulatively, these processes generated a large collection of candidates with limited professional political backgrounds, whose political viability was entirely due to their grassroots support.

Recruitment, Resources, and Training

Beginning in 2017, grassroots resistance groups began recruiting individuals to run for political office in their communities. This process involved identifying community leaders well suited for particular elections, convincing them to run, and helping them establish the resources to do so successfully. The EPDC methodically followed this process ahead of the 2018 midterms. In an interview conducted during the midterm election season, Winch noted, "I spend half my day recruiting. I'm trying to find where the holes are for this year and who I can plug into them."[27] The EPDC used its candidate recruitment to pursue its progressive goals by assembling a roster of potential progressive candidates and strategically supporting them when they ran for a winnable office. For example, although Winch had identified a "very progressive Pakistani-American female who want[ed] to run against an establishment Democrat for Mayor of Easton," Winch and the EPDC discouraged her from running because they didn't "want her to be associated with losing."[28] Winch affirmed her group's focus on municipal races, explaining that "you need to focus in on those races because no one is looking at them and you can really make a difference in a really fundamental way, particularly on school boards." These tactics reveal a highly organized effort to create a robust roster of progressive candidates at the most local level.

These efforts made an impression on the Democratic Party, which soon took notice of the large number of new candidates emerging through resistance groups. Surprised by the efficiency of the emerging grassroots recruitment infrastructure, Lehigh County Democratic chair Ed Hozza noted that "groups get information and different updates faster than we [do] as a party."[29] The efforts yielded impressive results: 2018 was "the first time in decades" that a Democratic candidate contested every State Assembly district in Lehigh County.[30] The same universal contestation occurred in neighboring Northampton County for the first time in ten years.[31] The Democrats were able to field more candidates than in previous years in part due to the cross-county and cross-district cooperation facilitated by groups like the EPDC, which kept a running list of all vacancies and all potential candidates. Grassroots groups also informed their members of school board and municipal executive positions for which they could run. "I've seen a lot of volunteers who now realize they hate what's happening on their school board, so they're going to run for School Board," remarked Perrapato of Turn PA Blue. "Or they're going to recruit somebody to run for school board."[32] Once such individuals decided they wanted to run for office, their grassroots groups gave them an immediately accessible political network, complete with tactical advisors, volunteers, and financial resources.

Several of the candidates who ran for office in the collar counties and Lehigh Valley in 2018 had precisely this start to their political careers. Marla Hexter, founder of Perkiomen Valley Women, decided to run for office in February 2017 after only three monthly meetings of her newly formed group. Her group wanted to "transition from being discussion-based to being more action-oriented," and members of the group ended up helping on her campaign.[33] She ultimately won her election with over 60 percent of the vote, taking her opponent "completely by surprise." State senate candidate Mark Pinsley, who challenged fourteen-year incumbent senator Pat Browne in the sixteenth senate district, followed a similar path as he sought office. After the 2016 election, Pinsley organized a group called Unite for America, from which he transitioned to Indivisible Berks, and "everything just snowballed from there," according to his campaign manager Hillary Kleinz.[34] Pinsely's campaign relied on the dedicated support of grassroots groups throughout Lehigh Valley. He ultimately lost his race to Pat Browne by 2 percent of the vote in a district in which Browne hadn't received less than 60 percent of the vote in over a decade.

State senate candidate Katie Muth's experience was a combination of the experiences of Hexter and Pinsley. Like Hexter, Muth's first involvement in politics was her Indivisible group, Indivisible MontCo, and like Pinsley, she was able to build on her early momentum to receive the support of a large number of grassroots groups in her senate campaign. Unlike Pinsley, she won her election against John Rafferty, a twelve-year Republican incumbent who had also won his previous elections with 60 percent of the vote and who in 2016 was the Republican nominee for Pennsylvania attorney general. Her victory as a complete political novice, self-described rape survivor, and outspoken feminist was one of the most surprising in Pennsylvania in 2018, and it was fueled by a coalition of grassroots and national resistance groups. To supplement the support she received from her own Indivisible group, Muth assiduously courted the support of other grassroots groups in her district. "She did it three people at a time," recalled Jane Palmer of Indivisible Berks. "She met with people. She met with me and my media team. She came to our meeting and talked to my members. She came to our events. She showed up over and over and over again."[35]

The groups with which she interacted repaid her dedication with the hard work of their volunteers. On Saturday before Election Day, eight volunteers stood together in the rain outside the Pink Moose Café on the banks of the Schuykill River in Royersford. Most of them were from Indivisible MontCo, though some were from Flippable. The Pink Moose Café was serving as a staging location for volunteers that day (the owner was a former member of Indivisible MontCo), and offering free coffee to anyone canvassing for "Katie." Over the course of the afternoon, over twenty volunteers, many clad in "Muth for Senate" apparel, came by the staging location to pick up canvass packets and talk to voters. When asked why they were volunteering, one couple responded, "This is the most important thing in politics right now! We would do anything for Katie."

In addition to directing volunteers to campaigns, grassroots resistance groups provided training and resources to their members seeking political office. Candidate trainings typically revolved around speech workshops, in which candidates could practice their public speaking and debate skills while honing their messages in front of informed audiences of their friends. In Lehigh County, Democratic Party chair Hozza recalled that "at their monthly meetings, [grassroots groups] ask for volunteers to give speeches, and then they're critiqued." Not only did these sessions help already-declared candidates, but they also helped the county party "identify people in those areas, potential candidates for those offices."[36] According to Winch, the EPDC ran such workshops because "a lot of folks that run for office, especially at the municipal level, don't really have that crisp, polished sound when they're talking to voters. So we definitely try to polish them up . . . so that they look like viable candidates."[37] Several groups also helped their candidates by producing flyers, videos, and social media content for their campaigns. For example, FIERCE Lehigh Valley had a "graphic design volunteer" who would create flyers for the group's events, but also for candidates as they decided to run.[38] Similarly, the EPDC had a group of graphic designers focused on helping candidates create professional-looking social media pages and campaign literature.

Grassroots resistance groups also increased the viability of their candidates by helping them fundraise, a feature of political campaigns that is often unpleasant for first-time office seekers without extensive political networks. A notable example of such support took place on October 17, when Lehigh Valley ROAR organized a music festival fundraiser in Bethlehem for its member and congressional candidate Susan Wild. Inspired by the city's annual summer concert series, "ROARfest" featured six bands and was hosted in a local bar. "We were rocking and roaring! It was great—the bands donated their time for free," recalled Morganelli. The event was free to all attendees but encouraged donations to the Wild campaign, which sent a representative to the event. The bar served a Wild-themed cocktail called the "Blue Wave," and the event generated over $2,000 for the candidate. "We were all participating," remembered Burkhardt, "and we all attended planning meetings and got it all set up."[39]

Valuable Volunteers

Throughout the 2018 election cycle, grassroots resistance groups never lost sight of their most significant political asset: their legions of dedicated and well-trained volunteers. The largest groups, like Lehigh Valley for All, Indivisible Berks, the EPDC, and Indivisible HOPE, all claimed to have mobilized over one hundred recurring volunteers who either canvassed directly for campaigns or advocated for progressive values more broadly. Groups like ROAR made up for their relatively smaller numbers (in ROAR's case, about forty volunteers) through their dedication, as members took vacation days to canvass for their favorite candidates. They were "small but mighty," according to Morganelli.

Grassroots groups were able to steer volunteers towards candidates by inviting candidates to address their assembled membership at monthly meetings. Several grassroots groups hosted some version of a candidate forum, in which candidates for every level of public office would speak to the group's membership, make their case, and take questions. In Berks County, Indivisible Berks developed a reputation for its size and the dedication of its volunteers, and its forums were therefore crucial campaign stops for candidates in the region. "All the Democratic congressional contenders came to us. They approached us. We did not approach them," described Palmer. "We'd let them have fifteen or twenty minutes to talk, and then we would have a wide open Q and A. Everybody could get right up close to the candidate; really sense what kind of people they were."[40] Other groups were more proactive in reaching out to candidates in the area. "As soon as a [candidate] name came up, Shirley [Morganelli] would always invite the person to speak to us, question and answer period, tell us what your issues are, tell us how you would react to this, that and the other thing," claimed Burkhardt. Regional columnist Bill White also noted that long after candidates had left, the ROAR membership remained for "Unhappy Hour," in which the candidates' pitches were discussed over wine and food. This affirmed "the idea that there are people in our community who have decided to do more than just sit despondently and watch our institutions unravel on cable TV."[41]

In contrast to the energetic grassroots support that some campaigns enjoyed, Scott Wallace, the Democratic nominee in the neighboring first district, had a harder time recruiting help from grassroots resistance networks. Widely perceived as an establishment candidate without much of a connection to the district (only 40 percent of voters believed him to be in touch with the needs of his constituents), Wallace had a difficult time against incumbent Brian Fitzpatrick, who campaigned as a moderate and emphasized his breaks with Trump.[42] It did not help that his campaign did not have the grassroots connections that powered Democratic candidates like Susan Wild.

This lack of grassroots support was in part a failure of the campaign's own making. As grassroots groups began looking for candidates to support, the Wallace campaign failed to respond to their outreach. Indivisible HOPE, one of the larger resistance groups active in the first district, hosted a candidate forum with local NPR satellite station WHYY, but didn't feature Wallace after his campaign declined the invitation. According to Christine Stenner, founder of Indivisible HOPE, "Scott Wallace was never [at our meetings] . . . during the primaries whenever we had something where we invited candidates, his campaign didn't even respond."[43] Although members of the group individually volunteered for the Wallace campaign in the final months of the election, Wallace never received the endorsement of Indivisible HOPE and therefore did not have access to the group's considerable organizational resources. Indivisible HOPE's 150 volunteers would probably have made a difference, as he ultimately lost the election by only nine thousand votes (a 2.5 percent margin).

In failing to reach out to grassroots groups, the Wallace campaign followed a pattern established by many high profile campaigns in the collar counties and Lehigh Valley. Both Wallace and the Clinton campaign of 2016 opted for campaigns managed by professional political operatives from outside of the region. Andrew Sklansky, the Wallace campaign's field director, had resided in first district for less than a year when he was tasked with establishing the campaign's canvassing operation. According to Vanessa Williams of FIERCE Lehigh Valley, this had happened before: "That's one of the ways I think that the Democratic Party has really faltered in the past is that they shipped people here from Washington or elsewhere, and tried to jump in three months before the election and figure out the region . . . there's a lot of nuance."[44] In Montgomery County, Marla Hexter had a similar opinion of the 2016 Clinton campaign, recalling that "there were so many things that the Hillary campaign did wrong. We knew we were going to the wrong neighborhoods, everything came down from Brooklyn."[45]

Familiarity with local political dynamics influenced how grassroots groups operated in the 2018 midterms, shaping the types of candidates they chose to support, the areas in which they chose to canvass, and what they said to voters when they arrived on their doorsteps. Unlike campaigns like Wallace's, which were "very top-down" and "just wanted to hit their [canvassing] targets," local grassroots groups were interested in building "progressive infrastructure in their community."[46] Though Wallace was ultimately endorsed by the national Indivisible umbrella organization, this turned out to be yet another example of an attempt to mobilize resources from the top-down, rather than the bottom up. While the national Indivisible organization had some influence on local groups, it was not a political party, and therefore groups like Indivisible HOPE felt free to act without much regard for this endorsement. "We were not involved because [the] Indivisible regional organizer mainly chats on Facebook Messenger, and when you don't pay attention for an hour you're totally lost," recalled Stenner. "I just decided to drop out of this and not pay attention anymore, to focus on our own work." By relying on the endorsement of the national Indivisible organization to shore up grassroots support, the Wallace campaign again overlooked the value of genuine engagement with grassroots resistance groups.

Scott Wallace lost his race, while Susan Wild won hers. Although grassroots support was not the only distinction between these candidates, the degree to which the campaigns engaged in grassroots outreach affected how they were viewed by their constituents and how easily they were able to mobilize dedicated volunteers. The contrast between these two candidates highlights a dynamic that was present throughout the collar counties and Lehigh Valley in the 2018 midterms, namely the degree to which grassroots engagement increased candidate viability and success. The Wallace campaign's failure to build bridges to grassroots resistance groups limited the extent to which it could rely on resistance volunteers.

In part, this was due to the fact that grassroots groups relied on personal connections between group members, group leadership, and individual campaigns to mobilize their volunteers for campaign involvement. In some cases, the leaders of grassroots groups were employed directly by campaigns, enabling them to facilitate close cooperation between the two. For example, in addition to being the founder and president of Indivisible HOPE, Christine Stenner was also the campaign manager for state representative candidate Josh Camden, a political novice running against a four-term Republican incumbent in the 147th state house district. To support his campaign, Stenner recruited both volunteers and staff from the membership of her Indivisible group. Similarly, Gabby Dietrich of Cumberland Valley Rising steered volunteers to campaigns by connecting them to other members who knew local candidates personally. Resistance groups also coordinated among themselves, sending their volunteers to other groups as necessary. At Turn PA Blue, for example, Perrapato noted "if I have somebody who's really interested in working for Chrissy Houlahan, I'm fine sending them to Swing Left because that also helps my candidate down ballot."[47] These various connections and interactions created a level of flexibility and responsiveness in volunteer assignments that doesn't typically exist in more hierarchical campaigns.

In addition to recruiting volunteers, grassroots groups also kept their members energized and focused. According to Pinsley's campaign manager Hillary Kleinz, although resistance groups can help recruit volunteers, they play a crucial role in "keeping people's morale up as well."[48] Keeping activists engaged over two years, from the election of Donald Trump to the 2018 elections, is no easy task. Yet Chair Hozza asserted that this was precisely what happened: "You could see it in the eyes of our female volunteers. Never have I seen such passion for volunteering, and working, giving up their Saturdays and Sundays, their weeknights, to get Democrats elected."

A New Landscape

This combination of candidate recruitment and support altered the electoral landscape of the collar counties and Lehigh Valley in favor of Democratic candidates. In Northampton County, Democrats won four of the five at-large county council seats up for election in 2017, all of which had been formerly held by Republicans. In Delaware County, on the southern border of Chester County, Democrats won their first seats on the county council in over forty years, breaking nearly a half-century of Republican hegemony.[49] Democrats in the Lehigh Valley fielded a candidate in every state assembly district, a feat they hadn't accomplished in over a decade.[50] Sitting in the Tri-County Democrats office on the eve of Election Day, a state assembly candidate put words to this phenomenon, stating, "since 2016, it's been different . . . We've had hundreds of volunteers come out of the woodwork . . . We're electing school board members and challenging Republican candidates who have been safe for years."[51]

The grassroots groups studied here contributed to this success not only by endowing traditional candidates with the resources necessary to win, but also by creating a new slate of candidates with strong community ties, something that mattered to voters in the collar counties and Lehigh Valley. A survey of Berks County Democratic Committee members found that a plurality of committee representatives considered a history of community activism to be the most important determinant of a candidate's success in local and state assembly elections, more important than previous political experience or involvement in the local Democratic Party. Lehigh County Democratic chair Hozza concurred: "the first thing the voter wants to see is that they were involved in the community."[52] Candidates that emerged from grassroots resistance groups met these criteria and were successful as a result.

The 2018 Democratic candidates for Pennsylvania State Senate further affirmed the impact of increased grassroots activity, particularly with regard to the number of women running for office. The number of women running for state senate in Pennsylvania increased by 60 percent from 2014 to 2018, from thirteen to twenty-one. Of the female candidates in 2018, fourteen were Democrats, and of those fourteen, eight were political novices, with little or no political experience prior to 2016. In contrast, no women without previous political experience ran for state senate in either 2014 or 2016.[53] In addition, six of the nine Democratic candidates for state senate who ran within the counties studied here had close relationships with grassroots groups. These relationships varied, but their existence was sufficient to connect the candidates to the energy of resistance groups. For example, Democratic incumbent Art Haywood, who ran for reelection in the fourth senate district, coordinated his reelection campaign with grassroots leaders even though he had his own existing political network.[54] The elevated number of political novices running for office and the connection these novices had to grassroots resistance groups suggest that the activities of grassroots groups described earlier was highly consequential in the 2018 election.

Voter registration and Democratic voter turnout levels also suggest that grassroots groups affected the electoral landscape of Pennsylvania. In counties throughout the state, both the percentage increase in Democratic voter registration and the percentage increase in Democratic turnout were highly correlated with the percentage of the female population that had graduate or professional degrees—the demographic group most overrepresented in grassroots resistance groups. Figure 12.1 shows a strong positive correlation between the percentage change in registered Democrats in 2018 and the percentage of women over twenty-five with a graduate or professional degree in each county. The correlation between the increase in registered Democrats and educated women (*R*-squared = .584, *P* <. 0001) is stronger than the correlation with the percentage of all people who hold advanced degrees, suggesting that women played a more significant role in this mobilization than men. Significantly, this correlation existed across a state with fourteen contested congressional races and hundreds of distinct voter registration efforts organized by political parties, nonprofit groups, public entities, and campaigns. The strength of this correlation affirms the relevance of educated women to the political mobilization that took place in Pennsylvania in 2018. While it does not independently demonstrate a causal link between grassroots groups and voter registration, the extensive voter

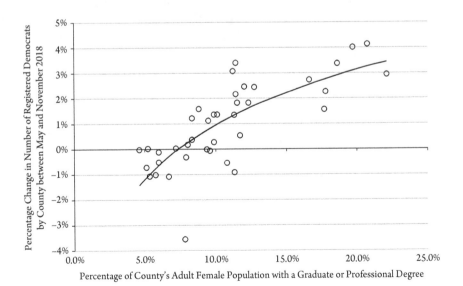

Figure 12.1 Educated Women and Democratic Voter Registration Gains in Pennsylvania.

Notes: Graph shows the percentage change in 2018 Democratic voter registration versus the percentage of adult women in a county with a graduate or professional degree. Data from US Census Bureau and the Pennsylvania Department of State.

registration activities of the resistance groups suggests that they might be the mechanism underlying this relationship.

The grassroots groups studied here undertook extensive voter registration efforts during 2017 and 2018, both in conjunction with the Democratic Party and independently. For many groups, voter registration was among their most significant initiatives, second only to canvassing. At the monthly meeting of Upper BuxMont Rising, group members reflected on their year's activities, noting how significant their voter registration efforts had been. "Our voter registration was so hot this year... maybe it was Kavanaugh," posited one member.[55] Upper BuxMont Rising had a variety of registration events throughout 2018, including trivia nights and debates. "We even hosted a big concert at a local bar—we had all kinds of events," recalled another member. Often, these events are co-hosted by a collection of groups. Turn PA Blue focused on coordinating events throughout the area, centralizing all events on its website and recruiting volunteers who would be available to various organizations on short notice should the need arise. Its website hosts a calendar on which users can find upcoming voter registration events from other organizations active in their area. In August of 2018, it advertised events from Indivisible Berks, NextGen, the Susan Wild congressional campaign, and the Bethlehem City Democratic Club. Although it is difficult to quantify the direct impact such efforts have, they likely contributed to the elevated rates of turnout that occurred in every county studied here.

Statewide data also suggest that grassroots resistance groups had a significant impact on Democratic voter turnout in the 2018 midterm elections. Figure 12.2 illustrates the strong positive correlation between the increase in Democratic voter turnout between the 2014 and 2018 gubernatorial election and the number of highly educated women in a county, using the same demographic data described earlier (R-squared $= .7059$, $P < .0001$). As in the case of the voter registration data, this correlation suggests that highly educated women played a role in increased Democratic mobilization, and again, the grassroots resistance groups appear to be a plausible mechanism of impact.

These data support the conclusions presented earlier in this chapter on the basis of interviews with grassroots leaders, party officials, and candidates—namely that grassroots resistance groups improved the electoral fortunes of Democrats by registering and turning out new voters through their electioneering efforts. Lehigh County Democratic chair Hozza didn't need statistical correlations to tell him what was behind the surge of Democratic activity. When asked what made the difference in the 2018 midterm elections, he was unequivocal: "It came down to our suburban, female, voters—and their distaste for the adulterous pumpkin in the White House."[56] His perspective, affirmed time and again by grassroots resistance leaders, reveals the potency of the resistance movement in the collar counties and Lehigh Valley.

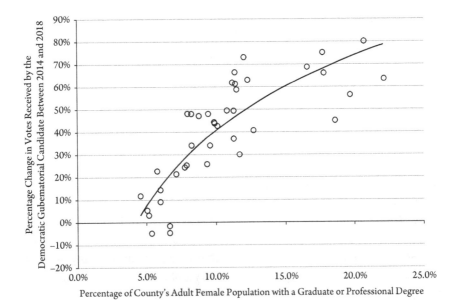

Figure 12.2 Educated Women and Democratic Voter Turnout in Pennsylvania.

Notes: Percentage change in Democratic gubernatorial voter turnout versus the percentage of adult women in a county with a graduate or professional degree. Data from US Census Bureau and the Pennsylvania Department of State.

Toward 2020 in Pennsylvania and Beyond

The groups that formed in the collar counties and Lehigh Valley emerged as part of a national wave of grassroots mobilization triggered by Donald Trump's election, one that encompassed a vast number of different organizations. Around the country and especially in the areas studied here, thousands of individuals awoke the day after the election and resolved to act in response to its outcome. The groups studied here did not emerge out of an existing political institution. Their affiliates sought each other out based on their dislike of President Trump and the political culture he represented. Activists met each other in living rooms, church basements, union halls, and diners. Their meetings started as opportunities to discuss the election, to make sense of the schisms it revealed in American culture, and to share their heartbreak and frustration about what that culture represented. In each other's company, these individuals found that they were not alone. As hundreds of people began coming to meetings and rallies, the groups began to organize. They elected leadership, defined their priorities, and began educating themselves about how best to get involved. They connected with each other in person and on social media, communicating on both a local and national level.

As their organization grew, so did their visibility. Events like the Women's March proved to many future grassroots leaders that organization and action could yield significant consequences, inspiring them to continue their activism upon their return home. Throughout 2017, resistance groups continued to grow and advocate for their agendas, mobilizing around the Affordable Care Act repeal attempt, the Trump travel ban, and the GOP-led tax reforms. Their members continued to learn about political processes at both national and local levels and used their knowledge to affect change where they could. Ultimately, they strengthened local Democratic Party organizations and increased the electoral success of Democratic and progressive candidates throughout the region.

The impact of these groups went beyond traditional indicators of party strength like voter registration and turnout numbers. In addition to strengthening the Democratic Party, they created an entirely new progressive infrastructure network. Groups like Indivisible Berks emphatically asserted their desire to remain independent of party politics and instead sought to change the minds of their neighbors in rural and suburban parts of the relatively conservative Berks County. Even groups that aligned more closely with the traditional party infrastructure recognized that the Democratic Party had flaws and inefficiencies, especially in the periods between major elections. By establishing themselves as independent of the Democratic Party to varying degrees, these groups raised questions about the future of progressive organizing in this region, especially with regard to Democratic Party cohesion and organization in major elections. The tension between hierarchical efficiency and decentralized flexibility is likely to be relevant to this movement going forward.

Features of this movement will likely endure in the coming years. The most visible example is the new class of elected officials that has emerged out of the resistance, at levels ranging from local municipal government to the US House of Representatives. All of the candidates who emerged out of the resistance groups of southeastern Pennsylvania, including Muth, Wild, and Hexter, will be in office until at least 2020. During this time, they will continue to engage with and lead their respective political networks, including their grassroots groups. The leadership of the resistance within this area has thus been partially institutionalized, insofar as it now holds political power within government. This institutionalization will likely change the tactics employed by the movement as protests against elected officials lose their obvious function. However, this does not necessarily mean that there will be a decline in grassroots political activity, as many activists have expressed a desire to continue holding elected officials accountable on policy matters ranging from health care to criminal justice reform.

The future of the resistance will also be influenced by the degree to which the leadership of the movement becomes integrated into the Democratic Party. This is particularly relevant in the cases of elected officials like Muth and Wild. Both enjoyed the support of comparable grassroots groups, but as of yet it is unclear whether this similarity is a salient part of their political identity as legislators. There is no national "Resistance Caucus" in Congress, unlike in the case of the Tea Party, which spawned a "Tea Party Caucus" in July 2010, even before any representatives of the movement had been elected to federal office. There has been no analogous effort among resistance Democrats since the most recent election.

Despite these novel dynamics among elected representatives of the resistance movement, the most consequential impact of the grassroots resistance groups in the collar counties and Lehigh Valley may be the symbiotic voter turnout infrastructure they have created with the Democratic Party. Donald Trump's narrow statewide margin of victory in 2016 and his inability to significantly increase his electoral appeal beyond his base mean that he has a relatively small margin for error in Pennsylvania in 2020. There are almost 800,000 more registered Democrats than Republicans in the state, so any significant change in voter turnout operations could return it to a Democratic presidential candidate. How these effects play out in 2020 remains to be seen.

Certain features of grassroots organizing modalities described in this chapter might inform future political endeavors and scholarly work as well. For example, this chapter described the use of social media by resistance groups not to coordinate across large geographies, but to maintain close communication within activist networks. Facebook groups in particular were a locus of this particular form of organizing, and the extent to which resistance groups relied on this medium sheds light on the interaction between face-to-face and online networking. In addition, this analysis illustrates the gaps in party infrastructure at the level of local politics that enabled resistance groups to circumvent local Democratic Party organizations when recruiting candidates and canvassing. The relatively low barrier to entry at the level of local elected office could inform the priorities of future grassroots groups and political parties.

Regardless of its future impact, the resistance has already made its mark on American political life. Members of the resistance join the ranks of Americans who have taken on the responsibility of political involvement for the benefit of their community and their country. In the data-driven world of twenty-first-century campaigns and social media bubbles, it is easy to assume that politics, like many other aspects of American culture, will dissolve into a series of ephemeral viral moments, as the algorithms of the established and powerful increasingly manipulate voters of all persuasions. The grassroots activists described in this study defy such categorization, demonstrating along the way that concerted and dedicated citizen action is still a consequential force in our political environment.

Notes

1. Katie Muth, Thomas Wolf, and Robert Casey, observed by author at Democratic Party rally, Thomas Paine Unitarian University Fellowship, November 3, 2018.
2. Clare Foran, "Republican Lawmakers Face Hostile Town-Hall Crowds," *The Atlantic*, February 23, 2017; Michael Malbin, "Does the Opening Predict a Wave?" Brookings Institution, July 25, 2017; Michelle Hackman, "Liberal Political Groups See Surge in Donations," *Wall Street Journal*, November 15, 2016; Geoffrey Skelley, "Record Voter Turnout in 2017 VA Primary Election," WVIR NBC29 Charlottesville, June 15, 2017.
3. Chris Walsh, "Together, We Flipped the West Coast Blue!" *Flippable*, November 7, 2017, https://blog.flippable.org/together-we-flipped-the-west-coast-blue-2521cd54ab64?_ga=2.9 7208605.364303419.1551302460-1729086919.1551115950.
4. David Weigel, "Left Out of AHCA Fight, Democrats Let Their Grass Roots Lead—and Win," *Washington Post*, March 24, 2017.
5. Charles Thompson, "Can Pa. Democrats Turn Anti-Trump Momentum into Actual Votes in 2018 Elections?" PennLive.com, January 30, 2018.
6. The collar counties and Lehigh Valley include the first, fourth, and seventh congressional districts, all of which were deemed competitive in the 2018 midterm elections.
7. Dennis Powell, "Geography of the Election: The Philadelphia Collar Counties—A Splash of Red," Newgeography.com, September 11, 2010, www.newgeography.com/content/001860-geography-election-the-philadelphia-collar-counties-a-splash-red.
8. Individuals interviewed as part of this study included Ruth Yeiser, outreach coordinator of Fair Districts PA; Naomi Winch, president of the East Penn Democratic Club; Shirley Morganelli, co-founder of Lehigh Valley ROAR; Barbara Burkhardt, member of Lehigh Valley ROAR; Phila Back, outreach director of Lehigh Valley Medicare for All; Jane Palmer, president and founder of Indivisible Berks; Christine Stenner, president and founder of Indivisible HOPE; Marla Hexter, Lower Fredrick Township supervisor and founder of Perkiomen Valley Women; Gabby Dietrich, president and founder of Cumberland Valley Rising; Vanessa Williams, president of FIERCE Lehigh Valley; leaders and members of the Tri-County Democrats; Jamie Perrapato, president and founder of Turn PA Blue; Chris Walsh, co-founder of Flippable; Kathy Harrington, founder of Lehigh Valley for All; Colleen Frank, founder of Upper BuxMont Rising and president of Pennridge Democrats; Jude-Laure Denis, former executive director of Power Northeast; Nancy Weston, founder and president of Bridle Path Resisters; Paige Van Wirt, Bethlehem city councilor and member of Lehigh Valley ROAR; name withheld, Democratic State Assembly candidate in a collar county district; Hillary Kleinz, campaign manager for state senate candidate Mark Pinsley; Rogette Harris, chair of the Dauphin County Democratic Party; Ed Hozza, chair of the Lehigh County Democratic Party; Matt Munsey, chair of the Northampton County Democratic Party; Stephen Schur, Zone 1 chair of the Chester County Democratic Party; Megan Angelo, grassroots activist; and Patty Bonner, grassroots activist.
9. Election results were obtained from Ballotopedia, an election analysis platform, while candidate records and precinct-level electoral data were obtained from county boards of election. Voter registration data were obtained from the Pennsylvania Department of State through its online portal.
10. With the exception of the Tri-County Democrats, each of the seventeen grassroots groups studied were founded or led by a woman at the time of the 2018 midterms (see note 8 in this chapter).
11. Chris Walsh, interview with Chris Walsh, Flippable, n.d.
12. "Introduction to the Guide | Indivisible," Indivisible.org, December 4, 2018, available at https://web.archive.org/web/20181204043022/https://indivisible.org/guide.
13. Michelle Merlin, "Shared Grief over Trump's Election Gives Rise to New Political Groups in Lehigh Valley," *Allentown Morning Call*, May 7, 2018.
14. Jamie Perrapato, interview with president and founder of Turn PA Blue, telephone, n.d.
15. Marla Hexter, interview with founder of Perkiomen Valley Women, telephone, n.d.
16. Jane Palmer, interview with president and founder of Berks County Indivisible, telephone, n.d.

17. Naomi Winch, interview with president of the East Penn Democratic Committee, telephone, n.d.
18. Naomi Winch, interview.
19. The figures cited here were obtained directly from the counties' boards of election via email outreach. These figures represent the best knowledge of county officials, who included both election results and party records in the data they provided.
20. Interview with founder and members of the Tri-County Democrats, in person, November 5, 2018.
21. Interview with founder and members of the Tri-County Democrats.
22. Perrapato, interview with president and founder of Turn PA Blue.
23. Perrapato, interview with president and founder of Turn PA Blue.
24. Matthew Munsey, interview with chair of the Northampton Democratic Party, telephone, n.d.
25. Vanessa Williams, interview with president and founder of FIERCE Lehigh Valley, telephone, n.d.
26. Barbara Burkhardt and Shirley Morganelli, interview with Lehigh Valley ROAR co-founders, in person, November 5, 2018.
27. Winch, interview with president of the East Penn Democratic Committee.
28. Winch, interview with president of the East Penn Democratic Committee.
29. Edward Hozza, interview with chair of Lehigh County Democratic Party, telephone, n.d.
30. Edward Hozza, interview with chair of Lehigh County Democratic Party.
31. Munsey, interview with chair of the Northampton Democratic Party.
32. Perrapato, interview with president and founder of Turn PA Blue.
33. Hexter, interview with founder of Perkiomen Valley Women.
34. Hillary Kleinz, interview with campaign manager of state senate candidate Mark Pinsely, in person, November 6, 2018.
35. Palmer, interview with president and founder of Berks County Indivisible.
36. Hozza, interview with chair of Lehigh County Democratic Party.
37. Winch, interview with president of the East Penn Democratic Committee.
38. Williams, interview with president and founder of FIERCE Lehigh Valley.
39. Burkhardt and Morganelli, interview with Lehigh Valley ROAR co-founders.
40. Palmer, interview with president and founder of Berks County Indivisible.
41. Bill White, "Lehigh Valley Women Asserting Themselves in Local Politics," *Allentown Morning Call*, March 7, 2018.
42. "Small GOP Lead in CD01," Monmouth University, October 3, 2018, www.monmouth.edu/polling-institute/reports/monmouthpoll_pa_100318/.
43. Christine Stenner, interview with Indivisible HOPE president and founder, telephone, September 26, 2018.
44. Vanessa Williams, interview with president and founder of FIERCE Lehigh Valley, telephone, n.d.
45. Marla Hexter, interview with founder of Perkiomen Valley Women, telephone, n.d.
46. Jane Palmer, interview with president and founder of Berks County Indivisible, telephone, n.d.
47. Perrapato, interview with president and founder of Turn PA Blue.
48. Kleinz, interview with campaign manager of state senate candidate Mark Pinsely.
49. Laura Benshoff, "Dems Vow More Transparency in Historic Delco Swearing-in Ceremony," WHYY, January 2, 2018.
50. Hozza, interview with chair of Lehigh County Democratic Party.
51. Interview with 2018 Pennsylvania State Assembly candidate, in-person, November 6, 2018.
52. Hozza, interview with chair of Lehigh County Democratic Party.
53. Candidates were designated as a novice if they had never previously run for political office and had no other significant history in public life. In practice, this often meant that they relied on activist mobilization to support their candidacies.
54. Perrapato, interview with president and founder of Turn PA Blue.
55. Upper Buxmont Rising monthly meeting, in person, November 4, 2018.
56. Hozza, interview with chair of Lehigh County Democratic Party.

13

Citizen Activism and the Democratic Party

THEDA SKOCPOL, LARA PUTNAM, AND CAROLINE TERVO

In a conservative area of Ohio on a winter weekday in January 2019, two of the authors met with the outgoing and incoming chairs of their county Democratic Party. Back in the summer of 2017, one of us first interviewed the older chairwoman—let's call her Elise—about her party's relationship to the new grassroots groups that had appeared "all of a sudden like boom" after November 2016. At that time, Elise described wary cooperation but also expressed skepticism. She had been active in the party since the 1980s, originally working with other women to open up an old-boy system to new as well as incumbent candidates. Above all, Elise was proud of her four years of work as county chair to maintain the local office while recruiting and supporting local candidates. The decline of labor unions was hampering her efforts, she acknowledged; and during the 2016 campaign, the Hillary Clinton operation had proved less effective than the previous Obama efforts. Given that she had to cope with such changes and soldier on, Elise wondered why additional independent groups were needed. Why couldn't people newly active after Trump's election just join the Democratic Party and loyally support all of its candidates?

By the time we returned to Ohio after the 2018 midterms, Elise had become much more welcoming of new liberal energy coursing through outside networks the party itself does not control. In the storefront office, we snapped a heart-warming picture of Elise hugging her newly elected successor—let's call her Melanie—a much younger woman who had recently moved to the area from California. Melanie volunteered for Clinton in 2016 and afterwards wondered "crap, what now?" On walks through town, she saw a yard sign for a new resistance group, knocked on the door, and soon found herself on the leadership team, where she eventually took responsibility for ensuring that someone would run for every state and local office in 2018. Except in a few pockets, Democrats

Theda Skocpol, Lara Putnam, and Caroline Tervo, Citizen Activism and the Democratic Party 2018 In: Upending American Politics Edited by: Theda Skocpol and Caroline Tervo, Oxford University Press (2020). © Oxford University Press
DOI: 10.1093/oso/9780190083526.003.0013

have not won in this part of Ohio for some time. Nevertheless, Melanie believes that having candidates for all offices is important to a "functioning democracy." When no one stepped up to challenge an incumbent GOP state legislator, she had what she calls a "look in the mirror moment" and decided to run herself, working with active resistance networks in even the remotest reaches of the district. She is proud she was part of statewide efforts to boost turnout in 2018 and "make Republicans work for their victories." In early 2019, with Elise's blessing, Melanie was elected the new county party chair.

The two women reflected on the changes they are seeing. Just as Elise once worked to open party structures to women and new candidates, now Melanie plans to take further steps. She intends to weave ties and do joint projects with independent allies, including the new activist networks and the recently expanded League of Women Voters that insists on presenting itself as non-partisan. Many of the newly engaged citizens, the two women agreed, stress values more than loyalty. They want to mount protests and contact officials about policy decisions, not just hand out bumper stickers during election seasons.

Even if efforts to open up this local party succeed, the county will not suddenly turn blue. Still, as we are about to see, this kind of party revitalization is happening in many places, and it could improve Democratic margins in national and state elections and enable local parties to serve as hubs for ongoing public discussion of vital issues.

A Democratic Party with Decayed Roots

Shifting to the national picture, America's Democratic Party has obviously been on a rollercoaster in recent years. The dizzying swings have not only been about electoral ups and downs, from the giddy heights of Barack Obama's victories to the bitter depths of the GOP waves of 2010 and 2014 and the shocking 2016 outcome. More than such ballot-box setbacks, the Democratic Party's reputation, organizational integrity, and abilities to connect with citizens have been increasingly on the line. After the 2008 elections marked "what seemed like the zenith of Democratic political participation," party leaders and outside advisors debated ways to translate Obama's massive grassroots campaign operation into enduring citizen-powered heft.[1] First, they tried subsuming a slightly renamed version under the Democratic National Committee; then they retooled it for Obama's reelection effort; and finally they set it up outside the party as a non-profit able to collect big donations to fund efforts to drum up support for the president's second-term policy initiatives.[2] None of these iterations really generated much citizen clout or engagement. Various autopsies tried to pin the blame differently, with most tagging the DNC as the villain.[3] Meanwhile, on the right, new waves of grassroots citizen activism were in fact roiling American politics. From 2009 on, conservative-minded Americans across all fifty states created more than one thousand local Tea Parties that met regularly to pressure elected officials and remake the Republican Party from below.[4]

In retrospect, hopes that a preserved version of Obama's campaign organization could somehow revitalize the Democratic Party seem naïve. To be sure, from 2007 to 2012 that innovative operation melded online and neighborhood-based "relational organizing" to engage 2.2 million volunteers led by some ten thousand neighborhood team leaders to register more than 1.8 million voters, hold regular house parties, make more than 150 million phone calls, and run more than five thousand get-out-the-vote staging areas.[5] Yet how could such a centrally coordinated operation originally tightly focused on a single overriding electoral goal have been expected to remake a federated US political party? As the research of political scientist Daniel Galvin has shown, Democratic presidents tend to turn quickly from campaigning to governing, from citizen mobilization to building legislative and administrative legacies, and so they have failed to translate campaign efforts into party-building projects.[6] Barack Obama and his top lieutenants did likewise, as they hustled to counter a deepening economic recession while addressing pent-up liberal demands for policy breakthroughs on health care and climate change. Then, after massive GOP gains in 2010, they became preoccupied with the president's reelection.

President Obama has been roundly criticized for his neglect of party building. Yet even if he had tried harder to reform the Democratic National Committee and sustain his campaign strategies, would such steps have sufficed? Could top-down efforts on the left have matched the burst of self-organized citizen energy expressed on the right in the grassroots Tea Party? Not likely. After all, the Republican Party itself did not create Tea Party groups, and neither did any other national power center. Rather, as conservative citizens formed local Tea Parties on their own, GOP leaders had to accommodate the new popular energies and demands—which they often did very reluctantly.

Meanwhile on the left, early discussions about continuing Obama's grassroots campaign organizations sparked worried discussions among leading Democrats. Would grassroots groups go off on their own and create chaos? It is hard, if not impossible, for people in powerful positions to translate a centrally managed endeavor into multi-purpose grassroots organizing. Self-managed groups of citizens are not easy to inspire or orchestrate from a Washington, DC, headquarters or an online cockpit. What is more, institutions like local, state, and national Democratic Parties are likely to open themselves to new participants and ideas only when they face pushes and pulls from groups at least partially perched outside of existing routines.

Unforeseen events have sharply shifted political equations since the Obama presidency. Ironically, many of the most promising opportunities for injecting new citizen energy into Democratic campaigns and organizations have emerged only after the 2016 defeat of Obama's heir apparent, Hillary Rodham Clinton. From that moment, as we have seen throughout this volume, hundreds of thousands of ordinary liberal-minded Americans decided to take responsibility themselves to fight for an inclusive, egalitarian US democracy. Emerging far and wide across the country, two thousand or more local groups responded to galvanizing events—the 2016 election and the January 2017 Women's Marches—by creating new grassroots organizations or supercharging the activism of older ones. Local resistance groups often take inspiration, cues, and bits and pieces of resources from professionally staffed advocacy or coordinating bodies. But for the most part, volunteers have organized locally—at the edges of and alongside existing Democratic Party organs, filling in gaps where party bodies are moribund or virtually nonexistent. Even as they fought Trump-GOP initiatives, most of these new grassroots resistance groups encouraged new candidates to run for public office and gave a big boost to Democratic campaigns. Their efforts helped build a massive "blue wave" that propelled resistance-backed candidates, especially women, into public office in 2017 and 2018. Furthermore, as Melanie's Ohio story illustrates, even when resisters' electoral efforts fell short, they have generated new people, tactics, and energy to reform and enlarge Democratic Party politics.

As of late 2019 and early 2020, it is too soon to tell how far this remaking of the roots of the Democratic Party will go—and what its overall impact will be on party agendas, structures, and electoral prospects. However, it is not too soon to document and explore the pathways of change unfolding at the intersection of grassroots resistance networks and party politics. That is what we do here, drawing in part on evidence gathered from various states and localities across the Midwest and upper South and relying especially on systematic information about some 225 local resistance groups operating in fifty-five of the state of Pennsylvania's sixty-seven counties.

The Keystone State has been, of course, pivotal to recent US electoral swings, and it is a highly varied place. Beyond the big cities of Philadelphia and Pittsburgh, each surrounded by suburbs and exurbs, the state also includes declining medium-sized industrial areas and vast stretches of small-town and rural areas in the center and across the top of the state. Indeed, with 2.7 million rural residents tallied in the 2010 census, Pennsylvania has a larger rural population than any state other than Texas and North Carolina. Beyond socioeconomic variety, there are blue, purple, and red partisan jurisdictions—and areas in rapid transition in one direction or another. In all of its variety, this vast state offers a remarkable window into the ways the Democratic Party is changing amidst the new citizen mobilizations sparked by the 2016 election.

Mapping the Resistance Terrain

By the middle of 2017, as we have discussed earlier in this volume, thousands of voluntarily organized grassroots resistance groups had established themselves as players in cities, suburbs, and towns across America. Exact numbers are hard to pin down, but late summer 2017 listings of many kinds of resistance contacts on the website map maintained by the national Indivisible organization can be sorted by jurisdictions. When this is done for the fifty states, we find that by August 2017 there were listings that ranged from a high of 8.3 per 100,000 voting-aged residents in Vermont to a low of one or fewer per 100,000 in Louisiana (1.0), Alabama (0.9) and Mississippi (0.8). The median falls between Ohio (2.24) and Michigan (2.22), and the state of Pennsylvania is slightly above the median, with a density score of 2.3 listings per 100,000 residents, ranked twenty-second among the fifty states.

Contact listings on the early Indivisible map should *not* be interpreted simply as actual grassroots resistance groups. Especially in the early phases, the Indivisible map included entities submitted by all kinds of people and organizations that wanted to declare themselves part of the burgeoning anti-Trump resistance. Those listings ranged from pre-2016 left-leaning organizations to a varied assortment of face-to-face, virtual, and mixed virtual and face-to-face entities that had popped into existence after November 2016. Many early listings referred to endeavors that never really got off the ground, while others were not real groups. Our best estimate is that about a third of early Indivisible map listings referred to actual groups of people who came together or refocused their activities after 2016, and have met at least periodically in 2017 and/or 2018. Still, the August 2017 listings we have tallied across the US states do give us a sense of vast extent and relative densities of early bursts of resistance activism. Even if only about a third of those early listings turned out to be "real" local groups, the listings themselves indicate aspirations to take part in the nationwide spread of anti-Trump activism. As of August 2017, people in forty-seven of Pennsylvania's sixty-seven counties had contributed listings of some sort to the Indivisible map.

To get a more precise sense of ongoing resistance activity, we have worked to identify and tally for each of the sixty-seven counties in Pennsylvania all of the named grassroots resistance groups whose core participants have met face-to-face for some stretches during 2017 and/or 2018. As of mid-2019, the master list we have developed contains some 225 local groups, one or more active in fifty-five Pennsylvania counties. To compile the list, we started with Indivisible map listings from early 2017 on—but we did not stop there. We also used internet searches, media reports, and interviews with leaders in Pennsylvania to ferret out as many names of local groups as we could; then we dug deeper to learn when and where each group has been active. Most of the groups on our master list are independent organizations voluntarily founded by sets of citizens after November 2016, but a small number are preexisting local membership groups that increased their activities after 2016 and chose to list themselves on the Indivisible map. Pre-2016 groups that we count as part of the grassroots resistance include a couple of Democratic Socialist chapters as well as several ideological or constituency auxiliaries linked to local Democratic parties.[7] However, we do *not* include any elected party committees with authority over party operations; nor do we include unions or statewide or national professional advocacy organizations, even though a few such entities registered themselves on the Indivisible map.

The twelve Pennsylvania counties that (as far as we can tell) have *not* generated any indigenous grassroots groups are mostly very sparsely populated rural areas with small shares of college-educated residents. Montour County is an exception. It has a relatively high share of educated residents but has not generated its own group, perhaps because it is nestled among neighbor counties where groups welcome Montour participants.[8] As this example suggests, neighbor effects can matter. Not just people living in a relatively highly educated county like Montour, but also residents of other counties without home-grown groups can be welcomed into resistance groups next door. For example, news articles about "Indivisible We Rise—West Central PA" (a group founded and still operating in the university town of Clarion in the county of the same name) call it "a nonpartisan watchdog group serving Clarion, Jefferson, Forest, Venango, and Clearfield counties."[9] However, most participants come from Clarion city and county, and on our master list we assign the group to just that county. We count groups in more than one county only if they are formally established as multicounty organizations or consortia.

Where did Pennsylvania citizens launch organized local resistance efforts? Grassroots groups are found almost everywhere, but—no surprise—the most substantial densities of Indivisible map listings and actual grassroots groups have appeared in Pennsylvania's two major metropolitan regions, greater Philadelphia and greater Pittsburgh, as well as in surrounding upscale suburbs and exurbs. Grassroots groups have also emerged in areas across the state with higher proportions of college-educated and economically well-to-do residents. In rural counties, where the residents tend to be less well-to-do and formally educated overall, groups tended to take shape just one or two at a time—and they often formed in towns with private colleges or branches of Penn State University. This makes sense, because colleges not only house students and employ teachers and college-educated staffers; they also attract educated retirees, serve knowledge-intensive businesses, and provide institutional spaces for community-wide public discussions. Forty-seven of Pennsylvania's sixty-seven counties are homes to hundreds of two- and four-year public and private institutions. Whereas eleven of the twenty Pennsylvania counties that have no colleges also failed to generate any indigenous resistance group, all but one of the counties with colleges did generate at least one group—often headquartered in the college town itself.[10]

Resistance Groups and Networks in Election 2018

Everywhere we have tracked grassroots resistance activities—across Pennsylvania and beyond—the first year, 2017, involved intense efforts to protest and push back against the policy initiatives of the Trump administration and the agendas of the GOP-dominated Congress. Speaking up for immigrants and refugees and agitating to prevent the repeal of ObamaCare were top efforts for almost all groups during that first year, although many groups also deployed subsets of members to deal with gerrymandering and educational and environmental issues. In states or districts that had off-year or special elections in 2017, resistance groups quickly got involved in election activities as well. By early 2018, the electoral turn was virtually universal, as almost all groups started focusing on what they could do to push back against Trump and the GOP by electing Democrats and new people to office. In the words of one leader of a large group in Waldo County, Maine, "as we have moved into this election year we have found ourselves increasingly involved with engagement rather than resistance, beginning with hosting candidate forums and now with a heavy focus on canvassing and GOTV."[11]

Varieties of Election Involvements

Grassroots resistance groups made various choices about election involvements. Like one organization we have tracked in a conservative part of North Carolina, a minority of groups chose to stand apart in order to maintain a non-partisan community profile. At the opposite end of the spectrum, some groups simply turned themselves into campaign organizations to support a member running for office or other local Democratic candidates.[12] Most groups positioned themselves somewhere in-between these poles, and it is important to note that even when resistance organizations themselves did not officially endorse candidates or perform a particular kind of electoral activity such as fundraising, they often helped members work individually and together on key election tasks. For

virtually all anti-Trump resisters, the 2017 special elections and the 2018 general
elections were all-hands-on-deck moments.

A Detailed Look at Electioneering in Pennsylvania

In early 2019, we gathered online questionnaire responses from leaders of eighty
grassroots resistance groups, plus comparable information from two additional
groups. These eighty-two responses provide a window into resistance group activities during the 2018 midterms in forty-nine Pennsylvania counties.[13] We used
a confidential online link to gather questionnaire responses from as many local
groups as possible, spreading the word through several coordinating networks—
including Pennsylvania Together and Action Together. Initial waves of responses
came from all over the state. After that, we recruited more respondents in other
areas by using online sources and interpersonal networks to reach into counties
where we knew additional groups had operated since 2016. We have not been
able to get questionnaire responses from every group we believe still exists, and
we do not claim that these responses describe the experiences of all anti-Trump
resistance groups in Pennsylvania. But this approach used in conjunction with
the master list we have assembled of ever-existing groups since late 2016 gives
us some assurance that we have heard from groups all over the state. The questionnaire respondents are group leaders (and often founders) who can offer an
informed overview. We posed seven open-ended questions, asking leaders to
describe their groups' "ups and downs" in 2018 member participation; types of
involvements (if any) in the 2018 elections; relationships with the Democratic
Party; and plans for the immediate post-2018 future. About the election specifically, we asked: "Was your organization involved in the 2018 midterm elections?
If yes, how? This can include supporting candidates, endorsing candidates,
donating money to campaigns, canvassing, registering people to vote, etc." In
addition, we asked people to reflect on anything that "surprised" them about
the 2018 election—and that query generated many colorful and insightful
reflections.

For the rest of this chapter, we draw upon questionnaire responses we received
from leaders of 82 groups, collated with additional data on groups and places in
Pennsylvania and beyond. When we use interviews, online answers, or emails
from people to whom we promised confidentiality, we either assign pseudonyms
or situate them without using their names. We name specific individuals, groups
or jurisdictions only when we have permission or can rely on information from
cited public sources such as news articles or public Facebook pages.

Figure 13.1 summarizes what we know about 2018 election activities from
eighty-two grassroots groups reporting from forty-nine Pennsylvania counties.
The first thing to notice is that almost all of the groups whose leaders filled

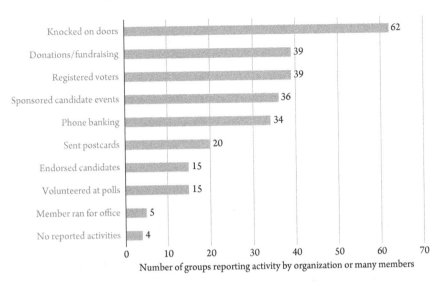

Figure 13.1 Activities in 2018 Elections Reported by Eighty-two Grassroots Resistance Groups in Forty-nine Pennsylvania Counties.

out our questionnaire were active in the 2018 elections—in fact, only four reported no election activities, fewer than the five groups that actually generated a member who ran for office in 2018. As Figure 13.1 tallies, more than a third of the groups—thirty out of eighty-two—said that their organization or many of its members got involved in seven or eight types of election activities (out of nine types). Forty-five groups indicated that they did four to six types of activities; and the remaining eleven groups mentioned one to three types of activities. In short, not only were almost all these groups active, the vast majority were engaged in an impressively wide range of activities during the 2018 elections. Some activities were not arduous—for example, when individual participants donated to candidates or volunteered on Election Day. Others required group efforts at key moments—for example to sponsor and arrange multi-candidate forums or candidate "meet and greets." Such events usually featured Democratic candidates running for offices at one or more levels; but a few groups invited Republican candidates as well. Remarkably, one group in rural Blair County actually co-sponsored a candidate forum with the local Tea Party.[14]

If such sporadic contributions were all that happened, we might assess the role of Pennsylvania resistance groups in the 2018 elections as important but routine. But this was far from the main storyline, because most groups reported undertakings that required members to make major commitments and learn new citizen skills most did not have before the Trump era. Voter registration drives, for example, require people to master often arcane or tricky legal rules before they contact potential voters. What is more, many local organizations—along with national and state organizers that provided various kinds of support—worked hard to prepare members to canvass neighborhoods and communities. "We had to calm down a lot of new canvassers who were anxious about knocking on doors out there," explained one leader, "and our message to them and anyone who would listen was don't imagine that areas that look bright red on a map are not full of folks who want to vote our way."

Despite big demands on volunteer time and emotions, "door knocking" was the kind of activity most frequently reported by our Pennsylvania respondents, as Figure 13.1 shows. More than three-quarters of the eighty-two groups said they engaged in this activity. The same thing happened far beyond Pennsylvania, as we know from media reports, field visits, and dozens of emails we have received from groups all over the United States. Grassroots resistance groups everywhere mounted major and repeated efforts to contact voters, and their commitments to door-knocking reshaped the social underpinnings of the 2018 elections. Four years earlier in the midterm elections of 2014, 96 million doors were knocked by all progressive groups and Democratic campaigns combined; and the total rose to 111 million in the presidential year of 2016. Canvassing for the 2018 cycle blew past both of those earlier totals—as some 155 million doors were knocked by Democrats and their allies, including the new grassroots volunteers.[15]

Most of the canvassing, phone-banking and postcard writing orchestrated by resistance groups was done directly on behalf of particular candidates—either to support the campaign of a group member or, more often, to boost the campaigns of local, state, and congressional candidates formally or informally endorsed by the group. As Maximilian Frank discussed in his analysis of the southeastern Pennsylvania counties in chapter 12, in many places where local Democratic organizations were not very adept at outreach, candidates themselves quickly realized that the new resistance groups were a valuable resource, full of volunteers who were eager and willing to provide ground troops for canvassing and get-out-the-vote operations. Candidates and groups willing to deploy canvassers often found each other early in the cycle. In southwestern Pennsylvania, for example, canvassing efforts by many resistance groups were on spectacular display in the run-up to the March 2018 special election that delivered a bare victory to Democrat Conor Lamb, who flipped a longtime GOP district that had gone for Trump in 2016 by nearly 20 points. During the 2018 primaries and special elections, many resistance groups similarly trained contingents of dozens to even hundreds of canvassers and deployed them every weekend starting months before Election Day—and then followed up with get-out-the-vote and poll-watching efforts when that day arrived. Depending in part on relationships between party leaders and resistance groups, the newly engaged volunteer door-knockers might, or might not, work from official campaign target lists. Some used lists from allied groups like unions; and some resistance volunteers simply canvassed entire neighborhoods, knocking on as many doors as possible to open conversations with fellow citizens of all partisan stripes.

Several respondents told us that their members started open-ended doorstep discussions long before they canvassed for particular candidates. Progressive-minded groups operating in conservative areas were especially likely to report doing this kind of values-oriented canvassing. As one explained, "We canvassed . . . leading with the question 'how can government make your life better?' and engaging in conversations with voters about what they care about. Then on the basis of shared values, we would suggest they vote for certain candidates . . . [B]ut we didn't lead with candidate or party. It made a huge difference in the quantity and quality of conversations we had."

The results of canvassing could be either shocking or gratifying, but either way the newly engaged volunteers gained new insights and spread them person-to-person across neighborhoods and districts. One respondent was "surprised at how red certain areas have become and how nasty people on the right are. There really does seem to be not only an education gap, but also a lack of empathy from many on the right." Yet even that respondent was glad to see that his "little" progressive group had positive effects on "certain candidates / races." Others reported pleasant discoveries. "In our canvassing efforts," explained a respondent from a GOP-leaning county, "a common response was, 'I didn't know there were any other Democrats in our township.'" "This district is very, very red," reported yet another leader. "People are actually afraid to put up yard signs for Democrats . . . [B]ut this year, people openly 'came out' as Democrats . . . They said they were glad to know . . . that they weren't all alone."

Did Volunteer Efforts Matter?

Despite some encouraging surprises, many resisters who did outreach in very conservative counties ended up chastened when voters they canvassed stuck with the GOP. Depending on the districts, election outcomes either disappointed or thrilled volunteers. Groups were elated when their members did a lot of canvassing in places where Democrats turned out in large numbers and either won or made major gains, as they did in Chester and Delaware Counties and in pockets of many other counties. But other group leaders were let down when last-minute GOP voter turnout surged to meet increased Democratic enthusiasm and most local voters followed established partisan identifications. As "hard as we worked for one particular charismatic, intelligent candidate for State House," explained one respondent from a rural county, "the results were very similar to the results two years before when the candidate was unimpressive and a fraction of doors were knocked." Despite "people declaring their support for him, when push came to shove, they apparently continued to vote straight ticket R."

Whatever the outcomes in 2018, many leaders expressed a quiet determination to keep at it. "Our candidate lost but we fought the good fight!" explained a respondent from a county where resisters supported one of their own running for Congress. Another woman reported that her group mounted a "massive GOTV / canvassing effort" and "despite having only 37 percent of registered voters being Democrats, [our candidate] lost by only a very small margin . . . This means we are on the right track—canvassing is a key!" Another respondent took the long view about a county where turnout was high and the GOP again prevailed. "I had hoped that some candidates . . . would win. At least one . . . But we . . . created a base in the county that we can build on for the future and we talked to people lots of people. And we will continue to do this."

As the questionnaire responses suggested, election trends show little evidence that newly nominated Democrats, especially progressives, made much headway in very red areas of Pennsylvania.[16] As the widely publicized case of Lancaster County illustrates, partisan gaps remained even when progressive candidates benefited from sustained and strong backing from the most avowedly progressive resistance groups.[17] Nevertheless, our preliminary quantitative explorations suggest that resistance activities and newly forged relationships between activist volunteers and local parties that were open to new energy may have contributed to modest 2018 boosts over previous vote shares for statewide Democratic headliners—for Senator Bob Casey compared to 2012, and for Governor Tom Wolf compared to 2014.[18] Casey and Wolf not only did better than Clinton in 2016, they also improved on their own previous vote shares in certain areas well beyond Democratic strongholds and recently blue-trending suburbs. The ironic bottom line is that it probably took extensive and determined mobilization by many local activists who consider themselves progressives to boost vote totals and shares, even slightly, for mainstream moderate Democrats. Still, as both 2016 and 2018 show, small shifts across many places can add up to very different statewide outcomes.

Democratic Party Changes amid the Activist Upsurge

Presidential elections are critical junctures for party organizations as well as candidates, and the defeat of Hillary Clinton and scores of other Democrats in 2016 certainly brought a jolting moment of reckoning for their party. The immediate emergence of grassroots resistance groups virtually everywhere meant that party officers and committees had to deal with persistent newcomers—just as existing GOP leaders had to cope with Tea Party activism after they lost big in 2008. In that case, Republican Party organizations were often taken over by Tea Partiers and pulled toward the hard right—during a decade when the GOP as a whole made major electoral gains. We cannot yet know whether similar or different processes are playing out for today's Democratic Party, but we can gain some purchase by tracking ways in which interactions with grassroots anti-Trump resistance groups are transforming party organizations and activities right now.

Online questionnaires we administered in early 2019 asked leaders of local groups that emerged or newly mobilized after November 2016 to characterize relationships to the local Democratic Party, and most local leaders who answered that query also made additional comments elsewhere. Responses referring to thirty-eight groups reported close, excellent, or good relationships with local parties; and respondents from another thirteen groups said that their relationships with local Democrats had changed for the better over the last year. By early 2019, in short, well over half (62 percent) of the eighty-two groups about which we were able to gather detailed information said that their relationships with local Democrats were positive or recently improving. Only about 15 percent of the groups said they had no ties at all to local Democrats or described their relations as tense or downright hostile. Wary cooperation has been the modal reality. "Working with our local Dems hasn't been easy, as we haven't been exactly welcomed with open arms," is how the leader of one group put it. And yet in that case, as in so many others, members of the group have won election to party committee seats; indeed, one of them is helping the local party update its website. In return, the respondent said, "we are pushing them to do better, be more transparent and inclusive and embrace a more progressive agenda" on issues like climate change and addressing racial inequalities in the schools.

The Pennsylvania Democratic Party holds elections every four years for official party committee slots (with one male and one female slot designated per ward precinct or township ward) as well as for county representatives to the State Committee. The first post-2016 party elections occurred in the May 2018 primaries, followed soon after by leadership "reorganizations" done by vote of the newly credentialed committeepersons. Resistance groups and networks were well-established by that time and many of their participants won election to party committees. Unfortunately, we did not specifically ask about party offices in our online questionnaire, but (as the comments quoted in the previous paragraph illustrate) many respondents—close to half—spontaneously reported that some or many of their members were serving on local Democratic committees. Usually starting in the summer of 2018, new grassroots activists and previously ensconced local Democratic regulars have found themselves sharing formal party authority in most parts of Pennsylvania. Like it or not, they have had to deal with each other as they make key choices about party procedures, nominations, and resource allocations.

Fitful rapprochements between new activists and prior party leadership may be happening statewide, but there are naturally many subthemes in such a vast and varied state. In this section, we look more deeply into patterns found in five Pennsylvania settings: (1) big city Democratic strongholds; (2) Democratic-leaning metropolitan suburbs; (3) upscale swing-district exurbs; (4) Republican-trending Rust Belt areas; and (5) conservative rural counties. In each context, relationships between organized grassroots resisters and Democrats have tended to follow characteristic patterns, captured in some local reporting and further illuminated by our questionnaire responses and interviews. For the Philadelphia and Pittsburgh metropolitan regions, our evidence often refers to sub-areas as well as entire counties, while in other parts of the state our data usually refer to county-wide organizations. Of course, none of Pennsylvania's counties is completely homogeneous and not every group or party story fits a single storyline. Nevertheless, we believe the following discussions capture important pathways of change unfolding in the Keystone State—and in other states with similar political geographies.

Inner City Democratic Machines Meet Rising Activism

One urban grassroots leader had a pointed comeback to our query about relations with the party: "Do you know the local Democratic Party in Philadelphia? It's ineffective except for its own very narrow interests." She went on to explain, we "did not coordinate at all with them" in 2018, "because they need new leadership to be effective. Rather, we coordinated with [other new progressive non-party groups] Indivisible and Turn PA Blue, and also Protect and Elect, which were populated by effective, active citizens willing to do the hard work of grass roots organizing."

The Democratic machine in big city Philadelphia is indeed long-entrenched and not very responsive to outsiders or newcomers. The party chair has been in his post for decades; and when our research group did an "audit study" in the fall of 2018 to see whether county parties would respond to a generic email asking for information about how to volunteer, the Philadelphia party was one of those that did not respond at all. In fact, it did not even have a workable email to convey the request for information about volunteer opportunities.[19] After the midterms, a local commentator observed that in "this fall's elections, there were dozens of ways for political newbies to get involved. Almost none of them were

Table 13.1 **Pennsylvania Political Geographies.**

Pennsylvania Political Geographies, with Examples	Social Characteristics	Legislators and Local Officials by 2016	Democrats in 2016 Election	Local/County Democratic Party by 2016	Post-2016 Relationships of Parties and Mobilized Grassroots Activists
Metropolitan inner cities: Pittsburgh & Philadelphia.	Heavily non-white & high poverty, with scattered white upscale areas.	All Democrats, uncontested by GOP.	Clinton 70–80% in primary; 80–90% in general. **Clinton slightly up from Obama.**	Loyalists fill slots; compete for primary endorsements but unite for general elections.	Initial tensions between party insiders, including persons of color, and upscale activists. Eventual alliances open doors for some progressive white and minority newcomers.
Metropolitan suburbs: Squirrel Hill & Mt. Lebanon in Allegheny County; parts of Philadelphia County plus nearby parts of collar counties.	Largely white & college educated.	All Democrats, rarely contested by GOP.	Clinton 45–60% in primary, 60–70% in general. **Clinton slightly up from Obama.**	Active party committees, some with affiliated club options in place.	New activists quickly focused on flipping GOP districts, supporting progressive challengers in inner Democratic areas and all Democrats in outer rings. Grassroots group members have run for committee slots or worked to create new affiliated party groups.

(continued)

Table 13.1 Continued

Pennsylvania Political Geographies, with Examples	Social Characteristics	Legislators and Local Officials by 2016	Democrats in 2016 Election	Local/County Democratic Party by 2016	Post-2016 Relationships of Parties and Mobilized Grassroots Activists
Upscale outer exurbs: North & South Hills in Allegheny County; parts of Lehigh County; Chester County, & other SE collar counties.	Largely white & college educated. Some high-status immigrant pockets.	Mostly GOP, 1/3 to 2/3 uncontested by Democrats.	Clinton 55–65% in primary, 45–55% in general. **Clinton way up from 2012, when Romney won in most places.**	Democratic committees with many open seats and occasional newcomers trying to promote citizen engagement.	Participants from many groups have run for county committees, filling mostly empty seats. Now work to foster openness and coordination.
Rust belt / declining industrial areas: Erie County in NW; Beaver & Washington Counties in SW; Luzerne County and surrounds in NE.	Largely white, non-college working-class; substantial clusters of Hispanic immigrants and some African American neighborhoods.	Mixed, trending GOP with some down-ballot longtime Democratic incumbents.	Clinton 50–60% in primary, 35–45% in general, sharply down after a decade of gradual Dem decline. **Flipped to Trump from Obama.**	Party committees with unfilled seats plus older unionists, patronage-oriented regulars. Some defections to Trump in 2016.	Scattered grassroots groups with professional women, Bernie supporters, and environmentalists have tense coexistence with longtime party insiders. Newcomers have filled some empty committee seats or displaced incumbents in some precincts.

Rural areas with small cities & towns: Most counties in central and northern Pennsylvania: Somerset, Warren, Indiana, Clarion, Armstrong, McKean.	Mostly white; predominately working and lower-middle class; small shares of college educated.	Almost all GOP, rarely contested by Democrats. Clinton 40–50% in primary, **new Dem lows of 20–30% in general election.**	Tiny Democratic committees; older women's groups often only active presence by 2010s.	Rarely more than one group in driving distance. Extensive overlap and synergy between groups and party committees. In some cases, local party or women's groups were active from the start. In other cases, newcomers have won seats and are working to build the party's community presence.

with the Philadelphia Democratic Party;" and "on the weekend before Election Day, the Democratic Party's Facebook page had not been updated in a month."[20]

Regnant Philadelphia Democrats face competition only in primaries. Factions may fight over nominations, but the party's candidates rack up huge margins in general elections. The only question—vitally important in statewide and presidential contests—is the level of voter turnout, especially among poorer and minority city residents. Many critics argued that ineffective turnout operations in Philadelphia were part of the reason Hillary Clinton fell short in Pennsylvania— so the goal of registering and turning out more voters moved front and center for citizen groups after November 2016.

Because Philadelphia was already home to both neighborhood-based and city-wide progressive and social justice groups operating outside of what they saw as a moribund Democratic Party, newly formed groups were supportive rather than central players.[21] As President Trump took office, new Indivisible-labeled groups joined already existing groups to pursue local reforms and voter contact along with pushback against the Trump-GOP agenda. "Reclaim Philadelphia," started by former Bernie staffers after the end of Sanders's 2016 primary run, swelled in membership after Trump's election, as did the 215 People's Alliance, another recently created economic justice-oriented community organizing group. Working alongside African American–led faith-based groups to support criminal justice reform advocate Larry Krasner for district attorney, these groups elbowed aside establishment alternatives in the May 2017 primary and went on to win 75 percent of the vote in November. Key players in the massive canvassing effort that carried Krasner to victory also included the Working Families Party, the Safety and Justice Political Action Committee (PAC), and the "Smart Justice" program of the American Civil Liberties Union.[22]

Post-Trump organizing in Philadelphia has thus been anchored outside of and to the left of the local Democratic Party establishment—a situation that challenges city incumbents yet also benefits statewide party candidates when it boosts voter registrations and election turnout. Summer 2018 saw the largest jump in Philadelphia voter registrations before a midterm election since 1970, the first year for which records exist; and voter turnout in the fall was the highest for any midterm since 1994, topping 50 percent in a city where 40 percent midterm turnout has been typical.[23] Despite the fact that both Senator Casey and Governor Wolf improved their performances statewide, neither improved in Philadelphia County.[24] Nevertheless, the turnout increment from a county that voted over 85 percent Democratic up and down the ballot was boon enough— and a reminder that the kind of increased activist and voter engagement that makes life difficult for local powerbrokers may be just what the Democratic Party needs in state and national contests.

How much change will occur in the Philadelphia Democratic Party remains an open question. After the midterms, newly engaged activists called for party reforms and mounted 2019 primary challenges. Nevertheless, even as party regulars have been rocked by scandals about sexual harassment and federal corruption charges, they have fended off most progressive challenges. "Philadelphia's Democratic Party shows it still has some punch in 2019 primary," is how a news headline summed up the continuing standoff.[25]

At the other end of the state, Pittsburgh likewise has an entrenched Democratic establishment full of not-very-progressive incumbents absorbed in factional divides. But the Pittsburgh regulars also face new challengers. Without as many preexisting left coalitions as in Philadelphia, Pittsburgh's newly engaged resistance activists have mounted more scattered, candidate-centered activities. During 2018, loose networks of new activists joined a shifting array of unions, newborn Democratic Socialists, and a few old-line progressive groups to elect left-leaning women to office, women of color in particular, in a city whose Democratic officeholders had long been much whiter, more male, older, and more conservative than the populace as a whole.

Pittsburgh's African American neighborhoods—home to about a quarter of the city's three hundred thousand residents—have been buffeted by gun violence, police violence, and gentrification. Even their most politically active residents have been marginalized within Democratic Party politics in the city, where a handful of largely white-ethnic family networks have long held sway.[26] "They sure don't listen to *us*," explained one frustrated African American Democratic committeeperson to the group of eager would-be citizen organizers who had begged a meeting with her ward committee in spring 2017. The disjuncture between the post-Trump surge of engagement among economically secure white women and the long-standing efforts of activists of color spurred intra-left contention early in 2017. Both the local Women's March and the first attempt to create an "Indivisible Pittsburgh" quickly stumbled into controversies.[27]

Skittishness over such debacles has contributed to the relative paucity and low profile of post-Trump grassroots groups formed by the city's upscale liberals. Nevertheless, new female activists and the (younger, majority white and male) Democratic Socialists have played important roles in fundraising and volunteering for progressive challengers to longtime Democratic incumbents. In 2018, Sara Innamorato and Summer Lee both won election as state representatives, ousting decades-long incumbents unaccustomed to political competition; and in 2019, Liv Bennett and Bethany Hallam likewise bested incumbents to win election to the county council.[28]

Elected in May 2018, the new Allegheny County Democratic Committee has more than five dozen grassroots-linked activists. As this change unfolded, the total number of men serving as county precinct persons held steady (down by one from 813 to 812), while the women serving increased significantly from 765 to 840.[29] Although some new committee people were elected within the city of Pittsburgh itself, many come from just outside. Only a quarter of Allegheny County's 1.2 million people live in the city proper. Countywide, adjustments in party-activist relations are happening relatively smoothly—along the lines of changes in the suburban and exurban areas to which we are about to turn. With fewer conflicts and stalemates than in Philadelphia, Allegheny County's Democratic Party is evolving from within in ways longtime powerbrokers are only beginning to recognize.

Democrats and Mobilized Progressives in the Suburbs

Some of Pennsylvania's prosperous suburbs close to metropolises have long had sizeable liberal populations voting Democratic and filling local party committee positions. This is the true for parts of Bucks, Chester, Delaware, and Montgomery, the "collar" counties immediately surrounding Philadelphia, as well as for communities like Squirrel Hill and Mt Lebanon in greater Pittsburgh.[30] Already home to good government civic groups adjacent to the party—such as Pittsburgh's 14th Ward Independent Democratic Club (going strong since 1964) and the Tri-County Dems at the junction of Berks, Chester, and Montgomery Counties—suburbs saw new surges of anti-Trump organizing led by people who had much in common with counterparts already leading local party and civic organizations.[31] Information flowed smoothly along preexisting networks, with new activists rapidly recruited to fill any empty committeeperson slots, and new groups benefiting from quick understanding of the informal and formal party processes.

Many of these areas also had Republican incumbents on township or county councils, judicial circuits, school boards, state house and senate districts, or US congressional districts. After Trump's election, newly energized liberal activists had the disposable time, income, and passion to support challengers across the board—and they often quickly flipped seats. November 2017 saw an unprecedented array of local offices fall to Democratic challengers in Philly's collar counties and Pittsburgh's northern suburbs.[32] Then in November 2018, Democrats flipped five state senate seats, one in Pittsburgh's northern suburbs and four in the Philly collar, plus fourteen state house seats in the collar counties. Three US congressional seats in the southeast also changed hands, along with a newly redistricted seat won by Conor Lamb in his second victory of 2018 in (a different set of) Pittsburgh suburbs.[33]

Allegheny County suburban grassroots groups endured defeats for all the Democratic state house challengers they backed, most of them progressive women recruited from their own ranks. Yet the organizing muscle the activists created was mobilized to help achieve a state senate victory for Pan Iovino just five months later. With her election, all of Allegheny County's state senate seats are now in Democratic hands for the first time in decades.[34]

Highly active grassroots groups like Indivisible Narberth and Beyond in Montgomery County and Partners for Progress SWPA in Pittsburgh's South Hills are moving forward with a 2020 strategy plus have immediate plans to elect Democratic judges and progressive school board slates. "Well aligned & mutually supportive—building inclusion and engagement among local voters: Democrats, Independents and some disaffected Republicans," wrote one Montgomery County grassroots leader in response to our query about relations with the local Democratic Party. "Completely aligned," wrote another. "Our group likely leans a little more progressive, but there is significant overlap in leadership (the local party recruited a bunch of us to be committee people, for example)." Even in cases where grassroots respondents expressed frustration with out-of-touch county-level Democratic establishments, they often reported good relations with their own township-level party committees, on which they frequently now serve. "The grassroots popped up, seemingly out of thin air, and the establishment didn't know what to make of us. We demanded to be heard and to their credit, they ultimately heard us," one leader explained in a response that nicely sums up the changes that unfolded over a year and a half between 2016 and 2018 in most of Pennsylvania's increasingly liberal inner suburbs.

Swinging the Exurbs

Pennsylvania's "country club" exurbs are located a few political miles beyond the inner suburbs—in more homogenous school districts and spacious neighborhoods a few steps up the income scale. Not long ago at all, these areas were firmly in the GOP column for national, state, and local elections—but things have changed. Statewide in 2018, the districts with the very largest swings towards Bob Casey from his 2012 reelection results included two in suburban Allegheny County, two in Chester County, and one in Centre County.[35] These wealthy districts went from deeply conservative to Democratic Party-friendly in a single decade, and much of that change happened between 2016 and 2018.

West of Philadelphia, Chester County saw a similarly radical transformation, not just in a single district but across the entire jurisdiction of half a million people. Registered Republicans have outnumbered Democrats in Chester County since at least the end of the Civil War, and Ronald Reagan carried 70 percent of the vote here in 1984. By the 2000s, this began to shift as the county attracted younger transplants. Chester now has the highest portion of college graduates of any county in Pennsylvania, 48 percent, nearly twice the statewide average; it also boasts the highest median income. The county voted for Barack Obama once, then for Mitt Romney, and in 2016 swung hard against Donald Trump—and has not looked back since.[36] In 2014, Pennsylvania Governor Tom Wolf carried Chester only narrowly, his support concentrated in the dense municipalities strung along Route 30. Four years later he steamrolled his GOP challenger by a 25 point margin, carrying every district except a dozen rural ones at the county's western edge.[37]

From 2015 to 2019, Chester Democrats have been closing a voter registration gap with Republicans, but turnout in primaries as well as general elections tells the real story. Although the May 2015 primary in Chester included only 15,126 Democrats to 24,198 Republican voters, by 2017 the Democrats came within two thousand votes of equaling the Republicans, and by May 2019, 30,000 Chester Democrats swamped the relatively unchanged GOP turnout of 26,272. The 2019 gains at the polls suggest that the massive 2018 midterm efforts of groups like Indivisible Chester County, along with others who volunteered for Chester native Chrissy Houlahan's winning campaign in the sixth congressional district, has helped to speed sustained partisan shifts in the wealthy exurbs.

Similar dynamics to those in Chester County are unfolding at slower speed and smaller volume in exurban areas of southwestern counties like Butler and Westmoreland and in Franklin County in the center of the state. In Pike County, a rural-to-exurban county on the state's northeast border, Donald Trump got 71 percent of the vote, but in 2018 Democrat Wolf improved on his 2014 performance. With evident pride, a local grassroots group leader informed us that Pike County's 20 percent increase in Democratic turnout in 2018 was the highest of any county in the state.

In many exurban counties and areas, grassroots groups report that significant numbers of their members have sought election to their local Democratic committees. Despite occasional tensions with previous party insiders, many such local party committees have become highly active and effectively run. "In 2017, we filled perhaps 40 percent of the Democratic Committee seats," one group leader reported. Now, in early 2019, "we have more or less filled out the seats [and] we have candidates running for four of the four municipal council seats . . . Knocked on perhaps 2500 doors. . . . Provided full coverage of every poll in municipality during primary, and . . . also provided full coverage in general election." The results? "We elected 4 of our 5 candidates. It was significant that simple organizing and lots of tedious work pays off."

Resisters and Beleaguered Democrats in Rust Belt Counties

If upscale exurban Chester County west of Philadelphia stands as a poster child for citizen mobilizations that drew formerly Republican and Independent

Pennsylvanians into the Democratic column, Luzerne County in the deindustrializing Northeast exemplifies opposite tendencies—sharp swings toward the Trump GOP amid partial, conflictual change in old-line Democratic county leadership. Even as Donald Trump repels many longtime business-oriented moderates in Chester, he has attracted and held enthusiastic support from many older unionists and absconding white-ethnic Democrats in Luzerne County. In 2016, Trump won Luzerne County with more than 58 percent of the vote, swinging it hard from Obama's 2012 numbers. As the map in Figure 13.2 indicates, Trump's vote shares here and in similar rust belt areas in northeastern and western Pennsylvania greatly exceeded the vote shares garnered by previous GOP presidential contenders from the Bushes to McCain and Romney—a sure indication that Trump is seen by many as a new species of Republican.

The Luzerne Democratic Party, meanwhile, has fallen on hard times—and seems to have been AWOL prior to the spring 2018 elections of new local officials. When one of the authors first visited Luzerne County in the spring of 2017, she quickly learned that the county chair at that time, a man from a longtime local political family, was not returning anyone's calls and had done little of late to build the party. The 2014–18 chair was employed outside the county and, according to knowledgeable local observers, probably supported Trump in 2016, as did many other old-line Democrats in the area. A veteran newsman told

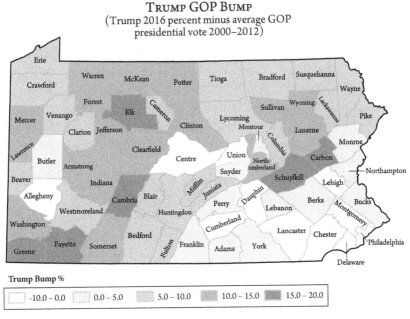

Trump GOP Bump
(Trump 2016 percent minus average GOP presidential vote 2000–2012)

Trump Bump %

-10.0 – 0.0	0.0 – 5.0	5.0 – 10.0	10.0 – 15.0	15.0 – 20.0

Figure 13.2 Trump-GOP Bump in Pennsylvania.

us he "knew what was happening" with defections to Trump when he saw long-time union guys cheering at Trump rallies.

Nevertheless, after November 2016 sprouts of new citizen activism popped up in Luzerne. In the city of Hazleton in the southern part of this huge county, Dominican immigrants had become the majority and their votes were beginning to weigh at all levels from school board elections to state and national contests. A tiny new resistance group formed in Hazleton and engaged in occasional joint efforts with a much larger group founded in Wilkes-Barre, the county seat in the northern part of the county. Part of a multi-county consortium called Action Together Northeast Pennsylvania (AT-NEPA), the Luzerne group was organized by middle-class Hillary supporters. It meets regularly, has a Facebook page, issues regular newsletters and email alerts, collects member dues, and has incorporated as a 501(c)(4). In Luzerne and beyond, AT-NEPA both pushes progressive causes from outside the Democratic Party and seeks (in the words of leaders) to "infiltrate" and reform party operations.

In contrast to developments elsewhere, the 2018 midterm elections did not see big Democratic gains in Luzerne County and surrounds—although an area Democratic congressman was reelected, Governor Wolf won the county, and the vote share for Senator Bob Casey improved over Hillary Clinton's dismal 2016 showing. Senator Casey actually flipped another Pennsylvania rust belt county, Erie, back into the Democratic column, and perhaps could have done the same in Luzerne were it not for the fact that his GOP opponent was the former mayor of Hazleton, Lou Barletta. As chapter 4 recounts, Barletta touted Trump's brand of anti-immigrant politics, which resonates with many older Luzerne whites who have watched their industrial jobs disappear–even as Dominican immigrants pour in to take jobs in giant fulfillment centers. The county has experienced rapid immigration since 2000, and economically precarious areas experiencing rapid ethnic transitions provide fertile ground for Trump-style Republicanism.

Democratic Party organizations are of course affected by all these changes. In 2018, a new Luzerne County Democratic chair was elected: John Pekarovsky, a longtime party regular who served as Larksville Borough councilman for 24 years.[38] Although not identified as progressive, the new chair has pledged to "make the party more inclusive" and seems to be looking for areas of cooperation to attract younger people, develop social media modalities, and reverse recent shifts in party registrations toward the GOP.[39] Pekarovsky is "willing to return our calls," says Alisha Hoffman-Mirilovich, one of Action Together-NEPA's founders and co-leaders.[40] In the spring of 2018, progressive-minded resisters ran for and won various county committee posts, and a higher proportion of Luzerne precinct slots are now filled by engaged citizens. Action Together has challenged previously insider-run nominations of some old-line Democrats, yet it has also canvassed and turned out votes for a number of local party candidates.

Perhaps not surprisingly, growing contact and shared responsibilities between resistance activists and longtime county party honchos do not immediately reduce conflicts in places like Luzerne. If anything, tensions rise at first, as traditionally minded leaders who think everyone should fall in line must deal with obstreperous activists who demand public transparency and maintain their separate extra-party organization to exert leverage for progressive causes and pick and choose to endorse like-minded candidates. The equation is complex. Bigger counties may be more diverse, and thus more likely to generate independent activist groups, yet they also control resources sufficient to make party regulars want to fight changes. Counties with larger budgets have very tangible rewards at stake in party conflicts over endorsements. Even where Democratic machines in de-unionizing rust belt areas are mere shadows of their former selves when it comes to mobilizing voters, they may very well still be able to channel valuables like regional development funds and no-bid contracts into grateful hands.

Even so, as new activists and longtime insiders both swim against regional tides running fast toward the GOP, discernable signs of greater Democratic Party openness are evident in Luzerne and other rust belt areas. Resistance activism is not destroying the Democratic Party in these challenging areas. Instead, it is gradually if fitfully reworking party practices, leaderships, and agendas, at least in some places.

In the southwestern parts of Pennsylvania, rust belt counties tend to have not just strong labor traditions but also many currently unionized workers along with younger well-educated residents in newly prosperous pockets. In these places, newly forged party-group alliances have fueled considerable electoral recovery for Democrats. Distinct yet complementary social networks can learn to work together, as happened when a post-November 2016 "Washington County Democrats" club formed after the established party declined to embrace the new activism. This group met monthly and drove intense outreach efforts in the Conor Lamb special election of March 2018. It also organized a training session on "How to Run for Precinct Person" attended by more than 100 people and went on to elect new county committee persons and leaders. Similarly, in Beaver County, the post-2016 Young Democrats played a similar role, serving as a launching pad from which new activists ran for the county Democratic committee in 2018. The Beaver County Democratic Committee's revitalization is now well underway, with new bylaws in process along with multiple subcommittees and professional candidate trainings open to all.[41]

In 2016, Donald Trump carried Beaver County by 19 points and Washington County by 24, accelerating two decades of electoral erosion in places that were once Democratic strongholds. Yet in 2018, amid hard-fought campaigns up and down the ballot, statewide Democrats performed unexpectedly well in both Washington and Beaver Counties, with Governor Wolf improving on his 2014 performance by three to four points, and Senator Casey hitting the marks set by his 2012 performance.[42] In short, certain rust belt regions that had seemed on track for a warm embrace of national Republican dominance now look like they may turn around, at least partly—with obvious consequences for Democrats' statewide fortunes.

Standing Up Together in Rural Pennsylvania

Finally, we turn to the spatially biggest part of Pennsylvania's political geography—to the vast "T" of small-city and town-focused rural and forested counties in the middle and across the top of the state. We cite only a few examples here, but all are variants of the same story. In very conservative places, Democrats, liberals, and other Trump skeptics are relatively few in number, and these women and men are usually as familiar with one another personally as their GOP neighbors are with them. In many such places citizens started to organize right after November 8, 2016, just as they did in cities, suburbs, and exurbs, but the rural activists often had previously worked with area Democratic organizations, such as they were.

In rural versions of the usual organizing scenario, new voluntary groups emerged by early to mid-2017, sometimes "Indivisible" groups but sometimes stand-alone endeavors like "Fayette New Deal Democrats" or "Democratic Women of Somerset County."[43] In rural areas the newly formed groups typically had significant membership overlap with whatever formal Democratic Party committees existed in their very red areas, and the newly organized people rarely got a lot of push back. In Indiana County, a new group called "Coalition of Women" transformed before long into the party committee; its activists gaining election to party leadership even as they spread across leadership teams of issue-oriented local groups. In McKean County, Kinzua Country Indivisible played a similar role.

No matter whether official Democrats and anti-Trump grassroots activists have been organizationally separate or not, they have mostly cooperated in rural America. To be sure, there can be long-simmering tensions between regulars and progressives. But in deep red Pennsylvania, Democratic Party "establishments" either hardly exist or have very little to defend. As in tiny Jefferson County, the challenge is often not to fend off would-be participants but to find anyone at all who is willing to take on official Democratic roles. In the past, rural Democrats have also felt neglected by the state party. By now, there are indications of supportive contacts, but the fact remains that these local parties are tiny organizations dependent on volunteer leaderships.

Consequently, when rural Democrats and anti-Trump citizen activists wanted to step up after 2016, the tasks at hand were both straightforward and daunting. Citizens on the center-left saw—and seized—opportunities to speak up in the community about education and the environment, ObamaCare, anti-immigrant policies, and shocking events like Charlottesville. As an increasingly vocal minority, they needed to build some solidarity and energy in or near the party and find new candidates to run and voters to turn out in 2018 and beyond. Older college-educated women generally led the way, the usual concatenations of teachers, social service workers, retirees, and small business owners, joined by some husbands and male friends. There may not be very many such people in each rural county, but it only took a critical mass of a dozen or two to get things going. In most rural and conservative places, overlapping leaderships and a loose division of labor have linked Democratic committees with the founders and leaders of stand-alone resistance groups and the leaders of other local groups such as redistricting reformers or green groups mobilizing against fracking and petrochemical plant expansion. Activists switch roles from time to time, furthering synergistic cooperation to sustain a public voice for liberal values.

Election activities were certainly part of the story for rural resistance groups. Almost all extra-party groups whose leaders responded to our questionnaire said they worked alongside party committees to make sure Democratic candidates contested more offices in 2018; many groups also mounted vigorous registration drives, canvassing efforts, and get out the vote operations. Yet as we have already noted, even major efforts failed to move 2018 vote margins much in heavily GOP-tilted counties. Nevertheless, the realization by some rural groups that, as one leader put it, we "can't change anything in our deep red area by just canvassing, letter writing and phone banking" does not mean such groups are going to quit. They are more likely to recalibrate than retreat. "We need to think outside the box if we want to make change here," this leader said in an email describing plans as of mid-2019 to move "more towards changing hearts and minds" by exposing issues of corruption in state government and local environmental problems of wide concern to people of all persuasions.

The group in Clarion County is labeled "Indivisible," but it is not taking directions from the national Indivisible cockpit. Instead, as national Indivisible leaders focus on the 2020 primary process and urge local groups to contact congressional representatives weekly about matters like presidential impeachment, this local group—like many others in the Indivisible network—is instead building lateral ties to statewide organizations and to other citizens' groups in its region. In June 2019, the Clarion group followed that strategy by orchestrating a "summit" of around one hundred activists called "Cultivating Progress in Rural Communities: A Summit of Ideas, Opportunities and Connections." Attendees spent the day in sessions about issues and values of special concern to rural people—and the event was reportedly so "enthusiastically received" that Indivisible We Rise plans to "hold more such events in the future."[44] Out of this meeting, moreover, came a commitment to start "a left leaning faith coalition" to counter the "evangelical right" that "screams out here."[45] The chair of a nearby county Democratic Party has decided to step down from that post in order to commit herself to this new endeavor.

Resilient experimentation with projects beyond electioneering is likely for many rural groups for a basic reason—a key point we want to drive home. Post-2016 grassroots activism across Pennsylvania was always about more than just winning elections or reforming party committees. Those goals matter everywhere, but "raising our voices" and creating and maintaining a community presence for liberals and liberal values was the most important underlying driver for the organizers and most committed participants. Commitment to maintaining collective voice in community affairs is what sustains newly active citizens between elections and despite losses, especially in deeply conservative rural areas.

The Trump-era grassroots resistance is both a new form of multipurpose citizen activism in twenty-first-century America, and a reprise of very old US forms stretching back to the early nineteenth century.[46] New technologies, such as Facebook and email, have facilitated the organizing. But the organizing activities are new versions of old classics, intended to influence state and national politics and revitalize political parties by starting with local voice and community-building.

Peering Over the Horizon

Everywhere, Americans of liberal or moderate bent woke up after the November 2016 election with a strong desire to work with others and speak publicly for their vision of America as an inclusive, egalitarian democracy. The same waves of citizen determination swept not only across Pennsylvania, but also into western North Carolina, conservative parts of Ohio and Wisconsin, and all parts of the vast state of Maine. They swept up the Hudson River in New York and stretched out west not just to the liberal Pacific coast, but also into conservative Utah, where "Mormon Women for Ethical Government" joined the rousing citizen chorus.[47] Suddenly, after 2016, people, led by women, wanted to speak up and reach out to their neighbors. Together, they were determined to say "No!" to this presidency and to the Washington, DC, regime backing it.

The effects are still roiling politics in and around the Democratic Party, and it will be some time before anyone, let alone this chapter's authors, can draw any firm bottom lines about party revitalization and transformation. Some say the new grassroots resistance is like the Tea Party, sure to pull Democrats to the hard left, toward an uncompromising and highly ideological style of politics.[48]

We think that outcome is unlikely, given the variety of people and groups we see across Pennsylvania and beyond—especially because the real energy in this movement is directed toward making change at the civic roots of the country, through outreach to fellow citizens and efforts tailored to play out differently in various communities and states.

In Pennsylvania, most (very real and important) changes in Democratic Party organizations and operations seem to be happening so far in county and township committees, not through any grand redirection of the state party. That party is showing some signs of responding to newly determined activists in the Progressive Caucus, the largest constituency caucus in the several-hundred-person State Committee. But the State Committee meets only briefly a few times a year, and nothing yet suggests that the leadership of the Pennsylvania Democratic Party is focused on anything other than raising money and working with the Democratic National Committee to prepare for the 2020 elections. That is an understandable preoccupation and does *not* mean that all Pennsylvania party leaders are some kind of closed "establishment" unwilling to work with new resistance networks. What the current dynamics do suggest is that the work of revitalizing civic life and local party organizations is likely to rest with volunteer citizens themselves. It will not be either blocked or propelled from above—not by the Democratic Party and not by any national professional advocacy organization, either.

The last query on our questionnaire asked the grassroots resistance respondents, "Looking ahead, what major challenges does your organization face? Will your organization continue to operate?" Many leaders from all parts of Pennsylvania reported plans to continue and pointed to pressing challenges of attracting new participants, keeping current ones engaged, raising funds for core group functions, and reorganizing leadership teams when key people leave. Virtually all of them stressed the challenge of coping with "burnout effects" when, as one put it, "each day seems to bring more of the same sorts of outrage."

"But we are going to persist!" that same person said. In fact, all but a tiny handful of local groups we surveyed echoed that same determination to keep going, at least for the next two years. "Yes, we're back with a vengeance, working on diversity issues and climate change," reported one leader in early 2019. "Yes, we have plans to continue at least through 2020" wrote another respondent who, as many did, described detailed plans for the 2020 election cycle. "We will start our listening canvass as soon as the weather is warm enough, and we will be active during the primary and the general this year [2019] and of course next." Not all continuing groups plan to specialize in election activities; some (as we have seen) are moving to a broader "hearts and minds" approach to try to shift public discourse in their communities. But 2020 looms as an inflection point for all. "The challenge is to keep the momentum up through 2020. Maybe even beyond."

Another leader summed up the grit and optimism expressed by many grassroots groups in the Keystone State—and she will get the last word here. Our biggest challenge, she said, is "dealing with pace and scope of destruction of Our country . . . and of a basic sense of decency and shared commitments to Democratic values." "Yes," we will continue—and "we will have an even greater impact!"

Acknowledgments

The authors wish to thank members of the Harvard University-based research team for their valuable assistance with this project: Caroline Cohen, Maximilian Frank, Leah Gose, Lainey Newman, and Elizabeth Thom. We are also grateful to Ben Forstate for his mapping and statistical assistance.

Notes

1. The quote comes from Joan Walsh, "The 7,383 Seat Strategy," *Nation*, March 22, 2018, an article that summarizes vast Democratic losses in state legislatures and governorships during the Obama presidency. Such losses have proved devastating because labor union decline amid economic shifts and GOP attacks often leaves local and state Democratic parties dependent on incumbent officeholders for support.
2. Sidney M. Milkis, "Are 'Organizing for Obama' and Successor Mobilization Efforts Building a Robust Progressive Movement?" Scholars Strategy Network brief, August 2013; and Ken Thomas, "New Nonprofit to Promote Obama Agenda," *U.S. News & World Report*, January 18, 2013. For an oppositional conservative perspective on this operation, see Matthew Vadum, "Organizing for America: The Democratic Party's Community Organizing Campaign to Promote Barack Obama," *Organization Trends*, May 1, 2010.
3. For examples, see Ari Berman, "What Became of Obama's Grassroots Political Movement?" *Nation*, October 19, 2010; and Micah L. Sifry, "Obama's Lost Army," *New Republic*, February 9, 2017.
4. Theda Skocpol and Vanessa Williamson, *The Tea Party and the Remaking of Republican Conservatism* (New York: Oxford University Press, 2012).
5. Quoted from Hahrie Han and Lara Putnam, "The Best Way for Democrats to Win in 2020? By Ignoring Candidates for Now," *Washington Post*, April 29, 2019. For a full analysis, see Elizabeth McKenna and Hahrie Han, *Groundbreakers: How Obama's 2.2 Million Volunteers Transformed Campaigning in America* (New York: Oxford University Press, 2014).
6. Daniel J. Galvin, *Presidential Party Building: Dwight D. Eisenhower to George W. Bush* (Princeton, NJ: Princeton University Press, 2010). In the book, Galvin contrasts Democratic presidents who have neglected party building to focus on building their legacies through legislation and Republican presidents who, for various reasons, have seen party-building as more important to cementing their White House achievements. More recently, Galvin extended his analysis through the Obama presidency in "Obama Built a Policy Legacy. But He Didn't Do Enough to Build the Democratic Party," *Monkey Cage*, November 16, 2016.
7. Pre-November 2016 groups also include a small set of Bernie Sanders–inspired voluntary citizen groups.

8. Reportedly, the February 9, 2017 founding meeting for Columbia County Indivisible, "attracted 70 attendees," including "at least a dozen . . . from Montour County." " 'Our ties with Montour County are very deep,' " said Dwayne Heisler, one of the group organizers, as quoted in Mary Bernath, "Anti-Trump Group Finds Allies in Danville Residents," *Danville News*, posted at dailyitem.com, March 15, 2017.

9. For articles that contain this multi-county description of the group, see Scott Shindledecker, "'Indivisible We Rise West Central PA' Organizes in Clarion," ExploreClarion.com, February 22, 2017; and Joann Bauer, "Indivisible We Rise—West Central PA Holds Summit for Issues Regarding Rural PA," ExploreClarion.com, June 7, 2019. Interviews and emails with a group leader indicate that most members come from the city and county of Clarion, but a handful have participated from neighboring Clearfield and Jefferson counties. As of mid-2019, one member of the group's steering committee is from Forest County, where she also serves on the Democratic committee. Nearby Venango County also has a home-grown group called "Oil Region Rising" that sometimes cooperates with the Clarion group.

10. The exception is interesting. Clearfield County is home to the DuBois branch of the University of Pennsylvania and thus might well have generated its own resistance group. However, we have learned from interviews and public records that there was already a vibrant, participatory local Democratic Party and local people felt they could work through that party after 2016.

11. Trudy Miller, administrator, August 22, 2018, post on the "Engage Waldo" Facebook page. Miller explained that her group's shift toward election activities was accompanied by a name change from "Indivisible Waldo" to "Engage Waldo." They felt it would be easier to do election work without the formal tie to "an independent expenditure organization" and noted that "we have had very little involvement with the national Indivisible organization in the past." Like many groups we have tracked, this one took early inspiration from the *Indivisible Guide*, but has not been very interested in the centrally coordinated efforts of the national Indivisible leadership.

12. This course was followed by a few groups in Pennsylvania, as well as by one group apiece we have followed in Ohio and Wisconsin. Some groups that turned into campaign projects intended to re-launch themselves as multi-purpose citizen groups after the election; others did not have that intention or, in any event, did not persist after November 2018.

13. For twelve counties in the state we have located no grassroots groups. Although we believe groups have existed in six more counties, we have not be able to obtain questionnaire responses from them.

14. This collaboration between the Blair County Tea Party and Indivisible Blair County is described in Anne Danahy, "Progressives, Tea Party Come Together for Candidate Forum for State Senate," WPSU Penn State, October 26, 2018. An unusually long-surviving group, the Blair County Tea Party celebrated its tenth anniversary in April 2019.

15. Data provided by NGP VAN, November 8, 2018. On the role of local grassroots groups in mobilizing volunteers for campaigns, see Marcy Miroff Rothenberg, "A Good Problem: Many Democratic Campaigns Are Awash in Blue Wave Volunteers," blog post, *Dem Write Press*, July 24, 2018, available at https://demwritepress.com/2018/07/24/a-good-problem-democratic-campaigns-are-awash-in-blue-wave-volunteers/; Nancy Solomon, "Meet the Women of the Suburban Resistance," WNYC News, October 17, 2018; Michael Scherer and David Weigel, "'Blue Wave' or 'Left-Wing Mob'? Anti-Trump Fervor Fuels a New Movement Aimed Squarely at Winning Elections," *Washington Post*, October 15, 2018; Daniel Drezner, "A New Kind of Grass-Roots Political Organization?" *Washington Post*, October 17, 2018; Charlotte Alter, "How the Anti-Trump Resistance Is Organizing Its Outrage," *Time*, October 18, 2018; Kate Zernike, "The Year of the Woman's Activism: Marches, Phone Banks, Postcards, More," *New York Times*, November 3, 2018; and Anesa Miller, "Swing State Saga: How We Fought on the Midterm Battleground," blog post, Dem Write Press, December 18, 2018, available at https://demwritepress.com/2018/12/18/swing-state-saga-how-we-fought-on-the-midterm-battleground/.

16. This conclusion is reinforced when precinct-level data are used, as explained in Jonathan Lai and Jared Whalen, "Pennsylvania, Polarized: How a Blue Wave and Red Response Deepened the State's Political Divisions," *Philadelphia Inquirer*, February 7, 2019.

17. Jimmy Tobias, "Can a Group of Scrappy Young Activists Build Real Progressive Power in Trump Country?" *Nation*, October 18, 2018; Ryan Grim, "Real Resistance: A Grassroots Uprising in Amish Country Begins to Find Meaning in Politics," *Intercept*, September 15, 2018; and Paul Blest, "Where Does the Democratic Left Go From Here?" *Splinter News*, December 19, 2018.
18. Across Pennsylvania counties that voted for Trump in 2016, an index capturing the presence and activities of resistance groups along with the openness of local parties to new volunteers correlates around 0.40 to 0.45 with gains in vote shares by the 2018 statewide Democratic headliners, especially Wolf. More rigorous statistical tests await further information from counties with known active grassroots groups that have not completed our questionnaire. Further quantitative work could also use precinct-level data. Maps we have done for key counties suggest close relationships between resistance group formation in relatively up-scale pockets and correlative shifts in both voting patterns and Democratic Party committee memberships.
19. Conducted in late September and early October 2018, our study covered both Democratic and Republican county parties in ten states. If we could find an online email address, we sent a generic message asking for information on volunteer opportunities, and then tallied whether county parties responded. Overall, Democratic county parties in Pennsylvania responded at the highest rate of either party in any of the ten states we surveyed. Nevertheless, we either could not find a contact email or got no response from twenty-four out of fifty-seven Democratic county parties in Pennsylvania. Small, rural, and very conservative counties predominated among the Pennsylvania non-respondents. But Philadelphia and Allegheny counties were also among the least responsive.
20. Terry Gillen, "Where Are You Philly Democrats?" *Philadelphia Citizen*, November 9, 2018.
21. For a list of groups, see "Philadelphia Resistance and Progressive Groups" *Michael Swayze's Community Resources Blog*, January 30, 2017. See also Mark Dent, "Turning Resistance into Action," *Philadelphia Citizen*, January 22, 2018.
22. Laura Clawson, "Beyond Coalition Politics as Usual: Five Questions with 215 People's Alliance's Bryan Mercer," *Daily Kos*, September 29, 2016; Alice Speri, "Can the Anti-Trump Resistance Take the Philadelphia DA's Office?" *Intercept*, May 15, 2017; and Harrison Jacobs, "The Inside Story of How Trump United a City of Activists to Elect the Most Progressive District Attorney in a Generation," *Business Insider*, November 12, 2017.
23. Claire Sasko, "Philly Voter Registration Is Way Up. What Does That Mean for Turnout?" *Philadelphia Magazine*, October 27, 2018.
24. Michael D'Onofrio, "Can Philly's High Voter Turnout Be Repeated in 2020?" *Philadelphia Tribune*, November 9, 2018.
25. See two articles by Dave Davies, "Philly Democratic Machine, Progressives Battle in Primary Tuesday," *Philadelphia Citizen*, May 20, 2019, and "Philadelphia' Democratic Party Shows It Still Has Some Punch in 2019 Primary," *Philadelphia Citizen*, May 22, 2019.
26. "Gentrification in Pittsburgh: A Tale of Two Cities," interviews by Virginia Alvino Young, WNYC, March 13, 2017, available at https://www.wnyc.org/story/gentrification-pittsburgh-tale-two-cities/; Felicity Williams, "Pittsburgh Is a Progressive City, But I'm Still Waiting for It to Be Pro-Black," *Public Source*, January 22, 2018; Ryan Deto, "Pittsburgh Is One of the Most Gentrified Cities in the U.S.," *Pittsburgh City Paper*, April 4, 2019; and Samantha Michaels, "As Antwon Rose's Death Looms Large, Pittsburgh's DA Faces Toughest Reelection Race in Decades," *Mother Jones*, May 21, 2019.
27. Alicia Salvadeo, "White Feminism Thing," *Medium* blog post, January 18, 2017. Available at https://medium.com/@icketmaster/white-feminism-thing-45cfc59a5dd; and Caitlyn Luce Christensen, "Indivisible Pittsburgh Will Destroy Itself," HuffPost, February 26, 2017.
28. Michelle Goldberg, "The Millennial Socialists Are Coming," *New York Times*, June 30, 2018; and Dan Majors and Andrew Goldstein, "John DeFazio, on County Council since 2000, Pinned to the Mat by Newcomer Bethany Hallam," *Pittsburgh Post-Gazette*, May 21, 2019.
29. We are grateful to research assistant Ben Forstate for compiling and mapping these statistics.
30. Arguably, this pattern also applies to select townships near Harrisburg, Lancaster City, and Wilkes-Barre.

31. Chris Zurawsky, "The Next Page: The 14th Ward Independent Democratic Club, Pittsburgh's Mavericks," *Pittsburgh Post-Gazette*, May 24, 2014.

32. Katie Meyer, "The Trump Resistance Works to Find Its Feet in Pa," WITF, May 15, 2017; Marc Levy, "Pennsylvania Democrats see Anti-Trump Zeal in Election Wins," Associated Press, November 8, 2017.

33. Marc Levy, "Philadelphia's Suburbs Roar in Another Post-Trump Election," Associated Press, November 8, 2018; Holly Otterbein, Andrew Seidman, and Jonathan Lai, "Think GOP's losses in Philly Suburbs Are Trump's Fault? It's More Complicated," *Philadelphia Inquirer*, November 18, 2018. For similar national patterns see Emma Green, "The Democrats' Most Radical Election Victory Was in the States," *The Atlantic*, November 7, 2018.

34. Campbell Robertson, "'I Don't Even Know What to Think': The Whiplash of Watching the Election Results," *New York Times*, November 7, 2018; Ryan Deto, "How Democrat Pam Iovino Flipped a Pittsburgh Area State Senate District," *Pittsburgh City Paper*, April 3, 2019; and Julian Routh, "Meet the Women Who Helped Elect Pam Iovino," *Pittsburgh Post-Gazette*, April 4, 2019.

35. In suburban Allegheny County, House District 28 had a 13.46 percent pro-Casey swing and House District 42 a 13.17 percent swing; in Centre County, House District 77 had a 12.79 percent swing; in Chester County, House District 167 had a 12.41 percent swing and House District 157 a 12.25 percent swing. Three of these rank among the ten wealthiest state house districts in Pennsylvania.

36. Michael P. Rellahan, "Will Chester County Voters Hop on the 'Blue' Wave, or Go 'Red?'" *Daily Local News*, November 3, 2018.

37. We are grateful to Ben Forstate for statistics and maps.

38. Bill O'Boyle, "Luzerne Democrats Elect Pekarovsky New Chairman," *Times Leader*, June 20, 2018.

39. Roger DuPuis, "On Politics: Chatting with Luzerne County's New Democratic Leader," *Times Leader*, June 25, 2018.

40. Interview and emails with Alisha Hoffman-Mirilovich, who gave permission to use her name.

41. Gavin Jenkins, "The Sessions Where Working-Class Democrats Learn to Take Down the GOP," Vice, Feb 19, 2019.

42. Likewise in 2018, midterm turnout in Erie County (which Trump had narrowly carried) was the highest it had been since 1994, and congressional candidate Ron DiNicola (running for a seat that Democrats had not even bothered to contest in 2016) carried the county by 20 points. Court-ordered redistricting in 2018 had made the seat slightly more attainable, but even the new district had been carried by Trump by 15 points. Ryan Briggs, "Analysts Increase Odds for Dem Congressional Upset in NW PA," *City & State Pennsylvania*, July 10, 2018; and Matthew Rink, "Midterm Turnout in Erie County Highest Since '94," GoErie.com, November 7, 2018.

43. Rural county Democratic Party organizations were not usually directly involved in launching new levels of activism after 2016, but there were exceptions. In Mifflin County, the county Democratic Committee simply signed itself up as the sole local resistance contact on the national Indivisible map. In Carbon County, media and Facebook sources suggest that ramped up activism was channeled through a long-standing party-linked club called the "Carbon County Democrats for Progress." In a few rural counties, people who might have either organized their own resistance group or participated in a nearby group were reportedly already active in their official county Democratic committee and kept working through it without feeling any need to organize a separate group.

44. Joanne Bauer, "Indivisible We Rise—West Central PA Holds Summit for Issues Regarding Rural PA," ExploreClarion.com, June 7, 2019. One of the authors of this chapter attended the summit, and another has exchanged emails with organizers about the resources for this event and the follow-ups likely to flow from it. Additional groups we are following in similarly rural and conservative parts of other states are also turning to organize around local issues—often over environmental concerns such as the issue of frack sand mines in Monroe County, Wisconsin.

45. Quote from summit attendee, in email communication with the authors, June 17, 2019.

46. See Theda Skocpol, *Protecting Soldiers and Mothers: The Political Origins of Social Policy in the United States* (Cambridge, MA: Harvard University Press, 1992); and Kristin A. Goss, *The Paradox of Gender Equality: How American Women's Groups Gained and Lost Their Public Voice* (Ann Arbor: University of Michigan Press, 2013).

47. We mention here places from which (mostly) women have written emails to us, after our earlier articles appear in places like *Democracy* magazine. The emailers, including from the Mormon group, wrote to tell us about their group's activities and say how pleased they were that someone in the national media has noticed what is going on at the democratic grass roots.

48. See for instance Tom Davis, "Are Democrats Facing Their Own Tea Party-Style Reckoning?" *Politico*, March 18, 2019.

Conclusion: America at a Crossroads

THEDA SKOCPOL AND CAROLINE TERVO

Americans are profoundly divided in political matters, but it is probably fair to say that regardless of party or ideology almost all were surprised when the 2016 presidential contest was called for Donald J. Trump on the evening of November 8, 2016. Tearful or elated, people woke up the next day with a sense that the United States was a different country than they had presumed. It was as if a national boat moving a bit erratically in a slow-moving river suddenly struck a hidden waterfall and tumbled into rocky rapids stretching as far as the eye could see. Would the country swirl out of control and break up on the rocks? Or would a recognizable version of the United States of America come through at the other end, with everyone rearranged and shaken up but safe?

With a bit of distance and a larger perspective, this sense of a sudden plunge over an unforeseeable 2016 waterfall appears illusory (although not entirely wrong, as we will soon consider). As this volume shows, early twenty-first century US politics had already undergone major reorganizations—especially on the right—well before TV-actor-turned-politician Donald Trump started his incessant domination of American television screens and Twitter feeds. Those prior changes turned November 2016 into a culmination of earlier radical shifts in conservative and Republican politics.

Now, American politics has entered a new, intense phase of contention over alternative possible futures for democratic governance and national identity. Will American voters in 2020 and beyond reconfirm the Trump-GOP's fusion of white ethnic defensiveness with ultra-free-market governance? Or will they repudiate that synthesis and redirect the country toward a future where governments at all levels further social inclusion and greater economic equality? The answers remain shrouded in the fog of ongoing political warfare, but the stakes are clear. The United States finds itself at a political crossroads as fateful as any juncture since the election of 1860. Beyond this or that policy proposal,

Theda Skocpol and Caroline Tervo, *Conclusion: America at a Crossroads* In: *Upending American Politics* Edited by: Theda Skocpol and Caroline Tervo, Oxford University Press (2020). © Oxford University Press
DOI: 10.1093/oso/9780190083526.003.0014

the country's basic identity—what America means and what it means to be American—is at stake.

The Shifting Organizational Terrain of US Politics

Contributions to Part I of this volume explained abrupt and radical shifts in recent Republican and conservative politics.[1] Outflanked by a massive, Koch political machine, the Republican Party effectively became—well before 2015—a wholly owned subsidiary of ultra-free-market ideologues. Republican Party elites were all-in for an unpopular agenda featuring upward-tilted tax cuts and the undercutting of government capacities to redistribute resources and regulate the market economy. As this shift in GOP policy agendas unfolded, the institutional Republican Party itself became a hollowed-out, weakened political shell from the point of view of democratic accountability. In many states, as well as in Washington, DC, GOP candidates, officeholders, and governing agendas were much more responsive to the concerted demands of collectively organized right-wing billionaires and multi-millionaires than they were accountable to the cultural or economic preferences of ordinary Republican voters, who were much more interested in immigration restriction and conservative Christian concerns than plutocratic Koch priorities such as tax cuts for the rich or reductions in middle-class social benefits. The post-2000 GOP was even more dismissive of the values and interests of the majority of Americans. Increasingly cut off from genuine popular support, by the mid-2010s the Republican Party was ripe for external takeover by a Trump-like figure touting supposedly populist priorities.

Meanwhile, the organizational reach of the Democratic Party and its liberal allies steadily declined—ironically, at an accelerating pace during the eight-year White House tenure of a popular Democratic president, Barack Obama. From 2008 to 2014, Democrats suffered massive electoral losses in state and local governments as well as Congress. Advocacy groups and think tanks mobilized or proliferated on the left, but in most states and districts inside the liberal coasts, such professionally managed progressive groups did not adequately fill the organizational deficits left by labor union decline spurred by economic shifts and unremitting right-wing attacks. Democrats suffered major losses in Congress and most states in 2010 and beyond, as most of their campaigns failed to replicate, even temporarily, anything close to neighborhood-level outreach achieved by the Obama presidential campaigns. As we have seen, even in a pivotal state like Florida, Democratic capacities for grassroots outreach were allowed to wither and regress, even as conservatives built local infrastructures and adapted Obama tactics to their own purposes.

Between 2008 and 2016 upsurges in US citizen engagement happened predominantly on the right, through new Tea Party organizing as well as continuing mobilizations of Americans enmeshed in Christian right churches and gun-rights networks. Some commentators touted Obama-era popular movements on the left such as the Occupy Wall Street effervescence of 2011, but once the urban tent cities pitched by Occupy protestors were abandoned, that outburst left little organizational residue. Occupy Wall Street's enduring reverberation in American politics is a catchphrase, "the 99 percent versus the 1 percent," rather than any widespread set of persistent citizen groups comparable to Christian right or pro-gun networks or the new local voluntary groups created under the Tea Party banner.

During the Obama years, grassroots citizen energy therefore played out at the culturally conservative right edge of the Republican Party. Tea Partiers and their successors—many of them hard-core Donald Trump enthusiasts—have indeed helped to change US politics and governance at all levels. Key chapters in this book have spelled out how grassroots conservative groups and networks intersected with elite free-market think tanks and the Koch network's federated juggernaut, Americans for Prosperity. Not just nationally but also in crucial swing states such as North Carolina and Wisconsin, elite free-market organizations formed ongoing alliances with geographically widespread popular conservative networks in ways that fueled both electoral gains for right-wing Republicans and major policy shifts once those GOPers took office.

Grassroots conservatives in the Tea Party and beyond have stoked and highlighted widespread anxiety and anger about immigrants, especially Mexican and Central American newcomers. "Ethno-nationalist populism" is the term this book has used to describe the grassroots prong of recent rightward pressures on Republicans. There is little question that popularly rooted movements pushing a nostalgic white-Christian American national identity have gained great political traction—originally through the post-2008 waves of local Tea Party organizing and, more recently, through pro-Trump rallies and movements reinforced by gun organizations and evangelical church networks. This passionate and widely organized populist radicalism has simultaneously helped conservative GOPers gain power and complicated their exercise of government authority once they have it. Thus far, Koch network plutocrats and GOP-backing Chamber of Commerce elites have tolerated immigration restrictions and some interferences with free markets, as long as electoral victories for the GOP lead to tax cuts and evisceration of government regulations.

Contributions to this book have spelled out why and how the Trump presidency has synthesized the elite and popular strains of GOP radicalism. Going into 2020, all indications suggest the Trump synthesis is more potent than ever, as ethno-nationalist followers roar approval at Trump rallies and conservative wealth-holders pour funds into dark money conservative conduits as well as GOP coffers.[2] The Trumpified GOP will be a potent nationwide contender, and it may benefit as much as Democrats from a potentially record level of voter turnout, especially if white working-class voters who sat out 2018 stick with the president and return to the polls.[3]

Will 2016 Turn Out to Be an Irrevocable Turning Point?

This brings us to the kernel of truth contained in the sense that November 2016 was an abrupt course shift for American politics. Although the analyses in this volume document many ways that juncture was more of a culmination—a predictable inflection point—than a freak change, it remains true that 2016 could signal a big, irrevocable redirection. Under the right circumstances, a tiny tipping point can change the course of history. In this case, an election decided by tens of thousands of votes in three states might enduringly tilt the arc of US history. That will prove true if—*if*—it turns out that the power shifts expressed and furthered by the narrow 2016 election result become cumulative and irreversible through subsequent political actions, choices, and outcomes. This kind of lock-in is likely if the next US elections confirm rather than begin to reverse the underlying organized power shifts expressed and furthered by 2016.

We cannot know yet what legacy the 2016 election will leave, but we can close this book by drawing on findings about liberal strengths and weaknesses, stirrings and divisions, to consider not just the prolegomenon to 2016, but also that election's aftermath, especially the remarkable grassroots resistance efforts that fed into major Democratic Party gains in 2018. Part II of this book brings the post-2016 developments into sharper view, and allows us to sketch alternative possibilities in the next phase of this period of intense and stark contention about the future of American democracy.

As of this writing, it is not at all clear whether Democrats will unite behind a credible 2020 presidential nominee after a contentious set of crowded primary contests. Still less is it knowable whether the party nominee will win the White House or whether Democrats will build on their 2018 gains in Congress and the states. These are the immediate 2020 stakes, for an election that could push the United States in very different directions for years to come. If Democrats fail to win the presidency, and especially if they should happen to lose all of Congress, the Trump synthesis of free-market and ethno-nationalist radical strands is likely to lock in for a long time to come. If, on the other hand, the 2018 turnarounds toward Democrats continue, if the Trump election turns out to have sparked the beginning of a deep, widespread, and enduring liberal and Democratic revival, then the coming trajectory of US politics and national identity will be very different. In that scenario, the Trumpist GOP will falter amid civic and political opposition that could usher in a prolonged era of more egalitarian and inclusive US government and an increasingly pluralist American national identity.

Such starkly different futures are possible because the two major US political parties are extremely polarized and closely balanced nationwide. With elites and popular supporters increasingly in lockstep, the two parties are clashing not just about contrasting approaches to government's role in the market economy, but also about opposite understandings of national identity and the sources of US vitality, past and future. Is the United States a country based on shared citizen principles, or is it a fundamentally white Christian ethnic community now fighting for continued sway? Because such fundamentals of Americanness are at stake, both the Tea Party movement and the anti-Trump resistance of recent times have rallied millions of ordinary citizens to "save America." On both ends of the US political divide, energized citizens are equally determined to fight for the country—but they act from very different moral understandings of what kind of polity and community the United States has been and should be.

For Republicans, grassroots conservatives and free-market elites alike, November 2016 looked like an across-the-board triumph, opening the door to full GOP control of all levers of institutional power in Washington, DC. Such full control would, it seemed, clear the way for the realization of the wish lists of the party's organized elite and populist backers—for massive tax cuts, regulatory rollbacks, substantial reductions in social spending, unfettered gun rights and restrictions on abortion, plus an endless stream of judicial appointments to reinforce all of these achievements. Especially important to all forces on the right has been the sense that the Donald Trump presidency is pulling America back from the brink of irrevocable liberal changes—both changes in the scope and purposes of government and changes in the authoritative projection of American power and purpose. Right-wing radical forces have adopted more and more extreme measures, countenancing fundamental abrogation of democratic voting rights and long-standing constitutional principles, because they believe, fervently, that America as they have known it and want it to be is at existential risk from rising ethnic diversity and liberal government actions. Majority preferences are not their lodestar, because they believe their vision for America is the right one. Under Trump, many of the right's preferred policy changes have, in fact, been shoved through, but not all and (in most cases) not yet irrevocably. Conservative elites and populists alike believe that 2020 will determine whether their project to "make America great again" falls short.

A lock-in of conservative gains followed by further leaps to the right will become highly probable if Trump and the GOP prevail again in 2020. In this scenario, an emboldened President Trump and Republican Party would not only go on to check off further policy changes on their wish list—repealing or permanently weakening ObamaCare, further transforming the federal judiciary, and making cuts to social insurance programs in order to preserve tax reductions. More consequentially, a repowered Trump-GOP juggernaut would double down on the use of state and national government to break up liberal organizational capacities and discourage potentially Democratic constituencies from voting. What is more, no one should underestimate the enduring normative and cultural impact of a Trump reelection. Many Americans of all economic and racial backgrounds would adjust expectations and behavior to the new dominant order. A politics of norm-flaunting and name-calling would proliferate. Citizen activists on the center left would be discouraged and many would stand down; and millions of other Americans would simply carry on, accepting that the power of the wealthy and an exclusionary national identity are here to stay.

Many expert observers see this outcome as an improbable dystopia and presume that because Donald Trump is a persistently unpopular president, he cannot win reelection. Maybe, but maybe not. As this book shows, opinion polls do not necessarily signify who enjoys organized clout in the right places to prevail in US political contests. Ironically, given the apparent weaknesses of the original 2016 Trump presidential campaign, Trump's political allies are preparing for 2020 by fully taking over and greatly strengthening Republican Party organizations at all levels. They have built formidable fundraising and social media operations, and they are training large numbers of volunteers for ground-level voter outreach operations.[4] Big donors are pouring millions into Trump campaign coffers—and even the Koch network, whose leaders once again are claiming they will not endorse Trump because they oppose his tariffs and immigration restrictions, are deploying huge resources to turn out Republican votes for Congress. Those votes will go to Donald Trump, too, so the Koch network prissiness about officially endorsing him is mostly a fig leaf.[5]

At the conservative grassroots, Trump is, if anything, in even better shape than he is with GOP-aligned elites, because his administration has consistently carried through on promises to restrict immigration and asylum for refugees, harass undocumented migrants, and issue regulations and appoint judges committed to abortion restrictions and other Christian right preferences. Perhaps "the Wall" on the southwestern border has not been built, and may never be, but for most hardcore Trump voters this is a symbolic rather than literal goal. It signals the president's larger intention to restrict the flow of non-whites into the United States—a goal most popular conservatives applaud and expect Trump would pursue even more successfully in a second term. Furthermore, the critical inter-organizational bargains Trump made in 2016 with Christian right pastors and church networks, with gun organizations, and with white-dominated unions of police and other law enforcement officers are, if anything, more firmly in place going into 2020 than they were the first time around. Once again, conservative Americans throughout non-big-city communities are going to hear President Trump's angry "us versus them" messages loud and clear; and once again, millions of them will be contacted and urged to vote by friends and neighbors who believe that Trump is "making America great again" and fear it could all be reversed if a Democrat wins in 2020. They are correct that the stakes are high, and they will turn out to try to reelect Trump—and in the process usually vote for most others listed on Republican tickets for local, state, and national offices.

For Democrats, 2020 looms as even more of a moment of truth than it does for the right—and the key question is not just whether the party will elect a president, but whether it can manage to sustain and build upon the efforts that played out after 2016 and led to broad-based gains in the 2018 midterms. Ironically, the very November 2016 election that marked a Democratic nadir also focused liberal-minded citizens on the need to organize everywhere to pre-pare for the next rounds of elections in 2017 and 2018. During this interval, liberal Americans had to stop focusing their hopes on presidential politics and power centers in Washington, DC. Americans alarmed by the Trump-GOP agenda had to build from the bottom up in all parts of the country.

To tell the story of liberal pushback against the Trump presidency, many media outlets and analysts have focused on the efforts of professionally run leftist advo-cacy organizations like the American Civil Liberties Union, Planned Parenthood, and environmental and immigrant rights groups. In contrast, contributors to this volume have documented the arguably much more important widespread efforts pursued in up to two thousand local grassroots resistance groups active during 2017 and 2018. Across all fifty states and in communities of all sizes and partisan leanings, local volunteer organizers and newly active citizens—while certainly taking cues from national sources like the *Indivisible Guide*—acted on their own to lobby legislators and mount public protests against efforts to repeal ObamaCare, destroy environmental protections, and harass immigrants. At the same time, and most important of all, the newly active liberal grassroots citizens formed ongoing organizations with members who not only used social media but also met periodically in person. Middle-class college-educated women predominated as leaders and active participants in these groups, which in turn generated new candidates and turnout boosts for Democrats in 2017 and 2018. These groups also forged alliances with other Democratic constituencies such as labor unionists and African American churchgoers, thereby adding new heft to party support overall.

The remarkable "blue wave" that crested in November 2018 built because un-precedented numbers of ordinary citizens, especially women, ran for city and town offices, state legislatures, and Congress, while tens of thousands went door-to-door to turn out voters for both moderate and progressive Democrats. Especially in suburban and exurban areas with relatively well-educated populations, enough of these candidates won in 2018 to give Democrats firm control of the US House of Representatives and allow Democratic net gains of seven governorships and more than three hundred state legislative seats. Seven states, Colorado, Connecticut, Illinois, Maine, Nevada, New Mexico, and New York, saw Democrats secure trifecta control of governorships and state legislative majorities in both chambers; and Democrats broke GOP majorities or super-majorities in many other state legislatures.[6] Even candidates who lost their races—as many did—provided choices and a voice in public discussions in conservative counties where Democrats may not even have run anyone for office in recent years.

As November 2020 approaches, will Democrats and liberal-leaning citizens remember and build upon the lessons of the 2016 to 2018 interval—or will the presidential nominating horserace shift everyone's focus toward national ideological battles that could undercut the gains of 2018? For Democrats, challenges abound. Early phases of the 2020 primaries have featured many contenders fighting it out in cable TV "town halls" and nationally touted debates—venues that shift attention away from state and congressional politics, even though the Democratic Party still has a very long way to go in building subnational strength and revitalizing its ongoing presence in many states and non-big-city areas. National debates can easily become detached from the core issues of economic advancement, environmental improvements, and access to affordable health care and good education that animate most potential Democratic voters. Presidential nominating contests on both sides tend to prioritize the concerns of activists at the extremes, but that may be especially true for Democrats, whose donors and advocacy organizations cluster in metropoles on the two coasts. To the degree that presidential nominating politics takes over, it becomes all too easy for citizen groups across the country to feel they are no longer where the crucial action is and put local activities on the backburner. Even more predictably, presidential primary fights induce donors and activists to privilege winning the nomination and downplay what it takes to win nationwide contests at all levels when the general election arrives. Media outlets play along, as in the chaotic mid-2019 Democratic primary debates where twenty contenders competed to take ultra-left issue stands—such as calls to open borders to all migrants and abolish private insurance —that could hinder the party's 2020 prospects.[7]

Will 2020 Democrats coalesce around a nationally appealing presidential and vice presidential ticket? Or will they drag ideological and identity fights into and beyond their nominating convention? If the latter happens, it could be very bad news for many congressional and state candidates, unless local citizen networks in most places continue to advance locally viable candidates and keep in touch with fellow citizens. Such tactics secured widespread Democratic gains in 2017 and 2018 and could lay the groundwork for all Democratic candidates along with the presidential ticket in 2020. But protracted, nationally televised fights that magnify extreme stands and highlight social group differences could very well leave citizen activists themselves discouraged—and divert resources from crucial efforts to register and contact voters and bolster local and state party capacities. As it has for Democrats in the past, presidential politics could end up undercutting broad-based center-left politics.

Despite these challenges, the Democratic Party's fortunes may benefit from potential continuing opportunities to strengthen party structures. As national nominating battles play out, the hitherto decaying Democratic Party may have a chance to augment its presence in oft-overlooked states and localities, free from immediate oversight by a presidential campaign. The Republican Party faced a similar opening in 2015, when the national organization built a data operation and voter contact behemoth long before a clear nominee emerged from a sprawling pool of candidates.[8] If done early and well, this strategy could be pivotal for rebuilding a long-term and robust Democratic Party infrastructure to help candidates up and down the ballot and in future elections. The extent to which this is done in states like Wisconsin, Michigan, Pennsylvania, Florida, and North Carolina could prove electorally decisive not just in 2020 but in later cycles as well. Rebuilding nationwide Democratic energy and sway is going to take more than one set of election victories.

What It Takes to Prevail in US Federal Democracy

In the United States, now as much as in the past, politics inescapably plays out across jurisdictions and levels in a federated polity. Media commentators and national analysts often speak as if the country is one big national mass democracy, where outcomes flow from appeals to the largest number of voters or from a politics of adding up demographic slices. But this is far from true. In a federated system, the key to political power is capacity to operate across disparate electoral geographies and levels of government. National majority support is simply not sufficient to win governing authority—or to connect with the concerns of people who live in very different states and communities. Instead, even for Democrats, victories in Congress, state politics, and the Electoral College depend not just on getting out the vote in congenial metropolitan areas, but also on winning majorities or hefty pluralities in heartland states and non-big-city areas.

Always and everywhere, politics is best understood as organized teamwork. For any given political system and juncture, analysts must ask: What kinds of organized alliances and team-building strategies are best suited to leveraging existing electoral and governing institutions? In the United States, political teams that want to prevail must be able to operate across jurisdictions and levels in the federated system. This requisite applies to all players, from organized sets of wealthy political donors like those assembled in the Koch network, to popularly rooted constituencies like the Christian right and gun rights advocates, to the two major political parties themselves. Political parties must also compete in long-shot districts and field candidates for every office. As the Doug Jones race for US Senate in Alabama shows, in order to prevail, the decision to run for office has to be made long before unanticipated events make a race that looked impossible actually winnable.[9]

Within the US federal system, moreover, state-level politics and the dynamics of legislative districts matter just as much as the presidency. From the 1980s to the early 2000s, conservatives learned that governorships and state legislatures are keys to building and sustaining political power, as Alexander Hertel-Fernandez discusses in his contribution to this volume and elaborates in detail in his important book, *State Capture: How Conservative Activists, Big Businesses, and Wealthy Donors Reshaped the American States—and the Nation.*[10] Right-wing donors have achieved sustained leverage over Republicans and US policy agendas by investing in nation-spanning networks of advocacy groups and think tanks that can contact voters and deploy money, ideas, and activists in public policy campaigns. As Republicans won key state offices—especially in wave elections such as 2010—they gained the power to draw legislative and congressional districts, weaken public-sector unions, limit access to the ballot box, and undermine federal laws, including those enacted during Barack Obama's two terms. Similarly, should a Democratic presidential nominee prevail in November of 2020, his or her first term will be severely hamstrung, to the point of near irrelevance, if the US Senate stays persistently in GOP hands and if conservative governors and state legislators can block or undermine ostensibly national policies that require their cooperation. Finally, of course, the 2020 Democratic presidential contender will not prevail at all if he or she cannot build majorities across many states, enough to win the Electoral College no matter how many votes accumulate in the most liberal states.

As the two leading US parties battle for control of the White House, they ignore at their peril the multi-level structure of US politics and the ways in which states and local districts influence national processes. In recent times, Democrats have often succumbed to this peril. Liberal voters are increasingly concentrated in rich states and large metropolises, and the same is true for most elite allies of Democrats, both professional advocates and high-income donors.[11] Party leaders feel the tug of metropolitan realities on issues ranging from health care to immigration, to housing realities and wage rates, and in the process they can become increasingly unresponsive to nonmetropolitan realities. Democrats risk fading permanently from public life and governance in too many of the states and districts that together control Congress, state legislatures, and the Electoral College.

After November 2016, this negative spiral for Democrats showed signs of reversal, because popular anti-Trump resistance efforts flared far and wide across the US political geography. Remarkably, as a number of chapters in this book have documented, the anti-Trump resistance was not restricted to big city marches or agitation by national advocacy organizations. Instead, ordinary liberal-minded citizens, especially middle-class women, created voluntary civic groups in suburbs, regional cities, and small towns, as well as in big cities, and these newly active citizens organized, spoke up, and did electoral outreach virtually everywhere. Widespread and persistently organized post-2016 activism by liberal-minded citizens has easily equaled that of conservative-minded grassroots Tea Parties after 2008. Anti-Trump resistance efforts became so politically consequential in 2017 and 2018 precisely because they included the organized activities of thousands of citizen groups committed to election outreach in every state and communities of all sizes. This remarkably widespread wave of citizen organizing from below gave Democrats a broader civic presence going into the pivotal 2018 midterm elections. As we have argued in this book, a key question is whether those post-2016 gains in citizen engagement will persist, revitalize local and state Democratic Parties, and boost Democratic electoral prospects from localities to states to Congress and the presidency in the years to come.

Organizations and changes in them matter in politics, and the hallmark of this volume has been to illuminate current US politics by probing shifting organizational configurations and alliances in the US federal polity. In the first two decades of the twenty-first century, American elite and grassroots actors on the US right have organized to synthesize big money, ideas, legislation, and popular engagement across most states and all three levels of government. Can any comparable alliances across places and levels be built and sustained on the American center-left? Tendencies toward broad Democratic teamwork emerged between 2016 and 2018, in a political opportunity structure that left little room for nationally focused campaigns and rewarded inter-linked efforts across many states and local districts. However, the political opportunity structure leading from 2018 to 2020 is quite different, putting front and center a fractious Democratic presidential nominating battle and the clash in Washington, DC, between the Trump White House and the Democratic-led House of Representatives. For many Democratic politicians, not to mention the national advocates urging them on via Twitter and the national media outlets covering everything, current incentives favor individual display and infighting over hot-button ideological and identity issues. Democratic Party teamwork and bridge building across left to center divides are not easy to accomplish in this juncture.

The stakes remain stark. If Democrats cannot build on the broad outreach of 2018, it may not matter very much in 2020 and beyond whether sheer majorities of voters—including urbanites, young people, immigrants, and growing ethnic minority groups—pile up ballots for Democrats in the bluest states and enclaves. Because the federated rules of US politics advantage political teams with a widespread presence, organized right-wing minority rule is one very possible future for American politics and governance. Given the ways in which they are organized and deployed across the US federal system, ultra-conservative Republicans are poised to overcome the unpopularity of their economic and cultural positions to keep winning (or gaining hefty pluralities) in enough jurisdictions to cement minority national power for decades to come.

That possible American political future—a future in which an older, whiter, much more right-wing GOP continues to hold defensive sway over an increasingly diverse, youthful, and liberal-minded nation—can be avoided only if the recent widespread upsurge of center-left citizen energy both persists and transforms the Democratic Party into a more truly nationwide public force. Going into 2020 and beyond, the leaders of the Democratic Party must continue the broad momentum of 2018 to enhance party teamwork in every state and across many kinds of districts where citizens live varied lives and do not always think along the same lines as the most liberal coastal Democrats. Only by finding the wisdom and savvy to build from 2018 can Democrats effectively counter today's ultra-conservative Republicans. Only that way can Democrats and the voters who look to them put their party in a position to maneuver effectively within US federal institutions and leverage governments at all levels to progressive ends.

Notes

1. Because much of this conclusion summarizes key findings from the body of the book, particular points are not documented again. References appear only for new assertions, recent publications, and empirical claims not previously covered in core chapters.
2. Annie Karni and Maggie Haberman, "Trump and R.N.C. Raised $105 Million in 2nd Quarter, a Sign He Will Have Far More Money Than in 2016," *New York Times*, July 2, 2019.
3. Nate Cohn, "Huge Turnout Is Expected in 2020. So Which Party Would Benefit?" *New York Times*, July 15, 2019.
4. See, for example, David Weigel, "The Trailer: From Crucial Waukesha County, the Battle for Wisconsin," *Washington Post*, July 25, 2019.
5. Josh Dawsey and Michelle Ye Hee Lee, "Koch Network Tells Donors It Plans to Stay Out of the 2020 Race, Once Again Declining to Back Trump," *Washington Post*, January 24, 2019.
6. Dylan Scott, "Democratic Wins in These 9 States Will Have Seismic Policy Consequences," *Vox*, November 10, 2018.
7. Of the stances taken in the first presidential primary debate, one Republican strategist noted, "Immigration and health care were gifts to our party, especially immigration," Matt Gorman

quoted in Shane Goldmacher, "What We Learned from the 2020 Democratic Debates," *New York Times*, June 28, 2019.

8. Eli Stokols, "Reince Priebus' Surrender," *Politico*, July 21, 2016.

9. Doug Jones, a former federal prosecutor, defeated Roy Moore after allegations of Moore's sexual misconduct emerged weeks before the general election. Janet Hook and Joshua Jamerson, "Democrat Doug Jones Beats Roy Moore to Win Alabama Senate Seat," *Wall Street Journal*, December 13, 2017.

10. Alexander Hertel-Fernandez, *State Capture: How Conservative Activists, Big Businesses, and Wealthy Donors Reshaped the American States—and the Nation* (New York: Oxford University Press, 2019).

11. For more on the interaction between long-standing US institutional realities and recent socioeconomic and party trends, see Jonathan A. Rodden, *Why Cities Lose: The Deep Roots of the Urban-Rural Political Divide* (New York: Basic Books, 2020).

INDEX

For the benefit of digital users, indexed terms that span two pages (e.g., 52–53) may, on occasion, appear on only one of those pages.